I0118013

Texas Public Information Act Handbook 2018

Written by
The Office of the Attorney General of Texas

Open, transparent, and accountable government is the cornerstone of a healthy and functional democracy. This book was written by The Office of The Attorney General of Texas to further the goal of accessing information from the State of Texas under the Public Information Act. Regardless of your political beliefs, I hope that you find this book helpful in the pursuit of information to understand and hold government accountable to the citizens.

Should you have suggestions or feedback on ways to improve this book please send email to Books@OcotilloPress.com

Edited 2021 Ocotillo Press
ISBN 978-1-954285-49-1

No rights reserved. The content of this book is believed to be in the public domain as it is a work of the office of the Texas Attorney General and is considered public information. It is being printed to further the goal of the document to empower transparent and accountable government. It has been adjusted to accomodate the printing and binding process.

Printed in the United States of America

Ocotillo Press
Houston, TX 77017
Books@OcotilloPress.com

Disclaimer: The user of this book is responsible for following safe and lawful practices at all times. The publisher assumes no responsibility for the use of the content of this book. The publisher has made an effort to ensure that the text is complete and properly typeset, however omissions, errors, and other issues may exist that the publisher is unaware of.

Dear Fellow Texans:

As the Texas Constitution states, "All political power is inherent in the people," and that means a free government should work for the people, not the other way around. One of my priorities when I became Texas Attorney General in 2015 was to encourage open government – and to enforce our laws that mandate it when necessary. The Texas Public Information Act sets requirements for the ability of citizens to access information on action taken by governmental bodies. Such transparency provides Texans with a more complete understanding of how their government works, and, when necessary, provides them an opportunity to hold their public officials accountable.

Open government is vital to a free and informed society, and this updated guide will help both public officials and the people they serve understand and comply with the Texas Public Information Act. You can view or download the handbook by visiting www.texasattorneygeneral.gov/files/og/publicinfo_hb.pdf. What's more, my office's Open Government Hotline is available to answer any questions about open government in Texas. The toll-free number is 877-OPEN TEX (877-673-6839).

Texans have a right to know how their government is spending their tax dollars and exercising the powers granted by the people. Transparency and open decision-making are fundamental principles of the Texas Public Information Act, and they are essential to ensuring continued trust and confidence in officials and our government.

Best regards,

Ken Paxton
Attorney General of Texas

TABLE OF CONTENTS

A PREFACE TO THE PUBLIC INFORMATION ACT HANDBOOK

The Act. The Texas Public Information Act (the "Public Information Act" or the "Act") gives the public the right to request access to government information. Below is a description of the basic procedures, rights and responsibilities under the Act.

Making a Request. The Act is triggered when a person submits a written request to a governmental body. The request must ask for records or information already in existence. The Act does not require a governmental body to create new information, to do legal research, or to answer questions. In preparing a request, a person may want to ask the governmental body what information is available.

Charges to the Requestor. A person may ask to view the information, get copies of the information, or both. If a request is for copies of information, the governmental body may charge for the copies. If a request is only for an opportunity to inspect information, then usually the governmental body may not impose a charge on the requestor. However, under certain limited circumstances a governmental body may impose a charge for access to information. All charges imposed by a governmental body for copies or for access to information must comply with the rules prescribed by the Office of the Attorney General ("OAG"), unless another statute authorizes a governmental body to set its own charges.

Exceptions to the Act. Although the Act makes most government information available to the public, some exceptions exist. If an exception might apply and the governmental body wishes to withhold the information, the governmental body generally must, within ten business days of receiving the open records request, refer the matter to the OAG for a ruling on whether an exception applies. If the OAG rules that an exception applies, the governmental body will not release the information. If a governmental body improperly fails to release information, the Act authorizes the requestor or the OAG to file a civil lawsuit to compel the governmental body to release the information.

Questions or Complaints. To reach the OAG's Open Government Hotline, call toll-free (877) 673-6839 (877-OPEN TEX). Hotline staff can answer questions about the proper procedures for using and complying with the Act and can assist both governmental bodies and people requesting information from a governmental body. Hotline staff also review written complaints about alleged violations of the Act. If a complaint relates to charges, contact the OAG's Cost Hotline toll-free at (888) 672-6787 (888-ORCOSTS) or forward a written complaint. Certain violations of the Act may involve possible criminal penalties. Those violations must be reported to the appropriate county attorney or criminal district attorney.

Federal Agencies. The Act does not apply to the federal government or to any of its departments or agencies. If you are seeking information from the federal government, the appropriate law is the federal Freedom of Information Act ("FOIA"). FOIA's rules and procedures are different from those of the Public Information Act.

Rights of Requestors

All people who request public information have the right to:

- Receive treatment equal to all other requestors
- Receive a statement of estimated charges in advance
- Choose whether to inspect the requested information, receive a copy of the information, or both
- Be notified when the governmental body asks the OAG for a ruling on whether the information may or must be withheld
- Be copied on the governmental body's written comments to the OAG stating the reason why the stated exceptions apply
- Lodge a complaint with the OAG regarding any improper charges for responding to a public information request
- Lodge a complaint with the OAG or the county attorney or criminal district attorney, as appropriate, regarding any alleged violation of the Act

Responsibilities of Requestors

All people who request public information have the responsibility to:

- Submit a written request according to a governmental body's reasonable procedures
- Include enough description and detail of the requested information so the governmental body can accurately identify and locate the requested items
- Cooperate with the governmental body's reasonable requests to clarify the type or amount of information requested
- Respond promptly in writing to all written communications from the governmental body (including any written estimate of charges)
- Make a timely payment for all valid charges
- Keep all appointments for inspection of records or for pick-up of copies

Rights of Governmental Bodies

All governmental bodies responding to information requests have the right to:

- Establish reasonable procedures for inspecting or copying information
- Request and receive clarification of vague or overly broad requests
- Request an OAG ruling regarding whether any information may or must be withheld
- Receive timely payment for all copy charges or other charges
- Obtain payment of overdue balances exceeding $100 or obtain a security deposit before processing additional requests from the same requestor
- Request a bond, prepayment or deposit if estimated costs exceed $100 (or, if the governmental body has fewer than 16 employees, $50)

Responsibilities of Governmental Bodies

All governmental bodies responding to information requests have the responsibility to:

- Treat all requestors equally
- Complete open records training as required by law
- Be informed of open records laws and educate employees on the requirements of those laws
- Inform the requestor of cost estimates and any changes in the estimates
- Confirm the requestor agrees to pay the costs before incurring the costs
- Provide requested information promptly
- Inform the requestor if the information will not be provided within ten business days and give an estimated date on which it will be provided
- Cooperate with the requestor to schedule reasonable times for inspecting or copying information
- Follow attorney general rules on charges; do not overcharge on any items; do not bill for items that must be provided without charge
- Inform third parties if their proprietary information is being requested from the governmental body
- Inform the requestor when the OAG has been asked to rule on whether information may or must be withheld
- Copy the requestor on written comments submitted to the OAG stating the reasons why the stated exceptions apply
- Comply with any OAG ruling on whether an exception applies or file suit against the OAG within 30 days
- Respond in writing to all written communications from the OAG regarding complaints about violations of the Act

This *Handbook* is available on the OAG's website at http://www.texasattorneygeneral.gov. The website also provides access to the following:

- Attorney General Opinions dating from 1939 through the present;
- all formal Open Records Decisions (ORDs); and
- most informal Open Records letter rulings (ORLs) issued since January 1989.

Additional tools found on the site include the *Open Meetings Act Handbook*, the text of the Public Information and Open Meetings Acts, and other valuable publications and resources for governmental bodies and citizens.

The following is a list of telephone numbers that may be helpful to those needing answers to open government questions.

Open Government Hotline *for questions regarding the Act and* *the Texas Open Meetings Act*	TOLL-FREE or	(877) OPEN TEX (512) 478-6736
Cost Hotline *for questions regarding charges under the Act*	TOLL-FREE or	(888) ORCOSTS (512) 475-2497
Freedom of Information Foundation *for questions regarding FOIA*		(800) 580-6651
State Library and Archives Commission Records Management Assistance *for records retention questions*		(512) 463-7610
U.S. Department of Education Family Policy Compliance Office *for questions regarding FERPA and education records*		(800) 872-5327
U.S. Department of Health and Human Services Office for Civil Rights *for questions regarding the Health Insurance Portability and* *Accountability Act of 1996 (HIPAA) and protected health information*		(800) 368-1019

Note on Terminology
In previous publications and rulings, the OAG has referred to chapter 552 of the Government Code as the "Open Records Act." The OAG, in conformity with the statute, has adopted the term "Public Information Act" to refer to the provisions of chapter 552. However, the OAG will continue, in this *Handbook* and elsewhere, to use the term "open records" in other contexts, such as "open records request" and "open records decision."

The ★ symbol is used throughout the *Handbook* to indicate sections that discuss significant changes in the law that have occurred since publication of the 2016 *Handbook*.

PART ONE: HOW THE PUBLIC INFORMATION ACT WORKS

I. OVERVIEW

A. Historical Background

The Texas Public Information Act (the "Public Information Act" or the "Act") was adopted in 1973 by the reform-minded 63rd Legislature.[1] The Sharpstown scandal, which occurred in 1969 and came to light in 1971, provided the motivation for several enactments opening up government to the people.[2]

The Act was initially codified as V.T.C.S. article 6252-17a, which was repealed in 1993[3] and replaced by the Public Information Act now codified in the Texas Government Code at chapter 552.[4] The codification of the Act was a nonsubstantive revision.[5]

B. Policy; Construction

The preamble of the Public Information Act is codified at section 552.001 of the Government Code. It declares the basis for the policy of open government expressed in the Public Information Act. It finds that basis in "the American constitutional form of representative government" and "the principle that government is the servant and not the master of the people." It further explains this principle in terms of the need for an informed citizenry:

---

[1] Act of May 19, 1973, 63rd Leg., R.S., ch. 424, 1973 Tex. Gen. Laws 1112.

[2] *See generally Mutscher v. State*, 514 S.W.2d 905 (Tex. Crim. App. 1974) (summarizing events of Sharpstown scandal); *see also* "Sharpstown Stock-Fraud Scandal," *Handbook of Texas Online*, published by the Texas State Historical Association, at http://www.tshaonline.org/handbook/online/articles/mqs01.

[3] Act of May 4, 1993, 73rd Leg., R.S., ch. 268, § 46, 1993 Tex. Gen. Laws 583, 986.

[4] Act of May 4, 1993, 73rd Leg., R.S., ch. 268, § 1, 1993 Tex. Gen. Laws 583, 594–607.

[5] Act of May 4, 1993, 73rd Leg., R.S., ch. 268, § 47, 1993 Tex. Gen. Laws 583, 986.

The people, in delegating authority, do not give their public servants the right to decide what is good for the people to know and what is not good for them to know. The people insist on remaining informed so that they may retain control over the instruments they have created.

The purpose of the Public Information Act is to maintain the people's control "over the instruments they have created." The Act requires the attorney general to construe the Act liberally in favor of open government.[6]

C.   Attorney General to Maintain Uniformity in Application, Operation and Interpretation of the Act

Section 552.011 of the Government Code authorizes the attorney general to prepare, distribute and publish materials, including detailed and comprehensive written decisions and opinions, in order to maintain uniformity in the application, operation and interpretation of the Act.[7]

D.   Section 552.021

Section 552.021 of the Government Code is the starting point for understanding the operation of the Public Information Act. It provides as follows:

Public information is available to the public at a minimum during the normal business hours of the governmental body.

This provision tells us information in the possession of a governmental body is generally available to the public. Section 552.002(a) of the Government Code defines "public information" as:

information that is written, produced, collected, assembled, or maintained under a law or ordinance or in connection with the transaction of official business:

  (1) by a governmental body;

  (2) for a governmental body and the governmental body:

   (A) owns the information;

   (B) has a right of access to the information; or

   (C) spends or contributes public money for the purpose of writing, producing, collecting, assembling, or maintaining the information; or

---

[6]   Gov't Code § 552.001(b); *see A & T Consultants v. Sharp*, 904 S.W.2d 668, 675 (Tex. 1995); *Abbott v. City of Corpus Christi*, 109 S.W.3d 113, 118 (Tex. App.—Austin 2003, no pet.); *Thomas v. Cornyn*, 71 S.W.3d 473, 480 (Tex. App.—Austin 2002, no pet.).

[7]   Gov't Code § 552.011.

(3) **by an individual officer or employee of a governmental body in the officer's or employee's official capacity and the information pertains to official business of the governmental body.**

If the governmental body wishes to withhold information from a member of the public, it must show that the requested information is within at least one of the exceptions to required public disclosure.[8] Subchapter C of the Act, sections 552.101 through 552.158, lists the specific exceptions to required public disclosure; these exceptions are discussed in Part Two of this *Handbook*.

E.   Open Records Training

The Act applies to every governmental body in Texas, yet prior to 2006 there was no uniform requirement or mechanism for public officials to receive training in how to comply with the law. The 79th Legislature enacted section 552.012 of the Government Code, which requires public officials to receive training in the requirements of the Public Information Act. The training requirement of the Public Information Act, codified at section 552.012, provides:

(a) **This section applies to an elected or appointed public official who is:**

(1) **a member of a multimember governmental body;**

(2) **the governing officer of a governmental body that is headed by a single officer rather than by a multimember governing body; or**

(3) **the officer for public information of a governmental body, without regard to whether the officer is elected or appointed to a specific term.**

(b) **Each public official shall complete a course of training of not less than one and not more than two hours regarding the responsibilities of the governmental body with which the official serves and its officers and employees under this chapter not later than the 90th day after the date the public official:**

(1) **takes the oath of office, if the person is required to take an oath of office to assume the person's duties as a public official; or**

(2) **otherwise assumes the person's duties as a public official, if the person is not required to take an oath of office to assume the person's duties.**

(c) **A public official may designate a public information coordinator to satisfy the training requirements of this section for the public official if the public information coordinator is primarily responsible for administering the responsibilities of the public official or governmental body under this chapter. Designation of a public information coordinator under this subsection does not relieve a public official from the duty to comply with any other requirement of this chapter that applies to the public official. The designated public information coordinator shall complete the training course regarding the responsibilities of the governmental body with which the coordinator**

---

[8]   Open Records Decision No. 363 (1983) (information is public unless it falls within specific exception).

serves and of its officers and employees under this chapter not later than the 90th day after the date the coordinator assumes the person's duties as coordinator.

(d) The attorney general shall ensure that the training is made available. The office of the attorney general may provide the training and may also approve any acceptable course of training offered by a governmental body or other entity. The attorney general shall ensure that at least one course of training approved or provided by the attorney general is available on videotape or a functionally similar and widely available medium at no cost. The training must include instruction in:

    (1) the general background of the legal requirements for open records and public information;

    (2) the applicability of this chapter to governmental bodies;

    (3) procedures and requirements regarding complying with a request for information under this chapter;

    (4) the role of the attorney general under this chapter; and

    (5) penalties and other consequences for failure to comply with this chapter.

(e) The office of the attorney general or other entity providing the training shall provide a certificate of course completion to persons who complete the training required by this section. A governmental body shall maintain and make available for public inspection the record of its public officials' or, if applicable, the public information coordinator's completion of the training.

(f) Completing the required training as a public official of the governmental body satisfies the requirements of this section with regard to the public official's service on a committee or subcommittee of the governmental body and the public official's ex officio service on any other governmental body.

(g) The training required by this section may be used to satisfy any corresponding training requirements concerning this chapter or open records required by law for a public official or public information coordinator. The attorney general shall attempt to coordinate the training required by this section with training required by other law to the extent practicable.

(h) A certificate of course completion is admissible as evidence in a criminal prosecution under this chapter. However, evidence that a defendant completed a course of training offered under this section is not prima facie evidence that the defendant knowingly violated this chapter.

Minimum Training Requirement: The law requires elected and appointed officials to attend, at a minimum, a one-hour educational course on the Public Information Act. This is a one-time-only training requirement; no refresher courses are required.

Compliance Deadlines: The law took effect on January 1, 2006. Officials who were in office before January 1, 2006 had one year—until January 1, 2007—to complete the required training. Officials who were elected or appointed after January 1, 2006, have 90 days within which to complete the required training.

Who Must Obtain the Training: The requirement applies to all governmental bodies subject to the Act. It requires the top elected and appointed officials from governmental bodies subject to these laws to complete a training course on the Act. Alternatively, public officials may designate a public information coordinator to attend training in their place so long as the designee is the person primarily responsible for the processing of open records requests for the governmental body. It is presumed most governmental bodies already have a designated public information coordinator; therefore, officials may choose to opt out of the training provided they designate their public information coordinator to receive the training in their place. However, officials are encouraged to complete the required training, and designation of a public information coordinator to complete training on their behalf does not relieve public officials of the responsibility to comply with the law.

May Not Opt Out of Training if Required by Other Law: Open government training is already required for the top officials of many state agencies under the Sunset Laws. The opt-out provisions of the training requirement would not apply to officials who are already required by another law to receive open government training.

Judicial Officials and Employees: Judicial officials and employees do not need to attend training regarding the Act because public access to information maintained by the judiciary is governed by Rule 12 of the Judicial Administration Rules of the Texas Supreme Court and by other applicable laws and rules.[9]

Training Curriculum: The basic topics to be covered by the training include:

1. the general background of the legal requirements for open records and public information;
2. the applicability of the Act to governmental bodies;
3. procedures and requirements regarding complying with open records requests;
4. the role of the attorney general under the Act; and
5. penalties and other consequences for failure to comply with the Act.

Training Options: The law contains provisions to ensure that training is widely available and free training courses are available so all officials in the state can have easy access to the training. The OAG provides a training video and "live" training courses.

Governmental Entities May Provide Training: Governmental entities that already provide their own internal training on the Act may continue to do so provided the curriculum meets the minimum requirements set forth by section 552.012 and is reviewed and approved by the OAG.[10]

---

[9] Gov't Code § 552.0035.

[10] Gov't Code § 552.012(d).

Other Entities May Provide Training: Officials may obtain the required training from any entity that offers a training course that has been reviewed and approved by the OAG. This encompasses courses by various interest groups, professional organizations, and continuing education providers.

Evidence of Course Completion: The trainer is required to provide the participant with a certificate of course completion. The official or public information coordinator's governmental body is then required to maintain the certificate and make it available for public inspection. The OAG does not maintain certificates for governmental bodies.

No Penalty for Failure to Receive Training: The purpose of the law is to foster open government by making open government education a recognized obligation of public service. The purpose is not to create a new civil or criminal violation, so there are no specific penalties for failure to comply with the mandatory training requirement. Despite the lack of a penalty provision, officials should be cautioned that a deliberate failure to attend training may result in an increased risk of criminal conviction should they be accused of violating the Act.

Training Requirements Will Be Harmonized: To avoid imposing duplicate training requirements on public officials, the attorney general is required to harmonize the training required by section 552.012 with any other statutory training requirements that may be imposed on public officials.

Please visit the attorney general's website at http://www.texasattorneygeneral.gov for more information on section 552.012.

II.   ENTITIES SUBJECT TO THE PUBLIC INFORMATION ACT

The Public Information Act applies to information of every "governmental body." "Governmental body" is defined in section 552.003(1)(A) of the Government Code to mean:

(i)   **a board, commission, department, committee, institution, agency, or office that is within or is created by the executive or legislative branch of state government and that is directed by one or more elected or appointed members;**

(ii)   **a county commissioners court in the state;**

(iii)   **a municipal governing body in the state;**

(iv)   **a deliberative body that has rulemaking or quasi-judicial power and that is classified as a department, agency, or political subdivision of a county or municipality;**

(v)   **a school district board of trustees;**

(vi)   **a county board of school trustees;**

(vii)   **a county board of education;**

(viii)   **the governing board of a special district;**

(ix)   **the governing body of a nonprofit corporation organized under Chapter 67, Water Code, that provides a water supply or wastewater service, or both, and is exempt from ad valorem taxation under Section 11.30, Tax Code;**

(x)   **a local workforce development board created under Section 2308.253;**

(xi)   **a nonprofit corporation that is eligible to receive funds under the federal community services block grant program and that is authorized by this state to serve a geographic area of the state; and**

(xii)   **the part, section, or portion of an organization, corporation, commission, committee, institution, or agency that spends or that is supported in whole or in part by public funds[.]**

The judiciary is expressly excluded from the definition of "governmental body."[11] The required public release of records of the judiciary is governed by Rule 12 of the Texas Rules of Judicial Administration.[12]

---

[11]   Gov't Code § 552.003(1)(B).

[12]   Rule 12 of the Texas Rules of Judicial Administration is located in Part Seven of this *Handbook*.

An entity that does not believe it is a "governmental body" within this definition may make a timely request for a decision from the attorney general under Subchapter G of the Act if there has been no previous determination regarding this issue and it wishes to withhold the requested information.[13]

A.   State and Local Governmental Bodies

The definition of the term "governmental body" encompasses all public entities in the executive and legislative branches of government at the state and local levels. Although a sheriff's office, for example, is not within the scope of section 552.003(1)(A)(i)–(xi), it is supported by public funds and is therefore a "governmental body" within section 552.003(1)(A)(xii).[14]

B.   Private Entities

1. Private Entities Supported by Public Funds

An entity that is supported in whole or in part by public funds or that spends public funds is a governmental body under section 552.003(1)(A)(xii) of the Government Code. Public funds are "funds of the state or of a governmental subdivision of the state."[15] The Texas Supreme Court has defined "'supported in whole or part by public funds' to include only those private entities or their sub-parts sustained, at least in part, by public funds, meaning they could not perform the same or similar services without the public funds."[16] Thus, section 552.003(1)(A)(xii) encompasses only those private entities that are dependent on public funds to operate as a going concern,[17] and only those entities acting as the functional equivalent of the government.[18]

2. Private Entities Deemed Governmental Bodies by Statute

Section 51.212 of the Education Code provides:

> **(f) A campus police department of a private institution of higher education is a law enforcement agency and a governmental body for purposes of Chapter 552, Government Code, only with respect to information relating solely to law enforcement activities.**[19]

There are no cases or formal opinions interpreting this subsection of the Education Code.

---

[13]   *See Blankenship v. Brazos Higher Educ. Auth., Inc.*, 975 S.W.2d 353, 362 (Tex. App.—Waco 1998, pet. denied) (entity does not admit it is governmental body by virtue of request for opinion from attorney general).

[14]   Open Records Decision No. 78 (1975) (discussing statutory predecessor to Gov't Code § 552.003(1)(A)(xii)); *see Permian Report v. Lacy*, 817 S.W.2d 175 (Tex. App.—El Paso 1991, writ denied) (suggesting county clerk's office is subject to Act as agency supported by public funds).

[15]   Gov't Code § 552.003(5).

[16]   *Greater Houston P'ship v. Paxton*, 468 S.W. 3d 51, 63 (Tex. 2015).

[17]   *Greater Houston P'ship v. Paxton*, 468 S.W. 3d 51, 61 (Tex. 2015).

[18]   *Greater Houston P'ship v. Paxton*, 468 S.W. 3d 51, 62 (Tex. 2015).

[19]   Educ. Code § 51.212(f).

C. Certain Property Owners' Associations Subject to Act

Section 552.0036 provides:

A property owners' association is subject to [the Act] in the same manner as a governmental body:

> **(1) if:**
>
> > **(A) membership in the property owners' association is mandatory for owners or for a defined class of owners of private real property in a defined geographic area in a county with a population of 2.8 million or more or in a county adjacent to a county with a population of 2.8 million or more;**
> >
> > **(B) the property owners' association has the power to make mandatory special assessments for capital improvements or mandatory regular assessments; and**
> >
> > **(C) the amount of the mandatory special or regular assessments is or has ever been based in whole or in part on the value at which the state or a local governmental body assesses the property for purposes of ad valorem taxation under Section 20, Article VIII, Texas Constitution; or**
>
> **(2) if the property owners' association:**
>
> > **(A) provides maintenance, preservation, and architectural control of residential and commercial property within a defined geographic area in a county with a population of 2.8 million or more or in a county adjacent to a county with a population of 2.8 million or more; and**
> >
> > **(B) is a corporation that:**
> >
> > > **(i) is governed by a board of trustees who may employ a general manager to execute the association's bylaws and administer the business of the corporation;**
> > >
> > > **(ii) does not require membership in the corporation by the owners of the property within the defined area; and**
> > >
> > > **(iii) was incorporated before January 1, 2006.**

The only county in Texas with a population of 2.8 million or more is Harris County. The counties adjoining Harris County are Waller, Fort Bend, Brazoria, Galveston, Chambers, Liberty, and Montgomery. Thus, property owners' associations located in those counties and otherwise within the parameters of section 552.0036 are considered to be governmental bodies for purposes of the Act.

D.   A Governmental Body Holding Records for Another Governmental Body

One governmental body may hold information on behalf of another governmental body. For example, state agencies may transfer noncurrent records to the Records Management Division of the Texas State Library and Archives Commission for storage.[20] State agency records held by the state library under the state records management program should be requested from the originating state agency, not the state library. The governmental body by or for which information is collected, assembled, or maintained pursuant to section 552.002(a) retains ultimate responsibility for disclosing or withholding information in response to a request under the Public Information Act, even though another governmental body has physical custody of it.[21]

E.   Private Entities Holding Records for Governmental Bodies

On occasion, when a governmental body has contracted with a private consultant to prepare information for the governmental body, the consultant keeps the report and data in the consultant's office, and the governmental body reviews it there. Although the information is not in the physical custody of the governmental body, the information is in the constructive custody of the governmental body and is therefore subject to the Act.[22] The private consultant is acting as the governmental body's agent in holding the records. Section 552.002(a) of the Act was amended in 1989 to codify this interpretation of the Act.[23]

The definition of "public information" in Government Code Section 552.002 read as follows:

(a) **information that is written, produced, collected, assembled, or maintained under a law or ordinance or in connection with the transaction of official business:**

   (1) **by a governmental body;**

   (2) **for a governmental body and the governmental body:**

      (A) **owns the information;**

      (B) **has a right of access to the information; or**

      (C) **spends or contributes public money for the purpose of writing, producing, collecting, assembling, or maintaining the information; or**

   (3) **by an individual officer or employee of a governmental body in the officer's or employee's official capacity and the information pertains to official business of the governmental body**

---

[20]   Open Records Decision No. 617 (1993); *see* Open Records Decision No. 674 (2001).

[21]   Open Records Decision No. 576 (1990).

[22]   Open Records Decision No. 462 (1987).

[23]   Act of May 29, 1989, 71st Leg., R.S., ch. 1248, § 9, 1989 Tex. Gen. Laws 4996, 5023.

(a-1) Information is in connection with the transaction of official business if the information is created by, transmitted to, received by, or maintained by an officer or employee of the governmental body in the officer's or employee's official capacity, or a person or entity performing official business or a governmental function on behalf of a governmental body, and pertains to official business of the governmental body.

The following decisions recognize that various records held for governmental bodies by private entities are subject to the Act:

Open Records Decision No. 585 (1991) — the city manager may not contract away the right to inspect the list of applicants maintained by a private consultant for the city;

Open Records Decision No. 499 (1988) — the records held by a private attorney employed by a municipality that relate to legal services performed at the request of the municipality;

Open Records Decision No. 462 (1987) — records regarding the investigation of a university football program prepared by a law firm on behalf of the university and kept at the law firm's office; and

Open Records Decision No. 437 (1986) — the records prepared by bond underwriters and attorneys for a utility district and kept in an attorney's office.[24]

Section 2252.907 of the Government Code contains specific requirements for a contract between a state governmental entity and a nongovernmental vendor involving the exchange or creation of public information.

F.   Judiciary Excluded from the Public Information Act

Section 552.003(1)(B) of the Government Code excludes the judiciary from the Public Information Act. Section 552.0035 of the Government Code specifically provides that access to judicial records is governed by rules adopted by the Supreme Court of Texas or by other applicable laws and rules.[25] (*See* Part Seven of this *Handbook* for Rule 12 of the Texas Rules of Judicial Administration.) This provision, however, expressly provides that it does not address whether particular records are judicial records.

The purposes and limits of section 552.003(1)(B) were discussed in *Benavides v. Lee*.[26] At issue in that case were applications for the position of chief juvenile probation officer submitted to the Webb County Juvenile Board. The court determined that the board was not "an extension of the judiciary"

---

[24] *See also Baytown Sun v. City of Mont Belvieu*, 145 S.W.3d 268 (Tex. App.—Houston [14th Dist.] 2004, no pet.) (municipality had right of access to employee salary information of company it contracted with to manage recreational complex); Open Records Decision No. 585 (1991) (overruling Open Records Decision Nos. 499 (1988), 462 (1987), 437 (1986) to extent they suggest governmental body can waive its right of access to information gathered on its behalf).

[25] Gov't Code § 552.0035; *see* R. Jud. Admin. 12; *see also, e.g., Ashpole v. Millard*, 778 S.W.2d 169, 170 (Tex. App.—Houston [1st Dist.] 1989, no writ) (public has right to inspect and copy judicial records subject to court's inherent power to control public access to its records); Attorney General Opinion DM-166 (1992); Open Records Decision No. 25 (1974).

[26] *Benavides v. Lee*, 665 S.W.2d 151 (Tex. App.—San Antonio 1983, no writ).

for purposes of the Public Information Act, even though the board consisted of members of the judiciary and the county judge. The court stated as follows:

> The Board is not a court. A separate entity, the juvenile court, not the Board, exists to adjudicate matters concerning juveniles. Nor is the Board directly controlled or supervised by a court.
>
> Moreover, simply because the legislature chose judges as Board members, art. 5139JJJ, § 1, does not in itself indicate they perform on the Board as members of the judiciary. . . . [C]lassification of the Board as judicial or not depends on the functions of the Board, not on members' service elsewhere in government.[27]

The decisions made by the board were administrative, not judicial, and the selection of a probation officer was part of the board's administration of the juvenile probation system, not a judicial act by a judicial body. The court continued:

> The judiciary exception, § 2(1)(G) [now section 552.003(1)(B) of the Government Code], is important to safeguard judicial proceedings and maintain the independence of the judicial branch of government, preserving statutory and case law already governing access to judicial records. But it must not be extended to every governmental entity having any connection with the judiciary.[28]

The Texas Supreme Court also addressed the judiciary exception in *Holmes v. Morales*.[29] In that case, the court found that "judicial power" as provided for in article V, section 1, of the Texas Constitution "embraces powers to hear facts, to decide issues of fact made by pleadings, to decide questions of law involved, to render and enter judgment on facts in accordance with law as determined by the court, and to execute judgment or sentence."[30] Because the court found the Harris County District Attorney did not perform these functions, it held the district attorney is not a member of the judiciary, but is a governmental body within the meaning of the Public Information Act.

In Open Records Decision No. 657 (1997), the attorney general concluded telephone billing records of the Supreme Court did not relate to the exercise of judicial powers but rather to routine administration and were not "records of the judiciary" for purposes of the Public Information Act. The Texas Supreme Court subsequently overruled Open Records Decision No. 657 (1997), finding the court was not a governmental body under the Act and its records were therefore not subject to the Act.[31]

---

27   *Benavides v. Lee*, 665 S.W.2d 151, 151–52 (Tex. App.—San Antonio 1983, no writ) (footnote omitted).

28   *Benavides v. Lee*, 665 S.W.2d 151, 152 (Tex. App.—San Antonio 1983, no writ).

29   *Holmes v. Morales*, 924 S.W.2d 920 (Tex. 1996).

30   *Holmes v. Morales*, 924 S.W.2d 920, 923 (Tex. 1996).

31   *Order and Opinion Denying Request Under Open Records Act*, No. 97-9141, 1997 WL 583726 (Tex. August 21, 1997) (not reported in S.W.2d).

The State Bar of Texas is a "public corporation and an administrative agency of the judicial department of government."[32] Section 81.033 of the Government Code provides that, with certain exceptions, all records of the State Bar are subject to the Public Information Act.[33]

The following decisions address the judiciary exclusion:

Open Records Decision No. 671 (2001) — the information contained in the weekly index reports produced by the Ellis County District Clerk's office is derived from a case disposition database that is "collected, assembled, or maintained . . . for the judiciary." Gov't Code § 552.0035(a). Therefore, the information contained in weekly index reports is not public information under the Act;

Open Records Decision No. 646 (1996) — a community supervision and corrections department is a governmental body and is not part of the judiciary for purposes of the Public Information Act. Administrative records such as personnel files and other records reflecting the day-to-day management of a community supervision and corrections department are subject to the Public Information Act.[34] On the other hand, specific records regarding individuals on probation and subject to the direct supervision of a court that are held by a community supervision and corrections department are not subject to the Public Information Act because such records are held on behalf of the judiciary;

Open Records Decision No. 610 (1992) — the books and records of an insurance company placed in receivership pursuant to article 21.28 of the Insurance Code are excluded from the Public Information Act as records of the judiciary;

Open Records Decision No. 572 (1990) — certain records of the Bexar County Personal Bond Program are within the judiciary exclusion;

Open Records Decision No. 513 (1988) — records held by a district attorney on behalf of a grand jury are in the grand jury's constructive possession and are not subject to the Public Information Act. However, records a district attorney collects, prepares, and submits to grand jury are not in the constructive possession of the grand jury when that information is held by the district attorney.

Open Records Decision No. 204 (1978) — information held by a county judge as a member of the county commissioners court is subject to the Public Information Act; and

Open Records Decision No. 25 (1974) — the records of a justice of the peace are not subject to the Public Information Act but may be inspected under statutory and common-law rights of access.

---

[32] Gov't Code § 81.011(a); *see* Open Records Decision No. 47 (1974) (records of state bar grievance committee were confidential pursuant to Texas Supreme Court rule; not deciding whether state bar was part of judiciary).

[33] *Compare* Open Records Decision No. 604 (1992) (considering request for list of registrants for Professional Development Programs) *with In re Nolo Press/Folk Law, Inc.*, 991 S.W.2d 768 (Tex. 1999) (Unauthorized Practice of Law Committee of state bar is judicial agency and therefore subject to Rule 12 of Texas Rules of Judicial Administration).

[34] *But see* Gov't Code § 76.006(g) (document evaluating performance of officer of community supervision and corrections department who supervises defendants placed on community supervision is confidential).

III. INFORMATION SUBJECT TO THE PUBLIC INFORMATION ACT

A. Public Information is Contained in Records of All Forms

Section 552.002(b) of the Government Code states the Public Information Act applies to recorded information in practically any medium, including: paper; film; a magnetic, optical, solid state or other device that can store an electronic signal; tape; Mylar; and any physical material on which information may be recorded, including linen, silk, and vellum.[35] Section 552.002(c) specifies that "[t]he general forms in which the media containing public information exist include a book, paper, letter, document, e-mail, Internet posting, text message, instant message, other electronic communication, printout, photograph, film, tape, microfiche, microfilm, photostat, sound recording, map, and drawing and a voice, data, or video representation held in computer memory."

B. Exclusion of Tangible Items

Despite the assumption in Open Records Decision No. 252 (1980) that the Public Information Act applies to physical evidence, the prevailing view is that tangible items such as a tool or a key are not "information" within the Act, even though they may be copied or analyzed to produce information. In Open Records Decision No. 581 (1990), the attorney general dealt with a request for the source code, documentation, and computer program documentation standards of computer programs used by a state university. The requested codes, documentation, and documentation standards contained security measures designed to prevent unauthorized access to student records. The attorney general noted the sole significance of the computer source code, documentation, and documentation standards was "as a tool for the storage, manipulation, and security of other information."[36] While acknowledging the comprehensive scope of the term "information," the attorney general nevertheless determined the legislature could not have intended that the Public Information Act compromise the physical security of information management systems or other government property.[37] The attorney general concluded that information used solely as a tool to maintain, manipulate, or protect public property was not the kind of information made public by the statutory predecessor to section 552.021 of the Public Information Act.[38]

---

[35] *See also* Open Records Decision Nos. 660 (1999) (Section 52(a) of article III of Texas Constitution does not prohibit Port of Corpus Christi Authority from releasing computer generated digital map), 492 (1988) (raw data collected by outside consultant, but accessed by comptroller through data link and stored on comptroller's computer system), 432 (1985) (photographic negatives), 413 (1984) (sketches), 364 (1983) (videotapes), 352 (1982) (computer tapes), 32 (1974) (tape recordings).

[36] Open Records Decision No. 581 at 6 (1990).

[37] Open Records Decision No. 581 at 5–6 (1990) (drawing comparison to door key, whose sole significance as "information" is its utility as tool in matching internal mechanism of lock).

[38] Open Records Decision No. 581 at 6 (1990) (overruling in part Open Records Decision No. 401 (1983), which had suggested implied exception to required public disclosure applied to requested computer programs); *see also* Attorney General Opinion DM-41 (1991) (formatting codes are not "information" subject to Act).

C.   Personal Notes and E-mail in Personal Accounts or Devices

A few early decisions of the attorney general found certain personal notes of public employees were not "information collected, assembled, or maintained by governmental bodies pursuant to law or ordinance or in connection with the transaction of official business."[39] Thus, such personal notes were not considered subject to the Public Information Act.[40] Governmental bodies are advised to use caution in relying on early open records decisions that address "personal notes."

More recent decisions have concluded personal notes are not necessarily excluded from the definition of "public information" and may be subject to the Act.[41] The characterization of information as "public information" under the Act is not dependent on whether the requested records are in the possession of an individual, rather than a governmental body, or whether a governmental body has a particular policy or procedure that establishes a governmental body's access to the information.[42] If information was made, transmitted, maintained, or received in connection with a governmental body's official business, the mere fact that the governmental body does not possess the information does not take the information outside the scope of the Act.[43] In *Adkisson v. Paxton*, the court of appeals considered a request for correspondence related to a county commissioner's official capacity from his personal and county e-mail accounts. The court concluded the information in the commissioner's official-capacity e-mails is necessarily connected with the transaction of the county's official business, and the county owns the information regardless of whether the information is created or received in a personal e-mail account or an official county e-mail account. Thus, the court held the requested information is "public information" subject to the Act. This case construes a prior version section 552.002 of the Act, which the 83rd Legislature amended, along with section 552.003, in 2013.[44]

The amended definition of "public information" in section 552.002(a-2) now specifically includes:

> **any electronic communication created, transmitted, received, or maintained on any device if the communication is in connection with the transaction of official business.**

---

[39]   Open Records Decision No. 77 (1975) (quoting statutory predecessor to Gov't Code § 552.021).

[40]   *See* Open Records Decision No. 116 (1975) (portions of desk calendar kept by governor's aide comprising notes of private activities and aide's notes made solely for his own informational purposes are not public information); *see also* Open Records Decision No. 145 (1976) (handwritten notes on university president's calendar are not public information).

[41]   *See, e.g.*, Open Records Decision Nos. 635 (1995) (public official's or employee's appointment calendar, including personal entries, may be subject to Act), 626 (1994) (handwritten notes taken during oral interview by Texas Department of Public Safety promotion board members are subject to Act), 450 (1986) (handwritten notes taken by appraiser while observing teacher's classroom performance are subject to Act), 120 (1976) (faculty members' written evaluations of doctoral student's qualifying exam are subject to Act).

[42]   *See* Open Records Decision No. 635 at 3-4 (1995) (information does not fall outside definition of "public information" in Act merely because individual member of governmental body possesses information rather than governmental body as whole); *see also* Open Records Decision No. 425 (1985) (information sent to individual school trustees' homes was public information because it related to official business of governmental body) (overruled on other grounds by Open Records Decision No. 439 (1986)).

[43]   *See* Open Records Decision No. 635 at 6-8 (1995) (information maintained on privately-owned medium and actually used in connection with transaction of official business would be subject to Act).

[44]   *Adkisson v. Paxton*, 459 S.W.3d 761 (Tex. App.—Austin 2015, no pet.).

Section 552.002(a-1) further defines "information . . . in connection with the transaction of official business" as:

> **information . . . created by, transmitted to, received by, or maintained by an officer or employee of the governmental body in the officer's or employee's official capacity, or a person or entity performing official business or a governmental function on behalf of a governmental body, and pertains to official business of the governmental body.**

Adopting the attorney general's long-standing interpretation, the definition of "public information" now takes into account the use of electronic devices and cellular phones by public employees and officials in the transaction of official business. The Act does not distinguish between personal or employer-issued devices, but rather focuses on the nature of the communication or document. If the information was created, transmitted, received, or maintained in connection with the transaction of "official business," meaning, "any matter over which a governmental body has any authority, administrative duties, or advisory duties," the information constitutes public information subject to disclosure under the Act.[45]

There are no cases or formal decisions applying these amendments to section 552.002 or 552.003.

D. Commercially Available Information

Section 552.027 provides:

(a) **A governmental body is not required under the Act to allow the inspection of or to provide a copy of information in a commercial book or publication purchased or acquired by the governmental body for research purposes if the book or publication is commercially available to the public.**

(b) **Although information in a book or publication may be made available to the public as a resource material, such as a library book, a governmental body is not required to make a copy of the information in response to a request for public information.**

(c) **A governmental body shall allow the inspection of information in a book or publication that is made part of, incorporated into, or referred to in a rule or policy of a governmental body.**

This section is designed to alleviate the burden of providing copies of commercially available books, publications, and resource materials maintained by governmental bodies, such as telephone directories, dictionaries, encyclopedias, statutes, and periodicals. Therefore, section 552.027 provides exemptions from the definition of "public information" under section 552.002 for commercially available research material. However, pursuant to subsection (c) of section 552.027, a governmental body must allow inspection of a publication that is made a part of, or referred to in, a rule or policy of the governmental body.

---

[45] Gov't Code § 552.003(2-a).

IV. PROCEDURES FOR ACCESS TO PUBLIC INFORMATION

A. Informing the Public of Basic Rights and Responsibilities Under the Act

Section 552.205 of the Government Code requires the officer for public information of a governmental body to display a sign, in the form required by the attorney general, that contains basic information about the rights of a requestor, the responsibilities of a governmental body, and the procedures for inspecting or obtaining a copy of public information under the Public Information Act.[46] The sign is to be displayed at one or more places in the administrative offices of the governmental body where it is plainly visible to members of the public requesting information and employees of the governmental body whose duties involve receiving or responding to requests under the Act. The sign's format as prescribed by the attorney general is available on the attorney general's website. In addition, a chart outlining various deadlines to which governmental bodies are subject can be found in Part Eight of this *Handbook*.

B. The Request for Public Information

A governmental body that receives a verbal request for information may require the requestor to submit that request in writing because the governmental body's duty under section 552.301(a) to request a ruling from the attorney general arises only after it receives a written request.[47] Open Records Decision No. 654 (1997) held the Public Information Act did not require a governmental body to respond to a request for information sent by electronic mail. However, the 75th Legislature amended section 552.301 by defining a written request for information to include "a request made in writing that is sent to the officer for public information, or the person designated by that officer, by electronic mail or facsimile transmission."[48] Therefore, Open Records Decision No. 654 (1997) is superseded by the 1997 amendment of section 552.301.

Generally, a request for information need not name the Act or be addressed to the officer for public information.[49] An overly technical reading of the Act does not effectuate the purpose of the Act; a written communication that reasonably can be judged to be a request for public information is a request for information under the Public Information Act.[50] However, a request made by electronic mail or facsimile transmission must be sent to the officer for public information or the officer's designee.[51] Requests for a state agency's records that are stored in the Texas State Library and Archives Commission's State and Local Records Management Division should be directed to the originating agency, rather than to the state library.[52]

A governmental body must make a good faith effort to relate a request to information that it holds.[53] A governmental body may ask a requestor to clarify a request for information if the request is

---

[46] Gov't Code § 552.205(a).

[47] Open Records Decision No. 304 at 2 (1982).

[48] Gov't Code § 552.301(c).

[49] *See* Open Records Decision Nos. 497 at 3 (1988), 44 at 2 (1974).

[50] Open Records Decision No. 44 at 2 (1974).

[51] Gov't Code § 552.301(c).

[52] Open Records Decision No. 617 (1993).

[53] Open Records Decision No. 561 at 8 (1990).

unclear.[54] Section 552.222(b) provides that if a large amount of information has been requested, the governmental body may discuss with the requestor how the scope of the request might be narrowed, but the governmental body may not inquire into the purpose for which information will be used.[55] Section 552.222 also provides that a request for information is considered withdrawn if the requestor does not respond in writing to a governmental body's written request for clarification or additional information within 61 days.[56] The governmental body's written request for clarification or additional information must include a statement as to the consequences of the failure by the requestor to timely respond.[57] If the requestor's original request for information was sent by electronic mail, a governmental body may consider the request for information withdrawn if the governmental body sends its request for clarification to the electronic mail address from which the original request was sent or another electronic mail address, and the governmental body does not receive a timely written response or response by electronic mail from the requestor.[58] If the requestor's original request for information was not sent by electronic mail, a governmental body may consider the request for information withdrawn if the governmental body sent its request for clarification by certified mail to the requestor's physical or mailing address, and the governmental body does not receive a timely written response from the requestor.[59] When a governmental body, acting in good faith, requests clarification or narrowing of an unclear or overbroad request, the ten business day period to request an attorney general ruling is measured from the date the requestor responds to the request for clarification or narrowing.[60] A governmental body may, however, make certain inquiries of a requestor who seeks information relating to motor vehicle records to determine if the requestor is authorized to receive the information under the governing statute.[61] Similarly, a governmental body may require a requestor seeking an interior photograph taken by an appraisal district for property tax appraisal purposes to provide additional information sufficient to determine whether the requestor is eligible to receive the photograph.[62] In addition, a governmental body may make inquiries of a requestor in order to establish proper identification.[63]

It is implicit in several provisions of the Act that it applies only to information already in existence.[64] Thus, the Act does not require a governmental body to prepare new information in response to a request.[65] Furthermore, the Act does not require a governmental body to inform a requestor if the requested information comes into existence after the request has been made.[66] Consequently, a governmental body is not required to comply with a continuing request to supply information on a

---

[54]   Gov't Code § 552.222(b).

[55]   Gov't Code § 552.222(b).

[56]   Gov't Code § 552.222(d).

[57]   Gov't Code § 552.222(e).

[58]   Gov't Code § 552.222(g).

[59]   Gov't Code § 552.222(f).

[60]   *City of Dallas v. Abbott*, 304 S.W.3d 380, 387 (Tex. 2010).

[61]   Gov't Code § 552.222(c) (referencing Transp. Code ch. 730).

[62]   Gov't Code § 552.222(c-1).

[63]   Gov't Code § 552.222(a).

[64]   *See* Gov't Code §§ 552.002, .021, .227, .351.

[65]   *A & T Consultants, Inc. v. Sharp*, 904 S.W.2d 668, 676 (Tex. 1995); *Fish v. Dallas Indep. Sch. Dist.*, 31 S.W.3d 678, 681 (Tex. App.—Eastland 2000, pet. denied); Attorney General Opinion H-90 (1973); Open Records Decision Nos. 452 at 2–3 (1986), 342 at 3 (1982), 87 (1975).

[66]   Open Records Decision No. 452 at 3 (1986).

periodic basis as such information is prepared in the future.[67] Moreover, the Act does not require a governmental body to prepare answers to questions or to do legal research.[68] Section 552.227 states that "[a]n officer for public information or the officer's agent is not required to perform general research within the reference and research archives and holdings of state libraries."

Section 552.232 provides for the handling of repetitious or redundant requests.[69] Under this section, a governmental body that receives a request for information for which it determines it has already furnished or made copies available to the requestor upon payment of applicable charges under Subchapter F may respond to the request by certifying to the requestor that it has already made the information available to the person. The certification must include a description of the information already made available; the date of the governmental body's receipt of the original request for the information; the date it furnished or made the information available; a certification that no changes have been made to the information; and the name, title, and signature of the officer for public information, or his agent, who makes the certification.

Section 552.0055 provides that a *subpoena duces tecum* or request for discovery issued in compliance with a statute or rule of civil or criminal procedure is not considered to be a request for information under the Public Information Act.

C. The Governmental Body's Duty to Produce Public Information Promptly

The Act designates the chief administrative officer and each elected county officer as the officer for public information for a governmental body.[70] In general, the officer for public information must protect public information and promptly make it available to the public for copying or inspecting.[71] Section 552.221 specifies the duties of the officer for public information upon receiving a request for public information. Section 552.221 reads in part:

(a) **An officer for public information of a governmental body shall promptly produce public information for inspection, duplication, or both on application by any person to the officer. In this subsection, "promptly" means as soon as possible under the circumstances, that is, within a reasonable time, without delay.**

(b) **An officer for public information complies with Subsection (a) by:**

(1) **providing the public information for inspection or duplication in the offices of the governmental body; or**

---

[67] Attorney General Opinion JM-48 at 2 (1983); Open Records Decision Nos. 476 at 1 (1987), 465 at 1 (1987).

[68] *See* Open Records Decision Nos. 563 at 8 (1990) (considering request for federal and state laws and regulations), 555 at 1–2 (1990) (considering request for answers to fact questions).

[69] Gov't Code § 552.232.

[70] *See* Gov't Code §§ 552.201, .202 (designating officer for public information and identifying department heads as agents for that officer); *see also Keever v. Finlan*, 988 S.W.2d 300, 301 (Tex. App.—Dallas 1999, pet. dism'd) (school district superintendent, rather than school board member, is chief administrative officer and custodian of public records).

[71] *See* Gov't Code § 552.203 (listing general duties of officer for public information).

(2) sending copies of the public information by first class United States mail if the person requesting the information requests that copies be provided and pays the postage and any other applicable charges that the requestor has accrued under Subchapter F.

(b-1) In addition to the methods of production described by Subsection (b), an officer for public information for a governmental body of this state complies with Subsection (a) by referring a requestor to an exact Internet location or uniform resource locator (URL) address on a website maintained by the governmental body and accessible to the public if the requested information is identifiable and readily available on that website. If the person requesting the information prefers a manner other than access through the URL, the governmental body must supply the information in the manner required by Subsection (b).

(b-2) If an officer for public information for a governmental body provides by e-mail an Internet location or uniform resource locator (URL) address as permitted by Subsection (b-1), the e-mail must contain a statement in a conspicuous font clearly indicating that the requestor may nonetheless access the requested information by inspection or duplication or by receipt through United States mail, as provided by Subsection (b).[72]

Thus, in order to comply with section 552.221, generally a governmental body must either provide the information for inspection or duplication in its offices or send copies of the information by first class United States mail. The 84th Legislature amended section 552.221 to provide an additional option for a "political subdivision."[73] The 85th Legislature expanded this option to apply to all governmental bodies.[74] A governmental body may comply with section 552.221 by referring the requestor to an exact Internet location or URL address maintained by the governmental body and accessible to the public, if the requested information is identifiable and readily accessible on the website.[75] If the governmental body uses e-mail to refer the requestor to an Internet location or URL address, the e-mail must contain a statement in a conspicuous font indicating the requestor may still choose to inspect the information or receive copies of the information.[76] If the requestor prefers to inspect the information or receive copies instead of accessing the information on the governmental body's website, the governmental body must either provide the information for inspection or duplication in its offices or send copies of the information by first class mail.[77] Although the attorney general has determined in a formal decision that a public information officer does not fulfill his or her duty under section 552.221 by simply referring a requestor to a governmental body's website, this decision is superseded by the amendment to section 552.221.

---

[72] Gov't Code § 552.221(b-1), (b-2).

[73] *See* Act of May 27, 2015, 84th Leg., R.S., ch. 692, § 1, 2015 Tex. Gen. Laws 2167.

[74] Gov't Code § 552.221(b-1), (b-2).

[75] Gov't Code § 552.221(b-1).

[76] Gov't Code § 552.221 (b-2).

[77] Gov't Code § 552.221(b-1).

An officer for public information is not responsible for how a requestor uses public information or for the release of information after it is removed from a record as a result of an update, a correction, or a change of status of the person to whom the information pertains.[78]

The officer for public information must "promptly" produce public information in response to an open records request.[79] "Promptly" means that a governmental body may take a reasonable amount of time to produce the information, but may not delay.[80] It is a common misconception that a governmental body may wait ten business days before releasing the information. In fact, as discussed above, the requirement is to produce information "promptly." What constitutes a reasonable amount of time depends on the facts in each case. The volume of information requested is highly relevant to what constitutes a reasonable period of time.[81]

If the request is to inspect the information, the Public Information Act requires only that the officer in charge of public information make it available for review within the "offices of the governmental body."[82] Temporarily transporting records outside the office for official use does not trigger a duty to make the records available to the public wherever they may be.[83]

Subsection 552.221(c) states:

> **If the requested information is unavailable at the time of the request to examine because it is in active use or in storage, the officer for public information shall certify this fact in writing to the requestor and set a date and hour within a reasonable time when the information will be available for inspection or duplication.**

The following decisions discuss when requested information is in "active use":

Open Records Decision No. 225 (1979) — a secretary's handwritten notes are in active use while the secretary is typing minutes of a meeting from them;

Open Records Decision No. 148 (1976) — a faculty member's file is not in active use the entire time the member's promotion is under consideration;

Open Records Decision No. 96 (1975) — directory information about students is in active use while the notice required by the federal Family Educational Rights and Privacy Act of 1974 is being given; and

Open Records Decision No. 57 (1974) — a file containing student names, addresses, and telephone numbers is in active use during registration.

---

[78]   Gov't Code § 552.204; Open Records Decision No. 660 at 4 (1999).

[79]   Gov't Code § 552.221(a); *see Dominguez v. Gilbert*, 48 S.W.3d 789, 792 (Tex. App.—Austin 2001, no pet.); Open Records Decision No. 665 (2000).

[80]   Gov't Code § 552.221(a); *see* Open Records Decision No. 467 at 6 (1987).

[81]   Open Records Decision No. 467 at 6 (1987).

[82]   Gov't Code § 552.221(b).

[83]   *Conely v. Peck*, 929 S.W.2d 630, 632 (Tex. App.—Austin 1996, no writ).

If an officer for public information cannot produce public information for inspection or duplication within ten business days after the date the information is requested, section 552.221(d) requires the officer to "certify that fact in writing to the requestor and set a date and hour within a reasonable time when the information will be available for inspection or duplication."

The 85th Legislature added section 552.221(e) of the Government Code, which provides:

> A request is considered to have been withdrawn if the requestor fails to inspect or duplicate the public information in the office of the governmental body on or before the 60th day after the date the information is made available or fails to pay the postage and any other applicable charges accrued under Subchapter F on or before the 60th day after the date the requestor is informed of the charges.[84]

A request may now be considered withdrawn if, after the 60th day, the requestor does not appear to inspect the information, fails to pick up the information, or fails to pay any applicable charges for the information.

D.   The Requestor's Right of Access

The Public Information Act prohibits a governmental body from inquiring into a requestor's reasons or motives for requesting information. In addition, a governmental body must treat all requests for information uniformly. Sections 552.222 and 552.223 provide as follows:

§ 552.222. Permissible Inquiry by Governmental Body to Requestor

(a) **The officer for public information and the officer's agent may not make an inquiry of a requestor except to establish proper identification or except as provided by Subsection (b), (c), or (c-1).[85]**

(b) **If what information is requested is unclear to the governmental body, the governmental body may ask the requestor to clarify the request. If a large amount of information has been requested, the governmental body may discuss with the requestor how the scope of a request might be narrowed, but the governmental body may not inquire into the purpose for which information will be used.**

(c) **If the information requested relates to a motor vehicle record, the officer for public information or the officer's agent may require the requestor to provide additional identifying information sufficient for the officer or the officer's agent to determine whether the requestor is eligible to receive the information under Chapter 730, Transportation Code. In this subsection, "motor vehicle record" has the meaning assigned that term by Section 730.003, Transportation Code.**

(c-1) **If the information requested includes a photograph described by Section 552.155(a), the officer for public information or the officer's agent may require the requestor to provide additional information sufficient for the officer or the officer's agent to**

---

[84]   Gov't Code § 552.221(e).

[85]   Gov't Code § 552.222(a).

determine whether the requestor is eligible to receive the information under Section 552.155(b).[86]

§ 552.223. Uniform Treatment of Requests for Information

The officer for public information or the officer's agent shall treat all requests for information uniformly without regard to the position or occupation of the requestor, the person on whose behalf the request is made, or the status of the individual as a member of the media.

Although section 552.223 requires an officer for public information to treat all requests for information uniformly, section 552.028 provides as follows:

(a) **A governmental body is not required to accept or comply with a request for information from:**

   (1) **an individual who is imprisoned or confined in a correctional facility; or**

   (2) **an agent of that individual, other than that individual's attorney when the attorney is requesting information that is subject to disclosure under this chapter.**

(b) **This section does not prohibit a governmental body from disclosing to an individual described by Subsection (a)(1), or that individual's agent, information held by the governmental body pertaining to that individual.**

(c) **In this section, "correctional facility" means:**

   (1) **a secure correctional facility, as defined by Section 1.07, Penal Code;**

   (2) **a secure correctional facility and a secure detention facility, as defined by Section 51.02, Family Code; and**

   (3) **a place designated by the law of this state, another state, or the federal government for the confinement of a person arrested for, charged with, or convicted of a criminal offense.**

Under section 552.028, a governmental body is not required to comply with a request for information from an inmate or his agent, other than the inmate's attorney, even if the requested information pertains to the inmate.[87] While subsection (b) does not prohibit a governmental body from complying with an inmate's request, it does not mandate compliance.[88]

---

[86] Gov't Code § 552.222(c-1).

[87] *See Harrison v. Vance*, 34 S.W.3d 660, 662–63 (Tex. App.—Dallas 2000, no pet.); *Hickman v. Moya*, 976 S.W.2d 360, 361 (Tex. App.—Waco 1998, pet. denied); *Moore v. Henry*, 960 S.W.2d 82, 84 (Tex. App.—Houston [1st Dist.] 1996, no writ).

[88] *Moore v. Henry*, 960 S.W.2d 82, 84 (Tex. App.—Houston [1st Dist.] 1996, no writ); Open Records Decision No. 656 at 3 (1997) (statutory predecessor to Gov't Code § 552.028 applies to request for voter registration information under Elec. Code § 18.008 when request is from incarcerated individual).

Generally, a requestor may choose to inspect or copy public information, or to both inspect and copy public information.[89] In certain circumstances, a governmental body may charge the requestor for access to or copies of the requested information.

1. Right to Inspect

Generally, if a requestor chooses to inspect public information, the requestor must complete the inspection within ten business days after the date the governmental body makes the information available or the request will be withdrawn by operation of law.[90] However, a governmental body is required to extend the inspection period by an additional 10 business days upon receiving a written request for additional time.[91] If the information is needed by the governmental body, the officer for public information may interrupt a requestor's inspection of public information.[92] When a governmental body interrupts a requestor's inspection of public information, the period of interruption is not part of the ten business day inspection period.[93] A governmental body may promulgate policies that are consistent with the Public Information Act for efficient, safe, and speedy inspection and copying of public information.[94]

2. Right to Obtain Copies

If a copy of public information is requested, a governmental body must provide "a suitable copy . . . within a reasonable time after the date on which the copy is requested."[95] However, the Act does not authorize the removal of an original copy of a public record from the office of a governmental body.[96] If the requested records are copyrighted, the governmental body must comply with federal copyright law.[97]

A governmental body may receive a request for a public record that contains both publicly available and excepted information. In a decision that involved a document that contained both publicly available information and information that was excepted from disclosure by the statutory predecessor to section 552.111, the attorney general determined the Act did not permit the governmental body to provide the requestor with a new document created in response to the request on which the publicly available information had been consolidated and retyped, unless the requestor agreed to receive a retyped document.[98] Rather, the attorney general concluded that the statutory predecessor to

---

89 Gov't Code §§ 552.221, .225, .228, .230.

90 Gov't Code § 552.225(a); *see also* Open Records Decision No. 512 (1988) (statutory predecessor to Gov't Code § 552.225 did not apply to requests for copies of public information or authorize governmental body to deny repeated requests for copies of public records).

91 Gov't Code § 552.225(b).

92 Gov't Code § 552.225(c).

93 Gov't Code § 552.225(c).

94 Gov't Code § 552.230; *see* Attorney General Opinion JM-757 (1987) (governmental bodies may deny requests for information when requests raise questions of safety or unreasonable disruption of business).

95 Gov't Code § 552.228(a).

96 Gov't Code § 552.226.

97 *See* Open Records Decision No. 660 at 5 (1999) (Federal Copyright Act "may not be used to deny access to or copies of the information sought by the requestor under the Public Information Act," but a governmental body may place reasonable restrictions on use of copyrighted information consistent with rights of copyright owner).

98 Open Records Decision No. 606 at 2–3 (1992).

section 552.228 required the governmental body to make available to the public copies of the actual public records the governmental body had collected, assembled, or maintained, with the excepted information excised.[99]

The public's right to suitable copies of public information has been considered in the following decisions:

Attorney General Opinion JM-757 (1987) — a governmental body may refuse to allow members of the public to duplicate public records by means of portable copying equipment when it is unreasonably disruptive of working conditions, when the records contain confidential information, when it would cause safety hazards, or when it would interfere with other persons' rights to inspect and copy records;

Open Records Decision No. 660 (1999) — section 52(a) of article III of the Texas Constitution does not prohibit the Port of Corpus Christi Authority from releasing a computer generated digital map, created by the Port with public funds, in response to a request made under Chapter 552 of the Government Code;

Open Records Decision No. 633 (1995) — a governmental body does not comply with the Public Information Act by releasing to the requestor another record as a substitute for any specifically requested portions of an offense report that are not excepted from required public disclosure, unless the requestor agrees to the substitution;

Open Records Decision No. 571 (1990) — the Public Information Act does not give a member of the public a right to use a computer terminal to search for public records; and

Open Records Decision No. 243 (1980) — a governmental body is not required to compile or extract information if the information can be made available by giving the requestor access to the records themselves.[100]

E.   Computer and Electronic Information

Section 552.228(b) provides:

If public information exists in an electronic or magnetic medium, the requestor may request a copy in an electronic medium, such as on diskette or on magnetic tape. A governmental body shall provide a copy in the requested medium if:

(1) the governmental body has the technological ability to produce a copy of the requested information in the requested medium;

(2) the governmental body is not required to purchase any software or hardware to accommodate the request; and

---

99   Open Records Decision No. 606 at 2–3 (1992).

100   *See also* Open Records Decision Nos. 512 (1988), 465 (1987), 144 (1976).

(3) provision of a copy of the information in the requested medium will not violate the terms of any copyright agreement between the governmental body and a third party.[101]

If a governmental body is unable to provide the information in the requested medium for any of the reasons described by section 552.228(b), the governmental body shall provide the information in another medium that is acceptable to the requestor.[102] A governmental body is not required to use material provided by a requestor, such as a diskette, but rather may use its own supplies to comply with a request.[103]

A request for public information that requires a governmental body to program or manipulate existing data is not considered a request for the creation of new information.[104] If a request for public information requires "programming or manipulation of data,"[105] and "compliance with the request is not feasible or will result in substantial interference with its ongoing operations,"[106] or "the information could be made available in the requested form only at a cost that covers the programming and manipulation of data,"[107] a governmental body is required to provide the requestor with a written statement describing the form in which the information is available, a description of what would be required to provide the information in the requested form, and a statement of the estimated cost and time to provide the information in the requested form.[108] The governmental body shall provide the statement to the requestor within twenty days after the date the governmental body received the request.[109] If, however, the governmental body gives written notice within the twenty days that additional time is needed, the governmental body has an additional ten days to provide the statement.[110] Once the governmental body provides the statement to the requestor, the governmental body has no obligation to provide the requested information in the requested form unless within thirty days the requestor responds to the governmental body in writing.[111] If the requestor does not respond within thirty days, the request is considered withdrawn.[112]

---

[101] Gov't Code § 552.228(b).

[102] Gov't Code § 552.228(b).

[103] Gov't Code § 552.228(c).

[104] *Fish v. Dallas Indep. Sch. Dist.*, 31 S.W.3d 678, 681–82 (Tex. App.—Eastland 2000, pet. denied); *see* Gov't Code § 552.231; Attorney General Opinion H-90 (1973); Open Records Decision Nos. 452 at 2–3 (1986), 87 (1975).

[105] Gov't Code § 552.231(a)(1); *see* Gov't Code § 552.003(2), (4) (defining "manipulation" and "programming").

[106] Gov't Code § 552.231(a)(2)(A).

[107] Gov't Code § 552.231(a)(2)(B).

[108] Gov't Code § 552.231(a), (b); *see Fish v. Dallas Indep. Sch. Dist.*, 31 S.W.3d 678, 682 (Tex. App.—Eastland 2000, pet. denied); Open Records Decision No. 661 at 6–8 (1999).

[109] Gov't Code § 552.231(c).

[110] Gov't Code § 552.231(c).

[111] Gov't Code § 552.231(d). *See also Fish v. Dallas Indep. Sch. Dist.*, 31 S.W.3d 678, 682 (Tex. App.—Eastland 2000, pet. denied); Open Records Decision No. 661 (1999) (Gov't Code § 552.231 enables governmental body and requestor to reach agreement as to cost, time and other terms of responding to request requiring programming or manipulation of data).

[112] Gov't Code § 552.231(d-1).

V. DISCLOSURE TO SELECTED PERSONS

A. General Rule: Under the Public Information Act, Public Information is Available to All Members of the Public

The Public Information Act states in several provisions that public information is available to "the people," "the public," and "any person."[113] Thus, the Public Information Act deals primarily with the general public's access to information; it does not, as a general matter, give an individual a "special right of access" to information concerning that individual that is not otherwise public information.[114] Information that a governmental body collects, assembles or maintains is, in general, either open to all members of the public or closed to all members of the public.

Additionally, section 552.007 prohibits a governmental body from selectively disclosing information that is not confidential by law but that a governmental body may withhold under an exception to disclosure. Section 552.007 provides as follows:

> **(a) This chapter does not prohibit a governmental body or its officer for public information from voluntarily making part or all of its information available to the public, unless the disclosure is expressly prohibited by law or the information is confidential under law.**
>
> **(b) Public information made available under Subsection (a) must be made available to any person.[115]**

If, therefore, a governmental body releases to a member of the public nonconfidential information, then the governmental body must release the information to all members of the public who request it. For example, in rendering an open records decision under section 552.306, the attorney general would not consider a governmental body's claim that section 552.111 authorized the governmental body to withhold a report from a requestor when the governmental body had already disclosed the report to another member of the public.[116]

B. Some Disclosures of Information to Selected Individuals or Entities Do Not Constitute Disclosures to the Public Under Section 552.007

As noted, the Public Information Act prohibits the selective disclosure of information to members of the public. A governmental body may, however, have authority to disclose records to certain persons or entities without those disclosures being voluntary disclosures to "the public" within the

---

[113] *See, e.g.*, Gov't Code §§ 552.001, .021, .221(a). The Act does not require a requestor be a Texas resident or an American citizen.

[114] Open Records Decision No. 507 at 3 (1988); *see also* Attorney General Opinion JM-590 at 4 (1986); Open Records Decision No. 330 at 2 (1982).

[115] *See also* Open Records Decision No. 463 at 1–2 (1987).

[116] *See* Open Records Decision No. 400 at 2 (1983) (construing statutory predecessor to Gov't Code § 552.111); *see also Cornyn v. City of Garland*, 994 S.W.2d 258, 265 (Tex. App.—Austin 1999, no pet.) (information released pursuant to discovery in litigation was not voluntarily released and thus was excepted from disclosure under Public Information Act).

meaning of section 552.007 of the Government Code. In these cases, the governmental body normally does not waive applicable exceptions to disclosure by transferring or disclosing the records to these specific persons or entities.

1. Special Rights of Access: Exceptions to Disclosure Expressly Inapplicable to a Specific Class of Persons

a. Special Rights of Access Under the Public Information Act

The following provisions in the Public Information Act provide an individual with special rights of access to certain information even though the information is unavailable to members of the general public: sections 552.008, 552.023, 552.026, and 552.114.

i. Information for Legislative Use

Section 552.008 of the Government Code states in pertinent part:

> **(a) This chapter does not grant authority to withhold information from individual members, agencies, or committees of the legislature to use for legislative purposes.**
>
> **(b) A governmental body on request by an individual member, agency, or committee of the legislature shall provide public information, including confidential information, to the requesting member, agency, or committee for inspection or duplication in accordance with this chapter if the requesting member, agency, or committee states that the public information is requested under this chapter for legislative purposes.**

Section 552.008 provides that a governmental body shall provide copies of information, including confidential information, to an individual member, agency, or committee of the legislature if requested for legislative purposes.[117] The section provides that disclosure of excepted or confidential information to a legislator does not waive or affect the confidentiality of the information or the right to assert exceptions in the future regarding that information, and provides specific procedures relating to the confidential treatment of the information.[118] An individual who obtains confidential information under section 552.008 commits an offense if that person misuses the information or discloses it to an unauthorized person.[119]

Subsections (b-1) and (b-2) of section 552.008 provide:

> **(b-1) A member, committee, or agency of the legislature required by a governmental body to sign a confidentiality agreement under Subsection (b) may seek a decision as provided by Subsection (b-2) about whether the information covered by the confidentiality agreement is confidential under law. A confidentiality agreement signed under Subsection (b) is void to the extent that the agreement covers**

---

[117] *See Tex. Comm'n on Envtl. Quality v. Abbott*, 311 S.W.3d 663 (Tex. App.—Austin 2010, pet. denied) (Gov't Code § 552.008 required commission to release to legislator for legislative purposes attorney-client privileged documents subject to confidentiality agreement).

[118] Gov't Code § 552.008(b).

[119] Gov't Code § 552.352(a-1).

information that is finally determined under Subsection (b-2) to not be confidential under law.

(b-2) The member, committee, or agency of the legislature may seek a decision from the attorney general about the matter. The attorney general by rule shall establish procedures and deadlines for receiving information necessary to decide the matter and briefs from the requestor, the governmental body, and any other interested person. The attorney general shall promptly render a decision requested under this subsection, determining whether the information covered by the confidentiality agreement is confidential under law, not later than the 45th business day after the date the attorney general received the request for a decision under this subsection. The attorney general shall issue a written decision on the matter and provide a copy of the decision to the requestor, the governmental body, and any interested person who submitted necessary information or a brief to the attorney general about the matter. The requestor or the governmental body may appeal a decision of the attorney general under this subsection to a Travis County district court. A person may appeal a decision of the attorney general under this subsection to a Travis County district court if the person claims a proprietary interest in the information affected by the decision or a privacy interest in the information that a confidentiality law or judicial decision is designed to protect.[120]

If a member of the legislature signs a confidentiality agreement but subsequently believes the information the governmental body has released pursuant to section 552.008 is not confidential, the member may request an attorney general decision regarding the confidentiality of the information.[121] If the attorney general determines the information is not confidential, any confidentiality agreement the member signed is void. The attorney general promulgated rules relating to its decisions under section 552.008(b-2).[122] These rules are available on the attorney general's website and in Part Four of this *Handbook*.

ii. Information About the Person Who Is Requesting the Information

Section 552.023 of the Government Code provides an individual with a limited special right of access to information about that individual. It states in pertinent part:

(a) A person or a person's authorized representative has a special right of access, beyond the right of the general public, to information held by a governmental body that relates to the person and that is protected from public disclosure by laws intended to protect that person's privacy interests.

(b) A governmental body may not deny access to information to the person, or the person's representative, to whom the information relates on the grounds that the information is considered confidential by privacy principles under this chapter but may assert as grounds for denial of access other provisions of this chapter or other law that are not intended to protect the person's privacy interests.

---

[120] Gov't Code § 552.008(b-1), (b-2).

[121] *See, e.g.*, Open Records Letter No. 2013-08637 (2013).

[122] *See* 1 T.A.C. §§ 63.1–.6.

Subsections (a) and (b) of section 552.023 prevent a governmental body from asserting an individual's own privacy as a reason for withholding records from that individual. However, the individual's right of access to private information about that individual under section 552.023 does not override exceptions to disclosure in the Public Information Act or confidentiality laws protecting some interest other than that individual's privacy.[123] The following decisions consider the statutory predecessor to section 552.023:

Open Records Decision No. 684 (2009) — when requestor is a person whose privacy interests are protected under section 552.130, concerning certain motor vehicle information, or section 552.136, concerning access device information, requestor has a right of access to the information under section 552.023;

Open Records Decision No. 587 (1991) — because former Family Code section 34.08, which made confidential reports, records, and working papers used or developed in an investigation of alleged child abuse, protected law enforcement interests as well as privacy interests, the statutory predecessor to section 552.023 did not provide the subject of the information a special right of access to the child abuse investigation file;

Open Records Decision No. 577 (1990) — under the Communicable Disease Prevention and Control Act, information in the possession of a local health authority relating to disease or health conditions is confidential but may be released with the consent of the person identified in the information; because this confidentiality provision is designed to protect the privacy of the subject of the information, the statutory predecessor to section 552.023 authorized a local health authority to release to the subject medical or epidemiological information relating to the person who signed the consent.

iii. Information in a Student or Education Record

Section 552.114 of the Government Code, which defines "student record" and deems such records confidential, states a governmental body must make such information available if the information is requested by: 1) educational institution personnel; 2) the student involved or the student's parent, legal guardian, or spouse; or 3) a person conducting a child abuse investigation pursuant to Subchapter D of Chapter 261 of the Family Code.[124] Section 552.026 of the Government Code, which conforms the Act to the requirements of the federal Family Educational Rights and Privacy

---

[123] *See* Open Records Decision No. 556 (1990) (predecessor statute to section 552.111 applied to requestor's claim information); *see also Abbott v. Tex. State Bd. of Pharmacy*, 391 S.W.3d 253, 260 (Tex. App.—Austin 2012, no pet.) (because Pharmacy Act confidentiality provision protected integrity of board's regulatory process, board's withholding of requestor's records was based on law not intended solely to protect requestor's privacy interest); *Tex. State Bd. of Chiropractic Exam'rs v. Abbott*, 391 S.W.3d 343, 351 (Tex. App.—Austin 2013, no pet.) (because provision making board's investigation records confidential protected integrity of board's regulatory process rather than requestor's privacy interest, section 552.023 did not prevent board from denying access to requested information).

[124] Gov't Code § 552.114(a), (b), (c).

Act of 1974[125] ("FERPA"), also incorporates the rights of access established by that federal law.[126] To the extent FERPA conflicts with state law, the federal statute prevails.[127][128]

b. Special Rights of Access Created by Other Statutes

Statutes other than the Act grant specific entities or individuals a special right of access to specific information. For example, section 901.160 of the Occupations Code makes information about a licensee held by the Texas State Board of Public Accountancy available for inspection by the licensee. Exceptions in the Act cannot authorize the board to withhold this information from the licensee because the licensee has a statutory right to the specific information requested.[129] As is true for the right of access provided under section 552.023 of the Act, a statutory right of access does not affect the governmental body's authority to rely on applicable exceptions to disclosure when the information is requested by someone other than an individual with a special right of access.

2. Intra- or Intergovernmental Transfers

The transfer of information within a governmental body or between governmental bodies is not necessarily a release to the public for purposes of the Act. For example, a member of a governmental body, acting in his or her official capacity, is not a member of the public for purposes of access to information in the governmental body's possession. Thus, an authorized official may review records of the governmental body without implicating the Act's prohibition against selective disclosure.[130] Additionally, a state agency may ordinarily transfer information to another state agency or to another governmental body subject to the Public Information Act without violating the confidentiality of the information or waiving exceptions to disclosure.[131]

On the other hand, a federal agency is subject to an open records law that differs from the Texas Public Information Act. A state governmental body, therefore, should not transfer non-disclosable information to a federal agency unless some law requires or authorizes the state governmental body

---

[125] 20 U.S.C. § 1232g.

[126] Open Records Decision No. 431 at 2–3 (1985).

[127] Open Records Decision No. 431 at 3 (1985).

[128] Open Records Decision No. 431 at 3 (1985).

[129] Open Records Decision No. 451 at 4 (1986); *see also* Open Records Decision Nos. 500 at 4–5 (1988) (considering property owner's right of access to appraisal records under Tax Code), 478 at 3 (1987) (considering intoxilyzer test subject's right of access to test results under statutory predecessor to Transp. Code § 724.018).

[130] *See* Attorney General Opinions JC-0283 at 3–4 (2000), JM-119 at 2 (1983); *see also* Open Records Decision Nos. 678 at 4 (2003) (transfer of county registrar's list of registered voters to secretary of state and election officials is not release to public prohibited by Gov't Code § 552.1175), 674 at 4 (2001) (information in archival state records that was confidential in custody of originating governmental body remains confidential upon transfer to commission), 666 at 4 (2000) (municipality's disclosure to municipally appointed citizen advisory board of information pertaining to municipally owned power utility does not constitute release to public as contemplated under Gov't Code § 552.007), 464 at 5 (1987) (distribution of evaluations by university faculty members among faculty members does not waive exceptions to disclosure with respect to general public) (overruled on other grounds by Open Records Decision No. 615 (1993)).

[131] *See* Attorney General Opinions H-917 at 1 (1976), H-242 at 4 (1974); Open Records Decision Nos. 667 at 3–4 (2000), 661 at 3 (1999). *But see* Attorney General Opinion JM-590 at 4–5 (1986) (comptroller's release to city prohibited where Tax Code made information confidential, enumerated entities to which information may be disclosed, and did not include city among enumerated entities).

to do so.[132] A federal agency may not maintain the state records with the "same eye towards confidentiality that state agencies would be bound to do under the laws of Texas."[133]

Where information is confidential by statute, the statute specifically enumerates the entities to which the information may be released, and the governmental body is not among those entities, the information may not be transferred to the governmental body.[134]

3. Other Limited Disclosures That Do Not Implicate Section 552.007

The attorney general has recognized other specific contexts in which a governmental body's limited release of information to certain persons does not constitute a release to "the public" under section 552.007:

Open Records Decision No. 579 at 7 (1990) — exchanging information among litigants in informal discovery was not a voluntary release under the statutory predecessor to section 552.007;

Open Records Decision No. 501 (1988) — while former article 9.39 of the Insurance Code prohibited the State Board of Insurance from releasing escrow reports to the public, the Board could release the report to the title company to which the report related;

Open Records Decision No. 454 at 2 (1986) — governmental body that disclosed information it reasonably concluded it had a constitutional obligation to do so could still invoke statutory predecessor to section 552.108; and

Open Records Decision No. 400 (1983) — the prohibition against selective disclosure does not apply when a governmental body releases confidential information to the public.

---

[132] Open Records Decision No. 650 at 4 (1996); *See, e.g.*, Open Records Letter No. 2017-09880 (2017) (United States Army provided right of access under federal law to criminal history record information in certain city police records).

[133] *Attorney General Opinion H-242 at 4 (1974); accord* Attorney General Opinion MW-565 at 4 (1982); Open Records Decision No. 561 at 6 (1990) (quoting with approval Attorney General Opinion H-242 (1974)).

[134] *See generally* Attorney General Opinion JM-590 at 5 (1986); Open Records Decision Nos. 661 at 3 (1999), 655 at 8 (1997), 650 at 3 (1996).

VI. ATTORNEY GENERAL DETERMINES WHETHER INFORMATION IS SUBJECT TO AN EXCEPTION

A. Duties of the Governmental Body and of the Attorney General Under Subchapter G

Sections 552.301, 552.302, and 552.303 set out the duty of a governmental body to seek the attorney general's decision on whether information is excepted from disclosure to the public.

Section 552.301, subsections (a), (b), and (c), provide that when a governmental body receives a written request for information the governmental body wishes to withhold, it must seek an attorney general decision within ten business days of its receipt of the request and state the exceptions to disclosure that it believes are applicable. Subsections (a), (b), and (c) read:

> **(a)   A governmental body that receives a written request for information that it wishes to withhold from public disclosure and that it considers to be within one of the exceptions under Subchapter C must ask for a decision from the attorney general about whether the information is within that exception if there has not been a previous determination about whether the information falls within one of the exceptions.**
>
> **. . .**
>
> **(b)   The governmental body must ask for the attorney general's decision and state the exceptions that apply within a reasonable time but not later than the 10th business day after the date of receiving the written request.**
>
> **(c)   For purposes of this subchapter, a written request includes a request made in writing that is sent to the officer for public information, or the person designated by that officer, by electronic mail or facsimile transmission.**

Thus, a governmental body that wishes to withhold information from the public on the ground of an exception generally must seek the decision of the attorney general as to the applicability of that exception.[135] In addition, an entity contending that it is not subject to the Act may timely request a decision from the attorney general to avoid the consequences of noncompliance if the entity is determined to be subject to the Act.[136] Therefore, when requesting such a decision, the entity should not only present its arguments as to why it is not subject to the Act, but should also raise any exceptions to required disclosure it believes apply to the requested information.

---

[135]   *Thomas v. Cornyn*, 71 S.W.3d 473, 480 (Tex. App.—Austin 2002, no pet.); *Dominguez v. Gilbert*, 48 S.W.3d 789, 792 (Tex. App.—Austin 2001, no pet.); Open Records Decision Nos. 452 at 4 (1986), 435 (1986) (referring specifically to statutory predecessors to Gov't Code §§ 552.103 and 552.111, respectively); *see Conely v. Peck*, 929 S.W.2d 630, 632 (Tex. App.—Austin 1996, no writ) (requirement to request open records decision within ten days comes into play when governmental body denies access to requested information or asserts exception to public disclosure of information).

[136]   *See Blankenship v. Brazos Higher Educ. Auth., Inc.*, 975 S.W.2d 353, 362 (Tex. App.—Waco 1998, pet. denied) (entity does not admit it is governmental body by virtue of request for opinion from attorney general).

A governmental body need not request an attorney general decision if there has been a previous determination that the requested material falls within one of the exceptions to disclosure.[137] What constitutes a "previous determination" is narrow in scope, and governmental bodies are cautioned against treating most published attorney general decisions as "previous determinations" to avoid the requirements of section 552.301(a). The attorney general has determined that there are two types of previous determinations.[138] The first and by far the most common instance of a previous determination pertains to specific information that is again requested from a governmental body when the attorney general has previously issued a decision that evaluates the public availability of the precise information or records at issue. This first instance of a previous determination does not apply to records that are substantially similar to records previously submitted to the attorney general for review, nor does it apply to information that may fall within the same category as any given records on which the attorney general has previously ruled. The first type of previous determination requires that all of the following criteria be met:

1. the information at issue is precisely the same information that was previously submitted to the attorney general pursuant to section 552.301(e)(1)(D) of the Government Code;

2. the governmental body that received the request for the information is the same governmental body that previously requested and received a ruling from the attorney general;

3. the attorney general's prior ruling concluded the precise information is or is not excepted from disclosure under the Act; and

4. the law, facts, and circumstances on which the prior attorney general ruling was based have not changed since the issuance of the ruling.[139]

Absent all four of the above criteria, and unless the second type of previous determination applies, a governmental body must ask for a decision from the attorney general if it wishes to withhold from the public information that is requested under the Act.

The second type of previous determination requires that all of the following criteria be met:

1. the information at issue falls within a specific, clearly delineated category of information about which the attorney general has previously rendered a decision;

2. the previous decision is applicable to the particular governmental body or type of governmental body from which the information is requested;[140]

---

[137] Gov't Code § 552.301(a); *Dominguez v. Gilbert*, 48 S.W.3d 789, 792–93 (Tex. App.—Austin 2001, no pet.).

[138] Open Records Decision No. 673 (2001).

[139] A governmental body should request a decision from the attorney general if it is unclear to the governmental body whether there has been a change in the law, facts or circumstances on which the prior decision was based.

[140] Previous determinations of the second type can apply to all governmental bodies if the decision so provides. *See, e.g.*, Open Records Decision No. 670 (2001) (all governmental bodies may withhold information subject to predecessor of Gov't Code § 552.117(a)(2) without necessity of seeking attorney general decision). On the other hand, if the decision is addressed to a particular governmental body and does not explicitly provide that it also applies to other governmental bodies or to all governmental bodies of a certain type, then only the particular governmental body to which the decision is addressed may rely on the decision as a previous determination. *See, e.g.*, Open Records Decision No. 662 (1999) (constituting second type of previous determination but only with respect to information held by Texas Department of Health).

3. the previous decision concludes the specific, clearly delineated category of information is or is not excepted from disclosure under the Act;

4. the elements of law, fact, and circumstances are met to support the previous decision's conclusion that the requested records or information at issue is or is not excepted from required disclosure; and[141]

5. the previous decision explicitly provides that the governmental body or bodies to which the decision applies may withhold the information without the necessity of again seeking a decision from the attorney general.

Absent all five of the above criteria, and unless the first type of previous determination applies, a governmental body must ask for a decision from the attorney general if it wishes to withhold requested information from the public under the Act.

An example of this second type of previous determination is found in Open Records Decision No. 670. In that decision, the attorney general determined that pursuant to the statutory predecessor of section 552.117(a)(2) of the Government Code, a governmental body may withhold the home address, home telephone number, personal cellular telephone number, personal pager number, social security number, and information that reveals whether the individual has family members, of any individual who meets the definition of "peace officer" without requesting a decision from the attorney general.

The governmental body may not unilaterally decide to withhold information on the basis of a prior open records decision merely because it believes the legal standard for an exception, as established in the prior decision, applies to the recently requested information.[142]

When in doubt, a governmental body should consult with the Open Records Division of the Office of the Attorney General prior to the ten business day deadline to determine whether requested information is subject to a previous determination.[143]

A request for an open records decision pursuant to section 552.301 must come from the governmental body that has received a written request for information.[144] Otherwise, the attorney general does not have jurisdiction under the Act to determine whether the information is excepted from disclosure to the public.

Section 552.301(f) expressly prohibits a governmental body from seeking an attorney general decision where the attorney general or a court has already determined that the same information must

---

[141] Thus, in addition to the law remaining unchanged, the facts and circumstances must also have remained unchanged to the extent necessary for all of the requisite elements to be met. With respect to previous determinations of the second type, a governmental body should request a decision from the attorney general if it is unclear to the governmental body whether all of the elements on which the previous decision's conclusion was based have been met with respect to the requested records or information.

[142] Open Records Decision No. 511 (1988) (no unilateral withholding of information under litigation exception).

[143] *See* Open Records Decision No. 435 at 2–3 (1986) (attorney general has broad discretion to determine whether information is subject to previous determination).

[144] Open Records Decision Nos. 542 at 3 (1990), 449 (1986).

be released. Among other things, this provision precludes a governmental body from asking for reconsideration of an attorney general decision that concluded the governmental body must release information. Subsection (f) provides:

(f) A governmental body must release the requested information and is prohibited from asking for a decision from the attorney general about whether information requested under this chapter is within an exception under Subchapter C if:

> **(1) the governmental body has previously requested and received a determination from the attorney general concerning the precise information at issue in a pending request; and**

> **(2) the attorney general or a court determined that the information is public information under this chapter that is not excepted by Subchapter C.**

Section 552.301(g) authorizes a governmental body to ask for another attorney general decision if: (1) a suit challenging the prior decision was timely filed against the attorney general; (2) the attorney general determines that the requestor has voluntarily withdrawn the request for the information in writing or has abandoned the request; and (3) the parties agree to dismiss the lawsuit.[145]

Section 552.301(d) provides that if the governmental body seeks an attorney general decision as to whether it may withhold requested information, it must notify the requestor not later than the 10th business day after its receipt of the written request that it is seeking an attorney general decision. Section 552.301(d) reads:

(d) A governmental body that requests an attorney general decision under Subsection (a) must provide to the requestor within a reasonable time but not later than the 10th business day after the date of receiving the requestor's written request:

> **(1) a written statement that the governmental body wishes to withhold the requested information and has asked for a decision from the attorney general about whether the information is within an exception to public disclosure; and**

> **(2) a copy of the governmental body's written communication to the attorney general asking for a decision or, if the governmental body's written communication to the attorney general discloses the requested information, a redacted copy of that written communication.**

The attorney general interprets section 552.301(d)(1) to mean that a governmental body substantially complies with subsection (d)(1) by sending the requestor a copy of the governmental body's written communication to the attorney general requesting a decision. Because governmental bodies may be required to submit evidence of their compliance with subsection (d), governmental bodies are encouraged to submit evidence of their compliance when seeking an attorney general decision. If a governmental body fails to comply with subsection (d), the requested information is presumed public pursuant to section 552.302.

---

[145] Gov't Code § 552.301(g).

B. Items the Governmental Body Must Submit to the Attorney General

Sections 552.301(e) and (e-1) read:

(e) **A governmental body that requests an attorney general decision under Subsection (a) must within a reasonable time but not later than the 15th business day after the date of receiving the written request:**

(1) **submit to the attorney general:**

(A) **written comments stating the reasons why the stated exceptions apply that would allow the information to be withheld;**

(B) **a copy of the written request for information;**

(C) **a signed statement as to the date on which the written request for information was received by the governmental body or evidence sufficient to establish that date; and**

(D) **a copy of the specific information requested, or submit representative samples of the information if a voluminous amount of information was requested; and**

(2) **label that copy of the specific information, or of the representative samples, to indicate which exceptions apply to which parts of the copy.**

(e-1) **A governmental body that submits written comments to the attorney general under Subsection (e)(1)(A) shall send a copy of those comments to the person who requested the information from the governmental body not later than the 15th business day after the date of receiving the written request. If the written comments disclose or contain the substance of the information requested, the copy of the comments provided to the person must be a redacted copy.**

Thus, subsection (e) of section 552.301 requires a governmental body seeking an attorney general decision as to whether it may withhold requested information to submit to the attorney general, no later than the fifteenth business day after receiving the written request, written comments stating why the claimed exceptions apply, a copy of the written request, a signed statement as to the date of its receipt of the request or sufficient evidence of that date, and a copy of the specific information it seeks to withhold, or representative samples thereof, labeled to indicate which exceptions are claimed to apply to which parts of the information. Within fifteen business days, a governmental body must also copy the requestor on those comments, redacting any portion of the comments that contains the substance of the requested information. Governmental bodies are cautioned against redacting more than that which would reveal the substance of the information requested from the comments sent to the requestor. A failure to comply with the requirements of section 552.301 can result in the information being presumed public under section 552.302 of the Government Code.

1. Written Communication from the Person Requesting the Information

A written request includes a request sent by electronic mail or facsimile transmission to the public information officer or the officer's designee.[146] A copy of the written request from the member of the public seeking access to the records lets the attorney general know what information was requested, permits the attorney general to determine whether the governmental body met its statutory deadlines in requesting a decision, and enables the attorney general to inform the requestor of the ruling.[147] These written communications are generally public information.[148]

2. Information Requested from the Governmental Body

Section 552.303(a) provides:

> **A governmental body that requests an attorney general decision under this subchapter shall supply to the attorney general, in accordance with Section 552.301, the specific information requested. Unless the information requested is confidential by law, the governmental body may disclose the requested information to the public or to the requestor before the attorney general makes a final determination that the requested information is public or, if suit is filed under this chapter, before a final determination that the requested information is public has been made by the court with jurisdiction over the suit, except as otherwise provided by Section 552.322.**

Governmental bodies should submit a clean, legible copy of the information at issue. Original records should not be submitted. If the requested records are voluminous and repetitive, a governmental body may submit representative samples.[149] If, however, each document contains substantially different information, a copy of each and every requested document or all information must be submitted to the attorney general.[150] For example, it is not appropriate to submit a representative sample of information when the proprietary information of third parties is at issue. In that circumstance, it is necessary to submit the information of each third party with a potential proprietary interest rather than submitting the information of one third party as a representative sample. The attorney general must not disclose the submitted information to the requestor or the public.[151]

3. Labeling Requested Information to Indicate Which Exceptions Apply to Which Parts of the Requested Information

When a governmental body raises an exception applicable to only part of the information, it must mark the records to identify the information it believes is subject to that exception. A general claim that an exception applies to an entire report or document, when the exception clearly does not apply

---

[146] Gov't Code § 552.301(c).

[147] *See* Gov't Code § 552.306(b); Open Records Decision No. 150 (1977).

[148] *Cf.* Gov't Code § 552.301(d)(2), (e-1) (requiring governmental body to provide requestor copies of its written communications to attorney general); Open Records Decision No. 459 (1987) (considering public availability of governmental body's letter to attorney general).

[149] Gov't Code § 552.301(e)(1)(d).

[150] Open Records Decision Nos. 499 at 6 (1988), 497 at 4 (1988).

[151] Gov't Code § 552.3035.

to all information in that report or document, does not conform to the Act.[152] When labeling requested information, a governmental body should mark the records in such a way that all of the requested information remains visible for the attorney general's review. For obvious reasons, the attorney general cannot make a determination on information it cannot read.

4. Statement or Evidence as to Date Governmental Body Received Written Request

The governmental body, in its submission to the attorney general, must certify or provide sufficient evidence of the date it received the written request.[153] This will enable the attorney general to determine whether the governmental body has timely requested the attorney general's decision within ten business days of receiving the written request, as required by section 552.301(b), and timely submitted the other materials that are required by section 552.301(e) to be submitted by the fifteenth business day after receipt of the request. Section 552.301 provides that if a governmental body receives a written request by United States mail and cannot adequately establish the actual date on which the governmental body received the request, the written request is considered to have been received by the governmental body on the third business day after the date of the postmark on a properly addressed request.[154]

The attorney general does not count skeleton crew days observed by a governmental body as business days for the purpose of calculating that governmental body's deadlines under the Public Information Act. A governmental body briefing the attorney general under section 552.301 must inform the attorney general in the briefing of any holiday, including skeleton crew days, observed by the governmental body. If the briefing does not notify the attorney general of holidays the governmental body observes, the deadlines will be calculated to include those days.

5. Letter from the Governmental Body Stating Which Exceptions Apply and Why

The letter from the governmental body stating which exceptions apply to the information and why they apply is necessary because the Public Information Act presumes that governmental records are open to the public unless the records are within one of the exceptions set out in Subchapter C.[155] This presumption is based on the language of section 552.021, which makes virtually all information in the custody of a governmental body available to the public. This language places on the governmental body the burden of proving that an exception applies to the records requested from it.[156] Thus, if the governmental body wishes to withhold particular information, it must establish that a particular exception applies to the information and must mark the records to identify the portion the governmental body believes is excepted from disclosure. Conclusory assertions that a particular exception applies to requested information will not suffice. The burden for establishing the applicability of each exception in the Public Information Act is discussed in detail in Part Two of

---

[152] Gov't Code § 552.301(e)(2); Open Records Decision Nos. 419 at 3 (1984), 252 at 3 (1980), 150 at 2 (1977).

[153] Gov't Code § 552.301(e)(1)(c).

[154] Gov't Code § 552.301(a-1).

[155] *See* Attorney General Opinion H-436 (1974); Open Records Decision Nos. 363 (1983), 150 (1977), 91 (1975).

[156] *See Thomas v. Cornyn*, 71 S.W.3d 473, 480–81 (Tex. App.—Austin 2002, no pet.); Open Records Decision Nos. 542 at 2–3 (1990) (burden is placed on governmental body when it requests ruling pursuant to statutory predecessor to Gov't Code § 552.301), 532 at 1 (1989), 363 (1983), 197 at 1 (1978).

this *Handbook*. If a governmental body does not establish how and why an exception applies to the requested information, the attorney general has no basis on which to pronounce it protected.[157]

The governmental body must send to the requestor a copy of its letter to the attorney general stating why information is excepted from public disclosure.[158] In order to explain how a particular exception applies to the information in dispute, the governmental body may find it necessary to reveal the content of the requested information in its letter to the attorney general. In such cases, the governmental body must redact comments containing the substance of the requested information in the copy of its letter it sends to the requestor.[159]

C. Section 552.302: Information Presumed Public if Submissions and Notification Required by Section 552.301 Are Not Timely

Section 552.302 provides:

> **If a governmental body does not request an attorney general decision as provided by Section 552.301 and provide the requestor with the information required by Sections 552.301(d) and (e-1), the information requested in writing is presumed to be subject to required public disclosure and must be released unless there is a compelling reason to withhold the information.**

Section 552.301(b) establishes a deadline of ten business days for the governmental body to request a decision from the attorney general and state the exceptions that apply.[160] Subsection (d) of section 552.301 requires that the governmental body notify the requestor within ten business days if it is seeking an attorney general decision as to whether the information may be withheld. Section 552.301(e) establishes a deadline of fifteen business days for the governmental body to provide the other materials required under that subsection to the attorney general. Subsection (e-1) of section 552.301 requires that the governmental body copy the requestor on its written comments, within fifteen business days, redacting any portion of the comments that contains the substance of the information requested.

Section 552.302 provides that if the governmental body does not make a timely request for a decision, notify and copy the requestor, and make the requisite submissions to the attorney general as required by section 552.301, the requested information will be presumed to be open to the public, and only the demonstration of a "compelling reason" for withholding the information can overcome that

---

[157] Open Records Decision No. 363 (1983).

[158] Gov't Code § 552.301(e-1).

[159] Gov't Code § 552.301(e-1).

[160] *See also* Gov't Code §§ 552.308 (timeliness of action by United States mail, interagency mail, or common or contract carrier), .309 (timeliness of action by electronic submission).

presumption.[161] In the great majority of cases, the governmental body will not be able to overcome that presumption and must promptly release the requested information. Whether failure to meet the respective ten and fifteen business day deadlines, and submit the requisite information within those deadlines, has the effect of requiring disclosure depends on whether the governmental body asserts a compelling reason that would overcome the presumption of openness arising from the governmental body's failure to meet the submission deadlines.

In *Paxton v. City of Dallas*, the Texas Supreme Court determined (1) the failure of a governmental body to timely seek a ruling from the OAG to withhold information subject to the attorney-client privilege does not constitute a waiver of the privilege, and (2) the attorney-client privilege constitutes a compelling reason to withhold information under section 552.302 of the Government Code.[162]

The supreme court's decision overrules a long line of attorney general decisions discussing the burden a governmental body must meet in order to overcome the legal presumption that the requested information is public and must be released unless there is a compelling reason to withhold the information from disclosure. However, notwithstanding *Paxton v. City of Dallas*, the section 552.302 presumption of openness is triggered as soon as the governmental body fails to meet any of the requisite deadlines for submissions or notification set out in section 552.301. Governmental bodies should review the determination in *Paxton v. City of Dallas* when considering the consequences of failing to comply with the procedures set out in section 552.301.

D. Section 552.303: Attorney General Determination that Information in Addition to that Required by Section 552.301 Is Necessary to Render a Decision

Section 552.303 provides for instances when the attorney general determines information other than that required to be submitted by section 552.301 is necessary to render a decision.[163] If the attorney general determines more information is necessary to render a decision, it must so notify the governmental body and the requestor. [164] If the additional material is not provided by the governmental body within seven calendar days of its receipt of the attorney general's notice, the information sought to be withheld is presumed public and must be disclosed unless a compelling reason for withholding the information is demonstrated.[165]

---

[161] Gov't Code § 552.302; *see Hancock v. State Bd. of Ins.*, 797 S.W.2d 379 (Tex. App.—Austin 1990, no writ); Open Records Decision Nos. 515 at 6 (1988), 452 (1986), 319 (1982); *see also Simmons v. Kuzmich*, 166 S.W.3d 342, 348-49 (Tex. App.—Fort Worth 2005, no pet.) (party seeking to withhold information has burden in trial court of proving exception from disclosure and presumably must comply with steps mandated by statute to seek and preserve such exception from disclosure); *Abbott v. City of Corpus Christi*, 109 S.W.3d 113, 122 n.6 (Tex. App.—Austin 2003, no pet.) (court need not decide whether law enforcement exception applies because city never submitted any reasons or comments as to how exception applied, and issue was not before it because city failed to meet Act's procedural requirements).

[162] *Paxton v. City of Dallas*, 509 S.W.3d 247, 262, 271 (Tex. 2017).

[163] Gov't Code § 552.303(b)–(e).

[164] Gov't Code § 552.303(c).

[165] Gov't Code § 552.303(d)–(e).

E.   Section 552.305:   When the Requested Information Involves a Third Party's Privacy or Property Interests

Section 552.305 reads as follows:

(a)   In a case in which information is requested under this chapter and a person's privacy or property interests may be involved, including a case under Section 552.101, 552.104, 552.110, or 552.114, a governmental body may decline to release the information for the purpose of requesting an attorney general decision.

(b)   A person whose interests may be involved under Subsection (a), or any other person, may submit in writing to the attorney general the person's reasons why the information should be withheld or released.

(c)   The governmental body may, but is not required to, submit its reasons why the information should be withheld or released.

(d)   If release of a person's proprietary information may be subject to exception under Section 552.101, 552.110, 552.113, or 552.131, the governmental body that requests an attorney general decision under Section 552.301 shall make a good faith attempt to notify that person of the request for the attorney general decision. Notice under this subsection must:

  (1)   be in writing and sent within a reasonable time not later than the 10th business day after the date the governmental body receives the request for the information; and

  (2)   include:

    (A)   a copy of the written request for the information, if any, received by the governmental body; and

    (B)   a statement, in the form prescribed by the attorney general, that the person is entitled to submit in writing to the attorney general within a reasonable time not later than the 10th business day after the date the person receives the notice:

      (i)   each reason the person has as to why the information should be withheld; and

      (ii)   a letter, memorandum, or brief in support of that reason.

(e)   A person who submits a letter, memorandum, or brief to the attorney general under Subsection (d) shall send a copy of that letter, memorandum, or brief to the person who requested the information from the governmental body. If the letter, memorandum, or brief submitted to the attorney general contains the substance of the information requested, the copy of the letter, memorandum, or brief may be a redacted copy.

Section 552.305 relieves the governmental body of its duty under section 552.301(b) to state which exceptions apply to the information and why they apply when (1) a third party's privacy or property interests may be implicated, (2) the governmental body has requested a ruling from the attorney general, and (3) the third party or any other party has submitted reasons for withholding or releasing the information.[166] However, section 552.305 does not relieve a governmental body of its duty to request a ruling within ten business days of receiving a request for information, notify the requestor in accordance with section 552.301(d), or provide the attorney general's office with the information required in section 552.301(e).[167] The language of section 552.305(b) is permissive and does not require a third party with a property or privacy interest to seek relief from the attorney general before filing suit against the attorney general under section 552.325. The opportunity to submit comments during the ruling process does not automatically provide access to the courts. A third party must still meet jurisdictional requirements for standing before it may file suit over a ruling that orders information to be disclosed.

Section 552.305(d) requires the governmental body to make a good faith effort to notify a person whose proprietary interests may be implicated by a request for information where the information may be excepted from disclosure under section 552.101, 552.110, 552.113, or 552.131. The governmental body is generally not required to notify a party whose privacy, as opposed to proprietary, interest is implicated by a release of information. The governmental body may itself argue that the privacy interests of a third party except the information from disclosure.

The required notice must be in writing and sent within ten business days of the governmental body's receipt of the request. It must include a copy of the written request for information and a statement that the person may, within ten business days of receiving the notice, submit to the attorney general reasons why the information in question should be withheld and explanations in support thereof. The form of the statement required by section 552.305(d)(2)(B), as prescribed by the attorney general, can be found in Part Nine of this *Handbook*. Subsection (e) of section 552.305 requires a person who submits reasons under subsection (d) for withholding information to send a copy of such communication to the requestor of the information, unless the communication reveals the substance of the information at issue, in which case the copy sent to the requestor may be redacted.

The following open records decisions have interpreted the statutory predecessor to section 552.305:

Open Records Decision No. 652 (1997) — if a governmental body takes no position pursuant to section 552.305 of the Government Code or has determined that requested information is not protected under a specific confidentiality provision, the attorney general will issue a decision based on a review of the information at issue and on any other information provided to the attorney general by the governmental body or third parties;

Open Records Decision No. 609 (1992) — the attorney general is unable to resolve a factual dispute when a governmental body and a third party disagree on whether information is excepted from disclosure based on the third party's property interests;

---

[166] Open Records Decision No. 542 at 3 (1990).

[167] *See* Gov't Code §§ 552.301(a)–(b), (e), .305.

Open Records Decision No. 575 (1990) — the Public Information Act does not require a third party to substantiate its claims of confidentiality at the time it submits material to a governmental body;

Open Records Decision No. 552 (1990) — explanation of how the attorney general deals with a request when, pursuant to the statutory predecessor to section 552.305 of the Public Information Act, a governmental body takes no position on a third party's claim that information is excepted from public disclosure by the third party's property interests and when relevant facts are in dispute; and

Open Records Decision No. 542 (1990) — the statutory predecessor to section 552.305 did not permit a third party to request a ruling from the attorney general.

F. Section 552.3035: Attorney General Must Not Disclose Information at Issue

Section 552.3035 expressly prohibits the attorney general from disclosing information that is the subject of a request for an attorney general decision.

G. Section 552.304: Submission of Public Comments

Section 552.304 of the Act permits any person to submit written comments as to why information at issue in a request for an attorney general decision should or should not be released. In order to be considered, such comments must be received before the attorney general renders a decision under section 552.306, and must be submitted pursuant to sections 552.308 and 552.309, as discussed below.

H. Rendition of Attorney General Decision

Pursuant to section 552.306 of the Act, the attorney general must render an open records decision "not later than the 45th business day after the date the attorney general received the request for a decision."[168] If the attorney general cannot render a decision by the 45 day deadline, the attorney general may extend the deadline by ten business days by informing the governmental body and the requestor of the reason for the delay.[169] The attorney general must provide a copy of the decision to the requestor.[170] The attorney general addressed this section in Open Records Decision No. 687 (2011), concluding section 552.306 imposes a duty on the attorney general to rule on a claimed exception to disclosure when, prior to the issuance of the decision, a party has brought an action before a Texas court posing the same open records question.

I. Timeliness of Action

Pursuant to section 552.308, when the Act requires a request, notice or other document to be submitted or otherwise given to a person within a specified period, the requirement is met in a timely

---

[168] Gov't Code § 552.306(a).

[169] Gov't Code § 552.306(a).

[170] Gov't Code § 552.306(b).

fashion if the document is sent by first class United States mail or common or contract carrier properly addressed with postage or handling charges prepaid and: (1) bears a post office cancellation mark or a receipt mark of the carrier indicating a time within that period; or (2) the submitting person furnishes satisfactory proof the document was deposited in the mail or with the carrier within that period.[171] If a state agency is required to submit information to the attorney general, the timeliness requirement is met if the information is sent by interagency mail and the state agency provides sufficient evidence to establish the information was deposited within the proper period.[172]

The attorney general has established an electronic filing system that allows governmental bodies and interested third parties to submit information electronically for a fee.[173] Information submitted through this designated system will be considered timely if it is electronically submitted within the proper time period.[174] The attorney general has promulgated rules to administer the designated system.[175] These rules are available on the attorney general's website and in Part Four of this *Handbook*. The creation of the electronic filing system does not affect the right of a person or governmental body to submit information to the attorney general under section 552.308.[176]

VII. COST OF COPIES AND ACCESS

Subchapter F of the Public Information Act, sections 552.261 through 552.275, generally provides for allowable charges for copies of and access to public information. All charges must be calculated in accordance with the rules promulgated by the attorney general under section 552.262.[177] The rules establish the charges, as well as methods of calculation for those charges. The rules also provide that a governmental body that is not a state agency may exceed the costs established by the rules of the attorney general by up to 25 percent.[178] The cost rules are available on the attorney general's website and in Part Four of this *Handbook*. Also available on the website is the Public Information Cost Estimate Model, a tool designed to assist the public and governmental bodies in estimating costs associated with public information requests.[179]

A.   Charges for Copies of Paper Records and Printouts of Electronic Records

Section 552.261(a) allows a governmental body to recover costs related to reproducing public information. A request for copies that results in more than fifty pages may be assessed charges for labor, overhead (which is calculated as a percentage of the total labor), and materials.[180]

---

[171]   Gov't Code § 552.308(a).

[172]   Gov't Code § 552.308(b).

[173]   *See* Gov't Code § 402.006(d).

[174]   Gov't Code § 552.309(a).

[175]   1 T.A.C. §§ 63.21–.24. These rules are available on the attorney general's website and in Part Four of this *Handbook*.

[176]   Gov't Code § 552.309(c).

[177]   *See* 1 T.A.C. §§ 70.1–.12.

[178]   Gov't Code § 552.262(a), (b).

[179]   http://www.texasattorneygeneral.gov/open/cost_page.shtml.

[180]   1 T.A.C. § 70.3(d), (e), (i).

Requests that require programming and/or manipulation of data may be assessed charges for those tasks also, as well as computer time to process the request.[181] The law defines "programming" as "the process of producing a sequence of coded instructions that can be executed by a computer."[182] "Manipulation" of data is defined as "the process of modifying, reordering, or decoding of information with human intervention."[183] Finally, "processing" means "the execution of a sequence of coded instructions by a computer producing a result."[184] The amount allowed for computer processing depends on the type of computer used and the time needed for the computer to process the request. The time is calculated in CPU minutes for mainframe and mid-range computers, and in clock hours for client servers and PCs. Computer processing time is not charged for the same time that a governmental body is charging for labor or programming. The use of a computer during this time period is covered by the overhead charge.

The 85th Legislature amended section 552.261 of the Government Code to allow requests to be combined in some instances. Section 552.261(e) states:

> (e) Except as otherwise provided by this subsection, all requests received in one calendar day from an individual may be treated as a single request for purposes of calculating costs under this chapter. A governmental body may not combine multiple requests under this subsection from separate individuals who submit requests on behalf of an organization.[185]

Therefore, a governmental body may now combine separate requests from one individual received within one calendar day when calculating costs.

Examples:

1.A governmental body receives a request for copies of the last 12 months' worth of travel expenditures for employees, including reimbursements and backup documentation. The records are maintained in the governmental body's main office. The governmental body determines there are 120 pages, and it will take one and a half hours to put the information together, redact drivers' license numbers pursuant to section 552.130 and credit card numbers pursuant to section 552.136, and make copies. The total allowable charges for this request would be:

Copies, 120 pages @ $.10/page	$12.00
Labor, 1.5 hours @ $15.00/hour	$22.50
Overhead, $22.50 x .20	$4.50
Total for copies & labor (paper records)	$39.00

2.In addition to the above request, the requestor sends a separate request for copies of all e-mails between two named individuals and members of the public for the same 12 month period. Pursuant to section 552.137, the governmental body will redact any e-mail addresses of members of the public. The governmental body's e-mail system allows electronic redaction of e-mail

---

[181]   1 T.A.C. § 70.3(c), (d), (h).

[182]   Gov't Code § 552.003(4).

[183]   Gov't Code § 552.003(2).

[184]   Gov't Code § 552.003(3).

[185]   Gov't Code § 552.261(e).

addresses by writing a program. Once the program is written it will take half of an hour to execute. The requestor wants the e-mails on a CD. The total charges for this request would be:

Labor, .50 hours to locate/compile responsive e-mails, @ $15.00/hour	$7.50
Labor, .50 hours to write program to redact, @ $28.50/hour	$14.25
Labor, .50 hours to prepare for and download to CD, @ $15.00/hour	$7.50
Overhead, $29.25 x .20	$5.85
Client Server, .50 hours to process program and make copy, @ $2.20/hour	$1.10
Materials, 1 CD @ $1.00/each	$1.00
Total for materials & labor (electronic redaction/electronic records)	$37.20

Postage charges may be added if the requestor wants the CD sent by mail.

3. The governmental body's system does not allow electronic redaction of e-mail addresses. To provide the requestor the records in electronic medium, the governmental body must print the e-mails, manually redact the e-mail addresses, and scan the redacted e-mails into a file. The governmental body may charge to print out and redact the e-mails that will be scanned. The requestor wants the e-mails on a CD. The total charges for this request would be:

Printouts to be scanned, 80 pages, @ $.10/page	$8.00
Labor, .50 hours to locate/compile/print responsive e-mails, @ $15.00/hour	$7.50
Labor, .50 hours to redact, @ $15.00/hour	$7.50
Labor, .25 hours to scan redacted copies, @ $15.00/hour	$3.75
Overhead, $18.75 x .20	$3.75
Client Server, .05 hours to copy to CD, @ $2.20/hour	$0.18
Materials, 1 CD @ $1.00/each	$1.00
Total for materials and labor (manual redaction/electronic records	$31.68

Postage charges may be added if the requestor wants the CD sent by mail.

B. Charges for Inspection of Paper Records and Electronic Records

Charges for inspection of paper records are regulated by section 552.271, and charges for inspection of electronic records are discussed in section 552.272. Section 552.271 allows charges for copies for any page that must be copied so that confidential information may be redacted to enable the requestor to inspect the information subject to release.[186] No other charges are allowed unless[187] (a) the records to be inspected are older than five years, or (b) the records completely fill, or when assembled will completely fill, six or more archival boxes, and (c) the governmental body estimates it will require more than five hours to prepare the records for inspection.[188] If a governmental body has fewer than 16 full-time employees, the criteria are reduced to: (a) the records are older than three years, or (b) the records fill, or when assembled will completely fill, three or more archival boxes, and (c) the governmental body estimates it will require more than two hours to prepare the records for inspection.[189] An "archival box" is a box that measures approximately 12.5" W x 15.5" L x 10" H.[190] Only records responsive to the request may be counted towards the number of boxes. Preparing records that fall under subsections 552.271(c) or (d) for inspection includes the time needed to locate and compile the records, redact the confidential information, and make copies of pages that require redaction. Overhead charges are not allowed on requests for inspection of paper records.[191]

Section 552.272 allows charges for labor when providing access to electronic information requires programming and/or manipulation of data, regardless of whether or not the information is available directly on-line to the requestor.[192] Searching and/or printing electronic records is neither programming nor manipulation of data. Overhead is not allowed on requests for inspection of electronic records.[193]

Example:

The requestor states she wants to inspect travel expenditure records for the past year, and then decide whether or not she wants copies. Of the 120 pages that are responsive, 112 pages have information that must be redacted, as required by sections 552.130 and 552.136, before the requestor may inspect the records. The total allowable charges for this request would be:

Redacted copies, 112 @ $.10/page	$11.20
Labor & Overhead	$0.00
Total for inspection (redacted copies)	$11.20

---

[186] Gov't Code § 552.271(b).
[187] Gov't Code § 552.271(b).
[188] Gov't Code § 552.271(c).
[189] Gov't Code § 552.271(d).
[190] 1 T.A.C. § 70.2(10).
[191] Gov't Code § 552.271(c), (d).
[192] Gov't Code § 552.271(a), (b).
[193] Gov't Code § 552.271(a), (b).

C. Waivers or Reduction of Estimated Charges

If a governmental body determines that producing the information requested is in the "public interest" because it will primarily benefit the general public, the governmental body shall waive or reduce the charges.[194] The determination of whether providing information is in the "public interest" rests solely with the governmental body whose records are requested.[195] Additionally, the law allows a governmental body to waive charges if the cost of collecting the amount owed exceeds the actual amount charged.[196]

D. Providing a Statement of Estimated Charges as Required by Law

If a governmental body estimates that charges will exceed $40.00, the governmental body is required to provide the requestor with a written itemized statement of estimated charges before any work is undertaken.[197] Additionally, the statement must advise the requestor if there is a less costly method of viewing the records.[198] The statement must also contain a notice that the request will be considered automatically withdrawn if the requestor does not respond in writing within ten business days of the date of the statement that the requestor: (a) accepts the charges, (b) modifies the request in response to the estimate, or (c) has sent, or is sending, a complaint regarding the charges to the attorney general.[199] If the governmental body has the ability to communicate with the general public by electronic mail and/or facsimile, the statement must also advise the requestor that a response may be sent by either of those methods, as well as by regular mail or in person.[200]

Governmental bodies are cautioned that an itemized statement lacking any of the required elements is considered to be "deficient" because it does not comply with the law. The consequences of providing a deficient statement may result in (a) limiting the amount the governmental body may recover through charges,[201] and/or (b) preventing the governmental body from considering the request withdrawn by operation of law.[202]

If after receiving agreement from the requestor for the charges, but before completing the request, the governmental body determines the actual charges will exceed the agreed-upon charges by more than 20 percent, the governmental body must provide the requestor an updated statement of estimated charges.[203] This updated statement has the same requirements as the initial statement. If the governmental body fails to provide the updated statement of estimated charges, charges for the entire request are limited to the initial agreed-upon estimate plus 20 percent.[204] If the requestor does not respond to the updated statement, the request is considered withdrawn.

---

[194] Gov't Code § 552.267(a).

[195] Gov't Code § 552.267(a).

[196] Gov't Code § 552.267(b).

[197] Gov't Code § 552.2615(a).

[198] Gov't Code § 552.2615(a).

[199] Gov't Code § 552.2615(b).

[200] Gov't Code § 552.2615(a)(3).

[201] 1 T.A.C. § 70.7(a).

[202] Gov't Code § 552.2615.

[203] Gov't Code § 552.2615(c).

[204] Gov't Code § 552.2615(c).

If a request is estimated to exceed $100.00 ($50.00 if a governmental body has fewer than 16 full-time employees), a governmental body that provides the statement of estimated charges with all its required elements may also require that the requestor prepay, deposit a percentage of the total amount, or provide a bond for the total amount.[205] Decisions about method of payment rest with the governmental body. A governmental body that requires a deposit or bond may consider the request withdrawn if payment is not received within ten business days of the date the governmental body requested the deposit or bond.[206] If the requestor makes payment within the required time, the request is considered received on the date the payment is made.[207] Additionally, a governmental body is not required to comply with a new request if a requestor owes more than $100.00 on unpaid charges for previous requests for which the requestor was provided, and accepted, an appropriate statement of estimated charges.[208] In such cases, the governmental body may require the requestor to pay the unpaid amounts before complying with that request. All unpaid charges must be duly documented.[209]

In addition to the statement of estimated charges required when a request will exceed $40.00, a governmental body is also required to provide a statement when it determines that a request will require programming and/or manipulation of data and (1) complying with the request is not feasible or will substantially interfere with the governmental body's ongoing operation, or (2) the request can only be fulfilled at a cost that covers the programming and/or manipulation of data.[210] Governmental bodies are cautioned that a statement under section 552.231, unlike section 552.2615, is not contingent on the charges being over a certain amount. Rather, the statement is mandated if the requisite conditions are present. The statement must include that the information is not available in the form requested, in which form it is available, any contracts or services needed to put the information in the form requested, the estimated charges calculated in accordance with the rules promulgated by the attorney general, and the estimated time of completion to provide the information in the form requested.[211] On provision of the statement, the governmental body is not required to provide the information in the form requested unless the requestor states, in writing, that the requestor agrees with the estimated charges and time parameters, or that the requestor will accept the information in the form that is currently available.[212] If the requestor fails to respond to the statement in writing within 30 days, the request is considered withdrawn.[213]

---

[205] Gov't Code § 552.263(c); 1 T.A.C. § 70.7(d), (e).

[206] Gov't Code § 552.263(f).

[207] Gov't Code § 552.263(e).

[208] Gov't Code § 552.263(c); 1 T.A.C. § 70.7(f).

[209] Gov't Code § 552.263(c); 1 T.A.C. § 70.7(f).

[210] Gov't Code § 552.231(a).

[211] Gov't Code § 552.231(b).

[212] Gov't Code § 552.231(d).

[213] Gov't Code § 552.231(d-1).

E. Cost Provisions Regarding Requests Requiring a Large Amount of Personnel Time

Section 552.275 authorizes a governmental body to establish a reasonable limit, not less than 15 hours for a one month period or 36 hours in a 12 month period, on the amount of time that personnel are required to spend producing public information for inspection or copies to a requestor, without recovering the costs attributable to the personnel time related to that requestor.[214] If a governmental body chooses to establish a time limit under this section, a requestor will be required to compensate the governmental body for the costs incurred in satisfying subsequent requests once the time limit has been reached. The 85th Legislature amended section 552.275 to allow county officials who have designated the same officer for public information to calculate time for purposes of this section collectively.[215] A limit under this section does not apply if the requestor is an elected official of the United States, the State of Texas, or a political subdivision of the State of Texas; or an individual who, for a substantial portion of the individual's livelihood or for substantial financial gain is seeking the information for (a) dissemination by a new medium or communication service provider, or (b) creation or maintenance of an abstract plant as described by section 2501.004 of the Insurance Code.[216] Section 552.275 does not replace or supersede other sections, and it does not preclude a governmental body from charging labor for a request for inspection or copies for inspection for which a charge is authorized under other sections of this law.

On establishing the time limit, a governmental body must make it clear to all requestors that the limit applies to all requestors equally, except as provided by the exemptions of subsections (j), (k), and (l). A governmental body that avails itself of section 552.275 must provide a requestor with a statement detailing the time spent in complying with the instant request and the cumulative amount of time the requestor has accrued towards the established limit.[217] A governmental body may not charge for the time spent preparing the statement.[218] If a requestor meets or exceeds the established limit, the governmental body may assess charges for labor, overhead, and material for all subsequent requests. The governmental body is required to provide a written estimate within ten business days of receipt of the request, even if the estimated total will not exceed $40.00. All charges assessed under section 552.275 must be in compliance with the rules promulgated by the attorney general.[219] If a governmental body provides the requestor with a written statement under this section, and the time limits prescribed have been met, the governmental body is not required to respond unless the requestor submits payment.[220] If a requestor fails to submit payment, the request is considered withdrawn.[221]

---

[214] Gov't Code §552.275(a), (b).

[215] Gov't Code §552.275(a-1).

[216] Gov't Code §552.275(j).

[217] Gov't Code § 552.275(d).

[218] Gov't Code § 552.275(d).

[219] Gov't Code § 552.275(e).

[220] Gov't Code § 552.275(g).

[221] Gov't Code § 52.275(h).

F. Complaints Regarding Alleged Overcharges

Estimates are, by their very nature, imperfect. Therefore, governmental bodies are encouraged to run tests on sample data and to rely on the results of those tests in calculating future charges. However, even when a governmental body has taken steps to ensure that a charge is appropriate, a requestor may still believe that the charges are too high. Section 552.269 states that a requestor who believes he or she has been overcharged may lodge a complaint with the attorney general.[222] The attorney general reviews, investigates, and makes determinations on complaints of overcharges. Complaints must be received within ten business days after the requestor knows of the alleged overcharge, and must include a copy of the original request, and any amendments thereto, as well as a copy of any correspondence from the governmental body stating the charges. If a complainant does not provide the required information within the established time frame, the complaint is dismissed.[223]

When a complaint is lodged against a governmental body, the attorney general will contact the governmental body, generally by mail, to obtain information on how the charges were calculated, and the physical location and state of the records. The governmental body may also be asked to provide copies of invoices, contracts, and any other relevant documents.[224] The attorney general may uphold the charges as presented to the requestor, require the issuance of an amended statement of estimated charges, or, if the requestor has already paid the charges, require the issuance of a refund for the difference between what was paid and the charges that are determined to be appropriate.[225] A governmental body may be required to pay three times the difference if it is determined that a requestor overpaid because the governmental body refused or failed to follow the attorney general rules and the charges were not calculated in good faith.[226]

G. Cost Provisions Outside the Public Information Act

The provisions of section 552.262 do not apply if charges for copies are established by another statute.[227] For example, section 550.065 of the Transportation Code establishes a charge of $6.00 for an accident report maintained by a governmental entity.[228] Section 118.011 of the Local Government Code establishes the charge for a non-certified copy of information obtained from the county clerk.[229] Section 118.144 of the Local Government Code also establishes a charge for copies obtained from the county treasurer.[230] Additionally, the attorney general has determined that section 191.008 of the Local Government Code prevails over section 552.272, by giving a county commissioners court the right to set charges regarding access to certain information held by the county.[231]

---

[222] Gov't Code § 552.269(a).

[223] 1 T.A.C. § 70.8(b).

[224] 1 T.A.C. § 70.8(c), (d), (e).

[225] 1 T.A.C. § 70.8(f).

[226] Gov't Code § 552.269(b); 1 T.A.C. § 70.8(h).

[227] Gov't Code § 552.262(a).

[228] Transp. Code § 550.065(d).

[229] Local Gov't Code § 118.011(a)(4).

[230] Local Gov't Code § 118.144.

[231] Local Gov't Code § 191.008; Open Records Decision No. 668 at 9 (2000).

VIII. PENALTIES AND REMEDIES

A. Informal Resolution of Complaints

The Office of the Attorney General maintains an Open Government Hotline staffed by personnel trained to answer questions about the Public Information Act. In addition to answering substantive and procedural questions posed by governmental bodies and requestors, the Hotline staff handles written, informal complaints concerning requests for information. While not meant as a substitute for the remedies provided in sections 552.321 and 552.3215, the Hotline provides an informal alternative for complaint resolution. In most cases, Hotline staff are able to resolve complaints and misunderstandings informally. The Hotline can be reached toll-free at (877) 673-6839 (877-OPEN TEX) or in the Austin area at (512) 478-6736 (478-OPEN). Questions concerning charges for providing public information should be directed to the attorney general's toll-free Cost Hotline at (888) 672-6787 (888-ORCOSTS) or in the Austin area at (512) 475-2497.

B. Criminal Penalties

The Public Information Act establishes criminal penalties for both the release of information that must not be disclosed and the withholding of information that must be released. Section 552.352(a) of the Act provides: "A person commits an offense if the person distributes information considered confidential under the terms of this chapter." This section applies to information made confidential by law.[232]

Section 552.353(a) provides:

> **An officer for public information, or the officer's agent, commits an offense if, with criminal negligence, the officer or the officer's agent fails or refuses to give access to, or to permit or provide copying of, public information to a requestor as provided by this chapter.**

Subsections (b) through (d) of section 552.353 set out various affirmative defenses to prosecution under subsection (a), including, for example, that a timely request for a decision from the attorney general is pending or that the officer for public information is pursuing judicial relief from compliance with a decision of the attorney general pursuant to section 552.324.[233] A violation of section 552.352 or section 552.353 constitutes official misconduct [234] and is a misdemeanor punishable by confinement in a county jail for not more than six months, a fine not to exceed $1,000, or both confinement and the fine.[235]

The Act also criminalizes the destruction, alteration or concealment of public records. Section 552.351 provides that the willful destruction, mutilation, removal without permission, or alteration of public records is a misdemeanor punishable by confinement in a county jail for a minimum of

---

[232] *See* Open Records Decision No. 490 (1988).

[233] Gov't Code § 552.353(b)(2-3). *See generally Hubert v. Harte-Hanks Tex. Newspapers, Inc.*, 652 S.W.2d 546, 548–49 (Tex. App.—Austin 1983, writ ref'd n.r.e.).

[234] Gov't Code §§ 552.352(c), .353(f).

[235] Gov't Code §§ 552.352(b), .353(e).

three days and a maximum of three months, a fine of a minimum of $25.00 and a maximum of $4,000, or both confinement and the fine.[236]

C. Civil Remedies

1. Writ of Mandamus

Section 552.321 of the Act provides for a suit for a writ of mandamus to compel a governmental body to release requested information. A requestor or the attorney general may seek a writ of mandamus to compel a governmental body to release requested information if the governmental body refuses to seek an attorney general decision, refuses to release public information or if the governmental body refuses to release information in accordance with an attorney general decision.[237] Section 552.321(b) provides that a mandamus action filed by a requestor under section 552.321 must be filed in a district court of the county in which the main offices of the governmental body are located. A mandamus suit filed by the attorney general under section 552.321 must be filed in a district court in Travis County, except if the suit is against a municipality with a population of 100,000 or less, in which case the suit must be filed in a district court of the county where the main offices of the municipality are located.[238]

Section 552.321 authorizes a mandamus suit to compel the release of information even if the attorney general has ruled such information is not subject to required public disclosure.[239] The courts have held a requestor may bring a mandamus action regardless of whether an attorney general decision has been requested.[240] Further, the Texas Supreme Court considered a requestor's mandamus action filed after the governmental body requested an attorney general decision, but prior to the attorney general's issuance of a decision.[241] The supreme court held a requestor is not required to defer a suit for mandamus until the attorney general issues a decision.[242] A requestor may counterclaim for mandamus as part of his or her intervention in a suit by a governmental body or third party over a ruling that orders information to be disclosed.[243]

2. Violations of the Act: Declaratory Judgment or Injunctive Relief; Formal Complaints

Section 552.3215 provides for a suit for declaratory judgment or injunctive relief brought by a local prosecutor or the attorney general against a governmental body that violates the Public Information Act.

---

[236] Gov't Code § 552.351(a); *see also* Penal Code § 37.10 (tampering with governmental record).

[237] Gov't Code § 552.321(a); *see Thomas v. Cornyn*, 71 S.W.3d 473, 482 (Tex. App.—Austin 2002, no pet.).

[238] Gov't Code § 552.321(b).

[239] *Thomas v. Cornyn*, 71 S.W.3d 473, 483 (Tex. App.—Austin 2002, no pet.); *Tex. Dep't of Pub. Safety v. Gilbreath*, 842 S.W.2d 408, 411 (Tex. App.—Austin 1992, no writ).

[240] *Thomas v. Cornyn*, 71 S.W.3d 473, 483 (Tex. App.—Austin 2002, no pet.); *Tex. Dep't of Pub. Safety v. Gilbreath*, 842 S.W.2d 408, 411 (Tex. App.—Austin 1992, no writ); *see* Open Records Decision No. 687 (2011) (attorney general will rule on claimed exceptions to disclosure when, prior to issuance of open records decision, party brings action before Texas court posing same open records question).

[241] *Kallinen v. City of Houston*, 462 S.W. 3d 25 (Tex. 2015). .

[242] *Kallinen v. City of Houston*, 462 S.W. 3d 25 (Tex. 2015).

[243] *Thomas v. Cornyn*, 71 S.W.3d 473, 482 (Tex. App.—Austin 2002, no pet.).

a. Venue and Proper Party to Bring Suit

An action against a governmental body located in only one county may be brought only in a district court in that county. The action may be brought either by the district or county attorney on behalf of that county, or by the attorney general on behalf of the state. If the governmental body is located in more than one county, such a suit must be brought in the county where the governmental body's administrative offices are located.[244] If the governmental body is a state agency, the Travis County district attorney or the attorney general may bring such suit only in a district court of Travis County.[245]

b. Suit Pursuant to Formal Complaint

Before suit may be filed under section 552.3215, a person must first file a complaint alleging a violation of the Act. The complaint must be filed with the district or county attorney of the county where the governmental body is located. If the governmental body is located in more than one county, the complaint must be filed with the district or county attorney of the county where the governmental body's administrative offices are located. If the governmental body is a state agency, the complaint may be filed with the Travis County district attorney. If the governmental body is the district or county attorney, the complaint must be filed with the attorney general.[246]

c. Procedures for Formal Complaint

A complaint must be in writing and signed by the complainant and include the name of the governmental body complained of, the time and place of the alleged violation, and a general description of the violation.[247] The district or county attorney receiving a complaint must note on its face the date it was filed and must, before the 31st day after the complaint was filed, determine whether the alleged violation was committed, determine whether an action will be brought under the section, and notify the complainant in writing of those determinations.[248] If the district or county attorney determines not to bring suit under the section, or determines that a conflict of interest exists that precludes his bringing suit, then he or she must include a statement giving the basis for such determination and return the complaint to the complainant by the 31st day after receipt of the complaint.[249]

If the county or district attorney decides not to bring an action in response to a complaint filed with that office, the complainant may, before the 31st day after the complaint is returned, file the complaint with the attorney general. On receipt of the complaint, the attorney general within the same time frame must make the determinations and notification required of a district or county attorney. The 85th Legislature amended section 552.3215 of the Government Code to also allow the complainant to file a complaint under this section with the attorney general if on or after the 90th day after the complainant files a complaint with the district or county attorney, the district or county

---

[244] Gov't Code § 552.3215(c).

[245] Gov't Code § 552.3215(d).

[246] Gov't Code § 552.3215(e).

[247] Gov't Code § 552.3215(e).

[248] Gov't Code § 552.3215(f)–(g).

[249] Gov't Code § 552.3215(h).

attorney has not brought an action.[250] If the attorney general decides to bring an action in response to a complaint against a governmental body located in only one county, the attorney general must file such action in a district court of that county.[251]

d.   Governmental Body Must Be Given Opportunity to Cure Violation

Actions for declaratory judgment or injunctive relief under section 552.3215 may be brought only if the official proposing to bring the action notifies the governmental body in writing of the determination that the alleged violation was committed and the governmental body does not cure the violation before the fourth day after the date it receives the notice.[252]

e.   Cumulative Remedy

Actions for declaratory judgment or injunctive relief authorized under section 552.3215 are in addition to any other civil, administrative, or criminal actions authorized by law.[253]

3.   Suits Over an Open Records Ruling

The Act provides judicial remedies for a governmental body seeking to withhold requested information or a third party asserting a privacy or proprietary interest in requested information when the attorney general orders such information to be disclosed.[254] The venue for these suits against the attorney general is Travis County. The issue of whether the information is subject to disclosure is decided by the court anew. The court is not bound by the ruling of the attorney general. However, the only exceptions to disclosure a governmental body may raise before the court are exceptions that it properly raised in a request for an attorney general decision under section 552.301, unless the exception is one based on a requirement of federal law or one involving the property or privacy interests of another person.[255]

The court of appeals in *Morales v. Ellen* affirmed that the district court had jurisdiction to decide a declaratory judgment action brought against a governmental body by a third party which asserted privacy interests in documents the attorney general had ruled should be released.[256] The court held the statutory predecessor to section 552.305(b)—which permitted a third party whose privacy or property interests would be implicated by the disclosure of the requested information to "submit in writing to the attorney general the party's reasons why the information should be withheld or released"—is permissive and does not require a third party with a property or privacy interest to exhaust this remedy before seeking relief in the courts. [257] The legislature then enacted section 552.325 which recognizes the legal interests of third parties and their right to sue the attorney general to challenge a ruling that information must be released.

---

[250] Gov't Code §552.3215(i).

[251] Gov't Code § 552.3215(i).

[252] Gov't Code § 552.3215(j).

[253] Gov't Code § 552.3215(k).

[254] Gov't Code §§ 552.324, .325.

[255] Gov't Code § 552.326; *City of Dallas v. Abbott*, 304 S.W.3d 380, 392 (Tex. 2010); *Tex. Comptroller of Pub. Accounts v. Attorney General of Tex.*, 354 S.W.3d 336, 340 (Tex. 2010).

[256] *Morales v. Ellen*, 840 S.W.2d 519, 523 (Tex. App.—El Paso 1992, writ denied).

[257] *Morales v. Ellen*, 840 S.W.2d 519, 523 (Tex. App.—El Paso 1992, writ denied).

Sections 552.324 and 552.325 prohibit a governmental body, officer for public information, or other person or entity that wishes to withhold information from filing a lawsuit against a requestor. The only suit a governmental body or officer for public information may bring is one against the attorney general.[258] Section 552.324(b) requires that a suit by a governmental body be brought no later than the 30th calendar day after the governmental body receives the decision it seeks to challenge. If suit is not timely filed under the section, the governmental body must comply with the attorney general's decision. The deadline for filing suit under section 552.324 does not affect the earlier ten day deadline required of a governmental body to file suit in order to establish an affirmative defense to prosecution of a public information officer under section 552.353(b)(3).[259]

Section 552.325 provides that a requestor may intervene in a suit filed by a governmental body or another entity to prevent disclosure. The section includes procedures for notice to the requestor of the right to intervene and of any proposed settlement between the attorney general and a plaintiff by which the parties agree that the information should be withheld.

Sometimes during the pendency of a suit challenging a ruling, the requestor will voluntarily withdraw his or her request, or the requestor may no longer be found. Section 552.327 authorizes a court to dismiss a suit challenging an attorney general ruling if all parties to the suit agree to the dismissal and the attorney general determines and represents to the court that the requestor has voluntarily withdrawn the request for information in writing, or has abandoned the request.[260] In such cases, a governmental body will not be precluded from asking for another ruling on the same information at issue after the suit is dismissed by the court.[261]

4. Discovery and Court's In Camera Review of Information Under Protective Order

Section 552.322 authorizes a court to order that information at issue in a suit under the Act may be discovered only under a protective order until a final determination is made. When suit is filed challenging a ruling, the attorney general will seek access to the information at issue either informally or by way of this section, because the attorney general returns the information to the governmental body upon issuance of a ruling.

Section 552.3221 permits a party to file the information at issue with the court for in camera inspection as necessary for the adjudication of cases.[262] When the court receives the information for review, the court must enter an order that prevents access to the information by any person other than the court, a reviewing court of appeals or parties permitted to inspect the information pursuant to a protective order.[263] Information filed with the court under section 552.3221 does not constitute court records under Rule 76a of the Texas Rules of Civil Procedure and shall not be available by the clerk or any custodian of record for public disclosure.[264]

---

[258] Gov't Code § 552.324(a).

[259] Gov't Code § 552.324(b).

[260] Gov't Code § 552.327.

[261] Gov't Code § 552.327.

[262] Gov't Code § 552.3221(a).

[263] Gov't Code § 552.3221(b).

[264] Gov't Code § 552.3221(c).

D. Assessment of Costs of Litigation and Reasonable Attorney's Fees

Section 552.323 of the Act provides that in a suit for mandamus under section 552.321 or for declaratory judgment or injunctive relief under section 552.3215, the court shall assess costs of litigation and reasonable attorney's fees incurred by a plaintiff who substantially prevails.[265] However, a court may not assess such costs and attorney's fees against the governmental body if the court finds that it acted in reasonable reliance on a judgment or order of a court applicable to that governmental body, the published opinion of an appellate court, or a written decision of the attorney general.[266] In addition, a requestor who is an attorney representing himself in a suit to require a governmental body to disclose requested information under the Act is not entitled to attorney's fees because the requestor did not incur attorney's fees.[267]

The court may assess attorney's fees and costs in a suit brought under section 552.324 by a governmental body against the attorney general challenging a ruling that ordered information to be disclosed.[268] The trial court has discretion to award attorney's fees and costs incurred by a plaintiff or defendant who substantially prevails in a suit brought under section 552.324.[269] In exercising its discretion as to the assessment of such costs and attorney's fees, a court must consider whether the conduct of the officer for public information of the governmental body had a reasonable basis in law and whether the suit was brought in good faith.[270]

IX. PRESERVATION AND DESTRUCTION OF RECORDS

Subject to state laws governing the destruction of state and local government records, section 552.004 of the Act addresses the preservation period of noncurrent records. Sections 441.180 through 441.205 of the Government Code provide for the management, preservation, and destruction of state records under the guidance of the Texas State Library and Archives Commission.[271] Provisions for the preservation, retention, and destruction of local government records under the oversight of the Texas State Library and Archives Commission are set out in chapters 201 through 205 of the Local Government Code.

Section 552.0215 of the Act provides that with the exception of information subject to section 552.147 or a confidentiality provision, information that is not confidential but merely excepted from required disclosure under the Act is public information and is available to the public on or after the 75th anniversary of the date the information was originally created or received by the

---

[265] Gov't Code § 552.323(a).

[266] Gov't Code § 552.323(a).

[267] *Jackson v. State Office of Admin. Hearings*, 351 S.W.3d 290, 300 (Tex. 2011).

[268] Gov't Code § 552.323(b).

[269] Gov't Code § 552.323(b); *Hudson v. Paxton*, No. 03-13-00368-CV, 2015 WL 739605 (Tex. App.—Austin Feb. 20, 2015, pet. denied) (mem. op.) (when requestor intervened in suit filed by governmental body under section 552.324 and governmental body voluntarily released documents rendering controversy moot, requestor did not "substantially prevail" so as to be eligible for attorney's fees under section 552.323(b)); *Dallas Morning News v. City of Arlington*, No. 03-10-00192-CV, 2011 WL 182886, at *4 (Tex. App.—Austin, Jan. 21, 2011, no pet.) (mem. op., not designated for publication) (city's voluntary release of requested public information does not make requestor prevailing party).

[270] Gov't Code § 552.323(b); *see City of Garland v. Dallas Morning News*, 22 S.W.3d 351, 367 (Tex. 2000).

[271] *See, e.g.*, Attorney General Opinions DM-181 at 3 (1992), JM-1013 at 2, 5–6 (1989), JM-229 at 5 (1984).

governmental body.[272] This section does not, however, limit the authority of a governmental body to establish retention periods for records under applicable law.[273]

Section 552.203 provides that the officer for public information, "subject to penalties provided in this chapter," has the duty to see that public records are protected from deterioration, alteration, mutilation, loss, or unlawful removal and that they are repaired as necessary.[274] Public records may be destroyed only as provided by statute.[275] A governmental body may not destroy records even pursuant to statutory authority while they are subject to an open records request.[276]

X. PUBLIC INFORMATION ACT DISTINGUISHED FROM CERTAIN OTHER STATUTES

A. Authority of the Attorney General to Issue Attorney General Opinions

The attorney general has authority pursuant to article IV, section 22, of the Texas Constitution and sections 402.041 through 402.045 of the Government Code to issue legal opinions to certain public officers. These officers are identified in sections 402.042 and 402.043 of the Government Code. The attorney general may not give legal advice or a written opinion to any other person.[277]

On the other hand, the Public Information Act requires a governmental body to request a ruling from the attorney general if it receives a written request for records that it believes to be within an exception set out in subchapter C of the Act, sections 552.101 through 552.158, and there has not been a previous determination about whether the information falls within the exception.[278] Thus, all governmental bodies have a duty to request a ruling from the attorney general under the circumstances set out in section 552.301. A much smaller group of public officers has discretionary authority to request attorney general opinions pursuant to chapter 402 of the Government Code. A school district, for example, is a governmental body that must request open records rulings as required by section 552.301 of the Public Information Act, but has no authority to seek legal advice on other matters from the attorney general.[279]

Additionally, the Public Information Act gives the attorney general the authority to issue written decisions and opinions in order to maintain uniformity in the application, operation, and interpretation of the Act.[280]

---

[272] Gov't Code § 552.0215(a).

[273] Gov't Code § 552.0215(b).

[274] *See also* Gov't Code § 552.351 (penalty for willful destruction, mutilation, removal without permission or alteration of public records).

[275] *See generally* Attorney General Opinions DM-40 (1991) (deleting records), JM-830 (1987) (sealing records), MW-327 (1981) (expunging or altering public records).

[276] Local Gov't Code § 202.002(b); Open Records Decision No. 505 at 4 (1988).

[277] Gov't Code § 402.045.

[278] Gov't Code § 552.301(a); *see* Open Records Decision No. 673 (2001) (defining previous determination).

[279] *See generally* Attorney General Opinion DM-20 at 3–6 (1991).

[280] Gov't Code § 552.011.

B. Texas Open Meetings Act

The Public Information Act, Government Code chapter 552, and the Open Meetings Act, Government Code chapter 551, both serve the purpose of opening government to the people. However, they operate differently, and each has a different set of exceptions. The exceptions in the Public Information Act do not furnish a basis for holding executive session meetings to discuss confidential records.[281] Furthermore, the mere fact that a document was discussed in an executive session does not make it confidential under the Public Information Act.[282] Since the Open Meetings Act has no provision comparable to section 552.301 of the Public Information Act, the attorney general may address questions about the Open Meetings Act only when such questions are submitted by a public officer with authority to request attorney general opinions pursuant to chapter 402 of the Government Code. (A companion volume to this *Handbook*, the *Open Meetings Act Handbook*, is also available from the Office of the Attorney General.) In Open Records Decision No. 684 (2009), the attorney general issued a previous determination to all governmental bodies authorizing them to withhold certified agendas and tapes of closed meetings under section 552.101 in conjunction with section 551.104 of the Government Code, without the necessity of requesting an attorney general decision.[283]

C. Discovery Proceedings

The Public Information Act differs in purpose from statutes and procedural rules providing for discovery of documents in administrative and judicial proceedings.[284] The Act's exceptions to required public disclosure do not create privileges from discovery of documents in administrative or judicial proceedings.[285] Furthermore, information that might be privileged from discovery is not necessarily protected from required public disclosure under the Act.[286]

---

[281] *See* Attorney General Opinion JM-595 at 4 (1986).

[282] *City of Garland v. Dallas Morning News*, 22 S.W.3d 351, 367 (Tex. 2000); Open Records Decision No. 485 at 9–10 (1987); *see also* Open Records Decision No. 605 at 2–3 (1992).

[283] Open Records Decision No. 684 at 5 (2009).

[284] Attorney General Opinion JM-1048 at 2 (1989); Open Records Decision Nos. 551 at 4 (1990), 108 (1975).

[285] Gov't Code § 552.005.

[286] *See* Open Records Decision No. 575 at 2 (1990) (discovery privileges in Texas Rules of Evidence not confidentiality provisions for purpose of Gov't Code § 552.101). *But see* Open Records Decision Nos. 677 (2002) (analyzing work product privilege in context of Act), 676 (2002) (analyzing attorney-client privilege in context of Act).

PART TWO: EXCEPTIONS TO DISCLOSURE

I. INFORMATION GENERALLY CONSIDERED TO BE PUBLIC

A. Section 552.022 Categories of Information

Section 552.022 of the Public Information Act provides that "[w]ithout limiting the amount or kind of information that is public information under this chapter, the following categories of information are public information and not excepted from required disclosure unless made confidential under this chapter or other law . . . ."[287] Section 552.022(a) then lists eighteen categories of information. Section 552.022(a) is not an exhaustive list of the types of information subject to the Public Information Act.[288] Rather, it is a list of information that generally may be withheld only if it is expressly confidential by law.[289] Thus, the Act's permissive exceptions to disclosure generally do not apply to the categories of information contained in section 552.022.[290]

1. Discovery Privileges

The laws under which information may be considered confidential for the purpose of section 552.022 are not limited simply to statutes and judicial decisions that expressly make information confidential.[291] The Texas Supreme Court has held that discovery privileges included in the Texas Rules of Civil Procedure and the Texas Rules of Evidence are also "other law" that may make information confidential for the purpose of section 552.022.[292] Therefore, even if information is included in one of the eighteen categories of information listed in section 552.022(a), and as a result the information cannot be withheld under an exception listed in the Act, the information is still protected from disclosure if a governmental body can demonstrate that the information is privileged under the Texas Rules of Evidence or the Texas Rules of Civil Procedure.[293]

Accordingly, a governmental body claiming the attorney-client privilege for a document that is subject to section 552.022 of the Government Code should raise Texas Rule of Evidence 503 in order to withhold the information. If the governmental body demonstrates that rule 503 applies to part of a communication, generally the entire communication will be protected.[294] However, a fee

---

[287] Gov't Code § 552.022.

[288] *See City of Garland v. Dallas Morning News*, 22 S.W.3d 351, 359 (Tex. 2000).

[289] Gov't Code § 552.022(a); *Thomas v. Cornyn*, 71 S.W.3d 473, 480 (Tex. App.—Austin 2002, no pet.).

[290] *See In re City of Georgetown*, 53 S.W.3d 328, 331 (Tex. 2001). *But see* Gov't Code §§ 552.022(a)(1) (completed report, audit or evaluation may be withheld under Gov't Code § 552.108), .104(b) (information subject to Gov't Code § 552.022 may be withheld under Gov't Code § 552.104(a)), .133(c) (information subject to Gov't Code § 552.022 may be withheld under Gov't Code § 552.133).

[291] *See* Gov't Code § 552.022(a); *In re City of Georgetown*, 53 S.W.3d 328, 332–37 (Tex. 2001).

[292] *In re City of Georgetown*, 53 S.W.3d 328, 337 (Tex. 2001); *see* Open Records Decision Nos. 677 at 9 (2002), 676 at 2 (2002); *see generally* TEX. R. EVID. 501–513; TEX. R. CIV. P. 192.5.

[293] *In re City of Georgetown*, 53 S.W.3d 328, 333–34, 337 (Tex. 2001).

[294] *See Huie v. DeShazo*, 922 S.W.2d 920, 923 (Tex. 1996) (privilege extends to entire communication, including facts contained therein); *In re Valero Energy Corp.*, 973 S.W.2d 453, 457 (Tex. App.—Houston [14th Dist.] 1998, orig. proceeding) (privilege attaches to complete communication, including factual information).

bill is not excepted in its entirety if a governmental body demonstrates that a portion of the fee bill contains or consists of an attorney-client communication.[295] Rather, information in an attorney fee bill may only be withheld to the extent the particular information in the fee bill is demonstrated to be subject to the attorney-client privilege.[296]

Similarly, a governmental body claiming the work product privilege for a document that is subject to section 552.022 of the Government Code should raise Rule 192.5 of the Texas Rules of Civil Procedure in order to withhold the information.[297] Moreover, information is confidential for the purpose of section 552.022 under rule 192.5 only to the extent the information implicates the core work product aspect of the privilege.[298] Other work product is discoverable under some circumstances and therefore is not considered to be confidential for the purpose of section 552.022.[299]

2. Court Order

Section 552.022(b) prohibits a court in this state from ordering a governmental body to withhold from public disclosure information in the section 552.022 categories unless the information is confidential under the Act or other law.[300] Thus, although section 552.107(2) of the Act excepts from disclosure information that a court has ordered to be kept confidential, section 552.022 effectively limits the applicability of that subsection and the authority of a court to order confidentiality.[301]

B.   Certain Investment Information

Section 552.0225 provides that certain investment information is public and not excepted from disclosure under the Act. The section provides:

(a) **Under the fundamental philosophy of American government described by Section 552.001, it is the policy of this state that investments of government are investments of and for the people and the people are entitled to information regarding those investments. The provisions of this section shall be liberally construed to implement this policy.**

(b) **The following categories of information held by a governmental body relating to its investments are public information and not excepted from disclosure under this chapter:**

(1) **the name of any fund or investment entity the governmental body is or has invested in;**

---

[295] Open Records Decision No. 676 at 5 (2002).
[296] Open Records Decision No. 676 at 5–6 (2002).
[297] Open Records Decision No. 677 at 9 (2002).
[298] Open Records Decision No. 677 at 10 (2002).
[299] Open Records Decision No. 677 at 9–10 (2002).
[300] Gov't Code § 552.022(b).
[301] *See Ford v. City of Huntsville*, 242 F.3d 235, 241 (5th Cir. 2001).

(2)   the date that a fund or investment entity described by Subdivision (1) was established;

(3)   each date the governmental body invested in a fund or investment entity described by Subdivision (1);

(4)   the amount of money, expressed in dollars, the governmental body has committed to a fund or investment entity;

(5)   the amount of money, expressed in dollars, the governmental body is investing or has invested in any fund or investment entity;

(6)   the total amount of money, expressed in dollars, the governmental body received from any fund or investment entity in connection with an investment;

(7)   the internal rate of return or other standard used by a governmental body in connection with each fund or investment entity it is or has invested in and the date on which the return or other standard was calculated;

(8)   the remaining value of any fund or investment entity the governmental body is or has invested in;

(9)   the total amount of fees, including expenses, charges, and other compensation, assessed against the governmental body by, or paid by the governmental body to, any fund or investment entity or principal of any fund or investment entity in which the governmental body is or has invested;

(10)   the names of the principals responsible for managing any fund or investment entity in which the governmental body is or has invested;

(11)   each recusal filed by a member of the governing board in connection with a deliberation or action of the governmental body relating to an investment;

(12)   a description of all of the types of businesses a governmental body is or has invested in through a fund or investment entity;

(13)   the minutes and audio or video recordings of each open portion of a meeting of the governmental body at which an item described by this subsection was discussed;

(14)   the governmental body's percentage ownership interest in a fund or investment entity the governmental body is or has invested in;

(15)   any annual ethics disclosure report submitted to the governmental body by a fund or investment entity the governmental body is or has invested in; and

(16) the cash-on-cash return realized by the governmental body for a fund or investment entity the governmental body is or has invested in.

(c)   This section does not apply to the Texas Mutual Insurance Company or a successor to the company.

(d)   This section does not apply to a private investment fund's investment in restricted securities, as defined in Section 552.143.[302]

There are no cases or formal opinions interpreting this section. Section 552.143 excepts certain investment information from disclosure that is not made public under section 552.0225.[303] The attorney general has determined in an informal letter ruling that section 552.143 is subject to the public disclosure requirements of section 552.0225.[304]

C.   Other Kinds of Information that May Not Be Withheld

As a general rule, a governmental body may not use one of the exceptions in the Act to withhold information that a statute other than the Act expressly makes public.[305] For example, a governmental body may not withhold the minutes of an open meeting under the Act's exceptions since such minutes are made public by statute.[306]

II.   EXCEPTIONS

A.   Section 552.101: Confidential Information

Section 552.101 of the Government Code provides as follows:

> **Information is excepted from [required public disclosure] if it is information considered to be confidential by law, either constitutional, statutory, or by judicial decision.**

This section makes clear that the Public Information Act does not mandate the disclosure of information that other law requires be kept confidential. Section 552.352(a) states: "A person commits an offense if the person distributes information considered confidential under the terms of this chapter."[307] A violation under section 552.352 is a misdemeanor constituting official

---

[302] Gov't Code § 552.0225.

[303] Gov't Code § 552.143.

[304] Open Records Letter No. 2005-6095 (2005).

[305] Open Records Decision No. 623 (1994); *see also* Open Records Decision Nos. 675 (2001) (federal statute requiring release of cost reports of nursing facilities prevails over claim that information is excepted from disclosure under Gov't Code § 552.110), 451 (1986) (specific statute that affirmatively requires release of information at issue prevails over litigation exception of Public Information Act); *cf. Houston Chronicle Publ'g Co. v. Woods*, 949 S.W.2d 492 (Tex. App.—Beaumont 1997, orig. proceeding) (concerning public disclosure of affidavits in support of executed search warrants).

[306] Gov't Code § 551.022; *see* Open Records Decision No. 225 (1979).

[307] Gov't Code § 552.352(a).

misconduct.[308] In its discretion, a governmental body may release to the public information protected under the Act's exceptions to disclosure but not deemed confidential by law.[309] On the other hand, a governmental body has no discretion to release information deemed confidential by law.[310] Because the Act prohibits the release of confidential information and because its improper release constitutes a misdemeanor, the attorney general may raise section 552.101 on behalf of a governmental body, although the attorney general ordinarily will not raise other exceptions that a governmental body has failed to claim.[311]

By providing that all information a governmental body collects, assembles, or maintains is public unless expressly excepted from disclosure, the Act prevents a governmental body from making an enforceable promise to keep information confidential unless the governmental body is authorized by law to do so.[312] Thus, a governmental body may rely on its promise of confidentiality to withhold information from disclosure only if the governmental body has specific statutory authority to make such a promise. Unless a governmental body is explicitly authorized to make an enforceable promise to keep information confidential, it may not make such a promise in a confidentiality agreement such as a contract[313] or a settlement agreement.[314] In addition, a governmental body may not pass an ordinance or rule purporting to make certain information confidential unless the governmental body is statutorily authorized to do so.[315]

1. Information Confidential Under Specific Statutes

Section 552.101 incorporates specific statutes that protect information from public disclosure. The following points are important for the proper application of this aspect of section 552.101:

1) The language of the relevant confidentiality statute controls the scope of the protection.[316]

2) To fall within section 552.101, a statute must explicitly require confidentiality; a confidentiality requirement will not be inferred from the statutory structure.[317]

a. State Statutes

The attorney general must interpret numerous confidentiality statutes. Examples of information made confidential by statute include the following noteworthy examples:

---

[308] Gov't Code § 552.352(b), (c).

[309] Gov't Code § 552.007; *see Dominguez v. Gilbert*, 48 S.W.3d 789, 793 (Tex. App.—Austin 2001, no pet.).

[310] *See* Gov't Code § 552.007; *Dominguez v. Gilbert*, 48 S.W.3d 789, 793 (Tex. App.—Austin 2001, no pet.). *But see* discussion of informer's privilege in Part Two, Section II, Subsection A.2.b of this *Handbook*.

[311] *See* Open Records Decision Nos. 455 at 3 (1987), 325 at 1 (1982).

[312] Attorney General Opinion H-258 at 3 (1974); *see* Attorney General Opinions JM-672 at 1–2 (1987), JM-37 at 2 (1983); Open Records Decision Nos. 585 at 2 (1991), 514 at 1 (1988), 55A at 2 (1975).

[313] *See* Attorney General Opinion JM-672 at 2 (1987); Open Records Decision No. 514 at 1 (1988).

[314] *See* Open Records Decision No. 114 at 1 (1975).

[315] *See Indus. Found. v. Tex. Indus. Accident Bd.*, 540 S.W.2d 668, 677 (Tex. 1976), *cert. denied*, 430 U.S. 931 (1977); *Envoy Med. Sys. v. State*, 108 S.W.3d 333, 337 (Tex. App.—Austin 2003, no pet.); Open Records Decision No. 594 at 3 (1991).

[316] *See* Open Records Decision No. 478 at 2 (1987).

[317] *See, e.g.*, Open Records Decision No. 465 at 4–5 (1987).

- medical records that a physician creates or maintains regarding the identity, diagnosis, evaluation, or treatment of a patient;[318]

- reports, records, and working papers used or developed in an investigation of alleged child abuse or neglect under Family Code chapter 261;[319]

- certain information relating to the provision of emergency medical services;[320]

- communications between a patient and a mental health professional and records of the identity, diagnosis, or treatment of a mental health patient created or maintained by a mental health professional;[321] and

- certain personal information in a government-operated utility customer's account records if the customer has requested that the utility keep the information confidential.[322]

In the following examples, the attorney general has interpreted the scope of confidentiality provided by Texas statutes under section 552.101:

Open Records Decision No. 658 (1998) — section 154.073 of the Civil Practice and Remedies Code does not make confidential a governmental body's mediated final settlement agreement;[323]

Open Records Decision No. 655 (1997) — concerning confidentiality of criminal history record information and permissible interagency transfer of such information;

Open Records Decision No. 649 (1996) — originating telephone numbers and addresses furnished on a call-by-call basis by a service supplier to a 9-1-1 emergency communication district established under subchapter D of chapter 772 of the Health and Safety Code are confidential under section 772.318 of the Health and Safety Code. Section 772.318 does not except from disclosure any other information contained on a computer-aided dispatch report that was obtained during a 9-1-1 call;

Open Records Decision No. 643 (1996) — section 21.355 of the Education Code makes confidential any document that evaluates, as that term is commonly understood, the performance

---

[318] Occ. Code § 159.002(b); *see Abbott v. Tex. State Bd. of Pharmacy*, 391 S.W.3d 253, 258 (Tex. App.—Austin 2012, no pet.) (Medical Practice Act does not provide patient general right of access to medical records from governmental body responding to request for information under Public Information Act); Open Records Decision No. 681 at 16–17 (2004).

[319] Fam. Code § 261.201(a).

[320] Health & Safety Code § 773.091; *see* Open Records Decision No. 681 at 17–18 (2004).

[321] Health & Safety Code § 611.002.

[322] Util. Code § 182.052(a).

[323] The 76th Legislature amended section 154.073 of the Civil Practice and Remedies Code by adding subsection (d), which provides that a final written agreement to which a governmental body subject to the Act is a signatory and that was reached as a result of a dispute resolution procedure conducted under chapter 154 of that code is subject to or excepted from required disclosure in accordance with the Act. Act of May 30, 1999, 76th Leg., R.S., ch. 1352, § 6, 1999 Tex. Gen. Laws 4578, 4582; *see* Gov't Code § 552.022(a)(18) (settlement agreement to which governmental body is party may not be withheld unless it is confidential under the Act or other law).

of a teacher or administrator. The term "teacher," as used in section 21.355, means an individual who is required to hold and does hold a teaching certificate or school district teaching permit under subchapter B of chapter 21, and who is engaged in teaching at the time of the evaluation; an "administrator" is a person who is required to hold and does hold an administrator's certificate under subchapter B of chapter 21 and is performing the functions of an administrator at the time of the evaluation;

Open Records Decision No. 642 (1996) — section 143.1214(b) of the Local Government Code requires the City of Houston Police Department to withhold documents relating to an investigation of a City of Houston fire fighter conducted by the City of Houston Police Department's Public Integrity Review Group when the Public Integrity Review Group has concluded that the allegations were unfounded; and

Open Records Decision No. 640 (1996) (replacing Open Records Decision No. 637 (1996)) — the Texas Department of Insurance must withhold any information obtained from audit "work papers" that are "pertinent to the accountant's examination of the financial statements of an insurer" under former section 8 of article 1.15 of the Insurance Code; former section 9 of article 1.15 makes confidential the examination reports and related work papers obtained during the course of an examination of a carrier; section 9 of article 1.15 did not apply to examination reports and work papers of carriers under liquidation or receivership.

b. Federal Statutes

Section 552.101 also incorporates the confidentiality provisions of federal statutes and regulations. In Open Records Decision No. 641 (1996), the attorney general ruled that information collected under the Americans with Disabilities Act, 42 U.S.C. §§ 12101 *et seq.*, from an applicant or employee concerning that individual's medical condition and medical history is confidential under section 552.101 of the Government Code, in conjunction with provisions of the Americans with Disabilities Act. This type of information must be collected and maintained separately from other information and may be released only as provided by the Americans with Disabilities Act.

In Open Records Decision No. 681 (2004), the attorney general addressed whether the Health Insurance Portability and Accountability Act of 1996 ("HIPAA") and the related Privacy Rule[324] adopted by the United States Department of Health and Human Services make information confidential for the purpose of section 552.101. The attorney general determined that when a governmental body that is a "covered entity"[325] subject to the Privacy Rule, receives a request for "protected health information"[326] from a member of the public, it must evaluate the disclosure under the Act rather than the Privacy Rule. The decision also determined that the Privacy Rule does not

---

[324] The United States Department of Health and Human Services promulgated the Privacy Rule under HIPAA to implement HIPAA's privacy requirements for setting national privacy standards for health information. *See* 42 U.S.C. § 1320d-2; 45 C.F.R. pts. 160, 164.

[325] The Privacy Rule only applies to a covered entity, that is, one of the following three entities defined in the Privacy Rule: (1) a health plan; (2) a health care clearinghouse; and (3) a health care provider who transmits any health information in electronic form in connection with certain transactions covered by subchapter C, subtitle A of title 45 of the Code of Federal Regulations. *See* 42 U.S.C. § 1320d-1(a); 45 C.F.R. § 160.103.

[326] *See* 45 C.F.R. § 160.103 (defining "protected health information"); Open Records Decision No. 681 at 5–7 (2004) (determination of whether requested information is protected health information subject to Privacy Rule requires consideration of definitions of three terms in rule).

make information confidential for purposes of section 552.101 of the Government Code. In *Abbott v. Tex. Dep't of Mental Health & Mental Retardation*, the Third Court of Appeals agreed with the attorney general's analysis of the interplay of the Act and the Privacy Rule.[327]

As a general rule, the mere fact that a governmental body in Texas holds certain information that is confidential under the federal Freedom of Information Act or the federal Privacy Act will not bring the information within the section 552.101 exception, as those acts govern disclosure only of information that federal agencies hold.[328] However, if an agency of the federal government shares its information with a Texas governmental entity, the Texas entity must withhold the information that the federal agency determined to be confidential under federal law.[329]

2. Information Confidential by Judicial Decision

a. Information Confidential Under Common Law or Constitutional Privacy Doctrine

i. Common-Law Privacy

(a) Generally

Section 552.101 also excepts from required public disclosure information held confidential under case law. Pursuant to the Texas Supreme Court decision in *Indus. Found. v. Tex. Indus. Accident Bd.*,[330] section 552.101 applies to information when its disclosure would constitute the common-law tort of invasion of privacy through the disclosure of private facts. To be within this common-law tort, the information must (1) contain highly intimate or embarrassing facts about a person's private affairs such that its release would be highly objectionable to a reasonable person and (2) be of no legitimate concern to the public.[331] Because much of the information that a governmental body holds is of legitimate concern to the public, the doctrine of common-law privacy frequently will not exempt information that might be considered "private." For example, information about public employees' conduct on the job is generally not protected from disclosure.[332] The attorney general has found that the doctrine of common-law privacy does not protect the specific information at issue in the following decisions:

Open Records Decision No. 625 (1994) — a company's address and telephone number;

Open Records Decision No. 620 (1993) — a corporation's financial information;

---

[327] *Abbott v. Tex. Dep't of Mental Health & Mental Retardation*, 212 S.W.3d 648 (Tex. App.—Austin 2006, no pet.).

[328] Attorney General Opinion MW-95 at 2 (1979); Open Records Decision No. 124 at 1 (1976).

[329] *See* Open Records Decision No. 561 at 6–7 (1990); *accord United States v. Napper*, 887 F.2d 1528, 1530 (11th Cir. 1989) (documents that Federal Bureau of Investigation lent to city police department remained property of Bureau and were subject to any restrictions on dissemination of Bureau-placed documents).

[330] *Indus. Found. v. Tex. Indus. Accident Bd.*, 540 S.W.2d 668 (Tex. 1976), *cert. denied*, 430 U.S. 931 (1977).

[331] *Indus. Found. v. Tex. Indus. Accident Bd.*, 540 S.W.2d 668, 685 (Tex. 1976), *cert. denied*, 430 U.S. 931 (1977); *see* Open Records Decision No. 659 (1999).

[332] *See* Open Records Decision No. 455 (1987).

Open Records Decision No. 616 (1993) — a "mug shot," unrelated to any active criminal investigation, taken in connection with an arrest for which an arrestee subsequently was convicted and is serving time;

Open Records Decision No. 611 (1992) — records held by law enforcement agencies regarding violence between family members unless the information is highly intimate and embarrassing and of no legitimate public interest;

Open Records Decision No. 594 (1991) — certain information regarding a city's drug testing program for employees; and

Open Records Decision No. 441 (1986) — job-related examination scores of public employees or applicants for public employment.

The attorney general has concluded that, with the exception of victims of sexual assault,[333] section 552.101 does not categorically except from required public disclosure, on common-law privacy grounds, the names of crime victims.[334]

In addition to the seminal Public Information Act privacy case of *Industrial Foundation,* courts in other cases have considered the common-law right to privacy in the context of section 552.101 of the Act. In two cases involving the *Fort Worth Star-Telegram* newspaper, the Texas Supreme Court weighed an individual's right to privacy against the right of the press to publish certain embarrassing information concerning an individual. In *Star-Telegram, Inc. v. Doe,*[335] a rape victim sued the newspaper, which had published articles disclosing the age of the victim, the relative location of her residence, the fact that she owned a home security system, that she took medication, that she owned a 1984 black Jaguar automobile, and that she owned a travel agency. The newspaper did not reveal her actual identity. The court held that the newspaper in this case could not be held liable for invasion of privacy for public disclosure of embarrassing private facts because, although the information disclosed by the articles made the victim identifiable by her acquaintances, it could not be said that the articles disclosed facts which were not of legitimate public concern.

In *Star-Telegram, Inc. v. Walker,*[336] the court addressed another case involving the identity of a rape victim. In this case, the victim's true identity could be gleaned from the criminal court records and testimony. The court found that because trial proceedings are public information, the order entered by the criminal court closing the files and expunging the victim's true identity from the criminal records (more than three months following the criminal trial) could not retroactively abrogate the press's right to publish public information properly obtained from open records. Once information is in the public domain, the court stated, the law cannot recall the information. Therefore, the court

---

[333] *See* Open Records Decision No. 339 at 2 (1982).

[334] Open Records Decision No. 409 at 2 (1984); *see also* Open Records Decision Nos. 628 (1994) (identities of juvenile victims of crime are not *per se* protected from disclosure by common-law privacy), 611 (1992) (determining whether records held by law-enforcement agency regarding violence between family members are confidential under doctrine of common-law privacy must be done on case-by-case basis). *But see* Gov't Code §§ 552.132 (excepting information about certain crime victims), .1325 (excepting information held by governmental body or files with court contained in victim impact statement or submitted for purpose of preparing such statement).

[335] *Star-Telegram, Inc. v. Doe*, 915 S.W.2d 471 (Tex. 1995).

[336] *Star-Telegram, Inc. v. Walker*, 834 S.W.2d 54 (Tex. 1992).

found that the newspaper could not be held liable for invasion of privacy for publication of information appearing in public court documents.

In *Morales v. Ellen*,[337] the court of appeals considered whether the statements and names of witnesses to and victims of sexual harassment in an employment context were public information under the Act. In Open Records Decision No. 579 (1990), the attorney general had concluded that an investigative file concerning a sexual harassment complaint was not protected by common-law privacy. The decision in *Ellen* modified that interpretation. The *Ellen* court found that the names of witnesses and their detailed affidavits were "highly intimate or embarrassing." Furthermore, the court found that, because information pertinent to the sexual harassment charges and investigation already had been released to the public in summary form, the legitimate public interest in the matter had been satisfied. Therefore, the court determined that, in this instance, the public did not possess a legitimate interest in the names of witnesses to or victims of the sexual harassment, in their statements, or in any other information that would tend to identify them. The *Ellen* court did not protect from public disclosure the identity of the alleged perpetrator of the sexual harassment.

In *Abbott v. Dallas Area Rapid Transit*,[338] the court of appeals considered a request for the investigation report pertaining to a claim of racial discrimination. The court concluded this information is in no way intimate or embarrassing and is not comparable to the information at issue in *Morales v. Ellen*. The court of appeals determined the report was not protected by common-law privacy and must be released without redaction.

(b) Financial Information

Governmental bodies frequently claim that financial information pertaining to an individual is protected under the doctrine of common-law privacy as incorporated into section 552.101. Resolution of these claims hinges upon the role the information plays in the relationship between the individual and the governmental body.

Information regarding a financial transaction between an individual and a governmental body is a matter of legitimate public interest; thus, the doctrine of common-law privacy does not generally protect from required public disclosure information regarding such a transaction.[339] An example of a financial transaction between a person and a governmental body is a public employee's participation in an insurance program funded wholly or partially by his or her employer.[340] In contrast, a public employee's participation in a voluntary investment program or deferred compensation plan that the employer offers but does not fund is not considered a financial transaction between the individual and the governmental body; information regarding such participation is considered intimate and of no legitimate public interest.[341] Consequently, the doctrine of common-law privacy generally excepts such financial information from required public disclosure.

[337] *Morales v. Ellen*, 840 S.W.2d 519, 524–25 (Tex. App.—El Paso 1992, writ denied).

[338] *Abbott v. Dallas Area Rapid Transit*, 410 S.W.3d 876 (Tex. App.—Austin 2013, no pet.).

[339] *See* Open Records Decision Nos. 590 at 3 (1991), 523 at 3–4 (1989).

[340] *See* Open Records Decision No. 600 at 9 (1992).

[341] *See* Open Records Decision No. 545 at 3–5 (1990).

The doctrine of common-law privacy does not except from disclosure the basic facts concerning a financial transaction between an individual and a governmental body.[342] On the other hand, common-law privacy generally protects the "background" financial information of the individual, that is, information about the individual's overall financial status and past financial history.[343] However, certain circumstances may justify the public disclosure of background financial information; therefore, a determination of the availability of background financial information under the Act must be made on a case-by-case basis.[344]

ii. Constitutional Privacy

Section 552.101 also incorporates constitutional privacy.[345] The United States Constitution protects two kinds of individual privacy interests: (1) an individual's interest in independently making certain important personal decisions about matters that the United States Supreme Court has stated are within the "zones of privacy," as described in *Roe v. Wade*[346] and *Paul v. Davis*[347] and (2) an individual's interest in avoiding the disclosure of personal matters to the public or to the government.[348] The "zones of privacy" implicated in the individual's interest in independently making certain kinds of decisions include matters related to marriage, procreation, contraception, family relationships, and child rearing and education.[349]

The second individual privacy interest that implicates constitutional privacy involves matters outside the "zones of privacy." To determine whether the constitutional right of privacy protects particular information, the release of which implicates a person's interest in avoiding the disclosure of personal matters, the attorney general applies a balancing test that weighs the individual's interest in privacy against the public's right to know the information. Although such a test might appear more protective of privacy interests than the common-law test, the scope of information considered private under the constitutional doctrine is far narrower than that under the common law; the material must concern the "most intimate aspects of human affairs."[350]

---

[342] *See, e.g.*, Open Records Decision Nos. 523 at 3–4 (1989), 385 at 2 (1983) (hospital's accounts receivable showing patients' names and amounts they owed were subject to public disclosure).

[343] *See* Open Records Decision Nos. 523 at 3–4 (1989) (credit reports and financial statements of individual veterans participating in Veterans Land Program are protected from disclosure as "background" financial information), 373 at 3 (1983) (sources of income, salary, mortgage payments, assets, and credit history of applicant for housing rehabilitation grant are protected by common-law privacy). *But see* Open Records Decision No. 620 at 4 (1993) (background financial information regarding corporation is not protected by privacy).

[344] Open Records Decision No. 373 at 4 (1983).

[345] *Indus. Found. v. Tex. Indus. Accident Bd.*, 540 S.W.2d 668, 678 (Tex. 1976), *cert. denied*, 430 U.S. 931 (1977).

[346] *Roe v. Wade*, 410 U.S. 113, 152 (1973).

[347] *Paul v. Davis*, 424 U.S. 693, 712–13 (1976).

[348] Open Records Decision No. 600 at 4–5 (1992); *see also Whalen v. Roe*, 429 U.S. 589, 599–600 (1977).

[349] *Indus. Found. v. Tex. Indus. Accident Bd.*, 540 S.W.2d 668, 678, 679 (Tex. 1976), *cert. denied*, 430 U.S. 931 (1977).

[350] *See* Open Records Decision No. 455 at 5 (1987) (citing *Ramie v. City of Hedwig Village*, 765 F.2d 490, 492 (5th Cir. 1985)).

iii. Privacy Rights Lapse upon Death of the Subject

Common-law and constitutional privacy rights lapse upon the death of the subject.[351] Consequently, common-law and constitutional privacy can be asserted on behalf of family members of a deceased individual only on the basis of their own privacy interests, not on the basis of the deceased individual's privacy.[352] If a governmental body believes that the release of information will implicate the privacy interests of the family members of a deceased individual, the governmental body should notify the deceased's family of their right to submit comments to the attorney general explaining how release will affect their privacy interests.[353] In this regard, governmental bodies should also be aware of section 552.1085 of the Government Code, which pertains to the confidentiality and release of sensitive crime scene images from closed criminal cases, as discussed more fully in Part Two, Section II, Subsection J of this *Handbook*.

iv. False-Light Privacy

The Texas Supreme Court has held false-light privacy is not an actionable tort in Texas.[354] In addition, in Open Records Decision No. 579 (1990), the attorney general determined the statutory predecessor to section 552.101 did not incorporate the common-law tort of false-light privacy, overruling prior decisions to the contrary.[355] Thus, the truth or falsity of information is not relevant under the Public Information Act.

v. Special Circumstances

Through formal decisions, the attorney general developed the "special circumstances" test under common-law privacy to withhold certain information from disclosure.[356] "Special circumstances" refers to a very narrow set of situations in which the release of information would likely cause someone to face "an imminent threat of physical danger."[357] Such "special circumstances" do not include "a generalized and speculative fear of harassment or retribution."[358] In *Tex. Dep't of Pub. Safety v. Cox Tex. Newspapers, L.P. & Hearst Newspapers, L.P.*, the Third Court of Appeals concluded it could not adopt the special circumstances analysis because it directly conflicts with the two-part test articulated in *Industrial Foundation*, which is the sole criteria for determining whether

[351] *Moore v. Charles B. Pierce Film Enters., Inc.*, 589 S.W.2d 489, 491 (Tex. Civ. App.—Texarkana 1979, writ ref'd n.r.e.); *Justice v. Belo Broadcasting Corp.*, 472 F. Supp. 145, 146–47 (N.D. Tex. 1979) ("action for invasion of privacy can be maintained only by a living individual whose privacy is invaded") (quoting Restatement of Torts 2d); Attorney General Opinion H-917 at 3–4 (1976); Open Records Decision No. 272 at 1 (1981); *see United States v. Amalgamated Life Ins. Co.*, 534 F. Supp. 676, 679 (S.D.N.Y. 1982) (constitutional right to privacy terminates upon death and does not descend to heirs of deceased).

[352] *Moore v. Charles B. Pierce Film Enters., Inc.*, 589 S.W.2d 489, 491 (Tex. Civ. App.—Texarkana 1979, writ ref'd n.r.e.); *see also Nat'l Archives & Records Admin. v. Favish*, 541 U.S. 157 (2004); *Justice v. Belo Broadcasting Corp.*, 472 F. Supp. 145, 146–47 (N.D. Tex. 1979); *United States v. Amalgamated Life Ins. Co.*, 534 F. Supp. 676, 679 (S.D.N.Y. 1982).

[353] *See* Gov't Code § 552.304 (any interested person may submit comments explaining why records should or should not be released).

[354] *Cain v. Hearst Corp.*, 878 S.W.2d 577, 579 (Tex. 1994).

[355] Open Records Decision No. 579 at 3–8 (1990).

[356] Open Records Decision Nos. 169 (1977), 123 (1976).

[357] Open Records Decision No. 169 at 6 (1977).

[358] Open Records Decision No. 169 at 6 (1997).

information is private under the common law.[359] The Texas Supreme Court, however, reversed the court of appeals' opinion.[360] The supreme court concluded freedom from physical harm is an independent interest protected under law, untethered to the right of privacy. Thus, the supreme court for the first time announced a common-law right of physical safety exception under the Act. The supreme court adopted the standard enunciated in section 552.152 requiring the withholding of information if disclosure would create a "substantial threat of physical harm."[361] As articulated by the court, the new common-law exception requires more than vague assertions of potential harm.

vi. Dates of Birth of Members of the Public

Dates of birth of members of the public are contained in a wide variety of public records. The attorney general has historically concluded that dates of birth of members of the public are not protected under common-law privacy.[362] However, in *Paxton v. City of Dallas*,[363] the Third Court of Appeals concluded public citizens' dates of birth are protected by common-law privacy pursuant to section 552.101 of the Government Code. In its opinion, the court of appeals looked to the supreme court's rationale in *Texas Comptroller of Public Accounts v. Attorney General of Texas*,[364] where the supreme court concluded public employees' dates of birth are private under section 552.102 of the Government Code because the employees' privacy interest substantially outweighed the negligible public interest in disclosure.[365] Based on *Texas Comptroller*, the court of appeals concluded the privacy rights of public employees apply equally to public citizens, and thus, public citizens' dates of birth are also protected by common-law privacy. Consequently, dates of birth of members of the public are generally protected under common-law privacy.

b. Informer's Privilege

As interpreted by the attorney general, section 552.101 of the Government Code incorporates the "informer's privilege." In *Roviaro v. United States*,[366] the United States Supreme Court explained the rationale underlying the informer's privilege:

> What is usually referred to as the informer's privilege is in reality the Government's privilege to withhold from disclosure the identity of persons who furnish *information of violations of law to officers charged with enforcement of that law.* The purpose of the privilege is the furtherance and protection of the public interest in effective law enforcement. The privilege recognizes the obligation of citizens to communicate their knowledge of the commission of

---

[359] *Tex. Dep't of Pub. Safety v. Cox Tex. Newspapers, L.P. & Hearst Newspapers, L.P.*, 287 S.W.3d 390, 394-95 (Tex. App.—Austin 2009), *rev'd*, 343 S.W.3d 112 (Tex. 2011).

[360] *Tex. Dep't of Pub. Safety v. Cox Tex. Newspapers, L.P. & Hearst Newspapers, L.P.*, 343 S.W.3d 112 (Tex. 2011).

[361] *See* Gov't Code § 552.152 (information in custody of governmental body that relates to employee or officer of governmental body is excepted from disclosure if, under circumstances pertaining to employee or officer, disclosure would subject employee or officer to substantial threat of physical harm).

[362] *See* Open Records Decision No. 455 at 7 (1987).

[363] *Paxton v. City of Dallas*, No. 03-13-00546-CV, 2015 WL 3394061, at *3 (Tex. App.—Austin May 22, 2015, pet. denied) (mem. op.).

[364] *Texas Comptroller of Public Accounts v. Attorney General of Texas*, 354 S.W.3d 336 (Tex. 2010).

[365] *Texas Comptroller of Public Accounts v. Attorney General of Texas*, 354 S.W.3d 336, 347-348 (Tex. 2010).

[366] *Roviaro v. United States*, 353 U.S. 53 (1957).

crimes to law-enforcement officials and, by preserving their anonymity, encourages them to perform that obligation.[367]

In accordance with this policy, the attorney general has construed the informer's privilege aspect of section 552.101 as protecting the identity only of a person who (1) reports a violation or possible violation of the law (2) to officials charged with the duty of enforcing the particular law. The informer's privilege facet of section 552.101 does not protect information about lawful conduct.[368] The privilege protects information reported to administrative agency officials having a duty to enforce statutes with civil or criminal penalties, as well as to law enforcement officers.[369]

The informer's privilege protects not only the informer's identity, but also any portion of the informer's statement that might tend to reveal the informer's identity.[370] Of course, protecting an informer's identity and any identifying information under the informer's privilege serves no purpose if the accused already knows the informer's identity. The attorney general has held that the informer's privilege does not apply in such a situation.[371]

The informer's privilege facet of section 552.101 of the Government Code serves to protect the flow of information to a governmental body; it does not serve to protect a third person.[372] Thus, because it exists to protect the governmental body's interest, this privilege, unlike other section 552.101 claims, may be waived by the governmental body.[373]

B. Section 552.102: Confidentiality of Certain Personnel Information

Section 552.102 of the Government Code provides as follows:

(a) Information is excepted from [required public disclosure] if it is information in a personnel file, the disclosure of which would constitute a clearly unwarranted invasion of personal privacy, except that all information in the personnel file of an employee of a governmental body is to be made available to that employee or the employee's designated representative as public information is made available under this chapter. The exception to public disclosure created by this subsection is in addition to any exception created by Section 552.024. Public access to personnel information covered by Section 552.024 is denied to the extent provided by that section.

(b) Information is excepted from [required public disclosure] if it is a transcript from an institution of higher education maintained in the personnel file of a professional public school employee, except that this section does not exempt from disclosure the degree obtained or the curriculum on a transcript in the personnel file of the employee.

---

[367] *Roviaro v. United States*, 353 U.S. 53, 59 (1957) (emphasis added) (citations omitted).

[368] *See* Open Records Decision Nos. 515 at 4–5 (1988), 191 at 1 (1978).

[369] *See* Open Records Decision No. 515 at 2 (1988).

[370] Open Records Decision No. 515 at 2 (1988).

[371] Open Records Decision No. 208 at 1–2 (1978).

[372] Open Records Decision No. 549 at 5 (1990).

[373] Open Records Decision No. 549 at 6 (1990).

1. Dates of Birth of Public Employees

In 1983, the Third Court of Appeals in *Hubert v. Harte-Hanks Tex. Newspapers, Inc.*[374] ruled the test to be applied under section 552.102 is the same as the test formulated by the Texas Supreme Court in *Industrial Foundation* for applying the doctrine of common-law privacy as incorporated by section 552.101. However, the Texas Supreme Court has held section 552.102(a) excepts from disclosure only the dates of birth of state employees in the payroll database of the Texas Comptroller of Public Accounts.[375] In light of the court's determination, a governmental body should not raise section 552.102(a) if it seeks to withhold its employees' personnel information under common-law privacy. The appropriate exception a governmental body should raise to protect its employees' personnel information under common-law privacy is section 552.101. Section 552.102(a) only excepts from disclosure a public employee's birth date that is contained in records maintained by the governmental body in an employment context.

Section 552.102 applies to former as well as current public employees.[376] However, section 552.102 does not apply to applicants for employment.[377] In addition, section 552.102 applies only to the personnel records of public employees, not the records of private employees.

2. Transcripts of Professional Public School Employees

Section 552.102 also protects from required public disclosure most information on a transcript from an institution of higher education maintained in the personnel files of professional public school employees. Section 552.102(b) does not except from disclosure information on a transcript detailing the degree obtained and the curriculum pursued.[378] Moreover, the attorney general has interpreted section 552.102(b) to apply only to the transcripts of employees of public schools providing public education under title 2 of the Education Code, not to employees of colleges and universities providing higher education under title 3 of the Education Code.[379]

C. Section 552.103: Litigation or Settlement Negotiations Involving the State or a Political Subdivision

Section 552.103(a) of the Act, commonly referred to as the "litigation exception," excepts from required public disclosure:

> **[I]nformation relating to litigation of a civil or criminal nature to which the state or a political subdivision is or may be a party or to which an officer or employee of the state or a political subdivision, as a consequence of the person's office or employment, is or may be a party.**

---

[374] *Hubert v. Harte-Hanks Tex. Newspapers, Inc.*, 652 S.W.2d 546, 550 (Tex. App.—Austin 1983, writ ref'd n.r.e.).

[375] *Tex. Comptroller of Pub. Accounts v. Attorney General of Tex.*, 354 S.W. 3d 336 (Tex. 2010).

[376] Attorney General Opinion JM-229 at 2 (1984).

[377] Open Records Decision No. 455 at 8 (1987).

[378] *See* Open Records Decision No. 526 (1989).

[379] *See, e.g.*, Open Records Letter Nos. 2013-11312 (2013), 2009-18243 (2009), 2008-10363 (2008), 2008-08137 (2008).

Section 552.103(a) was intended to prevent the use of the Public Information Act as a method of avoiding the rules of discovery used in litigation.[380] This exception enables a governmental body to protect its position in litigation "by forcing parties seeking information relating to that litigation to obtain it through discovery" procedures.[381] Section 552.103 is a discretionary exception to disclosure and does not make information confidential under the Act.[382] As such, section 552.103 does not make information confidential for the purposes of section 552.022. Further, a governmental body waives section 552.103 by failing to comply with the procedural requirements of section 552.301.[383]

1. Governmental Body's Burden

For information to be excepted from public disclosure by section 552.103(a), (1) litigation involving the governmental body must be pending or reasonably anticipated and (2) the information must relate to that litigation.[384] Therefore, a governmental body that seeks an attorney general decision has the burden of clearly establishing both prongs of this test.

For purposes of section 552.103(a), a contested case under the Administrative Procedure Act (APA), Government Code chapter 2001, constitutes "litigation."[385] Questions remain regarding whether administrative proceedings not subject to the APA may be considered litigation within the meaning of section 552.103(a).[386] In determining whether an administrative proceeding should be considered litigation for the purpose of section 552.103, the attorney general will consider the following factors: (1) whether the dispute is, for all practical purposes, litigated in an administrative proceeding where (a) discovery takes place, (b) evidence is heard, (c) factual questions are resolved, and (d) a record is made; and (2) whether the proceeding is an adjudicative forum of first jurisdiction.[387]

Whether litigation is reasonably anticipated must be determined on a case-by-case basis.[388] Section 552.103(a) requires concrete evidence that litigation is realistically contemplated; it must be more than conjecture.[389] The mere chance of litigation is not sufficient to trigger section 552.103(a).[390] The fact that a governmental body received a claim letter that it represents to the attorney general to be in compliance with the notice requirements of the Texas Tort Claims Act, Civil Practice and Remedies Code chapter 101, or applicable municipal ordinance, shows that litigation is reasonably

---

[380] *Thomas v. Cornyn*, 71 S.W.3d 473, 487 (Tex. App.—Austin 2002, no pet.); Attorney General Opinion JM-1048 at 4 (1989).

[381] Open Records Decision No. 551 at 3 (1990).

[382] *Dallas Area Rapid Transit v. Dallas Morning News*, 4 S.W.3d 469, 475–76 (Tex. App.—Dallas 1999, no pet.); Open Records Decision No. 665 at 2 n.5 (2000).

[383] Open Records Decision Nos. 663 at 5 (1999), 542 at 4 (1990).

[384] *Univ. of Tex. Law Sch. v. Tex. Legal Found.*, 958 S.W.2d 479, 481 (Tex. App.—Austin 1997, orig. proceeding); *Heard v. Houston Post Co.*, 684 S.W.2d 210, 212 (Tex. App.—Houston [1st Dist.] 1984, writ ref'd n.r.e.).

[385] Open Records Decision No. 588 at 7 (1991) (construing statutory predecessor to APA).

[386] Open Records Decision No. 588 at 6–7 (1991).

[387] *See* Open Records Decision No. 588 (1991).

[388] Open Records Decision No. 452 at 4 (1986).

[389] Attorney General Opinion JM-266 at 4 (1984); Open Records Decision Nos. 677 at 3 (2002), 518 at 5 (1989), 328 at 2 (1982).

[390] Open Records Decision Nos. 677 at 3 (2002), 518 at 5 (1989), 397 at 2 (1983), 361 at 2 (1983), 359 at 2 (1983).

anticipated.[391] If a governmental body does not make this representation, the claim letter is a factor the attorney general will consider in determining from the totality of the circumstances presented whether the governmental body has established that litigation is reasonably anticipated.

In previous open records decisions, the attorney general had concluded that a governmental body could claim the litigation exception only if it established that withholding the information was necessary to protect the governmental body's strategy or position in litigation.[392] However, Open Records Decision No. 551 (1990) significantly revised this test and concluded that the governmental body need only establish the relatedness of the information to the subject matter of the pending or anticipated litigation.[393] Therefore, to meet its burden under section 552.103(a) in requesting an attorney general decision under the Act, the governmental body must identify the issues in the litigation and explain how the information relates to those issues.[394] When the litigation is actually pending, the governmental body should also provide the attorney general a copy of the relevant pleadings.

2. Only Circumstances Existing at the Time of the Request

Subsection (c) of section 552.103 provides as follows:

> **Information relating to litigation involving a governmental body or an officer or employee of a governmental body is excepted from disclosure under Subsection (a) only if the litigation is pending or reasonably anticipated on the date that the requestor applies to the officer for public information for access to or duplication of the information.**

Consequently, in determining whether a governmental body has met its burden under section 552.103, the attorney general or a court can only consider the circumstances that existed on the date the governmental body received the request for information, not information about occurrences after the date of the request for information.[395]

3. Temporal Nature of Section 552.103

Generally, when parties to litigation have inspected the records pursuant to court order, discovery, or through any other means, section 552.103(a) may no longer be invoked.[396] In addition, once litigation is neither reasonably anticipated nor pending, section 552.103(a) is no longer applicable.[397] Once a governmental body has disclosed information relating to litigation, the governmental body is ordinarily precluded from invoking section 552.103(a) to withhold the same information. This is not the case, however, when a governmental body has disclosed information to a co-defendant in

---

[391]   Open Records Decision No. 638 at 4 (1996).

[392]   *See* Open Records Decision Nos. 518 at 5 (1989), 474 at 5 (1987).

[393]   Open Records Decision No. 551 at 5 (1990).

[394]   Open Records Decision No. 551 at 5 (1990).

[395]   Open Records Decision No. 677 at 2–3 (2002).

[396]   Open Records Decision No. 597 (1991) (statutory predecessor to Gov't Code § 552.103 did not except basic information in offense report that was previously disclosed to defendant in criminal litigation); *see* Open Records Decision Nos. 551 at 4 (1990), 511 at 5 (1988), 493 at 2 (1988), 349 (1982), 320 (1982).

[397]   Open Records Decision Nos. 551 at 4 (1990), 350 (1982); *see Thomas v. El Paso County Cmty. Coll. Dist.*, 68 S.W.3d 722, 726 (Tex. App.—El Paso 2001, no pet.).

litigation, where the governmental body believes in good faith that it has a constitutional obligation to disclose it.[398]

4. Scope of Section 552.103

Section 552.103 applies to information that relates to pending or reasonably anticipated litigation, which is a very broad category of information.[399] The protection of section 552.103 may overlap with that of other exceptions that encompass discovery privileges. However, the standard for proving that section 552.103 applies to information is the same regardless of whether the information is also subject to a discovery privilege.

For example, information excepted from disclosure under the litigation exception may also be subject to the work product privilege.[400] However, the standard for proving that the litigation exception applies is wholly distinct from the standard for proving that the work product privilege applies.[401] The work product privilege is incorporated into the Act by section 552.111 of the Government Code, not section 552.103.[402] If both section 552.103 and the work product privilege could apply to requested information, the governmental body has the discretion to choose to assert either or both of the exceptions.[403] However, the governmental body must meet distinct burdens depending on the exception it is asserting.[404] Under section 552.103, the governmental body must demonstrate that the requested information relates to pending or reasonably anticipated litigation.[405] Under the work product privilege, the governmental body must demonstrate that the requested information was created for trial or in anticipation of civil litigation by or for a party or a party's representative.[406]

5. Duration of Section 552.103 for Criminal Litigation

Subsection (b) of section 552.103 provides as follows:

> **For purposes of this section, the state or a political subdivision is considered to be a party to litigation of a criminal nature until the applicable statute of limitations has expired or until the defendant has exhausted all appellate and postconviction remedies in state and federal court.**

---

[398] Open Records Decision No. 454 at 3 (1986).

[399] *Univ. of Tex. Law Sch. v. Tex. Legal Found.*, 958 S.W.2d 479, 483 (Tex. App.—Austin 1997, orig. proceeding).

[400] *See* Open Records Decision No. 677 at 2 (2002).

[401] *See* Open Records Decision No. 677 at 2 (2002).

[402] *See* Open Records Decision No. 677 at 4 (2002).

[403] *See* Open Records Decision No. 677 at 2 (2002); Open Records Decision No. 647 at 3 (1996).

[404] Open Records Decision No. 677 at 2 (2002).

[405] *See* Open Records Decision No. 677 at 2 (2002); Gov't Code § 552.103; *Univ. of Tex. Law Sch. v. Tex. Legal Found.*, 958 S.W.2d 479, 481 (Tex. App.—Austin 1997, no pet.); *Heard v. Houston Post Co.*, 684 S.W.2d 210, 212 (Tex. App.—Houston [1st Dist.] 1984, writ ref'd n.r.e.).

[406] Open Records Decision No. 677 at 5–8 (2002).

The attorney general has determined that section 552.103(b) is not a separate exception to disclosure; it merely provides a time frame within which the litigation exception excepts information from disclosure.[407]

D. Section 552.104: Information Relating to Competition or Bidding

Section 552.104 of the Government Code provides as follows:

(a) **Information is excepted from the requirements of Section 552.021 if it is information that, if released, would give advantage to a competitor or bidder.**

(b) **The requirement of Section 552.022 that a category of information listed under Section 552.022(a) is public information and not excepted from required disclosure under this chapter unless expressly confidential under law does not apply to information that is excepted from required disclosure under this section.**

Section 552.104(a) of the Government Code excepts from disclosure information that, if released, would give advantage to a competitor or bidder. The Texas Supreme Court considered section 552.104 and held the "test under section 552.104 is whether knowing another bidder's [or competitor's information] would be an advantage, not whether it would be a decisive advantage."[408] The supreme court further held section 552.104 protection is not limited to governmental bodies, and therefore a private third party may also invoke this exception.[409] The supreme court's decision overrules a long line of attorney general decisions limiting the application of section 552.104 to governmental bodies and discussing the burden a governmental body must meet in order to withhold information under section 552.104. Both governmental bodies and third parties should therefore exercise caution in relying on prior attorney general decisions regarding the applicability of section 552.104. Section 552.104(b) provides that information excepted from disclosure under this section may be withheld even if it falls within one of the categories of information listed in section 552.022(a).

E. Section 552.105: Information Related to Location or Price of Property

Section 552.105 of the Government Code excepts from required public disclosure information relating to:

(1) **the location of real or personal property for a public purpose prior to public announcement of the project; or**

(2) **appraisals or purchase price of real or personal property for a public purpose prior to the formal award of contracts for the property.**

---

[407] Open Records Decision No. 518 at 5 (1989).

[408] *Boeing Co. v. Paxton*, 466 S.W. 3d 831, 841 (Tex. 2015).

[409] *Boeing Co. v. Paxton*, 466 S.W. 3d 831, 833 (Tex. 2015).

This exception protects a governmental body's planning and negotiating position with respect to particular real or personal property transactions,[410] and its protection is therefore limited in duration. The protection of section 552.105(1) expires upon the public announcement of the project for which the property is being acquired, while the protection of section 552.105(2) expires upon the governmental body's acquisition of the property in question.[411] Because section 552.105(2) extends to "information relating to" the appraisals and purchase price of property, it may protect more than just the purchase price or appraisal of a specific piece of property.[412] For example, the attorney general has held that appraisal information about parcels of land acquired in advance of others to be acquired for the same project could be withheld where this information would harm the governmental body's negotiating position with respect to the remaining parcels.[413] Similarly, the location of property to be purchased may be withheld under section 552.105(2) if releasing the location could affect the purchase price of the property. The exception for information pertaining to "purchase price" in section 552.105(2) also applies to information pertaining to a lease price.[414]

When a governmental body has made a good faith determination that the release of information would damage its negotiating position with respect to the acquisition of property, the attorney general in issuing a ruling under the Act will accept that determination, unless the records or other information show the contrary as a matter of law.[415]

F.   Section 552.106: Certain Legislative Documents

Section 552.106 of the Government Code provides as follows:

(a)   **A draft or working paper involved in the preparation of proposed legislation is excepted from [required public disclosure].**

(b)   **An internal bill analysis or working paper prepared by the governor's office for the purpose of evaluating proposed legislation is excepted from [required public disclosure].**

Section 552.106(a) protects documents concerning the deliberative processes of a governmental body relevant to the enactment of legislation.[416] The purpose of this exception is to encourage frank discussion on policy matters between the subordinates or advisors of a legislative body and the legislative body.[417] However, section 552.106(a) does not protect purely factual material.[418] If a draft or working paper contains purely factual material that can be disclosed without revealing protected judgments or recommendations, such factual material must be disclosed unless another

---

[410]   Open Records Decision No. 357 at 3 (1982).

[411]   Gov't Code § 552.105; *see* Open Records Decision No. 222 at 1–2 (1979).

[412]   *See Heidenheimer v. Tex. Dep't of Transp.*, No. 03-02-00187-CV, 2003 WL 124248, at *2 (Tex. App.—Austin Jan. 16, 2003, pet. denied) (mem. op., not designated for publication); Open Records Decision No. 564 (1990) (construing statutory predecessor to Gov't Code § 552.105).

[413]   Open Records Decision No. 564 (1990).

[414]   Open Records Decision No. 348 (1982).

[415]   Open Records Decision No. 564 at 2 (1990).

[416]   *See* Open Records Decision No. 429 at 5 (1985).

[417]   Open Records Decision No. 460 at 2 (1987).

[418]   Open Records Decision Nos. 460 at 2 (1987), 344 at 3–4 (1982), 197 at 3 (1978), 140 at 4 (1976).

exception to disclosure applies.[419] Section 552.106(a) protects drafts of legislation that reflect policy judgments, recommendations, and proposals prepared by persons with some official responsibility to prepare them for the legislative body.[420] In addition to documents actually created by the legislature, the attorney general has construed the term "legislation" to include certain documents created by a city or a state agency.[421]

The following open records decisions have held certain information to be excepted from required public disclosure under the statutory predecessor to section 552.106(a):

Open Records Decision No. 460 (1987) — a city manager's proposed budget prior to its presentation to the city council, where the city charter directed the city manager to prepare such a proposal and the proposal was comprised of recommendations rather than facts;

Open Records Decision No. 367 (1983) — recommendations of the executive committee of the Texas State Board of Public Accountancy for amendments to the Public Accountancy Act; and

Open Records Decision No. 248 (1980) — drafts of a municipal ordinance and resolution that were prepared by a city staff study group for discussion purposes and that reflected policy judgments, recommendations, and proposals.

The following open records decisions have held information not to be excepted from required public disclosure under the statutory predecessor to section 552.106(a):

Open Records Decision No. 482 (1987) — drafts and working papers incorporated into materials that are disclosed to the public;

Open Records Decision No. 429 (1985) — documents relating to the Texas Turnpike Authority's efforts to persuade various cities to enact ordinances, as the agency had no official authority to do so and acted merely as an interested third party to the legislative process; and

Open Records Decision No. 344 (1982) — certain information relating to the State Property Tax Board's biennial study of taxable property in each school district, for the reason that the nature of the requested information compiled by the board was factual.

Section 552.106(b) excepts from disclosure "[a]n internal bill analysis or working paper prepared by the governor's office for the purpose of evaluating proposed legislation[.]"[422] The purpose of section 552.106(b) is also to encourage frank discussion on policy matters; however, this section applies to information created or used by employees of the governor's office for the purpose of evaluating proposed legislation. Furthermore, like section 552.106(a), section 552.106(b) only protects policy

---

[419] Open Records Decision No. 460 at 2 (1987).

[420] Open Records Decision No. 429 at 5 (1985).

[421] *See* Open Records Decision Nos. 460 at 2–3 (1987), 367 (1983), 248 (1980).

[422] Gov't Code § 552.106(b).

judgments, advice, opinions, and recommendations involved in the preparation or evaluation of proposed legislation; it does not except purely factual information from public disclosure.[423]

Sections 552.106 and 552.111 were designed to achieve the same goals in different contexts.[424] The purpose of section 552.111 is "to protect from public disclosure advice and opinions on policy matters and to encourage frank and open discussion within the agency in connection with its decision-making processes."[425] Because the policies and objectives of each exception are the same, some decisions applying section 552.111 may be helpful in determining how section 552.106 should be construed.[426] Although the provisions protect the same type of information, section 552.106 is narrower in scope because it applies specifically to the legislative process.[427]

G.   Section 552.107:   Certain Legal Matters

Section 552.107 of the Government Code states that information is excepted from required public disclosure if:

> **(1)   it is information that the attorney general or an attorney of a political subdivision is prohibited from disclosing because of a duty to the client under the Texas Rules of Evidence or the Texas Disciplinary Rules of Professional Conduct; or**
>
> **(2)   a court by order has prohibited disclosure of the information.**

This section has two distinct aspects: subsection (1) protects information within the attorney-client privilege, and subsection (2) protects information a court has ordered to be kept confidential.

1.   Information Within the Attorney-Client Privilege

When seeking to withhold information not subject to section 552.022 of the Government Code based on the attorney-client privilege, a governmental body should assert section 552.107(1).[428] In Open Records Decision No. 676 (2002), the attorney general interpreted section 552.107 to protect the same information as protected under Texas Rule of Evidence 503.[429] Thus, the standard for demonstrating the attorney-client privilege under the Act is the same as the standard used in discovery under rule 503. In meeting this standard, a governmental body bears the burden of providing the necessary facts to demonstrate the elements of the attorney-client privilege.[430]

---

[423]   *See* House Comm. on State Affairs, Public Hearing, May 6, 1997, H.B. 3157, 75th Leg. (1997) (protection given to legislative documents under Gov't Code § 552.106(a) is comparable with protection given to governor's legislative documents under Gov't Code § 552.106(b)).

[424]   Open Records Decision No. 482 at 9 (1987).

[425]   *Austin v. City of San Antonio*, 630 S.W.2d 391, 394 (Tex. App.—San Antonio 1982, writ ref'd n.r.e.); Open Records Decision No. 222 (1979).

[426]   Open Records Decision No. 482 at 9 (1987). *But see* Open Records Decision No. 615 at 5 (1993) (agency's policymaking functions protected by statutory predecessor to section 552.111 do not encompass routine internal administrative and personnel matters).

[427]   *See* Open Records Decision Nos. 460 at 3 (1987), 429 at 5 (1985).

[428]   Open Records Decision Nos. 676 at 1–3 (2002), 574 at 2 (1990).

[429]   Open Records Decision No. 676 at 4 (2002).

[430]   Open Records Decision No. 676 at 6 (2002).

First, the governmental body must demonstrate that the information constitutes or documents a communication.[431] Second, the communication must have been made "to facilitate the rendition of professional legal services" to the client governmental body.[432] Third, the governmental body must demonstrate that the communication was between or among clients, client representatives, lawyers, and lawyer representatives.[433] Fourth, the governmental body must show that the communication was confidential; that is, the communication was "not intended to be disclosed to third persons other than those: to (A) whom disclosure is made to furtherance the rendition of professional legal services to the clients; or (B) reasonably necessary to transmit the communication."[434] Finally, because the client can waive the attorney-client privilege at any time, the governmental body must demonstrate that the communication has remained confidential.[435]

The privilege will not apply if the attorney or the attorney's representative was acting in a capacity "other than that of providing or facilitating professional legal services to the client."[436] In *Harlandale Indep. Sch. District v. Cornyn*,[437] the Third Court of Appeals addressed whether an attorney was working in her capacity as an attorney when she conducted a factual investigation, thus rendering factual information from the attorney's report excepted from public disclosure under section 552.107(1) of the Government Code. There, the Harlandale Independent School District hired an attorney to conduct an investigation into an alleged assault and render a legal analysis of the situation upon completion of the investigation.[438] The attorney produced a report that included a summary of the factual investigation as well as legal opinions.[439] While the court of appeals held the attorney-client privilege does not apply to communications between an attorney and a client "when the attorney is employed in a non-legal capacity, for instance as an accountant, escrow agency, negotiator, or notary public," the court also held the attorney in that case was acting in a legal capacity in gathering the facts because the ultimate purpose of her investigation was the rendition of legal advice.[440] Thus, when an attorney is hired to conduct an investigation in his or her capacity as an attorney, a report produced by an attorney containing both factual information and legal advice is excepted from disclosure in its entirety under section 552.107(1).

If a governmental body demonstrates that any portion of a communication is protected under the attorney-client privilege, then the entire communication will be generally excepted from disclosure

---

[431]   Open Records Decision No. 676 at 7 (2002).

[432]   Open Records Decision No. 676 at 7 (2002); TEX. R. EVID. 503(b)(1).

[433]   TEX. R. EVID. 503(b)(1)(A)–(E); Open Records Decision No. 676 at 8–10 (2002).

[434]   TEX. R. EVID. 503(a)(5); Open Records Decision No. 676 at 10 (2002); *see Osborne v. Johnson*, 954 S.W.2d 180, 184 (Tex. App.—Waco 1997, orig. proceeding) (whether communication was confidential depends on intent of parties involved at time information was communicated).

[435]   Open Records Decision No. 676 at 10–11 (2002).

[436]   Open Records Decision No. 676 at 7 (2002); *see also In re Tex. Farmers Ins. Exch.*, 990 S.W.2d 337, 340 (Tex. App.—Texarkana 1999, orig. proceeding) (attorney-client privilege does not apply if attorney acting in capacity other than that of attorney).

[437]   *Harlandale Indep. Sch. Dist. v. Cornyn*, 25 S.W.3d 328 (Tex. App.—Austin 2000, pet. denied).

[438]   *Harlandale Indep. Sch. Dist. v. Cornyn*, 25 S.W.3d 328, 330 (Tex. App.—Austin 2000, pet. denied).

[439]   *Harlandale Indep. Sch. Dist. v. Cornyn*, 25 S.W.3d 328, 330–331 (Tex. App.—Austin 2000, pet. denied).

[440]   *Harlandale Indep. Sch. Dist. v. Cornyn*, 25 S.W.3d 328, 332–35 (Tex. App.—Austin 2000, pet. denied).

under section 552.107.[441] However, section 552.107 does not apply to a non-privileged communication within a privileged communication, if the non-privileged communication is maintained by the governmental body separate and apart from the otherwise privileged communication. For example, if an e-mail string includes an e-mail or attachment that was received from or sent to a non-privileged party, and the e-mail or attachment that was received from or sent to the non-privileged party is separately responsive to the request for information when it is removed from the e-mail string and stands alone, the governmental body may not withhold the non-privileged e-mail or attachment under section 552.107.[442]

The scope of the attorney-client privilege and the work product privilege, which is encompassed by section 552.111 of the Government Code, are often confused. The attorney-client privilege covers certain communications made in furtherance of the rendition of professional legal services, while the work product privilege covers work prepared for the client's lawsuit.[443] For materials to be covered by the attorney-client privilege, they need not be prepared for litigation.

a.   Attorney Fee Bills

Attorney fee bills are subject to section 552.022(a)(16) and thus may not be withheld under section 552.107. Nonetheless, information contained in attorney fee bills may be withheld if it is protected under the attorney-client privilege as defined in rule 503 of the Texas Rules of Evidence, or is made confidential under the Act or other law for the purpose of section 552.022.[444] Because the express language of section 552.022(a)(16) provides "information that is *in* a bill for attorney's fees" is not excepted from disclosure unless it is confidential under the Act or other law, the entirety of an attorney fee bill cannot be withheld on the basis that it contains or is an attorney-client communication.[445]

b.   Information a Private Attorney Holds for the Governmental Body

If a governmental body engages a private attorney to perform legal services, information in the attorney's possession relating to the legal services is subject to the Public Information Act.[446]

---

[441]   *See Huie v. DeShazo*, 922 S.W.2d 920, 923 (Tex. 1996) (privilege extends to entire communication, including facts contained therein); *In re Valero Energy Corp.*, 973 S.W.2d 453, 457 (Tex. App.—Houston [14th Dist.] 1998, orig. proceeding) (privilege attaches to complete communication, including factual information).

[442]   *See, e.g.*, Open Records Letter Nos. 2013-12509 (2013), 2013-12111 (2013).

[443]   *See Nat'l Tank Co. v. Brotherton*, 851 S.W.2d 193, 200 (Tex. 1993); *Owens-Corning Fiberglas Corp. v. Caldwell*, 818 S.W.2d 749, 750 (Tex. 1991).

[444]   *See In re City of Georgetown*, 53 S.W.3d 328, 337 (Tex. 2001); Open Records Decision No. 676 at 5–6 (2002).

[445]   Gov't Code §552.022(a)(16) (emphasis added); *see also* Open Records Decision Nos. 676 at 5 (2002) (attorney fee bill cannot be withheld in entirety on basis it contains or is attorney-client communication pursuant to language in section 552.022(a)(16)), 589 (1991) (information in attorney fee bill excepted only to extent information reveals client confidences or attorney's legal advice).

[446]   Gov't Code § 552.002(a)(2), (a-1) (definition of public information includes information pertaining to official business of governmental body that was created by, transmitted to, received by, or is maintained by person or entity performing official business on behalf of governmental body); Open Records Decision Nos. 663 at 7–8 (1999), 499 at 5 (1988), 462 at 7 (1987).

c. Waiver of the Attorney-Client Privilege

Texas Rule of Evidence 511 provides that, except where a disclosure is itself privileged, the attorney-client privilege is waived if a holder of the privilege voluntarily discloses or consents to disclosure of any significant part of the matter.[447]

In *Paxton v. City of Dallas*, the Texas Supreme Court determined (1) the failure of a governmental body to timely seek a ruling from the OAG to withhold information subject to the attorney-client privilege does not constitute a waiver of the privilege, and (2) the attorney-client privilege constitutes a compelling reason to withhold information under section 552.302 of the Government Code.[448]

2. Information Protected by Court Order

Section 552.107(2) excepts from disclosure information a court has ordered a governmental body to keep confidential. Prior to the amendment of section 552.022 in 1999, governmental bodies often relied on section 552.107(2) to withhold from disclosure the terms of a settlement agreement if a court had issued an order expressly prohibiting the parties to the settlement agreement or their attorneys from disclosing the terms of the agreement.[449] Under the current version of section 552.022, however, a state court may not order a governmental body or an officer for public information to withhold from public disclosure any category of information listed in section 552.022 unless the information is confidential under this chapter or other law.[450] A settlement agreement to which a governmental body is a party is one category of information listed in section 552.022.[451]

With the exception of information subject to section 552.022, section 552.107(2) excepts from disclosure information that is subject to a protective order during the pendency of the litigation.[452] As with any other exception to disclosure, a governmental body must request a ruling from the attorney general if it wishes to withhold information under section 552.107(2) and should submit a copy of the protective order for the attorney general's review. A governmental body may not use a protective order as grounds for the exception once the court has dismissed the suit from which it arose.[453]

H. Section 552.108: Certain Law Enforcement, Corrections, and Prosecutorial Information

Section 552.108 of the Government Code, sometimes referred to as the "law enforcement" exception, provides as follows:

---

[447]   TEX. R. EVID. 511(a)(1); *see also Jordan v. Court of Appeals for Fourth Supreme Judicial Dist.*, 701 S.W.2d 644, 649 (Tex. 1985) (if matter for which privilege is sought has been disclosed to third party, thus raising question of waiver of privilege, party asserting privilege has burden of proving no waiver has occurred).

[448]   *Paxton v. City of Dallas*, 509 S.W.3d 247, 262, 271 (Tex. 2017).

[449]   *See* Open Records Decision No. 415 at 2 (1984).

[450]   Gov't Code § 552.022(b).

[451]   Gov't Code § 552.022(a)(18).

[452]   Open Records Decision No. 143 at 1 (1976).

[453]   Open Records Decision No. 309 at 5 (1982).

(a) **Information held by a law enforcement agency or prosecutor that deals with the detection, investigation, or prosecution of crime is excepted from the requirements of Section 552.021 if:**

(1) **release of the information would interfere with the detection, investigation, or prosecution of crime;**

(2) **it is information that deals with the detection, investigation, or prosecution of crime only in relation to an investigation that did not result in conviction or deferred adjudication;**

(3) **it is information relating to a threat against a peace officer or detention officer collected or disseminated under Section 411.048; or**

(4) **it is information that:**

(A) **is prepared by an attorney representing the state in anticipation of or in the course of preparing for criminal litigation; or**

(B) **reflects the mental impressions or legal reasoning of an attorney representing the state.**

(b) **An internal record or notation of a law enforcement agency or prosecutor that is maintained for internal use in matters relating to law enforcement or prosecution is excepted from the requirements of Section 552.021 if:**

(1) **release of the internal record or notation would interfere with law enforcement or prosecution;**

(2) **the internal record or notation relates to law enforcement only in relation to an investigation that did not result in conviction or deferred adjudication; or**

(3) **the internal record or notation:**

(A) **is prepared by an attorney representing the state in anticipation of or in the course of preparing for criminal litigation; or**

(B) **reflects the mental impressions or legal reasoning of an attorney representing the state.**

(c) **This section does not except from the requirements of Section 552.021 information that is basic information about an arrested person, an arrest, or a crime.**

1. **The Meaning of "Law Enforcement Agency" and the Applicability of Section 552.108 to Other Units of Government**

Section 552.108 generally applies to the records created by an agency, or a portion of an agency, whose primary function is to investigate crimes and enforce the criminal laws.[454] It generally does not apply to the records created by an agency whose chief function is essentially regulatory in nature.[455] For example, an agency that employs peace officers to investigate crime and enforce criminal laws may claim that section 552.108 excepts portions of its records from required public disclosure. On the other hand, an agency involved primarily in licensing certain professionals or regulating a particular industry generally may not use section 552.108 to except its records from disclosure.[456] An agency that investigates both civil and criminal violations of law but lacks criminal enforcement authority is not a law enforcement agency for purposes of section 552.108.[457]

Entities that have been found to be law enforcement agencies for purposes of section 552.108 include: the Texas Department of Criminal Justice (formerly the Texas Department of Corrections);[458] the Texas National Guard;[459] the Attorney General's Organized Crime Task Force;[460] a fire department's arson investigation division;[461] the El Paso Special Commission on Crime;[462] the Texas Lottery Commission;[463] the Texas Alcoholic Beverage Commission's Enforcement Division;[464] and the Texas Comptroller of Public Accounts for purposes of enforcing the Tax Code.[465]

The following entities are not law enforcement agencies for purposes of section 552.108: the Texas Department of Agriculture;[466] the Texas Board of Private Investigators and Private Security Agencies;[467] the Texas Board of Pharmacy;[468] and the Texas Real Estate Commission.[469]

---

[454] *See* Open Records Decision Nos. 493 at 2 (1988), 287 at 2 (1981).

[455] Open Records Decision No. 199 (1978).

[456] *See* Open Records Decision No. 199 (1978). *But see* Attorney General Opinion MW-575 at 1–2 (1982) (former Gov't Code § 552.108 may apply to information gathered by administrative agency when its release would unduly interfere with law enforcement); Open Records Decision No. 493 at 2 (1988).

[457] Open Records Letter No. 99-1907 (1999) (Medicaid Program Integrity Division of Health and Human Services Commission investigates both civil and criminal violations of Medicaid fraud laws and refers criminal violations to attorney general for criminal enforcement).

[458] Attorney General Opinion MW-381 at 3 (1981); Open Records Decision No. 413 at 1 (1984).

[459] Open Records Decision No. 320 at 1 (1982).

[460] Open Records Decision Nos. 211 at 3 (1978), 126 at 5 (1976).

[461] Open Records Decision No. 127 at 8 (1976).

[462] *See* Open Records Decision No. 129 (1976).

[463] *See* Gov't Code §§ 466.019(b) (Lottery Commission is authorized to enforce violations of lottery laws and rules), .020(a)-(b) (Lottery Commission is authorized to maintain department of security staffed by commissioned peace officers or investigators).

[464] *See* Alco. Bev. Code §§ 5.14 (Texas Alcoholic Beverage Commission may commission inspectors with police powers to enforce Alcoholic Beverage Code), .31 (powers and duties of commission), .36 (commission shall investigate violations of Alcoholic Beverage Code and other laws relating to alcoholic beverages), .361 (commission shall develop risk-based approach to enforcement).

[465] *A & T Consultants, Inc. v. Sharp*, 904 S.W.2d 668, 679 (Tex. 1995) (section 552.108 excepts records generated by comptroller in process of enforcing tax laws).

[466] Attorney General Opinion MW-575 at 1 (1982).

[467] Open Records Decision No. 199 (1978).

[468] Open Records Decision No. 493 (1988).

[469] Open Records Decision No. 80 (1975).

An agency that does not qualify as a law enforcement agency may, under limited circumstances, claim that section 552.108 excepts records in its possession from required public disclosure. For example, records that otherwise qualify for the section 552.108 exception, such as documentary evidence in a police file on a pending case, do not necessarily lose that status while in the custody of an agency not directly involved with law enforcement.[470] Where a non-law enforcement agency has in its custody information that would otherwise qualify for exception under section 552.108 as information relating to the pending case of a law enforcement agency, the custodian of the records may withhold the information if it provides the attorney general with a demonstration that the information relates to the pending case and a representation from the law enforcement entity that it wishes to withhold the information.[471]

Similarly, in construing the statutory predecessor to section 552.108, the attorney general concluded that if an investigation by an administrative agency reveals possible criminal conduct the agency intends to report to the appropriate law enforcement agency, then section 552.108 will apply to the information gathered by the administrative agency if the information relates to an open investigation or if the release would interfere with law enforcement.[472]

2. Application of Section 552.108

Section 552.108 excepts from required public disclosure four categories of information:

1) information the release of which would interfere with law enforcement or prosecution;

2) information relating to an investigation that did not result in a conviction or deferred adjudication;

3) information relating to a threat against a peace officer or detention officer collected or disseminated under section 411.048; and

4) information that is prepared by a prosecutor or that reflects the prosecutor's mental impressions or legal reasoning.

a. Interference with Detection, Investigation, or Prosecution of Crime

In order to establish the applicability of sections 552.108(a)(1) and 552.108(b)(1) to a requested criminal file, a law enforcement agency should inform the attorney general how and why release of the information would interfere with law enforcement.[473] The law enforcement agency must inform the attorney general of the status of the case the information concerns. Information relating to a pending criminal investigation or prosecution is one example of information that is excepted under

---

[470] Open Records Decision No. 272 at 1–2 (1981).

[471] Open Records Decision No. 474 at 4–5 (1987); *see, e.g.,* Open Records Letter No. 2004-1811 (2004).

[472] *See* Attorney General Opinion MW-575 at 1–2 (1982) (construing statutory predecessor); Open Records Decision No. 493 at 2 (1988) (same).

[473] *See Ex parte Pruitt,* 551 S.W.2d 706, 710 (Tex. 1977).

sections 552.108(a)(1) and 552.108(b)(1) because release of such information would presumptively interfere with the detection, investigation, or prosecution of crime.[474]

All of the formal open records decisions interpreting the law enforcement exception considered the predecessor statute rather than section 552.108 as it now reads. In these decisions, the attorney general permitted law enforcement agencies to withhold information in a closed criminal case only if its release would "unduly interfere" with law enforcement or crime prevention.[475] The following is a discussion of the "undue interference" standard under the predecessor statute. The reader may find this information useful in determining the types of information to provide to the attorney general when seeking to withhold information under the current provision's "interference" standard.

i. Information Relating to the Detection, Investigation, or Prosecution of Crime

To withhold information under former section 552.108, a governmental body had to demonstrate how release of the information would "unduly interfere" with law enforcement or prosecution.[476] For example, the names and statements of witnesses could be withheld if the law enforcement agency demonstrated that disclosure might either (1) subject the witnesses to possible intimidation or harassment or (2) harm the prospects of future cooperation by the witnesses.[477] However, to prevail on its claim that section 552.108 excepted the information from disclosure, a law enforcement agency had to do more than merely make a conclusory assertion that releasing the information would unduly interfere with law enforcement. Whether the release of particular records would unduly interfere with law enforcement was determined on a case-by-case basis.[478]

ii. Internal Records of a Law Enforcement Agency

To withhold internal records and notations of law enforcement agencies and prosecutors under former section 552.108, a governmental body had to demonstrate how release of the information would unduly interfere with law enforcement and crime prevention.[479] For example, the Department of Public Safety was permitted to withhold a list of stations that issue drivers' licenses and the corresponding code that designates each station on the drivers' licenses issued by that station.[480] Although the information did not on its face suggest that its release would unduly interfere with law enforcement, the Department of Public Safety explained that the codes are used by officers to determine whether a license is forged and argued that releasing the list of stations and codes would reduce the value of the codes for detecting forged drivers' licenses.[481] The attorney general previously held that release of routine investigative procedures, techniques that are commonly

---

[474] *See Houston Chronicle Publ'g Co. v. City of Houston*, 531 S.W.2d 177, 184–85 (Tex. Civ. App.—Houston [14th Dist.] 1975) (court delineates law enforcement interests that are present in active cases), *writ ref'd n.r.e. per curiam*, 536 S.W.2d 559 (Tex. 1976).

[475] *See* Open Records Decision Nos. 628 at 2 (1994), 313 at 2 (1982), 297 at 2 (1981).

[476] Open Records Decision Nos. 616 at 1 (1993), 434 at 2–3 (1986); *see Ex parte Pruitt*, 551 S.W.2d 706, 710 (Tex. 1977).

[477] *See* Open Records Decision No. 297 at 2 (1981).

[478] Open Records Decision No. 409 at 2 (1984).

[479] *See* Open Records Decision No. 508 at 2–4 (1988).

[480] Open Records Decision No. 341 at 2 (1982).

[481] Open Records Decision No. 341 at 1–2 (1982).

known, and routine personnel information would not unduly interfere with law enforcement and crime prevention.[482]

The Texas Supreme Court has addressed the applicability of former section 552.108 to the internal records and notations of the comptroller's office. In *A & T Consultants, Inc. v. Sharp*,[483] the supreme court stated that former section 552.108 has the same scope as section 552(b)(7) of the federal Freedom of Information Act,[484] which prevents the disclosure of investigatory records that would reveal law enforcement methods, techniques, and strategies, including those the Internal Revenue Service uses to collect federal taxes.[485] Some information, such as the date a taxpayer's name appeared on a generation list and the assignment date and codes in audits, is excepted from disclosure by former section 552.108 because it reflects the internal deliberations within the comptroller's office and would interfere with the comptroller's office's law enforcement efforts.[486] For audits that have been concluded, there is little harm in releasing some of this information.[487] The audit method and audit group remain excepted from disclosure before, during, and after the comptroller undertakes a taxpayer audit under former section 552.108.[488]

The attorney general also addressed whether internal records and notations could be withheld under the statutory predecessor to section 552.108 in the following decisions:

Open Records Decision No. 531 (1989) — detailed guidelines regarding a police department's use of force policy may be withheld, but not those portions of the procedures that restate generally known common-law rules, constitutional limitations, or Penal Code provisions; the release of the detailed guidelines would impair an officer's ability to arrest a suspect and would place individuals at an advantage in confrontations with police;

Open Records Decision No. 508 (1988) — the dates on which specific prisoners are to be transferred from a county jail to the Texas Department of Criminal Justice (formerly the Texas Department of Corrections) may be withheld prior to the transfer because release of this information could impair security, but these dates may not be withheld after the prisoner is transferred because the public has a legitimate interest in the information;

Open Records Decision No. 506 (1988) — the cellular telephone numbers assigned to county officials and employees with specific law enforcement duties may be withheld;

Open Records Decision No. 413 (1984) — a sketch showing the security measures that the Texas Department of Criminal Justice (formerly the Texas Department of Corrections plans to use for its next scheduled execution may be withheld because its release may make crowd control unreasonably difficult;

---

[482]   *See* Open Records Decision Nos. 216 at 4 (1978), 133 at 3 (1976).

[483]   *A & T Consultants, Inc. v. Sharp*, 904 S.W.2d 668 (Tex. 1995).

[484]   5 U.S.C. § 552(b)(7).

[485]   *A & T Consultants, Inc. v. Sharp*, 904 S.W.2d 668, 678 (Tex. 1995).

[486]   *A & T Consultants, Inc. v. Sharp*, 904 S.W.2d 668, 679–681 (Tex. 1995).

[487]   *A & T Consultants, Inc. v. Sharp*, 904 S.W.2d 668, 678 (Tex. 1995) (pre-audit generation and assignment dates not excepted under Gov't Code § 552.108 once audit completed).

[488]   *A & T Consultants, Inc. v. Sharp*, 904 S.W.2d 668, 679 (Tex. 1995).

Open Records Decision No. 394 (1983) — except for information regarding juveniles, a jail roster may not be withheld; a jail roster is an internal record that reveals information specifically made public in other forms, such as the names of persons arrested;

Open Records Decision No. 369 (1983) — notes recording a prosecutor's subjective comments about former jurors may be withheld; releasing these comments would tend to reveal future prosecutorial strategy; and

Open Records Decision Nos. 211 (1978), 143 (1976) — information that would reveal the identities of undercover agents or where employees travel on sensitive assignments may be withheld.

b. Concluded Cases

With regard to the second category of information, information relating to a criminal investigation or prosecution that ended in a result other than a conviction or deferred adjudication may be withheld under sections 552.108(a)(2) and 552.108(b)(2). Sections 552.108(a)(2) and 552.108(b)(2) cannot apply to an open criminal file because the investigation or prosecution for such a file has not concluded. If a case is still open and pending, either at the investigative or prosecution level, the sections that can apply are sections 552.108(a)(1) and 552.108(b)(1), not sections 552.108(a)(2) and 552.108(b)(2).

To establish the applicability of sections 552.108(a)(2) and 552.108(b)(2), a governmental body must demonstrate that the requested information relates to a criminal investigation that concluded in a final result other than a conviction or deferred adjudication.

c. Information Relating to a Threat Against a Peace Officer or Detention Officer

The third category of information protected under section 552.108(a)(3) consists of information relating to a threat against a peace officer or detention officer that is collected or disseminated under section 411.048 of the Government Code. Under section 411.048, the Department of Public Safety's Bureau of Identification and Records is required to create and maintain an index for the purpose of collecting and disseminating information regarding threats of serious bodily injury or death made against a peace officer.[489] The attorney general determined in an informal letter ruling that information provided to the Bureau of Identification and Records for potential inclusion in its database regarding threats made against a peace officer was excepted from disclosure under section 552.108(a)(3).[490]

d. Prosecutor Information

Under the fourth category of information, sections 552.108(a)(4) and 552.108(b)(3) protect information, including an internal record or notation, prepared by a prosecutor in anticipation of or in the course of preparing for criminal litigation *or* information that reflects the prosecutor's mental impressions or legal reasoning. When a governmental body asserts that the information reflects the

---

[489] Gov't Code § 411.048(b).

[490] Open Records Letter No. 2003-3988 (2003).

prosecutor's mental impressions or legal reasoning, the governmental body should, in its request for a ruling, explain how the information does so.

3. Limitations on Scope of Section 552.108

Section 552.108(c) provides that basic information about an arrested person, an arrest, or a crime may not be withheld under section 552.108.[491] The kinds of basic information not excepted from disclosure by section 552.108 are those that were deemed public in *Houston Chronicle Publ'g Co. v. City of Houston* and catalogued in Open Records Decision No. 127 (1976).[492] Basic information is information that ordinarily appears on the first page of an offense report, such as:

(a) the name, age, address, race, sex, occupation, alias, social security number, police department identification number, and physical condition of the arrested person;

(b) the date and time of the arrest;

(c) the place of the arrest;

(d) the offense charged and the court in which it is filed;

(e) the details of the arrest;

(f) booking information;

(g) the notation of any release or transfer;

(h) bonding information;

(i) the location of the crime;

(j) the identification and description of the complainant;

(k) the premises involved;

(l) the time of occurrence of the crime;

(m) the property involved, if any;

(n) the vehicles involved, if any;

(o) a description of the weather;

(p) a detailed description of the offense; and

---

[491] Gov't Code § 552.108(c).

[492] *Houston Chronicle Publ'g Co. v. City of Houston*, 531 S.W.2d 177 (Tex. Civ. App.—Houston [14th Dist.] 1975), *writ ref'd n.r.e. per curiam*, 536 S.W.2d 559 (Tex. 1976).

(q)   the names of the arresting and investigating officers.493

Generally, the identity of the complainant may not be withheld from disclosure under section 552.108. However, the identity of the complainant may be withheld in certain instances under other provisions of the law. For example, where the complainant is also the victim of a serious sexual offense, the identity of the complainant must be withheld from public disclosure pursuant to section 552.101 because such information is protected by common-law privacy.[494] The attorney general has also determined that, where the complainant is also an informer for purposes of the informer's privilege, the complainant's identity may be withheld under section 552.101 in conjunction with the common-law informer's privilege.[495]

Although basic information not excepted from disclosure by section 552.108 often is described by its location ("first-page offense report information"), the location of the information or the label placed on it is not determinative of its status under section 552.108. For example, radio dispatch logs or radio cards maintained by a police department that contain the type of information deemed public generally may not be withheld.[496] Likewise, basic information appearing in other records of law enforcement agencies, such as blotters, arrest sheets, and "show-up sheets," is not excepted from disclosure by section 552.108.[497] Conversely, a video of a booking that conveys information excepted from disclosure is not subject to disclosure when editing the tape is practically impossible and the public information on the tape is available in written form.[498]

Section 552.108 generally does not apply to information made public by statute or to information to which a statute grants certain individuals a right of access.[499] For example, even if an accident report completed pursuant to Chapter 550 of the Transportation Code relates to a pending criminal investigation, a law enforcement entity must release the accident report to a requestor given a statutory right of access to the report under section 550.065(c) of the Transportation Code.[500]

4.   Application of Section 552.108 to Information Relating to Police Officers and Complaints Against Police Officers

Because of their role in protecting the safety of the general public, law enforcement officers generally can expect a lesser degree of personal privacy than other public employees.[501] General information about a police officer usually is not excepted from required public disclosure by section 552.108.

---

[493]   Open Records Decision No. 127 at 3–5 (1976).

[494]   *See* Open Records Decision Nos. 440 (1986), 393 (1983), 339 (1982).

[495]   *See* Open Records Letter No. 2004-8297 (2004).

[496]   Open Records Decision No. 394 at 3–4 (1983); *see City of Lubbock v. Cornyn*, 993 S.W.2d 461 (Tex. App.—Austin 1999, no pet.).

[497]   *See* Open Records Decision No. 127 at 3–4 (1976).

[498]   Open Records Decision No. 364 (1983).

[499]   Open Records Decision Nos. 161 (1977), 146 at 2 (1976); *see also* Open Records Decision Nos. 613 at 4 (1993), 451 at 4 (1986).

[500]   Transp. Code § 550.065(c).

[501]   *See Tex. State Employees Union v. Tex. Dep't of Mental Health & Mental Retardation*, 746 S.W.2d 203, 206 (Tex. 1987); Open Records Decision No. 562 at 9 n.2 (1990).

For example, a police officer's age, law enforcement background, and previous experience and employment usually are not excepted from disclosure by section 552.108.[502]

Similarly, information about complaints against police officers generally may not be withheld under section 552.108. For example, the names of complainants, the names of the officers who are the subjects of complaints, an officer's written response to a complaint, and the final disposition of a complaint generally are not excepted from disclosure by section 552.108.[503] Information about complaints against public officers may be withheld under section 552.108 if the police department can demonstrate release of the information will interfere with the detection, investigation, or prosecution of crime. However, section 552.108 is inapplicable where a complaint against a law enforcement officer does not result in a criminal investigation or prosecution.[504]

a. Personnel Files of Police Officers Serving in Civil Service Cities

The disclosure of information from the personnel files of police officers serving in cities that have adopted chapter 143 of the Local Government Code (the fire fighters' and police officers' civil service law) is governed by section 143.089 of the Local Government Code.[505] Section 143.089 contemplates two different types of personnel files: (1) a police officer's civil service file that the civil service director is required to maintain pursuant to section 143.089(a) and (2) an internal file that the police department may maintain for its own use pursuant to section 143.089(g).[506] A police officer's civil service file must contain specified items, including commendations, documents relating to misconduct that resulted in disciplinary action and periodic evaluations by the officer's supervisor.[507] In cases in which a police department investigates a police officer's misconduct and takes disciplinary action[508] against a police officer, it is required by section 143.089(a)(2) to place all investigatory records relating to the investigation and disciplinary action, including background documents such as complaints, witness statements, and documents of like nature from individuals who were not in a supervisory capacity, in the police officer's civil service file maintained under section 143.089(a).[509] Records maintained in the police officer's civil service file are subject to release under chapter 552 of the Government Code.[510] Furthermore, pursuant to section 143.089(e), the police officer has a right of access to the records maintained in his civil service file.[511] However,

---

[502] *City of Fort Worth v. Cornyn*, 86 S.W.3d 320, 326–28 (Tex. App.—Austin 2002, no pet.); Open Records Decision Nos. 562 at 10 (1990), 329 at 1 (1982).

[503] Open Records Decision Nos. 350 at 3 (1982), 342 at 2 (1982), 329 at 2 (1982).

[504] *Morales v. Ellen*, 840 S.W.2d 519, 525–26 (Tex. App.—El Paso 1992, writ denied) (construing statutory predecessor).

[505] Local Gov't Code § 143.089; *see City of San Antonio v. San Antonio Express-News*, 47 S.W.3d 556 (Tex. App.—San Antonio 2000, pet. denied); *City of San Antonio v. Tex. Attorney Gen.*, 851 S.W.2d 946 (Tex. App.—Austin 1993, writ denied).

[506] Local Gov't Code § 143.089(a), (g).

[507] Local Gov't Code § 143.089(a).

[508] For the purpose of section 143.089 of the Local Government Code, the term "disciplinary action" includes removal, suspension, demotion, and uncompensated duty. Local Gov't Code §§ 143.051–.055. "Disciplinary action" does not include a written reprimand. *See* Attorney General Opinion JC-0257 at 5 (2000).

[509] *Abbott v. City of Corpus Christi*, 109 S.W.3d 113, 122 (Tex. App.—Austin 2003, no pet.).

[510] *See* Local Gov't Code § 143.089(f); Open Records Decision No. 562 at 6 (1990).

[511] Local Gov't Code § 143.089(e).

information maintained in a police department's internal file pursuant to section 143.089(g) is confidential and must not be released.[512]

Absent federal authority, a police department must not release to a federal law enforcement agency information made confidential under section 143.089(g).[513] A city police department should refer a request for information in a police officer's personnel file to the civil service director or the director's designee.[514]

5. Other Related Law Enforcement Records

a. Criminal History Information

Where an individual's criminal history information has been compiled or summarized by a governmental entity, the information takes on a character that implicates the individual's right of privacy in a manner that the same individual's records in an uncompiled state do not.[515] Thus, when a requestor asks for all information concerning a certain named individual and that individual is a suspect, arrestee, or criminal defendant in the information at issue, a law enforcement agency must withhold this information under section 552.101 of the Government Code as that individual's privacy right has been implicated.[516]

Federal law also imposes limitations on the dissemination of criminal history information obtained from the federal National Crime Information Center (NCIC) and its Texas counterpart, the Texas Crime Information Center (TCIC).[517] In essence, federal law requires each state to observe its own laws regarding the dissemination of criminal history information it generates, but requires a state to maintain as confidential any information from other states or the federal government that the state obtains by access to the Interstate Identification Index, a component of the NCIC.[518]

Chapter 411, subchapter F, of the Government Code contains the Texas statutes that govern the confidentiality and release of TCIC information obtained from the Texas Department of Public Safety. However, subchapter F "does not prohibit a criminal justice agency from disclosing to the public criminal history record information that is related to the offense for which a person is involved in the criminal justice system."[519] Moreover, the protection in subchapter F does not extend to driving record information maintained by the Department of Public Safety pursuant to subchapter C

---

[512] *See* Local Gov't Code § 143.089(g); *City of San Antonio v. Tex. Attorney Gen.*, 851 S.W.2d 946, 949 (Tex. App.—Austin 1993, writ denied).

[513] Open Records Decision No. 650 (1996).

[514] Local Gov't Code § 143.089(g).

[515] *Cf. United States Dep't of Justice v. Reporters Comm. for Freedom of the Press*, 489 U.S. 749, 764 (1989) (when considering prong regarding individual's privacy interest, court recognized distinction between public records found in courthouse files and local police stations and compiled summary of information and noted individual has significant privacy interest in compilation of one's criminal history).

[516] *See United States Dep't of Justice v. Reporters Comm. for Freedom of the Press*, 489 U.S. 749, 764 (1989); *cf.* Gov't Code § 411.083.

[517] *See* Open Records Decision No. 655 (1997).

[518] *See* 28 C.F.R. pt. 20; Open Records Decision No. 565 at 10–12 (1990).

[519] Gov't Code § 411.081(b).

of chapter 521 of the Transportation Code.[520] Any person is entitled to obtain from the Department of Public Safety information regarding convictions and deferred adjudications and the person's own criminal history information.[521]

b. Juvenile Law Enforcement Records

The 85th Legislature added Section 58.008 of the Family Code and repealed sections 58.007(c), 58.007(d), 58.007(e), and 58.007(f) of the Family Code.[522] Section 58.008 applies to records created before, on, or after September 1, 2017.[523] Accordingly, former sections 51.14(d) and 58.007(c) of the Family Code are no longer applicable to the analysis of juvenile law enforcement records.

The relevant language of Family Code section 58.008(b) provides as follows:

> **(b)   Except as provided by Subsection (d), law enforcement records concerning a child and information concerning a child that are stored by electronic means or otherwise and from which a record could be generated may not be disclosed to the public and shall be:**
>
> **(1) if maintained on paper or microfilm, kept separate from adult records;**
>
> **(2) if maintained electronically in the same computer system as adult records accessible only under controls that are separate and distinct from controls to access electronic data concerning adults; and**
>
> **(3) maintained on a local basis only and not sent to a central state or federal depository, except as provided by Subsection C or Subchapters B, D, and E.[524]**

Section 58.008(b) applies only to the records of a child[525] who is alleged to have engaged in delinquent conduct or conduct indicating a need for supervision.[526] Section 58.008(b) does not apply where the information in question involves a juvenile as only a complainant, witness, or individual party and not a juvenile as a suspect or offender. Section 58.008(b) applies to entire law enforcement records; therefore, a law enforcement entity is generally prohibited from releasing even basic information from an investigation file when section 58.008(b) applies.

However, section 58.008 provides:

> **(d)   Law enforcement records concerning a child may be inspected or copied by:**

---

[520] Gov't Code § 411.082(2)(B).

[521] Gov't Code §§ 411.083(b)(3), .135(a)(2).

[522] *See* Act of May 28, 2017, 85th Leg. R.S., S.B. 1304, §§ 13, 21.

[523] *See* Act of May 28, 2017, 85th Leg. R.S., S.B. 1304, § 22.

[524] Fam. Code § 58.008(b).

[525] Section 51.02 of the Family Code defines "child" as "a person who is: (A) ten years of age or older and under 17 years of age; or (B) seventeen years of age or older and under 18 years of age who is alleged or found to have engaged in delinquent conduct or conduct indicating a need for supervision as a result of acts committed before becoming 17 years of age." Fam. Code § 51.02(2).

[526] Fam. Code § 51.03(b); *see* Open Records Decision No. 680 at 4 (2003).

(1) a juvenile justice agency, as defined by Section 58.101;

(2) a criminal justice agency as defined by Section 411.082, Government Code;

(3) the child; or

(4) the child's parent or guardian.

(e) **Before a child or a child's parent or guardian may inspect or copy a record concerning the child under Subsection (d), the custodian of the record shall redact:**

(1) any personally identifiable information about a juvenile suspect, offender, victim, or witness who is not the child; and

(2) any information that is excepted from required disclosure under Chapter 552, Government Code, or any other law.[527]

Pursuant to section 58.008(d), a governmental body may not withhold a child's law enforcement records from the child's parent, guardian, or the child under section 58.008(b). However, pursuant to section 58.008(e)(2), a governmental body may raise other exceptions to disclosure. Also, pursuant to section 58.008(e)(1), personally identifiable information of a juvenile suspect, offender, witness, or victim who is not the child must be withheld. For purposes of section 58.008(e)(1), a juvenile victim or witness is a person under eighteen years of age.

c. Child Abuse and Neglect Records

The relevant language of Family Code section 261.201(a) provides:

(a) **Except as provided by Section 261.203, the following information is confidential, is not subject to public release under Chapter 552, Government Code, and may be disclosed only for purposes consistent with this code and applicable federal or state law or under rules adopted by an investigating agency:**

(1) a report of alleged or suspected abuse or neglect made under this chapter and the identity of the person making the report; and

(2) except as otherwise provided in this section, the files, reports, records, communications, audiotapes, videotapes, and working papers used or developed in an investigation under this chapter or in providing services as a result of an investigation.

Section 261.201(a) applies to a report of and information used or developed in an investigation of suspected abuse or neglect[528] of a child[529] and the identity of the individual who made the report of

---

[527] Fam. Code § 58.008(d), (e).

[528] Fam. Code § 261.001(1), (4).

[529] *See* Fam. Code § 101.003(a) (defining "child" for section 261.201 purposes).

abuse or neglect.[530]   Section 261.201(h), however, states section 261.201 does not apply to investigations of abuse or neglect in a home or facility regulated under chapter 42 of the Human Resources Code, such as a childcare facility.

Moreover, sections 261.201(k) and 261.201(l) provide:

(k)   **Notwithstanding Subsection (a), an investigating agency, other than the [Department of Family and Protective Services] or the Texas Juvenile Justice Department, on request, shall provide to the parent, managing conservator, or other legal representative of a child who is the subject of reported abuse or neglect, or to the child if the child is at least 18 years of age, information concerning the reported abuse or neglect that would otherwise be confidential under this section.   The investigating agency shall withhold information under this subsection if the parent, managing conservator, or other legal representative of the child requesting the information is alleged to have committed the abuse or neglect.**

(l)   **Before a child or a parent, managing conservator, or other legal representative of a child may inspect or copy a record or file concerning the child under Subsection (k), the custodian of the record or file must redact:**

(1) any personally identifiable information about a victim or witness under 18 years of age unless that victim or witness is:

(A)   the child who is the subject of the report; or

(B)   another child of the parent, managing conservator, or other legal representative requesting the information;

(2) any information that is excepted from required disclosure under Chapter 552, Government Code, or other law; and

(3) the identity of the person who made the report.

Pursuant to section 261.201(k), a governmental body may not withhold child abuse or neglect records from the parent, managing conservator, or other legal representative of the child, if the parent, managing conservator, or other legal representative is not accused of committing the abuse or neglect, or from the child if the child is at least eighteen years of age.   Pursuant to section 261.201(l)(2), a governmental body may raise other exceptions to disclosure for the child abuse or neglect records. Further, pursuant to sections 261.201(l)(1) and 261.201(l)(3), personally identifiable information of a victim or witness under eighteen years of age who is not the child or another child of the parent, managing conservator, or other legal representative and the identity of the reporting party must be withheld.

---

[530]   Open Records Decision No. 440 (1986) (construing statutory predecessors).

d. Sex Offender Registration Information

Under article 62.005 of the Code of Criminal Procedure, all information contained in either an adult or juvenile sex offender registration form and subsequently entered into the Department of Public Safety database is public information and must be released upon written request, except for the registrant's social security number, driver's license number, home, work, or cellular telephone number, information described by article 62.051(c)(7) or required by the Department of Public Safety under article 62.051(c)(9), and any information that would reveal the victim's identity.[531]

Local law enforcement authorities are required under article 62.053 of the Code of Criminal Procedure to provide school officials with "any information the authority determines is necessary to protect the public" regarding sex offenders except the person's social security number, driver's license number, home, work, or cellular telephone number, and any information that would identify the victim of the offense.[532]

Neither a school district official nor the general public is authorized to receive from local law enforcement authorities sex offender registration information pertaining to individuals whose reportable convictions or adjudication occurred prior to September 1, 1970.[533]

e. Records of 9-1-1 Calls

Originating telephone numbers and addresses of 9-1-1 callers furnished on a call-by-call basis by a telephone service supplier to a 9-1-1 emergency communication district established under subchapter B, C, or D of chapter 772 of the Health and Safety Code are confidential under sections 772.118, 772.218, and 772.318 of the Health and Safety Code, respectively.[534] Chapter 772 does not except from disclosure any other information contained on a computer aided dispatch report that was obtained during a 9-1-1 call.[535] Subchapter E, which applies to counties with populations over 2 million, does not contain a similar confidentiality provision. Other exceptions to disclosure in the Public Information Act may apply to information not otherwise confidential under section 772.118, section 772.218, or section 772.318 of the Health and Safety Code.[536]

f. Certain Information Related to Terrorism and Homeland Security

Sections 418.176 through 418.182 of the Government Code, part of the Texas Homeland Security Act, make confidential certain information related to terrorism or related criminal activity. The fact that information may relate to a governmental body's security concerns does not make the information *per se* confidential under the Texas Homeland Security Act. As with any exception to disclosure, a governmental body asserting one of the confidentiality provisions of the Texas

---

[531] Crim. Proc. Code art. 62.005(b); Open Records Decision No. 645 at 3 (1996) (construing statutory predecessor).

[532] Crim. Proc. Code art. 62.053(e), (f) (information must be released if restrictions under Crim. Proc. Code art. 62.054 are met).

[533] *See* Crim. Proc. Code art. 62.002(a).

[534] Open Records Decision No. 649 at 2–3 (1996).

[535] Open Records Decision No. 649 at 3 (1996).

[536] Open Records Decision No. 649 at 4 (1996).

Homeland Security Act must explain how the responsive records fall within the scope of the claimed provision.[537]

In *Texas Department of Public Safety v. Abbott*, the Texas Department of Public Safety challenged the conclusion of the attorney general and the trial court that videos recorded by security cameras in a Texas Capitol hallway were not confidential under section 418.182 of the Government Code.[538] In reversing this conclusion, the Third Court of Appeals found the Texas Department of Public Safety demonstrated the videos relate to the specifications of the capitol security system used to protect public property from an act of terrorism or related criminal activity because the legislature's use of "relates to" is a plain legislative choice to broadly protect information regarding security systems designed to protect public property. Thus, the court concluded the recorded images necessarily relate to the specifications of the security system that recorded them.

Release of certain information about aviation and maritime security is governed by federal law.[539] The attorney general has determined in several informal letter rulings that the decision to withhold or release such information rests with the head of the federal Transportation Security Administration (the "TSA") or the Coast Guard and that requests for such information should be referred to the TSA or Coast Guard for their decision concerning disclosure of the information.[540]

Section 660.2035 of the Government Code provides a voucher or other expense reimbursement form, and any receipt or other document supporting that voucher or other expense reimbursement form, that is submitted under section 660.027 is confidential for 18 months following the date of travel if the voucher or other expense reimbursement form is submitted for payment or reimbursement of a travel expense incurred by a peace officer while assigned to provide protection for an elected official or a member of the elected official's family.[541] At the expiration of the 18 months, the voucher or other expense reimbursement form and any supporting documents become subject to disclosure under the Public Information Act and are not excepted from public disclosure or confidential under the Act or other law.[542] However, subsection 660.2035(b) specifically lists seven exceptions in the Act that can apply to withhold information within a voucher, expense reimbursement form, and any supporting document.[543] In an informal letter ruling, the attorney general considered the Texas Department of Public Safety's claims that, after the expiration of the 18-month confidentiality period, sections 552.101 and 552.152 of the Government Code protected travel vouchers and supporting documentation submitted by agents of the Executive Protection Bureau for reimbursement of travel expenses.[544] Because section 552.101 is not one of the enumerated exceptions in subsection 660.2035(b), the attorney general determined section 552.101 did not apply to travel vouchers and supporting documentation.[545] However, as section 552.152 is an exception listed in subsection 660.2035(b), the attorney general considered the claim to withhold the information under section

---

[537] *See* Gov't Code § 552.301(e)(1)(A) (governmental body must explain how claimed exception to disclosure applies).

[538] *Tex. Dep't of Pub. Safety v. Abbott*, 310 S.W.3d 670 (Tex. App.—Austin 2010, no pet.).

[539] 49 U.S.C. § 114(r); 49 C.F.R. pt. 1520.

[540] Open Records Letter Nos. 2013-09028 (2013), 2009-11201 (2009), 2005-07525 (2005).

[541] Gov't Code § 660.2035(a).

[542] Gov't Code § 660.2035(b).

[543] Gov't Code § 660.2035(b).

[544] Open Records Letter No. 2014-02048 (2014).

[545] Open Records Letter No. 2014-02048 at 3 (2014).

552.152, and finding the claim had merit, concluded the travel vouchers and supporting documentation were excepted from disclosure under section 552.152.[546, 547]

g. Body Worn Camera Program

Subchapter N of chapter 1701 of the Occupations Code pertains to body worn cameras. Subchapter N revises the procedures associated with public information requests for body worn camera recordings. Generally, requestors need not use "magic words" when making requests to governmental bodies; however, when requestors seek access to body worn camera recordings, requestors must provide:

(1) the date and approximate time of the recording;
(2) the specific location where the recording occurred; and
(3) the name of one or more persons known to be a subject of the recording.[548]

Failure to provide this information does not preclude a requestor from requesting the same information again.[549] When properly requested, chapter 1701 provides for the confidentiality of body worn camera recordings under certain circumstances. A body worn camera recording is confidential if it was not required to be made under a law or policy adopted by the relevant law enforcement agency.[550]

Section 1701.660 makes confidential any recording from a body-worn camera that documents the use of deadly force or that is related to an administrative or criminal investigation of an officer until all criminal matters are finally adjudicated and all administrative investigations completed.[551] However, a law enforcement agency may choose to release such information if doing so furthers a law enforcement interest.[552] Before a law enforcement agency releases a body-worn camera recording that was made in a private place or in connection with a fine-only misdemeanor, the agency must receive authorization from the person who is the subject of the recording, or if that person is deceased, from the person's authorized representative.[553] A governmental body may continue to raise section 552.108 or any other applicable exception to disclosure or law for a body-worn camera recording.[554]

Section 1701.662 also extends the ten and fifteen business day deadlines associated with requesting a ruling from the attorney general to twenty and twenty-five business days, respectively.[555] Additionally, a governmental body that receives a "voluminous request" for body-worn camera

---

[546] Open Records Letter No. 2014-02048 at 3-4 (2014).
[547] Open Records Letter No. 2014-02048 at 3-4 (2014).
[548] Occ. Code § 1701.661(a).
[549] Occ. Code § 1701.661(b).
[550] Occ. Code § 1701.661(h).
[551] Occ. Code § 1701.660(a).
[552] Occ. Code § 1701.660(b).
[553] Occ. Code § 1701.661(f).
[554] Occ. Code § 1701.661(e).
[555] Occ. Code § 1701.662.

recordings is considered to have complied with the request if it provides the information no later than twenty-one business days after it receives the request.[556]

h.   Video Recordings of Arrests for Intoxication

Article 2.1396 of the Code of Criminal Procedure, redesignated by the 85th Legislature, provides as follows:

> **A person stopped or arrested on suspicion of an offense under Section 49.04, 49.045, 49.07, or 49.08, Penal Code, is entitled to receive from a law enforcement agency employing the peace officer who made the stop or arrest a copy of any video made by or at the direction of the officer that contains footage of:**
>
> **(1) the stop;**
>
> **(2) the arrest;**
>
> **(3) the conduct of the person stopped during any interaction with the officer, including during the administration of a field sobriety test; or**
>
> **(4) a procedure in which a specimen of the person's breath or blood is taken.**[557]

Article 2.1396 applies only to a recording of conduct that occurs on or after September 1, 2015.[558] A requestor's right of access to a video recording subject to article 2.1396 will generally prevail over the Act's general exceptions to disclosure.[559]

I.   Section 552.1081: Confidentiality of Certain Information Regarding Execution of Convict

Section 552.1081 of the Government Code provides as follows:

> **Information is excepted from the requirements of Section 552.021 if it contains identifying information under Article 43.14, Code of Criminal Procedure, including that of:**
>
> **(1) any person who participates in an execution procedure, including a person who uses, supplies, or administers a substance during the execution; and**
>
> **(2) any person or entity that manufactures, transports, tests, procures, compounds, prescribes, dispenses, or provides a substance or supplies used in an execution.**

There are no cases or formal opinions interpreting this section.

---

[556]   Occ. Code § 1701.663.

[557]   Crim. Proc. Code art. 2.1396.

[558]   Act of May 30, 2015, 84th Leg., R.S., H.B. 3791, § 2, 2015 Tex. Gen. Laws 3804, 3805 redesignated by Act of May 30, 2017, 85th Leg., R.S., H.B. 245, § 4.

[559]   *See* Open Records Decision Nos. 613 at 4 (1993), 451 (1986).

J. Section 552.1085: Confidentiality of Sensitive Crime Scene Image

(a) In this section:

(1) "Deceased person's next of kin" means:

(A) the surviving spouse of the deceased person;

(B) if there is no surviving spouse of the deceased, an adult child of the deceased person; or

(C) if there is no surviving spouse or adult child of the deceased, a parent of the deceased person.

(2) "Defendant" means a person being prosecuted for the death of the deceased person or a person convicted of an offense in relation to that death and appealing that conviction.

(3) "Expressive work" means:

(A) a fictional or nonfictional entertainment, dramatic, literary, or musical work that is a play, book, article, musical composition, audiovisual work, radio or television program, work of art, or work of political, educational, or newsworthy value;

(B) a work the primary function of which is the delivery of news, information, current events, or other matters of public interest or concern; or

(C) an advertisement or commercial announcement of a work described by Paragraph (A) or (B).

(4) "Local governmental entity" means a county, municipality, school district, charter school, junior college district, or other political subdivision of this state.

(5) "Public or private institution of higher education" means:

(A) an institution of higher education, as defined by Section 61.003, Education Code; or

(B) a private or independent institution of higher education, as defined by Section 61.003, Education Code.

(6) "Sensitive crime scene image" means a photograph or video recording taken at a crime scene, contained in or part of a closed criminal case, that depicts a deceased person in a state of dismemberment, decapitation, or similar mutilation or that depicts the deceased person's genitalia.

(7) "State agency" means a department, commission, board, office, or other agency that is a part of state government and that is created by the constitution or a statute of this state. The term includes an institution of higher education as defined by Section 61.003, Education Code.

(b) For purposes of this section, an Internet website, the primary function of which is not the delivery of news, information, current events, or other matters of public interest or concern, is not an expressive work.

(c) A sensitive crime scene image in the custody of a governmental body is confidential and excepted from the requirements of Section 552.021 and a governmental body may not permit a person to view or copy the image except as provided by this section. This section applies to any sensitive crime scene image regardless of the date that the image was taken or recorded.

(d) Notwithstanding Subsection (c) and subject to Subsection (e), the following persons may view or copy information that constitutes a sensitive crime scene image from a governmental body:

(1) the deceased person's next of kin;

(2) a person authorized in writing by the deceased person's next of kin;

(3) a defendant or the defendant's attorney;

(4) a person who establishes to the governmental body an interest in a sensitive crime scene image that is based on, connected with, or in support of the creation, in any medium, of an expressive work;

(5) a person performing bona fide research sponsored by a public or private institution of higher education with approval of a supervisor of the research or a supervising faculty member;

(6) a state agency;

(7) an agency of the federal government; or

(8) a local governmental entity.

(e) This section does not prohibit a governmental body from asserting an exception to disclosure of a sensitive crime scene image to a person identified in Subsection (d) on the grounds that the image is excepted from the requirements of Section 552.021 under another provision of this chapter or another law.

(f) Not later than the 10th business day after the date a governmental body receives a request for a sensitive crime scene image from a person described by Subsection (d)(4) or (5), the governmental body shall notify the deceased person's next of kin of the request in writing. The notice must be sent to the next of kin's last known address.

(g) A governmental body that receives a request for information that constitutes a sensitive crime scene image shall allow a person described in Subsection (d) to view or copy the image not later than the 10th business day after the date the governmental body receives the request unless the governmental body files a request for an attorney general decision under Subchapter G regarding whether an exception to public disclosure applies to the information.

There are no cases or formal opinions interpreting section 552.1085. However, in an informal letter ruling, the attorney general determined a governmental body failed to establish the applicability of section 552.1085 to the information at issue because the governmental body stated the information pertained to unresolved criminal cases that were ongoing.[560] In a separate letter ruling, the attorney general concluded the next of kin of the deceased person depicted in the photographs at issue would have a right to view or copy the photographs pursuant to section 552.1085(d)(1), because the governmental body may not use section 552.1085(c)(1) to withhold the photographs from the next of kin and raised no other exceptions to withhold the photographs.[561]

K. Section 552.109: Confidentiality of Certain Private Communications of an Elected Office Holder

Section 552.109 of the Government Code excepts from required public disclosure:

Private correspondence or communications of an elected office holder relating to matters the disclosure of which would constitute an invasion of privacy . . . .

The test to be applied to information under section 552.109 is the same as the common-law privacy standard under section 552.101 and decisions under section 552.109 and its statutory predecessor rely on the same tests applicable under section 552.101.[562] The common-law privacy standard is laid out in *Indus. Found. v. Tex. Indus. Accident Bd.*, and protects information if it (1) contains highly intimate or embarrassing facts, the publication of which would be highly objectionably to a reasonable person, and (2) is not of legitimate concern to the public.[563] Both prongs of this test must be established.[564] Section 552.109 only protects the privacy interests of elected office holders.[565] It does not protect the privacy interests of their correspondents.[566] Certain records of communications between citizens and members of the legislature or the lieutenant governor may not be subject to the Act.[567]

In the following open records decisions, the attorney general determined that certain information was not excepted from required public disclosure under the statutory predecessor to section 552.109:

---

[560] Open Records Letter No. 2014-04454 at 13 (2014).

[561] Open Records Letter No. 2013-21155 at 4 (2013).

[562] Open Records Decision Nos. 506 at 3 (1988), 241 (1980), 212 (1978).

[563] *Indus. Found. v. Tex. Indus. Accident Bd.*, 540 S.W.2d 668, 685 (Tex. 1976), *cert. denied*, 430 U.S. 931 (1977).

[564] *Indus. Found. v. Tex. Indus. Accident Bd.*, 540 S.W.2d 668, 681–685 (Tex. 1976), *cert. denied*, 430 U.S. 931 (1977).

[565] Open Records Decision No. 473 at 3 (1987).

[566] *See* Open Records Decision No. 332 at 2 (1982).

[567] *See* Gov't Code §§ 306.003, .004; Open Records Decision No. 648 (1996); Open Records Letter Nos. 2012-14193 (2012), 2012-06238 (2012).

Open Records Decision No. 506 (1988) — cellular telephone numbers of county officials where county paid for installation of service and for telephone bills, and which service was intended to be used by officials in conducting official public business, because public has a legitimate interest in the performance of official public duties;

Open Records Decision No. 473 (1987) — performance evaluations of city council appointees, because this section was intended to protect the privacy only of elected office holders; although city council members prepared the evaluations, the evaluations did not implicate their privacy interests;

Open Records Decision No. 332 (1982) — letters concerning a teacher's performance written by parents to school trustees, because nothing in the letters constituted an invasion of privacy of the trustees;

Open Records Decision No. 241 (1980) — correspondence of the governor regarding potential nominees for public office, because the material was not protected by a constitutional right of privacy; furthermore, the material was not protected by common-law right of privacy because it did not contain any highly embarrassing or intimate facts and there was a legitimate public interest in the appointment process;[568] and

Open Records Decision No. 40 (1974) — itemized list of long distance calls made by legislators and charged to their contingent expense accounts, because such a list is not a "communication."

L. Section 552.110: Confidentiality of Trade Secrets and Confidentiality of Certain Commercial or Financial Information

Section 552.110 of the Government Code provides as follows:

(a) **A trade secret obtained from a person and privileged or confidential by statute or judicial decision is excepted from [required public disclosure].**

(b) **Commercial or financial information for which it is demonstrated based on specific factual evidence that disclosure would cause substantial competitive harm to the person from whom the information was obtained is excepted from [required public disclosure].**

Section 552.110 refers to two types of information: (1) trade secrets and (2) confidential commercial or financial information obtained from a person. The Act requires a governmental body to make a good faith attempt to notify in writing a person whose proprietary information may be subject to section 552.110 within ten business days after receiving the request for the information.[569] A person so notified bears the burden of establishing the applicability of section 552.110.[570] A copy of the form the Act requires the governmental body to send to a person whose information may be subject

---

[568] *See* Open Records Decision No. 212 at 4 (1978).

[569] Gov't Code § 552.305.

[570] Gov't Code § 552.305.

to section 552.110, as well as section 552.101, section 552.113, or section 552.131, can be found in Part Nine of this *Handbook*.

1. Trade Secrets

The Texas Supreme Court has adopted the definition of the term "trade secret" from the Restatement of Torts, section 757 (1939).[571] The determination of whether any particular information is a trade secret is a determination of fact.[572] Noting that an exact definition of a trade secret is not possible, the Restatement lists six factors to be considered in determining whether particular information constitutes a trade secret:

(1)   the extent to which the information is known outside of [the company's] business;

(2)   the extent to which it is known by employees and others involved in [the company's business];

(3)   the extent of measures taken by [the company] to guard the secrecy of the information;

(4)   the value of the information to [the company] and to [its] competitors;

(5)   the amount of effort or money expended by [the company] in developing the information; [and]

(6)   the ease or difficulty with which the information could be properly acquired or duplicated by others.[573]

A party asserting the trade secret prong of section 552.110 is not required to satisfy all six factors listed in the Restatement in order to prevail on its claim.[574] In addition, other circumstances may be relevant in determining whether information qualifies as a trade secret.[575] Open Records Decision No. 552 (1990) noted that the attorney general is unable to resolve disputes of fact regarding the status of information as "trade secrets" and must rely upon the facts alleged or upon those facts that are discernible from the documents submitted for inspection. For this reason, the attorney general will accept a claim for exception as a trade secret when a *prima facie* case is made that the information in question constitutes a trade secret and no argument is made that rebuts that assertion as a matter of law.[576] In Open Records Decision No. 609 (1992), there was a factual dispute between the governmental body and the proponent of the trade secret protection as to certain elements of a *prima facie* case. Because the attorney general cannot resolve such factual disputes, the matter was referred back to the governmental body for fact-finding.

---

[571] *Hyde Corp. v. Huffines*, 314 S.W.2d 763, 776 (Tex.), *cert. denied*, 358 U.S. 898 (1958).

[572] Open Records Decision No. 552 at 2 (1990); *see Envoy Med. Sys. v. State*, 108 S.W.3d 333, 337 (Tex. App.—Austin 2003, no pet.).

[573] RESTATEMENT OF TORTS § 757 cmt. b (1939); *see Ctr. for Econ. Justice v. Am. Ins. Ass'n*, 39 S.W.3d 337, 344–45 (Tex. App.—Austin 2001, no pet.); *Birnbaum v. Alliance of Am. Insurers*, 994 S.W.2d 766, 783 (Tex. App.—Austin 1999, pet. denied).

[574] *See In re Bass*, 113 S.W.3d 735, 740 (Tex. 2003).

[575] *See In re Bass*, 113 S.W.3d 735, 740 (Tex. 2003).

[576] Open Records Decision Nos. 669 at 2 (2000), 552 at 5 (1990).

2. Commercial or Financial Information Privileged or Confidential by Law

Section 552.110 now expressly includes the standard for excepting from disclosure commercial and financial information.[577] An interested person must demonstrate "based on specific factual evidence that disclosure would cause substantial competitive harm to the person from whom the information was obtained." This standard resembles part of the test for applying the correlative exemption in the federal Freedom of Information Act, 5 U.S.C. § 552(b)(4), as set out in *Nat'l Parks & Conservation Ass'n v. Morton*.[578] That part of the *National Parks* test states that commercial or financial information is confidential if disclosure of the information is likely to cause substantial harm to the competitive position of the person from whom the information was obtained.[579] The current commercial and financial information branch of section 552.110 does not incorporate the part of the *National Parks* test for information that is likely to impair the government's ability to obtain necessary information in the future. Like the federal standard, section 552.110(b) requires the business enterprise whose information is at issue to make a specific factual or evidentiary showing, not conclusory or generalized allegations, that substantial competitive injury would likely result from disclosure.[580]

M. Section 552.111: Agency Memoranda

Section 552.111 of the Government Code excepts from required public disclosure:

> **An interagency or intraagency memorandum or letter that would not be available by law to a party in litigation with the agency . . . .**

To be protected under section 552.111, information must consist of interagency or intraagency communications. Although information protected by section 552.111 is most commonly generated by agency personnel, information created for an agency by outside consultants acting on behalf of the agency in an official capacity may be within section 552.111.[581] An agency's communications with other agencies and third parties, however, are not protected unless the agency demonstrates that the parties to the communications share a privity of interest.[582] For example, correspondence between a licensing agency and a licensee is not excepted under section 552.111.[583]

---

[577] The former section 552.110 excepted "commercial and financial information . . . privileged or confidential by statute or judicial decision." It did not set out the standard for excepting commercial or financial information. In 1996, the attorney general followed the test for applying section 552(b)(4) of the federal Freedom of Information Act as set forth in *Nat'l Parks & Conservation Ass'n v. Morton*, 498 F.2d 765 (D.C. Cir. 1974). *See* Open Records Decision No. 639 at 2–3 (1996). However, the Third Court of Appeals held that *National Parks* was not a judicial decision within the meaning of the former section 552.110. *Birnbaum v. Alliance of Am. Insurers*, 994 S.W.2d 766 (Tex. App.—Austin 1999, pet. denied). Consequently, after the *Birnbaum* decision, the attorney general no longer used the *National Parks* standard for excepting commercial or financial information under former section 552.110.

[578] *Nat'l Parks & Conservation Ass'n v. Morton*, 498 F.2d 765 (D.C. Cir. 1974).

[579] *See Nat'l Parks & Conservation Ass'n v. Morton*, 498 F.2d 765, 770 (D.C. Cir. 1974).

[580] *See* Open Records Decision No. 661 at 6 (1999).

[581] Open Records Decision No. 462 (1987) (construing statutory predecessor).

[582] *See* Open Records Decision No. 561 at 9 (1990) (correspondence from Federal Bureau of Investigation officer to city was not protected by statutory predecessor to Gov't Code § 552.111, where no privity of interest or common deliberative process existed between federal agency and city).

[583] Open Records Decision No. 474 at 5 (1987) (construing statutory predecessor).

Also, to be protected under section 552.111, an interagency or intraagency communication must be privileged from discovery in civil litigation involving the agency.[584] The attorney general has interpreted section 552.111 to incorporate both the deliberative process privilege and the work product privilege.[585]

1. Deliberative Process Privilege

Section 552.111 has been read to incorporate the deliberative process privilege into the Public Information Act for intraagency and interagency communications.[586] The deliberative process privilege, as incorporated into the Public Information Act, protects from disclosure intraagency and interagency communications consisting of advice, opinion or recommendations on policymaking matters of the governmental body at issue.[587] The purpose of withholding advice, opinion or recommendations under section 552.111 is "to encourage frank and open discussion within the agency in connection with its decision-making processes" pertaining to policy matters.[588] "An agency's policymaking functions do not encompass routine internal administrative and personnel matters; disclosure of information relating to such matters will not inhibit free discussion among agency personnel as to policy issues."[589] An agency's policymaking functions do include, however, administrative and personnel matters of broad scope that affect the governmental body's policy mission.[590] For example, because the information at issue in Open Records Decision No. 615 (1993) concerned the evaluation of a university professor's job performance, the statutory predecessor to section 552.111 did not except this information from required public disclosure. On the other hand, the information at issue in Open Records Decision No. 631 (1995) was a report addressing allegations of systematic discrimination against African-American and Hispanic faculty members in the retention, tenure, and promotion process at a university. Rather than pertaining solely to the internal administration of the university, the scope of the report was much broader and involved the university's educational mission. Accordingly, section 552.111 excepted from required public disclosure the portions of the report that constituted advice, recommendations or opinions.[591]

Even when an internal memorandum relates to a governmental body's policy functions, the deliberative process privilege excepts from disclosure only the advice, recommendations, and

---

[584] Open Records Decision Nos. 677 at 4 (2002), 615 at 2–3 (1993).

[585] Open Records Decision Nos. 647 at 5–6 (1996), 615 at 5 (1993); *see City of Garland v. Dallas Morning News*, 22 S.W.3d 351, 360 (Tex. 2000).

[586] *City of Garland v. Dallas Morning News*, 22 S.W.3d 351, 360 (Tex. 2000); *Lett v. Klein Indep. Sch. Dist.,* 917 S.W.2d 455, 456 (Tex. App.—Houston [14th Dist.] 1996, writ denied); *Tex. Dep't of Pub. Safety v. Gilbreath*, 842 S.W.2d 408, 412–13 (Tex. App.—Austin 1992, no writ); Open Records Decision No. 615 at 5 (1993).

[587] *City of Garland v. Dallas Morning News*, 22 S.W.3d 351, 361, 364 (Tex. 2000); *Arlington Indep. Sch. Dist. v. Tex. Attorney Gen.*, 37 S.W.3d 152, 158 (Tex. App.—Austin 2001, no pet.); Open Records Decision No. 615 at 5 (1993).

[588] *Austin v. City of San Antonio*, 630 S.W.2d 391, 394 (Tex. App.—San Antonio 1982, writ ref'd n.r.e.); *see also City of Garland v. Dallas Morning News*, 22 S.W.3d 351, 361 (Tex. 2000); *Lett v. Klein Indep. Sch. Dist.,* 917 S.W.2d 455, 456, 457 (Tex. App.—Houston [14th Dist.] 1996, writ denied); *Tex. Dep't of Pub. Safety v. Gilbreath*, 842 S.W.2d 408, 412 (Tex. App.—Austin 1992, no writ).

[589] Open Records Decision No. 615 at 5 (1993); *see City of Garland v. Dallas Morning News*, 22 S.W.3d 364 (Tex. 2000); *Lett v. Klein Indep. Sch. Dist.,* 917 S.W.2d 455, 456 (Tex. App.—Houston [14th Dist.] 1996, writ denied).

[590] Open Records Decision No. 631 at 3 (1995); *City of Garland v. Dallas Morning News*, 969 S.W.2d 548, 557 (Tex. App.—Dallas 1998), *aff'd*, 22 S.W.3d 351 (Tex. 2000).

[591] Open Records Decision No. 631 at 3 (1995).

opinions found in that memorandum. The deliberative process privilege does not except from disclosure purely factual information that is severable from the opinion portions of the memorandum.[592]

Before June 29, 1993, the attorney general did not confine the application of the statutory predecessor to section 552.111 solely to communications relating to agencies' policymaking functions. Given the change in the interpretation of the scope of section 552.111, a governmental body that receives a request for information should exercise caution in relying on attorney general decisions regarding the applicability of this exception written before June 29, 1993. For example, in Open Records Decision No. 559 (1990), the attorney general held that the predecessor statute to section 552.111 also protects drafts of a document that has been or will be released in final form to the public and any comments or other notations on the drafts because they necessarily represent advice, opinion, and recommendations of the drafter as to the form and content of the final document. However, the rationale and scope of this open records decision have been modified implicitly to apply only to those records involving an agency's policy matters.

2. Work Product Privilege

The attorney general has also concluded that section 552.111 incorporates the privilege for work product found in Texas Rule of Civil Procedure 192.5.[593] Rule 192.5 defines work product as:

> **(1)   material prepared or mental impressions developed in anticipation of litigation or for trial by or for a party or a party's representatives, including the party's attorneys, consultants, sureties, indemnitors, insurers, employees, or agents; or**

> **(2)   a communication made in anticipation of litigation or for trial between a party and the party's representatives or among a party's representatives, including the party's attorneys, consultants, sureties, indemnitors, insurers, employees, or agents.[594]**

A governmental body raising the work product privilege under section 552.111 bears the burden of providing the relevant facts in each case to demonstrate the elements of the privilege.[595] One element of the work product test is that the information must have been made or developed for trial or in anticipation of litigation.[596] In order for the attorney general to conclude that information was created for trial or in anticipation of litigation, the governmental body must demonstrate that at the time the information was created or acquired:

> a) a reasonable person would have concluded from the totality of the circumstances . . . that there was a substantial chance that litigation would ensue; and b) the party resisting discovery

---

[592]   *See* Open Records Decision No. 615 at 4–5 (1993); *City of Garland v. Dallas Morning News*, 22 S.W.3d 351 (Tex. 2000).

[593]   Open Records Decision No. 677 at 4–8 (2002).

[594]   TEX. R. CIV. P. 192.5(a).

[595]   *See* Open Records Decision No. 677 at 6 (2002).

[596]   TEX. R. CIV. P. 192.5(a); Open Records Decision No. 677 at 6 (2002)

believed in good faith that there was a substantial chance that litigation would ensue and [created or obtained the information] for the purpose of preparing for such litigation.[597]

A "substantial chance" of litigation does not mean a statistical probability, but rather "that litigation is more than merely an abstract possibility or unwarranted fear."[598]

Also, as part of the work product test, material or a mental impression must have been prepared or developed by or for a party or a party's representatives.[599] Similarly, in the case of a communication, the communication must have been between a party and the party's representatives.[600] Thus, a governmental body claiming the work product privilege must identify the parties or potential parties to the litigation, the person or entity that prepared the information, and any individual with whom the information was shared.[601]

If a requestor seeks a governmental body's entire litigation file, the governmental body may assert the file is excepted from disclosure in its entirety because such a request implicates the core work product aspect of the attorney work product privilege.[602] In such an instance, if the governmental body demonstrates the file was created in anticipation of litigation or for trial, the attorney general will presume the entire file is within the scope of the privilege.[603]

N. Section 552.112: Certain Information Relating to Regulation of Financial Institutions or Securities

Section 552.112 of the Government Code provides as follows:

(a) Information is excepted from the requirements of Section 552.021 if it is information contained in or relating to examination, operating, or condition reports prepared by or for an agency responsible for the regulation or supervision of financial institutions or securities, or both.

(b) In this section, "securities" has the meaning assigned by The Securities Act (Article 581-1 et seq., Vernon's Texas Civil Statutes).

(c) Information is excepted from the requirements of Section 552.021 if it is information submitted by an individual or other entity to the Texas Legislative Council, or to any state agency or department overseen by the Finance Commission of Texas and the

---

[597] *Nat'l Tank Co. v. Brotherton*, 851 S.W.2d 193, 207 (Tex. 1993); *In re Monsanto Co.*, 998 S.W.2d 917, 923–24 (Tex. App.—Waco 1999, orig. proceeding).

[598] *Nat'l Tank Co. v. Brotherton*, 851 S.W.2d 193, 204, 207 (Tex. 1993); *see* Open Records Decision No. 677 at 7 (2002).

[599] TEX. R. CIV. P. 192.5(a)(1); Open Records Decision No. 677 at 7 (2002).

[600] TEX. R. CIV. P. 192.5(a)(2); Open Records Decision No. 677 at 7–8 (2002).

[601] Open Records Decision No. 677 at 8 (2002).

[602] Open Records Decision No. 677 at 5–6 (2002).

[603] *See* Open Records Decision No. 647 at 5 (1996) (citing *Nat'l Union Fire Ins. Co. v. Valdez*, 863 S.W.2d 458, 461 (Tex. 1993)) (organization of attorney's litigation file necessarily reflects attorney's thought processes); *see also Curry v. Walker*, 873 S.W.2d 379, 380 (Tex. 1994) ("the decision as to what to include in [the file] necessarily reveals the attorney's thought processes concerning the prosecution or defense of the case").

information has been or will be sent to the Texas Legislative Council, for the purpose of performing a statistical or demographic analysis of information subject to Section 323.020. However, this subsection does not except from the requirements of Section 552.021 information that does not identify or tend to identify an individual or other entity and that is subject to required public disclosure under Section 323.020(e).

This section protects specific examination, operating, or condition reports prepared or obtained by agencies in regulating or supervising financial institutions or securities or information that indirectly reveals the contents of such reports.[604] Such reports typically disclose the financial status and dealings of the institutions that file them. Section 552.112 does not protect general information about the overall condition of an industry if the information does not identify particular institutions under investigation or supervision.[605] An entity must be a "financial institution" for its examination, operating, or condition reports to be excepted by section 552.112; it is not sufficient that the entity is regulated by an agency that regulates or supervises financial institutions.[606] The attorney general has stated that the term "financial institution" means "any banking corporation or trust company, building and loan association, governmental agency, insurance company, or related corporation, partnership, foundation, or the other institutions engaged primarily in lending or investing funds."[607] Notably, a Texas appeals court decision, *Birnbaum v. Alliance of Am. Insurers*,[608] held that insurance companies are not "financial institutions" under section 552.112, overruling the determination in Open Records Decision No. 158 (1977) that insurance companies were "financial institutions" under the statutory predecessor to the section. Section 552.112 is a permissive exception that a governmental body may waive at its discretion.[609] Thus, section 552.112 only protects the interests of a governmental body, rather than the interests of third parties.

The following open records decisions have considered whether information is excepted from required public disclosure under section 552.112:

> Open Records Decision No. 483 (1987) — Texas Savings and Loan Department report containing a general discussion of the condition of the industry that does not identify particular institutions under investigation or supervision is not excepted from disclosure;

> Open Records Decision No. 392 (1983) — material collected by the Consumer Credit Commissioner in an investigation of loan transactions was not protected by the statutory predecessor to section 552.112 when the requested information did not consist of a detailed description of the complete financial status of the company being investigated but rather consisted of the records of the company's particular transactions with persons filing consumer complaints;

> Open Records Decision No. 261 (1980) — form acknowledgment by bank board of directors that Department of Banking examination report had been received is excepted from disclosure where acknowledgment would reveal the conclusions reached by the department;

---

[604] *See generally* Open Records Decision Nos. 261 (1980), 29 (1974).

[605] Open Records Decision No. 483 at 9 (1987).

[606] Open Records Decision No. 158 at 4–5 (1977).

[607] Open Records Decision No. 158 at 5 (1977); *see also* Open Records Decision No. 392 at 3 (1983).

[608] *Birnbaum v. Alliance of Am. Insurers*, 994 S.W.2d 766 (Tex. App.—Austin 1999, pet. denied).

[609] *Birnbaum v. Alliance of Am. Insurers*, 994 S.W.2d 766 (Tex. App.—Austin 1999, pet. denied).

Open Records Decision No. 194 (1978) — pawn shop license application that includes information about applicant's net assets to assess compliance with Texas Pawnshop Act is not excepted from disclosure because such information does not qualify as an examination, operating, or condition report;

Open Records Decision No. 187 (1978) — property development plans submitted by a credit union to the Credit Union Department were excepted from disclosure by the statutory predecessor to section 552.112 because submission included detailed presentation of credit union's conditions and operations and the particular proposed investment; and

Open Records Decision No. 130 (1976) — investigative file of the enforcement division of the State Securities Board is excepted from disclosure.

O. Section 552.113: Confidentiality of Geological or Geophysical Information

Section 552.113 makes confidential electric logs under Subchapter M, Chapter 91, of the Natural Resources Code, and geological or geophysical information or data, including maps concerning wells, except when filed in connection with an application or proceeding before an agency. This exception also applies to geological, geophysical, and geochemical information, including electric logs, filed with the General Land Office, and includes provisions for the expiration of confidentiality of "confidential material," as that term is defined, and the use of such material in administrative proceedings before the General Land Office.

Section 552.113 of the Government Code provides as follows:

(a)   **Information is excepted from the requirements of Section 552.021 if it is:**

  (1) **an electric log confidential under Subchapter M, Chapter 91, Natural Resources Code;**

  (2) **geological or geophysical information or data, including maps concerning wells, except information filed in connection with an application or proceeding before an agency; or**

  (3) **confidential under Subsections (c) through (f).**

(b)   **Information that is shown to or examined by an employee of the General Land Office, but not retained in the land office, is not considered to be filed with the land office.**

(c)   **In this section:**

  (1) **"Confidential material" includes all well logs, geological, geophysical, geochemical, and other similar data, including maps and other interpretations of the material filed in the General Land Office:**

(A) in connection with any administrative application or proceeding before the land commissioner, the school land board, any board for lease, or the commissioner's or board's staff; or

(B) in compliance with the requirements of any law, rule, lease, or agreement.

(2) "Electric logs" has the same meaning as it has in Chapter 91, Natural Resources Code.

(3) "Administrative applications" and "administrative proceedings" include applications for pooling or unitization, review of shut-in royalty payments, review of leases or other agreements to determine their validity, review of any plan of operations, review of the obligation to drill offset wells, or an application to pay compensatory royalty.

(d) Confidential material, except electric logs, filed in the General Land Office on or after September 1, 1985, is public information and is available to the public under Section 552.021 on and after the later of:

(1) five years from the filing date of the confidential material; or

(2) one year from the expiration, termination, or forfeiture of the lease in connection with which the confidential material was filed.

(e) Electric logs filed in the General Land Office on or after September 1, 1985, are either public information or confidential material to the same extent and for the same periods provided for the same logs by Chapter 91, Natural Resources Code. A person may request that an electric log that has been filed in the General Land Office be made confidential by filing with the land office a copy of the written request for confidentiality made to the Railroad Commission of Texas for the same log.

(f) The following are public information:

(1) electric logs filed in the General Land Office before September 1, 1985; and

(2) confidential material, except electric logs, filed in the General Land Office before September 1, 1985, provided, that Subsection (d) governs the disclosure of that confidential material filed in connection with a lease that is a valid and subsisting lease on September 1, 1995.

(g) Confidential material may be disclosed at any time if the person filing the material, or the person's successor in interest in the lease in connection with which the confidential material was filed, consents in writing to its release. A party consenting to the disclosure of confidential material may restrict the manner of disclosure and the person or persons to whom the disclosure may be made.

(h) Notwithstanding the confidential nature of the material described in this section, the material may be used by the General Land Office in the enforcement, by administrative proceeding or litigation, of the laws governing the sale and lease of public lands and minerals, the regulations of the land office, the school land board, or of any board for lease, or the terms of any lease, pooling or unitization agreement, or any other agreement or grant.

(i) An administrative hearings officer may order that confidential material introduced in an administrative proceeding remain confidential until the proceeding is finally concluded, or for the period provided in Subsection (d), whichever is later.

(j) Confidential material examined by an administrative hearings officer during the course of an administrative proceeding for the purpose of determining its admissibility as evidence shall not be considered to have been filed in the General Land Office to the extent that the confidential material is not introduced into evidence at the proceeding.

(k) This section does not prevent a person from asserting that any confidential material is exempt from disclosure as a trade secret or commercial information under Section 552.110 or under any other basis permitted by law.

Open Records Decision No. 627 (1994) interpreted the predecessor to the current version of section 552.113 as follows:

[S]ection 552.113 excepts from required public disclosure all "geological or geophysical information or data including maps concerning wells," unless the information is filed in connection with an application or proceeding before an agency . . . . We interpret "geological or geophysical information" as section 552.113(2) uses the term to refer only to geological and geophysical information regarding the exploration or development of natural resources. [Footnote omitted] Furthermore, we reaffirm our prior determination that section 552.113 protects only geological and geophysical information that is commercially valuable. *See* Open Records Decision Nos. 504 (1988) at 2; 479 (1987) at 2. Thus, we conclude that section 552.113(2) protects from public disclosure only (i) geological and geophysical information regarding the exploration or development of natural resources that is (ii) commercially valuable.[610]

The decision explained that the phrase "information regarding the exploration or development of natural resources" signifies "information indicating the presence or absence of natural resources in a particular location, as well as information indicating the extent of a particular deposit or accumulation."[611]

Open Records Decision No. 627 (1994) overruled Open Records Decision No. 504 (1988) to the extent the two decisions are inconsistent. In Open Records Decision No. 504 (1988), the attorney general had interpreted the statutory predecessor to section 552.113 of the Government Code to require the application of a test similar to the test used at that time to determine whether the statutory

---

[610] Open Records Decision No. 627 at 3–4 (1994) (footnote omitted).
[611] Open Records Decision No. 627 at 4 n.4 (1994).

predecessor to section 552.110 protected commercial information (including trade secrets) from required public disclosure. Under that test, commercial information was "confidential" for purposes of the exemption if disclosure of the information was likely to have either of the following effects: (1) to impair the government's ability to obtain necessary information in the future; or (2) to cause substantial harm to the competitive position of the person from whom the information was obtained.[612]

Following the issuance of Open Records Decision No. 504 (1988), the attorney general articulated new tests for determining whether section 552.110 of the Government Code protects trade secret information and commercial and financial information from required public disclosure.[613] Thus, Open Records Decision No. 627 (1994) re-examined the attorney general's reliance upon the former tests for section 552.110 to determine the applicability of section 552.113. That decision noted that section 552.113, as the legislature originally enacted it, differed from its federal counterpart[614] in that the statutory predecessor to section 552.113 excepted from its scope "information filed in connection with an application or proceeding before any agency."[615] Thus, the state exception to required public disclosure exempted a more limited class of information than did the federal exemption.[616] Consequently, the decision determined that grafting the balancing test used to limit the scope of the federal exemption to the plain language of section 552.113 was unnecessary.[617] Since the current version of section 552.113 took effect on September 1, 1995, there have been no published court decisions interpreting the amended statute or the validity of Open Records Decision No. 627 (1994) in light of the amendments to the statute.

The attorney general, however, has interpreted the term "commercially valuable" in a subsequent decision. In Open Records Decision No. 669 (2000), the attorney general applied section 552.113 to digital mapping information supplied to the General Land Office by a third party. The specific information at issue was information that the third party allowed to be disclosed to the public.[618] The attorney general held that the information was not protected under section 552.113 because the information was publicly available and thus was not commercially valuable.[619] Therefore, in order to be commercially valuable for purposes of Open Records Decision No. 627 (1994) and section 552.113, information must not be publicly available.[620]

When a governmental body believes requested information of a third party may be excepted under this exception, the governmental body must notify the third party in accordance with section 552.305. The notice the governmental body must send to the third party is found in Part Nine of this *Handbook*.

---

[612] Open Records Decision No. 504 at 4 (1988).

[613] *See* Open Records Decision Nos. 592 at 2–8 (1991), 552 at 2–5 (1990).

[614] 5 U.S.C. § 552(b)(9).

[615] Open Records Decision No. 627 at 2–3 (1994).

[616] Open Records Decision No. 627 at 2–3 (1994).

[617] Open Records Decision No. 627 at 2–3 (1994).

[618] Open Records Decision No. 669 at 6 (2000).

[619] Open Records Decision No. 627 at 2–3 (1994).

[620] Open Records Decision No. 627 at 2–3 (1994).

P.   Sections 552.026 and 552.114:   Confidentiality of Student Records

The Public Information Act includes two provisions relating to student records, sections 552.026 and 552.114 of the Government Code.

1.   Family Educational Rights and Privacy Act of 1974

Section 552.026 incorporates into the Texas Public Information Act the federal Family Educational Rights and Privacy Act of 1974,[621] also known as "FERPA" or the "Buckley Amendment."[622] FERPA governs the availability of student records held by educational institutions or agencies that receive federal funds under programs administered by the federal government. It prohibits, in most circumstances, the release of personally identifiable information contained in a student's education records without a parent's written consent.[623] It also gives parents a right to inspect the education records of their children.[624] If a student has reached age 18 or is attending an institution of post-secondary education, the rights established by FERPA attach to the student rather than to the student's parents.[625] "Education records" for purposes of FERPA are records that contain information directly related to a student and that are maintained by an educational institution or agency.[626]

Information must be withheld from required public disclosure under FERPA only to the extent "reasonable and necessary to avoid personally identifying a particular student."[627] Personally identifying information is defined as including, but not limited to, the following information:

(a)   The student's name;

(b)   The name of the student's parent or other family members;

(c)   The address of the student or student's family;

(d)   A personal identifier, such as the student's social security number, student number, or biometric record;

(e)   Other indirect identifiers, such as the student's date of birth, place of birth, and mother's maiden name;

(f)   Other information that, alone or in combination, is linked or linkable to a specific student that would allow a reasonable person in the school community, who does not have personal knowledge of the relevant circumstances, to identify the student with reasonable certainty; or

---

[621]   20 U.S.C. § 1232g.

[622]   *See* Open Records Decision No. 72 (1975) (compliance with federal law was required before enactment of statutory predecessor to Gov't Code § 552.026).

[623]   20 U.S.C. § 1232g(b)(1).

[624]   20 U.S.C. § 1232g(a)(1).

[625]   20 U.S.C. § 1232g(d).

[626]   20 U.S.C. § 1232g(a)(4)(A).

[627]   Open Records Decision Nos. 332 (1982), 206 (1978).

(g) Information requested by a person who the educational agency or institution reasonably believes knows the identity of the student to whom the education record relates.628

An educational institution or agency may, however, release "directory information" to the public if the educational institution or agency complies with certain procedures.[629] Directory information includes, but is not limited to, the following information: "the student's name; address; telephone listing; electronic mail address; photograph; date and place of birth; major field of study; grade level; enrollment status (*e.g.,* undergraduate or graduate, full-time or part-time); dates of attendance; participation in officially recognized activities and sports; weight and height of members of athletic teams; degrees, honors, and awards received; and the most recent educational agency or institution attended."[630] The attorney general has determined that marital status and expected date of graduation also constitute directory information.[631]

University police department records concerning students previously were held to be education records for the purposes of FERPA.[632] However, FERPA was amended, effective July 23, 1992, to provide that the term "education records" does not include "records maintained by a law enforcement unit of the educational agency or institution that were created by that law enforcement unit for the purpose of law enforcement."[633] On the basis of this provision, records created by a campus police department are not excepted from required public disclosure by section 552.026 of the Government Code.[634]

FERPA applies only to records at educational institutions or agencies receiving federal funds and does not govern access to records in the custody of governmental bodies that are not educational institutions or agencies.[635] An "educational agency or institution" is "any public or private agency or institution" that receives federal funds under an applicable program.[636] Thus, an agency or institution need not instruct students in order to qualify as an educational agency or institution under FERPA. If education records are transferred by a school district or state institution of higher education to a state administrative agency concerned with education, federal regulations provide that the education records in the administrative agency's possession are subject to FERPA.[637]

If there is a conflict between the provisions of the state Public Information Act and FERPA, the federal statute prevails.[638] However, the attorney general has been informed by the Family Policy

---

628 34 C.F.R. § 99.3.

629 *See* 20 U.S.C. § 1232g(a)(5)(B).

630 34 C.F.R. § 99.3.

631 Open Records Decision No. 96 (1975); *see also* Open Records Decision Nos. 244 (1980) (student rosters public), 242 (1980) (student parking permit information public), 193 (1978) (report of accident insurance claims paid to identifiable students not public).

632 *See* Open Records Decision Nos. 342 at 2–3 (1982), 205 at 2 (1978).

633 20 U.S.C. § 1232g(a)(4)(B)(ii).

634 Open Records Decision No. 612 at 2 (1992) (campus police department records were not excepted by statutory predecessor to Gov't Code § 552.101, incorporating FERPA, or statutory predecessor to Gov't Code § 552.114).

635 *See* Open Records Decision No. 390 at 3 (1983) (City of Fort Worth is not "educational agency" within FERPA).

636 20 U.S.C. § 1232g(a)(3).

637 20 U.S.C. § 1232g(b)(1)(E), (b)(4)(B); 34 C.F.R. §§ 99.31, .33, .35.

638 Open Records Decision No. 431 (1985).

Compliance Office of the United States Department of Education that parents' rights to information about their children under FERPA do not prevail over school districts' rights to assert the attorney-client and work product privileges.[639] As a general rule, however, exceptions to disclosure under the Public Information Act do not apply to a request by a student or parent for the student's own education records pursuant to FERPA.[640]

In Open Records Decision No. 634 (1995), the attorney general stated that an educational agency or institution that seeks a ruling under the Public Information Act should, before submitting "education records" to the attorney general, either obtain parental consent to the disclosure of personally identifiable nondirectory information in the records or edit the records to make sure that they contain no personally identifiable nondirectory information. Subsequent correspondence from the United States Department of Education advised that educational agencies and institutions may submit personally identifiable information subject to FERPA to the attorney general for purposes of obtaining rulings as to whether information contained therein must be withheld under FERPA or state law.[641] In 2006, however, the United States Department of Education Family Policy Compliance Office informed the attorney general that FERPA does not permit state and local educational authorities to disclose to the attorney general, without parental consent, unredacted, personally identifiable information contained in education records for the purpose of our review in the open records ruling process under the Public Information Act.[642] Consequently, state and local educational authorities that receive a request for education records from a member of the public under the Public Information Act must not submit education records to the attorney general in unredacted form, that is, in a form in which "personally identifiable information" is disclosed.[643] Because the attorney general is prohibited from reviewing these education records to determine whether appropriate redactions under FERPA have been made, the attorney general will not address the applicability of FERPA to any records submitted as part of a request for decision. Such determinations under FERPA must be made by the educational authority in possession of the education records.[644] Questions about FERPA should be directed to the following agency:

> Family Policy Compliance Office
> U.S. Department of Education
> 400 Maryland Ave., S.W.
> Washington, D.C. 20202-5920
> 1-800-USA-LEARN (1-800-872-5327)

---

[639] Letter from LeRoy S. Rooker, Director, Family Policy Compliance Office, United States Dep't of Educ., to Keith B. Kyle (July 1999) (on file with the Open Records Division, Office of the Attorney General).

[640] Open Records Decision No. 431 at 3 (1985).

[641] *See* Letter from LeRoy S. Rooker, Director, Family Policy Compliance Office, United States Dep't of Educ., to David Anderson, Chief Counsel, Tex. Educ. Agency (April 29, 1998) (on file with the Open Records Division, Office of the Attorney General).

[642] This letter is available on the attorney general's website at: https://www.texasattorneygeneral.gov/files/og/20060725usdoe.pdf.

[643] *See* 34 C.F.R. § 99.3 (defining "personally identifiable information").

[644] In the future, if an educational authority does obtain parental consent to submit unredacted education records and the educational authority seeks a ruling from the attorney general on the proper redaction of those education records in compliance with FERPA, we will rule accordingly.

2. Section 552.114: Confidentiality of Student Records

(a) In this section, "student record" means:

    (1) information that constitutes education records as that term is defined by the Family Educational Rights and Privacy Act of 1974 (20 U.S.C. Section 1232g(a)(4)); or

    (2) information in a record of an applicant for admission to an educational institution, including a transfer applicant.

(b) Information is confidential and excepted from the requirements of Section 552.021 if it is information in a student record at an educational institution funded wholly or partly by state revenue. This subsection does not prohibit the disclosure or provision of information included in an education record if the disclosure or provision is authorized by 20 U.S.C. Section 1232g or other federal law.

(c) A record covered by Subsection (b) shall be made available on the request of:

    (1) educational institution personnel;

    (2) the student involved or the student's parent, legal guardian, or spouse; or

    (3) a person conducting a child abuse investigation required by Subchapter D, Chapter 261, Family Code.

(d) Except as provided by Subsection (e), an educational institution may redact information covered under Subsection (b) from information disclosed under Section 552.021 without requesting a decision from the attorney general.

(e) If an applicant for admission to an educational institution described by Subsection (b) or a parent or legal guardian of a minor applicant to an educational institution described by Subsection (b) requests information in the record of the applicant, the educational institution shall disclose any information that:

    (1) is related to the applicant's application for admission; and

    (2) was provided to the educational institution by the applicant.

"Student record" means both information that constitutes an education record under FERPA and information in the record of an applicant for admission to an educational institution, including a transfer applicant.[645] Section 552.114(b) deems information in a student record confidential and states subsection (b) does not prohibit the release of an education record authorized by FERPA or other federal law.[646] Section 552.114(c) recognizes a right of access to student records for certain

---

[645] Gov't Code § 552.114(a).

[646] Gov't Code § 552.114(b).

enumerated individuals.[647] Subsection (d) permits an educational institution to redact information in a student record without requesting an attorney general decision.[648] Subsection (e) gives an applicant for admission, or the parent or legal guardian of a minor applicant, a right of access to information that is related to the applicant's admission application and was provided to the educational institution by the applicant.[649]

Q. Section 552.115: Confidentiality of Birth and Death Records

Section 552.115 of the Government Code provides as follows:

(a) **A birth or death record maintained by the vital statistics unit of the Texas Department of State Health Services or a local registration official is excepted from [required public disclosure], except that:**

   (1) **a birth record is public information and available to the public on and after the 75th anniversary of the date of birth as shown on the record filed with the bureau of vital statistics or local registration official;**

   (2) **a death record is public information and available to the public on and after the 25th anniversary of the date of death as shown on the record filed with the vital statistics unit or local registration official, except that if the decedent is unidentified, the death record is public information and available to the public on and after the first anniversary of the date of death;**

   (3) **a general birth index or a general death index established or maintained by the vital statistics unit or a local registration official is public information and available to the public to the extent the index relates to a birth record or death record that is public information and available to the public under Subdivision (1) or (2);**

   (4) **a summary birth index or a summary death index prepared or maintained by the vital statistics unit or a local registration official is public information and available to the public; and**

   (5) **a birth or death record is available to the chief executive officer of a home-rule municipality or the officer's designee if:**

      (A) **the record is used only to identify a property owner or other person to whom the municipality is required to give notice when enforcing a state statute or an ordinance;**

      (B) **the municipality has exercised due diligence in the manner described by Section 54.035(e), Local Government Code, to identify the person; and**

---

[647] Gov't Code § 552.114(c).

[648] Gov't Code § 552.114(d).

[649] Gov't Code § 552.114(e).

(C) the officer or designee signs a confidentiality agreement that requires that:

(i) the information not be disclosed outside the office of the officer or designee, or within the office for a purpose other than the purpose described by Paragraph (A);

(ii) the information be labeled as confidential;

(iii) the information be kept securely; and

(iv) the number of copies made of the information or the notes taken from the information that implicate the confidential nature of the information be controlled, with all copies or notes that are not destroyed or returned remaining confidential and subject to the confidentiality agreement.

(b) Notwithstanding Subsection (a), a general birth index or a summary birth index is not public information and is not available to the public if:

(1) the fact of an adoption or paternity determination can be revealed by the index; or

(2) the index contains specific identifying information relating to the parents of a child who is the subject of an adoption placement.

(c) Subsection (a)(1) does not apply to the microfilming agreement entered into by the Genealogical Society of Utah, a nonprofit corporation organized under the laws of the State of Utah, and the Archives and Information Services Division of the Texas State Library and Archives Commission.

(d) For the purposes of fulfilling the terms of the agreement in Subsection (c), the Genealogical Society of Utah shall have access to birth records on and after the 50th anniversary of the date of birth as shown on the record filed with the bureau of vital statistics or local registration official, but such birth records shall not be made available to the public until the 75th anniversary of the date of birth as shown on the record.

Section 552.115 specifically applies to birth and death records of a local registration official as well as to those of the Texas Department of State Health Services.[650] This section does not apply to birth or death records maintained by other governmental bodies.[651] Until the time limits set out above have passed, a birth or death record may be obtained from the Vital Statistics Unit (the "Unit") of the Texas Department of State Health Services only in accordance with chapter 192 of the Health and Safety Code.[652] While birth records over seventy-five years old and death records over twenty-five years old are not excepted from disclosure under the Public Information Act, a local registrar of

[650] Gov't Code § 552.115(a).

[651] *See* Open Records Decision No. 338 (1982).

[652] *See generally* Open Records Decision No. 596 (1991) (regarding availability of adoption records).

the Unit[653] is required by title 3 of the Health and Safety Code and rules promulgated thereunder to deny physical access to these records and to provide copies of them for a certain fee.[654] These specific provisions prevail over the more general provisions in the Act regarding inspection and copying of public records.[655]

Section 552.115 specifically makes public a summary birth index and summary death index and also makes public a general birth index or general death index to the extent that it relates to birth or death records that would be public information under the section.[656] However, a general or summary birth index is not public information if it reveals the fact of an adoption or paternity determination or contains identifying information relating to the parents of a child who is the subject of an adoption placement.[657] Although the Act contains no language that defines the categories of information that comprise each type of index, the Texas Department of State Health Services has promulgated administrative rules that define each type of index.[658] In pertinent part, the current rule, which took effect August 11, 2013, provides as follows:

(b) Birth indexes.

(1) General birth indexes maintained or established by the Vital Statistics Unit or a local registration official shall be prepared by event year, in alphabetical order by surname of the registrant, followed by any given names or initials, the date of the event, the county of occurrence, the state or local file number, the name of the father, the maiden name of the mother, and sex of the registrant.

(2) A general birth index is public information and available to the public to the extent the index relates to a birth record that is public on or after the 75th anniversary of the date of birth as shown on the record unless the fact of an adoption or paternity determination can be revealed or broken or if the index contains specific identifying information relating to the parents of the child who is the subject of an adoption placement. The Vital Statistics Unit and local registration officials shall expunge or delete any state or local file numbers included in any general birth index made available to the public because such file numbers may be used to discover information concerning specific adoptions, paternity determinations, or the identity of the parents of children who are the subjects of adoption placements.

---

[653]   *See* Health & Safety Code § 191.022(c), (f).

[654]   *See* Attorney General Opinion DM-146 at 2 (1992); *see also* Attorney General Opinion MW-163 (1980).

[655]   Attorney General Opinion DM-146 at 5 (1992).

[656]   Gov't Code § 552.115(a).

[657]   Gov't Code § 552.115(b).

[658]   Absent specific authority, a governmental body may not generally promulgate a rule that makes information confidential so as to except the information from required public disclosure pursuant to section 552.101 of the Act. *See* Gov't Code § 552.101; *see also* Open Records Decision Nos. 484 (1987), 392 (1983), 216 (1978). In the instant case, however, the attorney general has found the predecessor agency to the Texas Department of State Health Services has been granted specific authority by the legislature to promulgate administrative rules that dictate the public availability of information contained in and derived from vital records. *See* Open Records Decision No. 596 (1991).

(3) A summary birth index maintained or established by the Vital Statistics Unit or a local registration official shall be prepared by event year, in alphabetical order by surname of the registrant, followed by any given names or initials, the date of the event, the county of occurrence, and sex of the registrant. A summary birth index or any listings of birth records are not available to the public for searching or inspection if the fact of adoption or paternity determination can be revealed from specific identifying information.

(c) **Death indexes.**

(1) A general death index maintained or established by the Vital Statistics Unit or a local registration official shall be prepared by event year, in alphabetical order by surname of the registrant, followed by any given names or initials; the date of the event; the county of occurrence; the registrant's social security number, sex, and marital status; the name of the registrant's spouse, if applicable; and the state or local file number.

(2) A general death index is public information and available to the public to the extent the index relates to a death record that is public on or after the 25th anniversary of the date of death as shown on the record.

(3) A summary death index maintained or established by the Vital Statistics Unit or a local registration official shall be prepared by event year, in alphabetical order by surname of the registrant, followed by any given names or initials, the date of the event, the county of occurrence, and sex of the registrant.[659]

Thus, the term "summary birth index" as used in section 552.115 refers to a list in alphabetical order by surname of the child, and its contents are limited to the child's name, date of birth, county of birth, and sex. Additionally, the term "general birth index" refers to a list containing only those categories of information that comprise a "summary birth index," with the additional categories of the file number and the parents' names. The term "summary death index" as used in section 552.115 refers to a list in alphabetical order by surname of the deceased, and its contents are limited to the deceased's name or initials, date of death, county of death, and sex. Furthermore, the term "general death index" refers to the same categories of information that comprise a "summary death index," with the additional categories of marital status, name of the deceased's spouse, if applicable, and file number.

Section 552.115 also provides that a birth or death record may be made available in certain circumstances to the chief executive officer of a home rule municipality to aid in the identification of a property owner.[660]

---

[659] 25 T.A.C. § 181.23(b)–(c).

[660] Gov't Code § 552.115(a).

R. Section 552.116: Audit Working Papers

Section 552.116 provides as follows:

> **(a) An audit working paper of an audit of the state auditor or the auditor of a state agency, an institution of higher education as defined by Section 61.003, Education Code, a county, a municipality, a school district, a hospital district, or a joint board operating under Section 22.074, Transportation Code, including any audit relating to the criminal history background check of a public school employee, is excepted from the requirements of Section 552.021. If information in an audit working paper is also maintained in another record, that other record is not excepted from the requirements of Section 552.021 by this section.**
>
> **(b) In this section:**
>
> > **(1) "Audit" means an audit authorized or required by a statute of this state or the United States, the charter or an ordinance of a municipality, an order of the commissioners court of a county, the bylaws adopted by or other action of the governing board of a hospital district, a resolution or other action of a board of trustees of a school district, including an audit by the district relating to the criminal history background check of a public school employee, or a resolution or other action of a joint board described by Subsection (a) and includes an investigation.**
> >
> > **(2) "Audit working paper" includes all information, documentary or otherwise, prepared or maintained in conducting an audit or preparing an audit report, including:**
> >
> > > **(A) intra-agency and interagency communications; and**
> > >
> > > **(B) drafts of the audit report or portions of those drafts.**

"Audit working paper" is defined as including all information prepared or maintained in conducting an audit or preparing an audit report including intra-agency or interagency communications and drafts of audit reports.[661] A governmental body that invokes section 552.116 must demonstrate the audit working papers are from an audit authorized or required by an authority mentioned in section 552.116(b)(1) and must identify that authority. To the extent that information in an audit working paper is also maintained in another record, such other record is not excepted by section 552.116, although such other record may be withheld from public disclosure under the Act's other exceptions.[662] There are no cases or formal opinions interpreting the current version of section 552.116.

---

[661] Gov't Code § 552.116(b).

[662] Gov't Code § 552.116(a).

S. Section 552.117: Confidentiality of Certain Addresses, Telephone Numbers, Social Security Numbers, and Personal Family Information

The 85th Legislature passed three different bills, Senate Bills 1576 and 42 and House Bill 1278, amending section 552.117 of the Government Code. Section 552.117 excepts from required public disclosure:

(a)   [I]nformation that relates to the home address, home telephone number, emergency contact information, or social security number of the following person or that reveals whether the person has family members:

   (1)   a current or former official or employee of a governmental body, except as otherwise provided by Section 552.024;

   (2)   a peace officer as defined by Article 2.12, Code of Criminal Procedure, or a security officer commissioned under Section 51.212, Education Code, regardless of whether the officer complies with Section 552.024 or 552.1175, as applicable;

   (3)   a current or former employee of the Texas Department of Criminal Justice or of the predecessor in function of the department or any division of the department, regardless of whether the current or former employee complies with Section 552.1175;

   (4)   a peace officer as defined by Article 2.12, Code of Criminal Procedure, or other law, a reserve law enforcement officer, a commissioned deputy game warden, or a corrections officer in a municipal, county, or state penal institution in this state who was killed in the line of duty, regardless of whether the deceased complied with Section 552.024 or 552.1175;

   (5)   a commissioned security officer as defined by Section 1702.002, Occupations Code, regardless of whether the officer complies with Section 552.024 or 552.1175, as applicable;

   (6)   an officer or employee of a community supervision and corrections department established under Chapter 76 who performs a duty described by Section 76.004(b), regardless of whether the officer or employee complies with Section 552.024 or 552.1175;

   (7)   a current or former employee of the office of the attorney general who is or was assigned to a division of that office the duties of which involve law enforcement, regardless of whether the current or former employee complies with Section 552.024 or 552.1175;

   (8)   a current or former employee of the Texas Juvenile Justice Department or of the predecessors in function of the department, regardless of whether the current or former employee complies with Section 552.024 or 552.1175;

(9) a current or former juvenile probation or supervision officer certified by the Texas Juvenile Justice Department, or the predecessors in function of the department, under Title 12, Human Resources Code, regardless of whether the current or former officer complies with Section 552.024 or 552.1175;

(10) a current or former employee of a juvenile justice program or facility, as those terms are defined by Section 261.405, Family Code, regardless of whether the current or former employee complies with Section 552.024 or 552.1175;

(11) a current or former member of the Texas military forces, as that term is defined by Section 437.001; or

Text of (a)(12), as added by Acts 2017, 85th Leg., ch. 34 (S.B. 1576), § 12

(12) a current or former employee of the Texas Civil Commitment Office or of the predecessor in function of the office or a division of the office, regardless of whether the current or former employee complies with Section 552.024 or 552.1175.

Text of (a)(12), as added by Acts 2017, 85th Leg., ch. 190 (S.B. 42), § 17

(12) a current or former federal judge or state judge, as those terms are defined by Section 13.0021(a), Election Code, or a spouse of a current or former federal judge or state judge; or

Text of (a)(12), as added by Acts 2017, 85th Leg., ch. 1006 (H.B. 1278), § 1

(12) a current or former district attorney, criminal district attorney, or county or municipal attorney whose jurisdiction includes any criminal law or child protective services matters, regardless of whether the current or former attorney complies with Section 552.024 or 552.1175; or

Text of (a)(13), as added by Acts 2017, 85th Leg., ch. 190 (S.B. 42), § 17

(13) a current or former district attorney, criminal district attorney, or county attorney whose jurisdiction includes any criminal law or child protective services matter.

Text of (a)(13), as added by Acts 2017, 85th Leg., ch. 1006 (H.B. 1278), § 1

(13) a current or former employee of a district attorney, criminal district attorney, or county or municipal attorney whose jurisdiction includes any criminal law or child protective services matters, regardless of whether the current or former employee complies with Section 552.024 or 552.1175.

(b) All documents filed with a county clerk and all documents filed with a district clerk are exempt from this section.

Generally, a governmental body may not invoke section 552.117 as a basis for withholding an official's or an employee's home address and telephone number if another law, such as a state statute expressly authorizing child support enforcement officials to obtain information to locate absent parents, requires the release of such information.[663] Because the subsections of section 552.117 deal with different categories of officials and employees and differ in their application, they are discussed separately below.

1. Subsections (a)(1), (11), and (12): Public Officials and Employees, Members of the Texas Military Forces, and Federal or State Judges and their Spouses

Section 552.117, subsections (a)(1) and (11) and subsection (a)(12) as added by the 85th Legislature in Senate Bill 42 must be read together with section 552.024, which provides as follows:

(a) **Except as provided by Subsection (a-1), each employee or official of a governmental body and each former employee or official of a governmental body shall choose whether to allow public access to the information in the custody of the governmental body that relates to the person's home address, home telephone number, emergency contact information, or social security number, or that reveals whether the person has family members.**

(a-1) **A school district may not require an employee or former employee of the district to choose whether to allow public access to the employee's or former employee's social security number.**

(b) **Each employee and official and each former employee and official shall state that person's choice under Subsection (a) to the main personnel officer of the governmental body in a signed writing not later than the 14th day after the date on which:**

(1) **the employee begins employment with the governmental body;**

(2) **the official is elected or appointed; or**

(3) **the former employee or official ends service with the governmental body.**

(c) **If the employee or official or former employee or official chooses not to allow public access to the information:**

(1) **the information is protected under Subchapter C; and**

(2) **the governmental body may redact the information from any information the governmental body discloses under Section 552.021 without the necessity of requesting a decision from the attorney general under Subchapter G.**

---

[663] *See* Open Records Decision No. 516 at 3 (1989).

(c-1) If, under Subsection (c)(2), a governmental body redacts or withholds information without requesting a decision from the attorney general about whether the information may be redacted or withheld, the requestor is entitled to seek a decision from the attorney general about the matter. The attorney general by rule shall establish procedures and deadlines for receiving information necessary to decide the matter and briefs from the requestor, the governmental body, and any other interested person. The attorney general shall promptly render a decision requested under this subsection, determining whether the redacted or withheld information was excepted from required disclosure to the requestor, not later than the 45th business day after the date the attorney general received the request for a decision under this subsection. The attorney general shall issue a written decision on the matter and provide a copy of the decision to the requestor, the governmental body, and any interested person who submitted necessary information or a brief to the attorney general about the matter. The requestor or the governmental body may appeal a decision of the attorney general under this subsection to a Travis County district court.

(c-2) A governmental body that redacts or withholds information under Subsection (c)(2) shall provide the following information to the requestor on a form prescribed by the attorney general:

(1) a description of the redacted or withheld information;

(2) a citation to this section; and

(3) instructions regarding how the requestor may seek a decision from the attorney general regarding whether the redacted or withheld information is excepted from required disclosure.

(d) If an employee or official or a former employee or official fails to state the person's choice within the period established by this section, the information is subject to public access.

(e) An employee or official or former employee or official of a governmental body who wishes to close or open public access to the information may request in writing that the main personnel officer of the governmental body close or open access.

(f) This section does not apply to a person to whom Section 552.1175 applies.

Subsection (a)(1) pertains to a current or former official or employee of a governmental body. Subsection (a)(11) pertains to a current or former member of the Texas military forces. Subsection (a)(12), as added by the 85th Legislature in Senate Bill 42, pertains to a current or former federal judge or state judge as defined by section 13.0021(a) of the Election Code, or a spouse of a current or former federal judge or state judge. To obtain the protection of section 552.117(a), the individuals identified in subsections (a)(1) and (11) and subsection (a)(12) as added by Senate Bill 42 must comply with section 552.024(c). If these individuals elect to withhold their home addresses, home telephone numbers, emergency contact information, social security numbers, and information that reveals whether they have family members, the governmental body may redact such information without the necessity of requesting an attorney general decision. If a governmental body chooses to redact this information without requesting an attorney general decision, it must notify the requestor as prescribed section 552.024(c-2) on the form created by the attorney general. The notice must include instructions regarding how the requestor may seek an attorney general's review of the governmental body's redactions. The form for notifying the requestor is published on the attorney general's website. The legislation enacting these provisions authorized the attorney general to promulgate rules establishing procedures for review under section 552.024(c-1). These rules were promulgated in Subchapter B of chapter 63 of title 1 of the Texas Administrative Code.[664] These rules are available on the attorney general's website and in Part Four of this *Handbook*.

Subsection (a)(11) pertains to a current or former member of the Texas military forces, which are defined as the Texas National Guard, the Texas State Guard, and any other military forces organized under state law.[665] In addition, section 437.232 of the Government Code protects certain information pertaining to service members[666] and provides as follows:

(a) **In this section, "military personnel information" means a service member's name, home address, rank, official title, pay rate or grade, state active duty orders, deployment locations, military duty addresses, awards and decorations, length of military service, and medical records.**

(b) **A service member's military personnel information is confidential and not subject to disclosure under Chapter 552.[667]**

In conjunction with section 552.024(a-1), section 552.147 of the Government Code makes social security numbers of school district employees confidential. Thus, the social security number of an employee of a school district is confidential in the custody of the school district even if the employee does not elect confidentiality under section 552.024.

Significant decisions of the attorney general regarding sections 552.024 and 552.117 prior to the recent amendments include the following:

Open Records Decision No. 622 (1994) — statutory predecessor to section 552.117(a)(1) excepts employees' former home addresses and telephone numbers from required public disclosure;

Open Records Decision No. 530 (1989) — addressing the time at which an employee may exercise the options under the statutory predecessor to section 552.024;

Open Records Decision No. 506 (1988) — these provisions do not apply to telephone numbers of mobile telephones that are provided to employees by a governmental body for work purposes; and

---

[664] *See* 1 T.A.C. §§ 63.11–.16.

[665] Gov't Code § 437.001(14).

[666] *See* Gov't Code § 437.001(8) (defining "service member" for purposes of chapter 437 of the Government Code).

[667] Gov't Code § 437.232.

Open Records Decision No. 455 (1987) — statutory predecessor to section 552.117(a)(1) continued to except an employee's home address and telephone number from required public disclosure after the employment relationship ends; it did not except, as a general rule, applicants' or other private citizens' home addresses and telephone numbers.

In addition, the attorney general has determined in informal rulings that section 552.117 can apply to personal cellular telephone numbers of government employees as well as telephone numbers that provide access to personal home facsimile machines of government employees.[668] The attorney general has also determined that section 552.117 does not protect a post office box number.[669]

2. Subsections (a)(2), (3), (4), (5), (6), (7), (8), (9), (10), (12), (12), and (13): Other Categories of Officers and Employees

As noted above, to obtain the protection of section 552.117, subsection (a)(1), the individuals identified in subsections (a)(1) and (11) and subsection (a)(12) as added by Senate Bill 42 must comply with the provisions of section 552.024. No action is necessary, however, on the part of the personnel listed in subsections (a)(2), (3), (4), (5), (6), (7), (8), (9), and (10), as well as subsection (a)(12) as added by Senate Bill 1576 of the 85th Legislature and subsections (a)(12) and (13) as added by House Bill 1278 of the 85th Legislature.

In Open Records Decision No. 670 (2001), the attorney general determined that all governmental bodies may withhold the home address, home telephone number, personal cellular phone number, personal pager number, social security number, and information that reveals whether the individual has family members, of any individual who meets the definition of "peace officer" set forth in article 2.12 of the Texas Code of Criminal Procedure or "security officer" in section 51.212 of the Texas Education Code, without the necessity of requesting an attorney general decision as to whether the exception under section 552.117(a)(2) applies. This decision may be relied on as a "previous determination" for the listed information.

T. Section 552.1175: Confidentiality of Certain Personal Information of Peace Officers, County Jailers, Security Officers, Employees of Certain State Agencies or Certain Criminal or Juvenile Justice Agencies or Offices, and Federal and State Judges[670]

The 85th Legislature amended section 552.1175 of the Government Code, which provides as follows:

(a) **This section applies only to:**

(1) **peace officers as defined by Article 2.12, Code of Criminal Procedure;**

(2) **county jailers as defined by Section 1701.001, Occupations Code;**

---

[668] *See, e.g.*, Open Records Letter Nos. 2002-1488 (2002), 2001-0050 (2001).

[669] *See* Open Records Decision No. 622 at 6 (1994) (legislative history makes clear that purpose of section 552.117 is to protect public employees from being harassed at *home*) (citing House Comm. on State Affairs, Bill Analysis, H.B. 1979, 69th Leg. (1985) (emphasis added)).

[670] Gov't Code § 552.1175.

(3) current or former employees of the Texas Department of Criminal Justice or of the predecessor in function of the department or any division of the department;

(4) commissioned security officers as defined by Section 1702.002, Occupations Code;

(5) a current or former district attorney, criminal district attorney, or county or municipal attorney whose jurisdiction includes any criminal law or child protective services matters;[671]

(5-a) a current or former employee of a district attorney, criminal district attorney, or county or municipal attorney whose jurisdiction includes any criminal law or child protective services matters;[672]

(6) officers and employees of a community supervision and corrections department established under Chapter 76 who perform a duty described by Section 76.004(b);

(7) criminal investigators of the United States as described by Article 2.122(a) , Code of Criminal Procedure;

(8) police officers and inspectors of the United States Federal Protective Service;

(9) current and former employees of the office of the attorney general who are or were assigned to a division of that office the duties of which involve law enforcement;

(10) current or former juvenile probation and detention officers certified by the Texas Juvenile Justice Department, or the predecessors in function of the department, under Title 12, Human Resources Code;

(11) current or former employees of a juvenile justice program or facility, as those terms are defined by Section 261.405, Family Code;

(12) current or former employees of the Texas Juvenile Justice Department or the predecessors in function of the department; and

(13) federal judges and state judges as defined by Section 13.0021, Election Code; and

---

[671] Gov't Code § 552.1175(a)(5).

[672] Gov't Code § 552.1175(a)(5-a).

(14) current or former employees of the Texas Civil Commitment Office or of the predecessor in function of the office or a division of this office.[673]

(b) Information that relates to the home address, home telephone number, emergency contact information, date of birth, or social security number of an individual to whom this section applies, or that reveals whether the individual has family members is confidential and may not be disclosed to the public under this chapter if the individual to whom the information relates:

    (1) chooses to restrict public access to the information; and

    (2) notifies the governmental body of the individual's choice on a form provided by the governmental body, accompanied by evidence of the individual's status.

(c) A choice made under Subsection (b) remains valid until rescinded in writing by the individual.

(d) This section does not apply to information in the tax appraisal records of an appraisal district to which Section 25.025, Tax Code, applies.

(e) All documents filed with a county clerk and all documents filed with a district clerk are exempt from this section.

(f) A governmental body may redact information that must be withheld under Subsection (b) from any information the governmental body discloses under Section 552.021 without the necessity of requesting a decision from the attorney general under Subchapter G.

(g) If, under Subsection (f), a governmental body redacts or withholds information without requesting a decision from the attorney general about whether the information may be redacted or withheld, the requestor is entitled to seek a decision from the attorney general about the matter. The attorney general by rule shall establish procedures and deadlines for receiving information necessary to decide the matter and briefs from the requestor, the governmental body, and any other interested person. The attorney general shall promptly render a decision requested under this subsection, determining whether the redacted or withheld information was excepted from required disclosure to the requestor, not later than the 45th business day after the date the attorney general received the request for a decision under this subsection. The attorney general shall issue a written decision on the matter and provide a copy of the decision to the requestor, the governmental body, and any interested person who submitted necessary information or a brief to the attorney general about the matter. The requestor or the governmental body may appeal a decision of the attorney general under this subsection to a Travis County district court.

---

[673] Gov't Code § 552.1175(a)(14).

(h) **A governmental body that redacts or withholds information under Subsection (f) shall provide the following information to the requestor on a form prescribed by the attorney general:**

    (1) **a description of the redacted or withheld information;**

    (2) **a citation to this section; and**

    (3) **instructions regarding how the requestor may seek a decision from the attorney general regarding whether the redacted or withheld information is excepted from required disclosure.**

Section 552.1175 excepts from public disclosure a listed person's home address, home telephone number, emergency contact information, date of birth, social security number, and family member information. The attorney general has stated in numerous informal rulings that the protection of section 552.117 only applies to information a governmental body holds in its capacity as an employer.[674] On the other hand, section 552.1175 affords the listed persons the opportunity to withhold personal information contained in records maintained by any governmental body in any capacity.[675] However, these individuals may not elect under section 552.1175 to withhold personal information contained in records maintained by county and district clerks or tax appraisal records of an appraisal district subject to section 25.025 of the Tax Code.[676]

In Open Records Decision No. 678 (2003), the attorney general determined that notification provided to a governmental body under section 552.1175 "imparts confidentiality to information only in the possession of the notified governmental body."[677] If the information is transferred to another governmental body, the individual must provide a separate notification to the receiving governmental body in order for the information in its hands to remain confidential.[678]

Also, unlike the requirement under section 552.117(a)(1) that an election to keep information confidential be made before a governmental body receives the request for information,[679] an election under section 552.1175 can be made after a governmental body's receipt of the request for information.

Subsection (f) allows a governmental body to redact without the necessity of requesting an attorney general decision the home address, home telephone number, emergency contact information, date of birth, social security number, and family member information of a person described in section 552.1175(a). Subsection (h) states that if a governmental body redacts in accordance with subsection (f), it must provide the requestor with certain information on the form prescribed by the attorney general, including instructions regarding how the requestor may seek an attorney general review of the governmental body's redactions. The form for notifying the requestor is located on the attorney general's website. The legislation enacting these provisions authorized the attorney

---

[674] *See, e.g.,* Open Records Letter Nos. 99-3302 (1999), 96-2452 (1996).

[675] *See, e.g.,* Open Records Letter No. 2002-6335 (2002).

[676] Gov't Code § 552.1175(d)–(e).

[677] Open Records Decision No. 678 at 4 (2003).

[678] Open Records Decision No. 678 at 4–5 (2003).

[679] Open Records Decision No. 530 at 5 (1989).

general to promulgate rules establishing procedures for its review under section 552.1175(g). These rules are available on the attorney general's website and in Part Four of this *Handbook*.[680]

U. Section 552.1176: Confidentiality of Certain Information Maintained by State Bar

Section 552.1176 to the Government Code provides as follows:

(a) **Information that relates to the home address, home telephone number, electronic mail address, social security number, or date of birth of a person licensed to practice law in this state that is maintained under Chapter 81 is confidential and may not be disclosed to the public under this chapter if the person to whom the information relates:**

　　(1) **chooses to restrict public access to the information; and**

　　(2) **notifies the State Bar of Texas of the person's choice, in writing or electronically, on a form provided by the state bar.**

(b) **A choice made under Subsection (a) remains valid until rescinded in writing or electronically by the person.**

(c) **All documents filed with a county clerk and all documents filed with a district clerk are exempt from this section.**

The protections of section 552.1176 only apply to records maintained by the State Bar.[681] There are no cases or formal opinions interpreting this exception.

V. Section 552.118: Confidentiality of Official Prescription Program Information

Section 552.118 of the Government Code excepts from required public disclosure:

(1) **information on or derived from an official prescription form or electronic prescription record filed with the Texas State Board of Pharmacy under Section 481.075, Health and Safety Code; or**

(2) **other information collected under Section 481.075 of that code.**

Under the Official Prescription Program, health practitioners who prescribe certain controlled substances must record certain information about the prescription on the official form, including the name, address, and date of birth or age of the person for whom the controlled substance is prescribed.[682] The dispensing pharmacist is required to complete the form and provide a copy to the

---

[680] *See* 1 T.A.C. §§ 63.11–.16.

[681] Open Records Letter No. 2009-13358 (2009).

[682] Health & Safety Code § 481.075(a), (e).

Texas State Board of Pharmacy.[683] Section 481.076 of the Health and Safety Code provides that the board may release this information only to certain parties, including named state entities charged with investigating health professionals or a law enforcement or prosecutorial official charged with investigating or enforcing laws governing illicit drugs.[684] Under section 552.118, copies of the prescription forms filed with the board, any information derived from the forms, and any other information collected under section 481.075 of the Health and Safety Code, are excepted from public disclosure.

W. Section 552.119:   Confidentiality of Certain Photographs of Peace Officers

Section 552.119 of the Government Code provides as follows:

(a)   **A photograph that depicts a peace officer as defined by Article 2.12, Code of Criminal Procedure, the release of which would endanger the life or physical safety of the officer, is excepted from the requirements of Section 552.021 unless:**

   (1) the officer is under indictment or charged with an offense by information;

   (2) the officer is a party in a civil service hearing or a case in arbitration; or

   (3) the photograph is introduced as evidence in a judicial proceeding.

(b)   **A photograph excepted from disclosure under Subsection (a) may be made public only if the peace officer gives written consent to the disclosure.**

In Open Records Decision No. 502 (1988), the attorney general held that there need not be a threshold determination that release of a photograph would endanger an officer before the statutory predecessor to section 552.119(a) could be invoked.[685] However, in 2003, the attorney general re-evaluated its interpretation of this provision and determined that, in order to withhold a peace officer's or security officer's photograph under section 552.119, a governmental body must demonstrate that release of the photograph would endanger the life or physical safety of the officer.[686]

Under section 552.119, a photograph of a peace officer cannot be withheld if (1) the officer is under indictment or charged with an offense by information; (2) the officer is a party in a civil service hearing or a case in arbitration; (3) the photograph is introduced as evidence in a judicial proceeding; or (4) the officer gives written consent to the disclosure. Furthermore, in Open Records Decision No. 536 (1989), the attorney general concluded that the statutory predecessor to section 552.119 did not apply to photographs of officers who are no longer living.[687] This opinion reasoned that the section was inapplicable after an officer's death because its purpose was to protect peace officers from life-threatening harassment and to ensure this protection would be effective by granting the

---

[683]   Health & Safety Code § 481.075(i).
[684]   Health & Safety Code § 481.076.
[685]   Open Records Decision No. 502 at 4–6 (1988).
[686]   Open Records Letter Nos. 2003-8009 (2003), 2003-8002 (2003).
[687]   Open Records Decision No. 536 at 2 (1989).

discretionary authority to release the photograph only to the subject of the photograph.[688] Protecting the photographs of deceased officers would not serve this purpose.[689]

X. Section 552.120: Confidentiality of Certain Rare Books and Original Manuscripts

Section 552.120 of the Government Code excepts from required public disclosure:

> **A rare book or original manuscript that was not created or maintained in the conduct of official business of a governmental body and that is held by a private or public archival and manuscript repository for the purpose of historical research . . . .**

The attorney general has not issued an open records decision on this provision. A similar provision applicable to state institutions of higher education is found in the Education Code:

> **Rare books, original manuscripts, personal papers, unpublished letters, and audio and video tapes held by an institution of higher education for the purposes of historical research are confidential, and the institution may restrict access by the public to those materials to protect the actual or potential value of the materials and the privacy of the donors.[690]**

Y. Section 552.121: Confidentiality of Certain Documents Held for Historical Research

Section 552.121 of the Government Code excepts from required public disclosure:

> **An oral history interview, personal paper, unpublished letter, or organizational record of a nongovernmental entity that was not created or maintained in the conduct of official business of a governmental body and that is held by a private or public archival and manuscript repository for the purpose of historical research . . . to the extent that the archival and manuscript repository and the donor of the interview, paper, letter, or record agree to limit disclosure of the item.**

The attorney general has not issued an open records decision on this provision. The Education Code sets out a similar provision applicable to institutions of higher education. It states as follows:

> **An oral interview that is obtained for historical purposes by an agreement of confidentiality between an interviewee and a state institution of higher education is not public information. The interview becomes public information when the conditions of the agreement of confidentiality have been met.[691]**

An attorney general opinion requested by a committee of the legislature that enacted section 51.910(a) states that the Public Information Act prevents an institution of higher education from agreeing to

---

[688] Open Records Decision No. 536 at 2 (1989).

[689] Open Records Decision No. 536 at 2 (1989).

[690] Educ. Code § 51.910(b).

[691] Educ. Code § 51.910(a).

keep oral history information confidential unless the institution has specific authority under law to make such agreements.[692]

Z.   Section 552.122: Test Items

Section 552.122 of the Government Code excepts from required public disclosure:

(a)   **A test item developed by an educational institution that is funded wholly or in part by state revenue . . . [; and]**

(b)   **A test item developed by a licensing agency or governmental body . . . .**

The attorney general considered the scope of the phrase "test items" in Open Records Decision No. 626 (1994). That decision considered whether employee evaluations and records used for determining promotions were "test items" under section 552.122(b). "Test item" was defined as "any standard means by which an individual's or group's knowledge or ability in a particular area is evaluated."[693] The opinion held that in this instance the evaluations of the applicant for promotion and the answers to questions asked of the applicant by the promotion board in evaluating the applicant were not "test items" and that such a determination under section 552.122 had to be made on a case-by-case basis.[694]

AA.   Section 552.123:   Confidentiality of Name of Applicant for Chief Executive Officer of Institution of Higher Education

Section 552.123 of the Government Code excepts from required public disclosure:

The name of an applicant for the position of chief executive officer of an institution of higher education, and other information that would tend to identify the applicant, . . . , except that the governing body of the institution must give public notice of the name or names of the finalists being considered for the position at least 21 days before the date of the meeting at which final action or vote is to be taken on the employment of the person.

Thus, section 552.123 expressly permits the withholding of any identifying information about candidates, not just their names.[695] Before the addition of the statutory predecessor to section 552.123, the names of all persons being considered for public positions were available under the Public Information Act.[696] The addition of this section changed the law only in respect to applicants for the position of university president.[697] The exception protects the identities of all applicants for

---

[692]   Attorney General Opinion JM-37 at 2 (1983).

[693]   Open Records Decision No. 626 at 6 (1994).

[694]   Open Records Decision No. 626 at 6–8 (1994).

[695]   Gov't Code § 552.123; *see also* Open Records Decision No. 540 at 3–4 (1990) (construing statutory predecessor to Gov't Code § 552.123).

[696]   *See Hubert v. Harte-Hanks Tex. Newspapers, Inc.,* 652 S.W.2d 546, 551 (Tex. App.—Austin 1983, writ ref'd n.r.e.); Open Records Decision No. 439 at 2 (1986).

[697]   *See* Open Records Decision No. 585 (1991) (availability of names of applicants for position of city manager).

the position of university president, whether they apply on their own initiative or are nominated.[698] Section 552.123 does not protect the names of finalists for the university president position.

BB. Section 552.1235: Confidentiality of Identity of Private Donor to Institution of Higher Education

Section 552.1235 of the Government Code provides as follows:

(a) **The name or other information that would tend to disclose the identity of a person, other than a governmental body, who makes a gift, grant, or donation of money or property to an institution of higher education or to another person with the intent that the money or property be transferred to an institution of higher education is excepted from the requirements of Section 552.021.**

(b) **Subsection (a) does not except from required disclosure other information relating to gifts, grants, and donations described by Subsection (a), including the amount or value of an individual gift, grant, or donation.**

(c) **In this section, "institution of higher education" has the meaning assigned by Section 61.003, Education Code.**

There are no cases or formal opinions interpreting this exception. However, in an informal ruling, the attorney general interpreted the term "person," as used in this exception, to include a "corporation, organization, government or governmental subdivision or agency, business trust, estate, trust, partnership, association, and any other legal entity."[699]

CC. Section 552.124: Confidentiality of Records of Library or Library System

Section 552.124 of the Government Code provides as follows:

(a) **A record of a library or library system, supported in whole or in part by public funds, that identifies or serves to identify a person who requested, obtained, or used a library material or service is excepted from the requirements of Section 552.021 unless the record is disclosed:**

(1) **because the library or library system determines that disclosure is reasonably necessary for the operation of the library or library system and the record is not confidential under other state or federal law;**

(2) **under Section 552.023; or**

(3) **to a law enforcement agency or a prosecutor under a court order or subpoena obtained after a showing to a district court that:**

---

[698] *See* Open Records Decision No. 540 at 5 (1990).

[699] Open Records Letter No. 2003-8748 (2003) (citing to Gov't Code § 311.005402.006(2)).

>   **(1) disclosure of the record is necessary to protect the public safety; or**
>
>   **(2) the record is evidence of an offense or constitutes evidence that a particular person committed an offense.**
>
> **(b)   A record of a library or library system that is excepted from required disclosure under this section is confidential.**

The legislative history suggests that the purpose of this section is to codify, clarify, and extend a prior decision of the attorney general.[700] This section protects the identity of the individual library user while allowing law enforcement officials access to such information by court order or subpoena. An individual has a special right of access under section 552.023 to library records that relate to that individual. There are no cases or formal opinions interpreting this exception. However, in an informal ruling, the attorney general interpreted section 552.124 to except from disclosure any information that specifically identifies library patrons.[701] In a separate informal ruling, the attorney general determined that section 552.124 does not except from disclosure information identifying library employees or other persons not requesting, obtaining, or using a library material or service.[702] In another informal ruling, the attorney general concluded section 552.124 is designed to protect individual privacy.[703] Therefore, because the right to privacy lapses at death, identifying information that pertains solely to a deceased person may not be withheld under section 552.124.[704]

DD.   Section 552.125:   Certain Audits

The 85th Legislature amended section 552.125 of the Government Code, which provides as follows:

> **Any documents or information privileged under Chapter 1101, Health and Safety Code, are excepted from the requirements of Section 552.021.[705]**

Information considered privileged under chapter 1101 of the Health and Safety Code includes audit reports.[706] Section 1101.051(a) describes an audit report as "a report that includes each document and communication ... produced from an environmental or health and safety audit."[707] An environmental or health and safety audit is defined under section 1101.003(a)(3) as:

> **a systematic voluntary evaluation, review, or assessment of compliance with environmental or health and safety laws or with any permit issued under an environmental or health and**

---

[700]   *See* Senate Comm. on State Affairs, Bill Analysis, S.B. 360, 73rd Leg., R.S. (1993); Open Records Decision No. 100 (1975) (identity of library user in connection with library materials he or she has reviewed was protected from public disclosure under statutory predecessor to Gov't Code § 552.101).

[701]   Open Records Letter No. 99-1566 (1999).

[702]   Open Records Letter No. 2000-3201 (2000).

[703]   Open Records Letter No. 2014-13140 at 4 (2014).

[704]   Open Records Letter No. 2014-13140 at 4 (2014).

[705]   Gov't Code § 552.125); *see also* Act of May 19, 2017, 85th Leg., R.S., S.B. 1488, § 20.002(b) (repealing Texas Environmental, Health, and Safety Audit Privilege Act, Tex. Rev. Civ. Stat. art. 4447cc).

[706]   Health and Safety Code § 1101.101(a)(3).

[707]   Health and Safety Code § 1101.051(a).

safety law conducted by an owner or operator, an employee of the owner or operator, a person, including an employee or independent contractor of the person, that is considering the acquisition of a regulated facility or operation, or an independent contractor of:

> (A)   a . . . facility or operation [regulated under an environmental or health and safety law]; or

> (B)   an activity at a . . . facility or operation [regulated under an environmental or health and safety law].[708]

There are no cases or formal opinions interpreting section 552.125.

EE.   Section 552.126:   Confidentiality of Name of Applicant for Superintendent of Public School District

Section 552.126 of the Government Code provides as follows:

> The name of an applicant for the position of superintendent of a public school district is excepted from the requirements of Section 552.021, except that the board of trustees must give public notice of the name or names of the finalists being considered for the position at least 21 days before the date of the meeting at which a final action or vote is to be taken on the employment of the person.

There are no cases or formal opinions interpreting this exception. However, in an informal ruling, the attorney general determined section 552.126 protects all identifying information about superintendent applicants, not just their names.[709] Section 552.126 does not protect the names of the finalists for a superintendent position.

FF.   Section 552.127: Confidentiality of Personal Information Relating to Participants in Neighborhood Crime Watch Organization

Section 552.127 of the Government Code provides as follows:

> (a)   Information is excepted from [required public disclosure] if the information identifies a person as a participant in a neighborhood crime watch organization and relates to the name, home address, business address, home telephone number, or business telephone number of the person.

> (b)   In this section, "neighborhood crime watch organization" means a group of residents of a neighborhood or part of a neighborhood that is formed in affiliation or association with a law enforcement agency in this state to observe activities within the neighborhood or part of a neighborhood and to take other actions intended to reduce crime in that area.

---

[708]   Health and Safety Code § 1101.003(a)(3).

[709]   Open Records Letter No. 99-2495 (1999).

There are no cases or formal opinions interpreting this exception. In an informal ruling, the attorney general found section 552.127 excepts from disclosure the name, home address, business address, home telephone number, or business telephone number of a participant in a neighborhood crime watch program.[710] However, the attorney general also found the name, address, or contact information of an organization participating in the neighborhood crime watch program is not protected under section 552.127 unless the information relates to or identifies an individual participant's name, home or business address, or home or business telephone number.[711]

GG. Section 552.128: Confidentiality of Certain Information Submitted by Potential Vendor or Contractor

Section 552.128 of the Government Code provides as follows:

(a) **Information submitted by a potential vendor or contractor to a governmental body in connection with an application for certification as a historically underutilized or disadvantaged business under a local, state, or federal certification program is excepted from [required public disclosure], except as provided by this section.**

(b) **Notwithstanding Section 552.007 and except as provided by Subsection (c), the information may be disclosed only:**

(1) **to a state or local governmental entity in this state, and the state or local governmental entity may use the information only:**

(A) **for purposes related to verifying an applicant's status as a historically underutilized or disadvantaged business; or**

(B) **for the purpose of conducting a study of a public purchasing program established under state law for historically underutilized or disadvantaged businesses; or**

(2) **with the express written permission of the applicant or the applicant's agent.**

(c) **Information submitted by a vendor or contractor or a potential vendor or contractor to a governmental body in connection with a specific proposed contractual relationship, a specific contract, or an application to be placed on a bidders list, including information that may also have been submitted in connection with an application for certification as a historically underutilized or disadvantaged business, is subject to required disclosure, excepted from required disclosure, or confidential in accordance with other law.**

There are no cases or formal opinions interpreting this exception. However, in informal rulings, the attorney general has determined that the exception does not apply to documents created by the governmental body rather than submitted by the potential vendor or contractor.[712] Additionally, the

---

[710] Open Records Letter No. 99-2830 (1999).

[711] Open Records Letter No. 99-2830 (1999).

[712] Open Records Letter Nos. 99-0565 (1999), 98-0782 (1998).

exception may cover information submitted orally by an applicant.[713] Subsection (c) of the exception does not make confidential a potential contractor's bid proposals, but states that bidding information is subject to public disclosure unless made confidential by law.[714]

HH. Section 552.129: Confidentiality of Certain Motor Vehicle Inspection Information

Section 552.129 of the Government Code provides as follows:

> **A record created during a motor vehicle emissions inspection under Subchapter F, Chapter 548, Transportation Code, that relates to an individual vehicle or owner of an individual vehicle is excepted from [required public disclosure].**

There are no cases or formal opinions interpreting this exception.

II. Section 552.130: Confidentiality of Certain Motor Vehicle Records

Section 552.130 of the Government Code provides as follows:

> **(a) Information is excepted from [required public disclosure] if the information relates to:**
>
> > **(1) a motor vehicle operator's or driver's license or permit issued by an agency of this state or another state or country;**
> >
> > **(2) a motor vehicle title or registration issued by an agency of this state or another state or country; or**
> >
> > **(3) a personal identification document issued by an agency of this state or another state or country or a local agency authorized to issue an identification document.**
>
> **(b) Information described by Subsection (a) may be released only if, and in the manner, authorized by Chapter 730, Transportation Code.**
>
> **(c) Subject to Chapter 730, Transportation Code, a governmental body may redact information described by Subsection (a) from any information the governmental body discloses under Section 552.021 without the necessity of requesting a decision from the attorney general under Subchapter G.**
>
> **(d) If, under Subsection (c), a governmental body redacts or withholds information without requesting a decision from the attorney general about whether the information may be redacted or withheld, the requestor is entitled to seek a decision from the attorney general about the matter. The attorney general by rule shall establish procedures and deadlines for receiving information necessary to decide the matter and briefs from the requestor, the governmental body, and any other interested person.**

---

[713] Open Records Letter Nos. 99-0979 (1999), 99-0922 (1999).
[714] Open Records Letter No. 99-1511 (1999).

The attorney general shall promptly render a decision requested under this subsection, determining whether the redacted or withheld information was excepted from required disclosure to the requestor, not later than the 45th business day after the date the attorney general received the request for a decision under this subsection. The attorney general shall issue a written decision on the matter and provide a copy of the decision to the requestor, the governmental body, and any interested person who submitted necessary information or a brief to the attorney general about the matter. The requestor or the governmental body may appeal a decision of the attorney general under this subsection to a Travis County district court.

(e)   **A governmental body that redacts or withholds information under Subsection (c) shall provide the following information to the requestor on a form prescribed by the attorney general:**

    (1) a description of the redacted or withheld information;

    (2) a citation to this section; and

    (3) instructions regarding how the requestor may seek a decision from the attorney general regarding whether the redacted or withheld information is excepted from required disclosure.

Examples of information excepted from required public disclosure under section 552.130(a)(1) include the license number, class, restrictions, and expiration date of a driver's license issued by an agency of the State of Texas.[715] Examples of information excepted from disclosure under section 552.130(a)(2) include a vehicle identification number and license plate number relating to a title or registration issued by an agency of the State of Texas.[716] Section 552.130 protects information relating to a license, title, or registration issued by this state, a state other than Texas, or another country. However, section 552.130 does not apply to motor vehicle record information found in a CR-3 accident report form. Access to a CR-3 accident report is specifically governed by section 550.065 of the Transportation Code, not section 552.130.[717]

Because, section 552.130 was enacted to protect privacy interests, an individual or his authorized representative has a special right of access to his motor vehicle record information, and such information may not be withheld from that individual under section 552.130.[718] Furthermore, information otherwise protected under section 552.130 may be released if the governmental body is authorized to release the information under chapter 730 of the Transportation Code. Section 552.222(c) of the Government Code permits the officer for public information or the officer's agent to require the requestor to provide additional identifying information sufficient for the officer or the officer's agent to determine whether the requestor is eligible to receive the information under chapter 730 of the Transportation Code. It should be noted that a deceased person's interest under

---

[715] *See, e.g.,* Open Records Letter Nos. 2002-7018 (2002), 2001-3659 (2001).

[716] *See, e.g.,* Open Records Letter Nos. 2000-4847 (2000), 2000-1083 (2000).

[717] *See* discussion of section 550.065 of the Transportation Code in Part Two, Section II, Subsection H of this *Handbook*.

[718] *See* Gov't Code § 552.023; Open Records Decision Nos. 684 at 12-13 (2009), 481 at 4 (1987) (privacy theories not implicated when individual requests information concerning himself).

section 552.130 lapses upon the person's death, but section 552.130 would protect the interest of a living person who has a co-ownership in the vehicle.[719]

Section 552.130(c) provides that subject to chapter 730 of the Transportation Code, a governmental body may redact without the necessity of requesting an attorney general decision information that is subject to subsection (a) of section 552.130. If a governmental body chooses to redact this information without requesting an attorney general decision, it must notify the requestor as prescribed by section 552.130(e) on the form created by the attorney general. The notice must include instructions regarding how the requestor may seek an attorney general's review of the governmental body's redactions. The form for notifying the requestor is located on the attorney general's website. Pursuant to section 552.130(d), the attorney general promulgated rules establishing procedures for review of a governmental body's redactions.[720] These rules are available on the attorney general's website and in Part Four of this *Handbook*.

If a governmental body lacks the technological capability to redact the motor vehicle record information from a requested video, it must seek a ruling from the attorney general if it wishes to withhold the information from disclosure.

JJ. Section 552.131: Confidentiality of Certain Economic Development Information

Section 552.131 of the Government Code reads as follows:

(a) **Information is excepted from the requirements of Section 552.021 if the information relates to economic development negotiations involving a governmental body and a business prospect that the governmental body seeks to have locate, stay, or expand in or near the territory of the governmental body and the information relates to:**

(1) **a trade secret of the business prospect; or**

(2) **commercial or financial information for which it is demonstrated based on specific factual evidence that disclosure would cause substantial competitive harm to the person from whom the information was obtained.**

(b) **Unless and until an agreement is made with the business prospect, information about a financial or other incentive being offered to the business prospect by the governmental body or by another person is excepted from the requirements of Section 552.021.**

(c) **After an agreement is made with the business prospect, this section does not except from the requirements of Section 552.021 information about a financial or other incentive being offered to the business prospect:**

---

[719] Open Records Decision No. 684 at 13 (2009). *See generally Moore v. Charles B. Pierce Film Enters., Inc.*, 589 S.W.2d 489, 491 (Tex. Civ. App.—Texarkana 1979, writ ref'd n.r.e.); *Justice v. Belo Broadcasting Corp.*, 472 F. Supp. 145, 146-47 (N.D. Tex. 1979); Attorney General Opinions JM-229 at 3 (1984), H-917 at 2-3(1976); Open Records Decision No. 272 at 1 (1981) (privacy rights lapse upon death).

[720] *See* 1 T.A.C. §§ 63.11–.16.

(1) by the governmental body; or

(2) by another person, if the financial or other incentive may directly or indirectly result in the expenditure of public funds by a governmental body or a reduction in revenue received by a governmental body from any source.

Section 552.131(a) applies to the same two types of information excepted from disclosure under section 552.110: (1) trade secrets; and (2) commercial or financial information for which it is demonstrated based on specific factual evidence that disclosure would cause substantial competitive harm to the person from whom the information was obtained. However, unlike section 552.110, section 552.131(a) applies only to information that relates to economic development negotiations between a governmental body and a business prospect. Section 552.131(b) excepts from public disclosure any information relating to a financial or other incentive that a governmental body or another person offers to a business prospect that seeks to have locate, stay, or expand in or near the territory of the governmental body. After the governmental body reaches an agreement with the business prospect, information about a financial or other incentive offered the business prospect is no longer excepted under section 552.131. There are no formal cases or opinions interpreting this exception.

When a governmental body believes requested information of a third party may be excepted under this exception, the governmental body must notify the third party in accordance with section 552.305. The notice the governmental body must send to the third party is found in Part Nine of this *Handbook*.

KK. Section 552.132: Confidentiality of Crime Victim or Claimant Information

Section 552.132 of the Government Code provides as follows:

(a) **Except as provided by Subsection (d), in this section, "crime victim or claimant" means a victim or claimant under Subchapter B, Chapter 56, Code of Criminal Procedure, who has filed an application for compensation under that subchapter.**

(b) **The following information held by the crime victim's compensation division of the attorney general's office is confidential:**

(1) **the name, social security number, address, or telephone number of a crime victim or claimant; or**

(2) **any other information the disclosure of which would identify or tend to identify the crime victim or claimant.**

(c) **If the crime victim or claimant is awarded compensation under Section 56.34, Code of Criminal Procedure, as of the date of the award of compensation, the name of the crime victim or claimant and the amount of compensation awarded to that crime victim or claimant are public information and are not excepted from the requirements of Section 552.021.**

(d) **An employee of a governmental body who is also a victim under Subchapter B, Chapter 56, Code of Criminal Procedure, regardless of whether the employee has filed an application for compensation under that subchapter, may elect whether to allow public access to information held by the attorney general's office or other governmental body that would identify or tend to identify the victim, including a photograph or other visual representation of the victim. An election under this subsection must be made in writing on a form developed by the governmental body, be signed by the employee, and be filed with the governmental body before the third anniversary of the latest to occur of one of the following:**

(1) **the date the crime was committed;**

(2) **the date employment begins; or**

(3) **the date the governmental body develops the form and provides it to employees.**

(e) **If the employee fails to make an election under Subsection (d), the identifying information is excepted from disclosure until the third anniversary of the date the crime was committed. In case of disability, impairment, or other incapacity of the employee, the election may be made by the guardian of the employee or former employee.**

Section 552.132 makes both the victim's and claimant's identifying information confidential without either party having to submit an election for non-disclosure to the Crime Victims' Compensation Division of the Office of the Attorney General. The attorney general has found that crime victims have a special right of access to their own information under section 552.023 of the Government Code.[721] There are no cases or formal opinions interpreting this exception.

---

[721] Open Records Letter No. 2001-0821 (2001).

LL. Section 552.1325: Crime Victim Impact Statement: Certain Information Confidential

Section 552.1325 of the Government Code provides as follows:

(a) **In this section:**

  (1) **"Crime victim" means a person who is a victim as defined by Article 56.32, Code of Criminal Procedure.**

  (2) **"Victim impact statement" means a victim impact statement under Article 56.03, Code of Criminal Procedure.**

(b) **The following information that is held by a governmental body or filed with a court and that is contained in a victim impact statement or was submitted for purposes of preparing a victim impact statement is confidential:**

  (1) **the name, social security number, address, and telephone number of a crime victim; and**

  (2) **any other information the disclosure of which would identify or tend to identify the crime victim.**

There are no cases or formal opinions interpreting this exception.

MM. Section 552.133: Confidentiality of Public Power Utility Competitive Matters

Section 552.133 of the Government Code provides as follows:

(a) **In this section, "public power utility" means an entity providing electric or gas utility services that is subject to the provisions of this chapter.**

(a-1) **For purposes of this section, "competitive matter" means a utility-related matter that is related to the public power utility's competitive activity, including commercial information, and would, if disclosed, give advantage to competitors or prospective competitors. The term:**

  (1) **means a matter that is reasonably related to the following categories of information:**

  (A) **generation unit specific and portfolio fixed and variable costs, including forecasts of those costs, capital improvement plans for generation units, and generation unit operating characteristics and outage scheduling;**

  (B) **bidding and pricing information for purchased power, generation and fuel, and Electric Reliability Council of Texas bids, prices, offers, and related services and strategies;**

(C) effective fuel and purchased power agreements and fuel transportation arrangements and contracts;

(D) risk management information, contracts, and strategies, including fuel hedging and storage;

(E) plans, studies, proposals, and analyses for system improvements, additions, or sales, other than transmission and distribution system improvements inside the service area for which the public power utility is the sole certificated retail provider; and

(F) customer billing, contract, and usage information, electric power pricing information, system load characteristics, and electric power marketing analyses and strategies; and

(2) does not include the following categories of information:

(A) information relating to the provision of distribution access service, including the terms and conditions of the service and the rates charged for the service but not including information concerning utility-related services or products that are competitive;

(B) information relating to the provision of transmission service that is required to be filed with the Public Utility Commission of Texas, subject to any confidentiality provided for under the rules of the commission;

(C) information for the distribution system pertaining to reliability and continuity of service, to the extent not security-sensitive, that relates to emergency management, identification of critical loads such as hospitals and police, records of interruption, and distribution feeder standards;

(D) any substantive rule or tariff of general applicability regarding rates, service offerings, service regulation, customer protections, or customer service adopted by the public power utility as authorized by law;

(E) aggregate information reflecting receipts or expenditures of funds of the public power utility, of the type that would be included in audited financial statements;

(F) information relating to equal employment opportunities for minority groups, as filed with local, state, or federal agencies;

(G) information relating to the public power utility's performance in contracting with minority business entities;

(H) information relating to nuclear decommissioning trust agreements, of the type required to be included in audited financial statements;

(I) **information relating to the amount and timing of any transfer to an owning city's general fund;**

(J) **information relating to environmental compliance as required to be filed with any local, state, or national environmental authority, subject to any confidentiality provided under the rules of those authorities;**

(K) **names of public officers of the public power utility and the voting records of those officers for all matters other than those within the scope of a competitive resolution provided for by this section;**

(L) **a description of the public power utility's central and field organization, including the established places at which the public may obtain information, submit information and requests, or obtain decisions and the identification of employees from whom the public may obtain information, submit information or requests, or obtain decisions;**

(M) **information identifying the general course and method by which the public power utility's functions are channeled and determined, including the nature and requirements of all formal and informal policies and procedures;**

(N) **salaries and total compensation of all employees of a public power utility; or**

(O) **information publicly released by the Electric Reliability Council of Texas in accordance with a law, rule, or protocol generally applicable to similarly situated market participants.**

(b) **Information or records are excepted from the requirements of Section 552.021 if the information or records are reasonably related to a competitive matter, as defined in this section. Information or records of a municipally owned utility that are reasonably related to a competitive matter are not subject to disclosure under this chapter, whether or not, under the Utilities Code, the municipally owned utility has adopted customer choice or serves in a multiply certificated service area. This section does not limit the right of a public power utility governing body to withhold from disclosure information deemed to be within the scope of any other exception provided for in this chapter, subject to the provisions of this chapter.**

(c) **The requirement of Section 552.022 that a category of information listed under Section 552.022(a) is public information and not excepted from required disclosure under this chapter unless expressly confidential under law does not apply to information that is excepted from required disclosure under this section.**

Section 552.133 excepts from disclosure a public power utility's information related to a competitive matter. The exception defines "competitive matter" as a utility-related matter that is related to the public power utility's competitive activity. In order to be "utility-related," the matter must relate to the six enumerated categories of information. Section 552.133 lists fifteen categories of information that may not be deemed competitive matters. In Open Records Decision No. 666 (2000), the attorney general determined that a municipality may disclose information pertaining to a municipally-owned power utility to a municipally-appointed citizen advisory board without waiving its right thereafter to assert an exception under the Act in response to a future public request for information.[722]

NN. Section 552.134: Confidentiality of Certain Information Relating to Inmate of Department of Criminal Justice

Section 552.134 of the Government Code reads as follows:

(a) **Except as provided by Subsection (b) or by Section 552.029, information obtained or maintained by the Texas Department of Criminal Justice is excepted from the requirements of Section 552.021 if it is information about an inmate who is confined in a facility operated by or under a contract with the department.**

(b) **Subsection (a) does not apply to:**

(1) **statistical or other aggregated information relating to inmates confined in one or more facilities operated by or under a contract with the department; or**

(2) **information about an inmate sentenced to death.**

(c) **This section does not affect whether information is considered confidential or privileged under Section 508.313.**

(d) **A release of information described by Subsection (a) to an eligible entity, as defined by Section 508.313(d) , for a purpose related to law enforcement, prosecution, corrections, clemency, or treatment is not considered a release of information to the public for purposes of Section 552.007 and does not waive the right to assert in the future that the information is excepted from required disclosure under this section or other law.**

This section should be read with two other provisions concerning the required public disclosure of Texas Department of Criminal Justice information, sections 552.029 and 508.313 of the Government Code. Section 508.313 of the Government Code generally makes confidential all information the Texas Department of Criminal Justice obtains and maintains about certain classes of inmates, including an inmate of the institutional division subject to release on parole, release to mandatory supervision, or executive clemency. Section 508.313 also applies to information about a releasee and a person directly identified in any proposed plan of release for an inmate. Section 508.313 requires the release of the information it covers to the governor, a member of the Board of Pardons and Paroles, the Criminal Justice Policy Council, or an eligible entity requesting information for a law enforcement, prosecutorial, correctional, clemency, or treatment purpose.[723] Thus, both sections 552.134 and 508.313 make certain information confidential.

On the other hand, section 552.029 of the Government Code provides that certain specified information cannot be withheld under sections 552.134 and 508.313.

---

[722] Open Records Decision No. 666 at 4 (2000).

[723] Gov't Code § 508.313(c).

Section 552.029 of the Government Code reads as follows:

Notwithstanding Section 508.313 or 552.134, the following information about an inmate who is confined in a facility operated by or under a contract with the Texas Department of Criminal Justice is subject to required disclosure under Section 552.021:

(1)   **the inmate's name, identification number, age, birthplace, department photograph, physical description, or general state of health or the nature of an injury to or critical illness suffered by the inmate;**

(2)   **the inmate's assigned unit or the date on which the unit received the inmate, unless disclosure of the information would violate federal law relating to the confidentiality of substance abuse treatment;**

(3)   **the offense for which the inmate was convicted or the judgment and sentence for that offense;**

(4)   **the county and court in which the inmate was convicted;**

(5)   **the inmate's earliest or latest possible release dates;**

(6)   **the inmate's parole date or earliest possible parole date;**

(7)   **any prior confinement of the inmate by the Texas Department of Criminal Justice or its predecessor; or**

(8)   **basic information regarding the death of an inmate in custody, an incident involving the use of force, or an alleged crime involving the inmate.**

The Texas Department of Criminal Justice has the discretion to release information otherwise protected under section 552.134 to voter registrars for the purpose of maintaining accurate voter registration lists.[724]

OO. Section 552.135: Confidentiality of Certain Information Held by School District

Section 552.135 of the Government Code provides as follows:

(a)   **"Informer" means a student or a former student or an employee or former employee of a school district who has furnished a report of another person's possible violation of criminal, civil, or regulatory law to the school district or the proper regulatory enforcement authority.**

(b)   **An informer's name or information that would substantially reveal the identity of an informer is excepted from the requirements of Section 552.021.**

---

[724]   Open Records Decision No. 667 at 4 (2000).

(c) **Subsection (b) does not apply:**

   (1) **if the informer is a student or former student, and the student or former student, or the legal guardian, or spouse of the student or former student consents to disclosure of the student's or former student's name; or**

   (2) **if the informer is an employee or former employee who consents to disclosure of the employee's or former employee's name; or**

   (3) **if the informer planned, initiated, or participated in the possible violation.**

(d) **Information excepted under Subsection (b) may be made available to a law enforcement agency or prosecutor for official purposes of the agency or prosecutor upon proper request made in compliance with applicable law and procedure.**

(e) **This section does not infringe on or impair the confidentiality of information considered to be confidential by law, whether it be constitutional, statutory, or by judicial decision, including information excepted from the requirements of Section 552.021.**

A school district that seeks to withhold information under this exception must clearly identify to the attorney general's office the specific civil, criminal, or regulatory law that is alleged to have been violated. The school district must also identify the individual who reported the alleged violation of the law. There are no cases or formal opinions interpreting this exception.

PP. Section 552.136: Confidentiality of Credit Card, Debit Card, Charge Card, and Access Device Numbers

Section 552.136 of the Government Code provides as follows:

(a) **In this section, "access device" means a card, plate, code, account number, personal identification number, electronic serial number, mobile identification number, or other telecommunications service, equipment, or instrument identifier or means of account access that alone or in conjunction with another access device may be used to:**

   (1) **obtain money, goods, services, or another thing of value; or**

   (2) **initiate a transfer of funds other than a transfer originated solely by paper instrument.**

(b) **Notwithstanding any other provision of this chapter, a credit card, debit card, charge card, or access device number that is collected, assembled, or maintained by or for a governmental body is confidential.**

(c) **A governmental body may redact information that must be withheld under Subsection (b) from any information the governmental body discloses under**

Section 552.021 without the necessity of requesting a decision from the attorney general under Subchapter G.

(d) **If, under Subsection (c), a governmental body redacts or withholds information without requesting a decision from the attorney general about whether the information may be redacted or withheld, the requestor is entitled to seek a decision from the attorney general about the matter. The attorney general by rule shall establish procedures and deadlines for receiving information necessary to decide the matter and briefs from the requestor, the governmental body, and any other interested person. The attorney general shall promptly render a decision requested under this subsection, determining whether the redacted or withheld information was excepted from required disclosure to the requestor, not later than the 45th business day after the date the attorney general received the request for a decision under this subsection. The attorney general shall issue a written decision on the matter and provide a copy of the decision to the requestor, the governmental body, and any interested person who submitted necessary information or a brief to the attorney general about the matter. The requestor or the governmental body may appeal a decision of the attorney general under this subsection to a Travis County district court.**

(e) **A governmental body that redacts or withholds information under Subsection (c) shall provide the following information to the requestor on a form prescribed by the attorney general:**

(1) **a description of the redacted or withheld information;**

(2) **a citation to this section; and**

(3) **instructions regarding how the requestor may seek a decision from the attorney general regarding whether the redacted or withheld information is excepted from required disclosure.**

A governmental body that raises section 552.136 must demonstrate how the "access device number" it seeks to withhold is used alone or in combination to obtain money, goods, services, or another thing of value or initiate a transfer of funds. The attorney general has interpreted this exception to include bank account and routing numbers, full and partial credit card numbers and their expiration dates, and insurance policy numbers.[725] Because section 552.136 protects privacy interests, a governmental body may not invoke this exception to withhold an access device from the person to whom the device belongs or that person's authorized representative.[726]

Pursuant to section 552.136(c), a governmental body may redact without the necessity of requesting an attorney general decision information that is subject to section 552.136. If a governmental body chooses to redact this information without requesting an attorney general decision, it must notify the requestor as prescribed by section 552.136(e) on the form created by the attorney general. The notice must include instructions regarding how the requestor may seek an attorney general's review of the

---

[725] Open Records Decision No. 684 at 9 (2009).

[726] Open Records Decision No. 684 at 12 (2009); *see* Gov't Code § 552.023.

governmental body's redactions. The form for notifying the requestor is located on the attorney general's website. The legislation enacting this provision authorized the attorney general to promulgate rules establishing procedures for review under section 552.136(d). These rules were promulgated in subchapter B of chapter 63 of title 1 of the Texas Administrative Code.[727] These rules are available on the attorney general's website and in Part Four of this *Handbook*.

QQ. Section 552.137: Confidentiality of Certain E-mail Addresses

Section 552.137 of the Government Code provides as follows:

(a) **Except as otherwise provided by this section, an e-mail address of a member of the public that is provided for the purpose of communicating electronically with a governmental body is confidential and not subject to disclosure under this chapter.**

(b) **Confidential information described by this section that relates to a member of the public may be disclosed if the member of the public affirmatively consents to its release.**

(c) **Subsection (a) does not apply to an e-mail address:**

(1) **provided to a governmental body by a person who has a contractual relationship with the governmental body or by the contractor's agent;**

(2) **provided to a governmental body by a vendor who seeks to contract with the governmental body or by the vendor's agent;**

(3) **contained in a response to a request for bids or proposals, contained in a response to similar invitations soliciting offers or information relating to a potential contract, or provided to a governmental body in the course of negotiating the terms of a contract or potential contract;**

(4) **provided to a governmental body on a letterhead, cover sheet, printed document, or other document made available to the public; or**

(5) **provided to a governmental body for the purpose of providing public comment on or receiving notices related to an application for a license as defined by Section 2001.003(2) of this code, or receiving orders or decisions from a governmental body.**

(d) **Subsection (a) does not prevent a governmental body from disclosing an e-mail address for any reason to another governmental body or to a federal agency.**

In addition to the exceptions found in amended section 552.137(c), the attorney general has determined that section 552.137 does not protect a government employee's work e-mail address or an institutional e-mail address or website address.[728] Further, this section does not apply to the

---

[727] *See* 1 T.A.C. §§ 63.11–.16

[728] Open Records Decision No. 684 at 10 (2009).

private e-mail addresses of government officials who use their private e-mail addresses to conduct official government business.[729] Because a person may consent to the disclosure of his or her e-mail address under the statute, the person has a right to his or her own e-mail address.[730] The attorney general issued Open Records Decision No. 684 (2009), a previous determination to all governmental bodies authorizing them to withhold an e-mail address of a member of the public without the necessity of requesting an attorney general decision.[731]

RR. Section 552.138: Confidentiality of Family Violence Shelter Center, Victims of Trafficking Shelter Center, and Sexual Assault Program Information

Section 552.138 of the Government Code provides as follows:

(a)   **In this section:**

   (1) **"Family violence shelter center" has the meaning assigned by Section 51.002, Human Resources Code.**

   (2) **"Sexual assault program" has the meaning assigned by Section 420.003.**

   (3) **"Victims of trafficking shelter center" means:**

      (A)   **a program that:**

         (i) **is operated by a public or private nonprofit organization; and**

         (ii) **provides comprehensive residential and nonresidential services to persons who are victims of trafficking under Section 20A.02, Penal Code; or**

      (B)   **a child-placing agency, as defined by Section 42.002, Human Resources Code, that provides services to persons who are victims of trafficking under Section 20A.02, Penal Code.**

(b)   **Information maintained by a family violence shelter center, victims of trafficking shelter center, or sexual assault program is excepted from the requirements of Section 552.021 if it is information that relates to:**

   (1) **the home address, home telephone number, or social security number of an employee or a volunteer worker of a family violence shelter center, victims of trafficking shelter center, or sexual assault program, regardless of whether the employee or worker complies with Section 552.024;**

---

[729]   *Austin Bulldog v. Leffingwell*, 490 S.W.3d 240 (Tex. App.—Austin 2016, no pet.).

[730]   Open Records Decision No. 684 at 10 (2009).

[731]   Open Records Decision No. 684 at 10 (2009).

(2) the location or physical layout of a family violence shelter center or victims of trafficking shelter center;

(3) the name, home address, home telephone number, or numeric identifier of a current or former client of a family violence shelter center, victims of trafficking shelter center, or sexual assault program;

(4) the provision of services, including counseling and sheltering, to a current or former client of a family violence shelter center, victims of trafficking shelter center, or sexual assault program;

(5) the name, home address, or home telephone number of a private donor to a family violence shelter center, victims of trafficking shelter center, or sexual assault program; or

(6) the home address or home telephone number of a member of the board of directors or the board of trustees of a family violence shelter center, victims of trafficking shelter center, or sexual assault program, regardless of whether the board member complies with Section 552.024.

(c) A governmental body may redact information maintained by a family violence shelter center, victims of trafficking shelter center, or sexual assault program that may be withheld under Subsection (b)(1) or (6) from any information the governmental body discloses under Section 552.021 without the necessity of requesting a decision from the attorney general under Subchapter G.

(d) If, under Subsection (c), a governmental body redacts or withholds information without requesting a decision from the attorney general about whether the information may be redacted or withheld, the requestor is entitled to seek a decision from the attorney general about the matter. The attorney general by rule shall establish procedures and deadlines for receiving information necessary to decide the matter and briefs from the requestor, the governmental body, and any other interested person. The attorney general shall promptly render a decision requested under this subsection, determining whether the redacted or withheld information was excepted from required disclosure to the requestor, not later than the 45th business day after the date the attorney general received the request for a decision under this subsection. The attorney general shall issue a written decision on the matter and provide a copy of the decision to the requestor, the governmental body, and any interested person who submitted necessary information or a brief to the attorney general about the matter. The requestor or the governmental body may appeal a decision of the attorney general under this subsection to a Travis County district court.

(e) A governmental body that redacts or withholds information under Subsection (c) shall provide the following information to the requestor on a form prescribed by the attorney general:

(1) a description of the redacted or withheld information;

(2) a citation to this section; and

(3) instructions regarding how the requestor may seek a decision from the attorney general regarding whether the redacted or withheld information is excepted from required disclosure.

Thus, section 552.138 allows a governmental body to redact the following information maintained by a family violence shelter center, victims of trafficking shelter center, or sexual assault program without the necessity of requesting an attorney general decision: the home address, home telephone number, or social security number of an employee or volunteer worker. Section 552.138 also allows the redaction of the home address or telephone number of a member of the board of directors or the board of trustees without the necessity of requesting an attorney general decision. If a governmental body chooses to redact this information without requesting an attorney general decision, it must notify the requestor as prescribed section 552.138(e) on the form created by the attorney general. The notice must include instructions regarding how the requestor may seek an attorney general's review of the governmental body's redactions. The form for notifying the requestor is published on the attorney general's website. The legislation enacting these provisions authorized the attorney general to promulgate rules establishing procedures for review under section 552.138(d). These rules are available on the attorney general's website and in Part Four of this *Handbook*.[732]

SS.   Section 552.139: Confidentiality of Government Information Related to Security or Infrastructure Issues for Computers

The 85th Legislature amended Section 552.139 of the Government Code to provide as follows:

(a)   Information is excepted from the requirements of Section 552.021 if it is information that relates to computer network security, to restricted information under Section 2059.055, or to the design, operation, or defense of a computer network.

(b)   The following information is confidential:

(1) a computer network vulnerability report;

(2) any other assessment of the extent to which data processing operations, a computer, a computer program, network, system, or system interface, or software of a governmental body or of a contractor of a governmental body is vulnerable to unauthorized access or harm, including an assessment of the extent to which the governmental body's or contractor's electronically stored information containing sensitive or critical information is vulnerable to alteration, damage, erasure, or inappropriate use;

(3) a photocopy or other copy of an identification badge issued to an official or employee of a governmental body; and

---

[732]   *See* 1 T.A.C. §§ 63.11–.16.

(4) information directly arising from a governmental body's routine efforts to prevent, detect, investigate, or mitigate a computer security incident, including information contained in or derived from an information security log.[733]

(b-1) Subsection (b)(4) does not affect the notification requirements related to a breach of system security as defined by Section 521.053, Business & Commerce Code.[734]

(c) Notwithstanding the confidential nature of the information described in this section, the information may be disclosed to a bidder if the governmental body determines that providing the information is necessary for the bidder to provide an accurate bid. A disclosure under this subsection is not a voluntary disclosure for purposes of Section 552.007.

Text of (d), as added by Acts 2017, 85th Leg., ch. 683 (H.B. 8), § 4

(d) When posting a contract on an Internet website as required by Section 2261.253, a state agency shall redact information made confidential by this section or excepted from public disclosure by this section. Redaction under this subsection does not except information from the requirements of Section 552.021.

Text of (d), as added by Acts 2017, 85th Leg., ch. 683 (H.B. 1861), § 1

(d) A state agency shall redact from a contract posted on the agency's Internet website under Section 2261.253 information that is made confidential by, or excepted from required public disclosure under, this section. The redaction of information under this subsection does not exempt the information from the requirements of Section 552.021 or 552.221.

There are no cases or formal opinions interpreting this exception.

TT. Section 552.140: Confidentiality of Military Discharge Records

Section 552.140 of the Government Code provides as follows:

(a) This section applies only to a military veteran's Department of Defense Form DD-214 or other military discharge record that is first recorded with or that otherwise first comes into the possession of a governmental body on or after September 1, 2003.

(b) The record is confidential for the 75 years following the date it is recorded with or otherwise first comes into the possession of a governmental body. During that period the governmental body may permit inspection or copying of the record or disclose information contained in the record only in accordance with this section or in accordance with a court order.

---

[733] Gov't Code § 552.139(b).

[734] Gov't Code § 552.139(b-1).

(c)   On request and the presentation of proper identification, the following persons may inspect the military discharge record or obtain from the governmental body free of charge a copy or certified copy of the record:

   (1) the veteran who is the subject of the record;

   (2) the legal guardian of the veteran;

   (3) the spouse or a child or parent of the veteran or, if there is no living spouse, child, or parent, the nearest living relative of the veteran;

   (4) the personal representative of the estate of the veteran;

   (5) the person named by the veteran, or by a person described by Subdivision (2), (3), or (4), in an appropriate power of attorney executed in accordance with Subchapters A and B, Chapter 752, Estates Code;

   (6) another governmental body; or

   (7) an authorized representative of the funeral home that assists with the burial of the veteran.

(d)   A court that orders the release of information under this section shall limit the further disclosure of the information and the purposes for which the information may be used.

(e)   A governmental body that obtains information from the record shall limit the governmental body's use and disclosure of the information to the purpose for which the information was obtained.

In Open Records Decision No. 684 (2009), the attorney general issued a previous determination to all governmental bodies authorizing them to withhold, a Form DD-214 or other military discharge record that is first recorded with or that otherwise first comes into the possession of the governmental body on or after September 1, 2003, under section 552.140 of the Government Code, without the necessity of requesting an attorney general decision.[735]

UU. Section 552.141: Confidentiality of Information in Application for Marriage License

Section 552.141 of the Government Code provides as follows:

(a)   Information that relates to the social security number of an individual that is maintained by a county clerk and that is on an application for a marriage license, including information in an application on behalf of an absent applicant and the affidavit of an absent applicant, or is on a document submitted with an application for a marriage license is confidential and may not be disclosed by the county clerk to the public under this chapter.

---

[735] Open Records Decision No. 684 at 11 (2009).

(b)   If the county clerk receives a request to make information in a marriage license application available under this chapter, the county clerk shall redact the portion of the application that contains an individual's social security number and release the remainder of the information in the application.

This exception applies only to an application for a marriage license that is filed on or after September 1, 2003.[736] There are no cases or formal opinions interpreting this exception.

VV. Section 552.142: Confidentiality of Records Subject to Order of Nondisclosure

Section 552.142 of the Government Code provides as follows:

(a)   Information is excepted from the requirements of Section 552.021 if an order of nondisclosure of criminal history record information with respect to the information has been issued under Subchapter E-1, Chapter 411.

(b)   A person who is the subject of information that is excepted from the requirements of Section 552.021 under this section may deny the occurrence of the criminal proceeding to which the information relates and the exception of the information under this section, unless the information is being used against the person in a subsequent criminal proceeding.

There are no cases or formal opinions interpreting this exception.

WW. Section 552.1425: Civil Penalty: Dissemination of Certain Criminal History Information

Section 552.1425 of the Government Code provides as follows:

(a)   A private entity that compiles and disseminates for compensation criminal history record information may not compile or disseminate information with respect to which the entity has received notice that:

(1)   an order of expunction has been issued under Article 55.02, Code of Criminal Procedure; or

(2)   an order of nondisclosure of criminal history record information has been issued under Subchapter E-1, Chapter 411.

(b)   A district court may issue a warning to a private entity for a first violation of Subsection (a). After receiving a warning for the first violation, the private entity is liable to the state for a civil penalty not to exceed $1,000 for each subsequent violation.

---

[736] *See* Act of May 21, 2003, 78th Leg., R.S., ch. 804, § 2, 2003 Tex. Gen. Laws 2356.

(c)   The attorney general or an appropriate prosecuting attorney may sue to collect a civil penalty under this section.

(d)   A civil penalty collected under this section shall be deposited in the state treasury to the credit of the general revenue fund.

There are no cases or formal opinions interpreting this section.

XX.   Section 552.143: Confidentiality of Certain Investment Information

Section 552.143 of the Government Code provides as follows:

(a)   All information prepared or provided by a private investment fund and held by a governmental body that is not listed in Section 552.0225(b) is confidential and excepted from the requirements of Section 552.021.

(b)   Unless the information has been publicly released, pre-investment and post-investment diligence information, including reviews and analyses, prepared or maintained by a governmental body or a private investment fund is confidential and excepted from the requirements of Section 552.021, except to the extent it is subject to disclosure under Subsection (c).

(c)   All information regarding a governmental body's direct purchase, holding, or disposal of restricted securities that is not listed in Section 552.0225(b)(2)–(9), (11), or (13)–(16) is confidential and excepted from the requirements of Section 552.021. This subsection does not apply to a governmental body's purchase, holding, or disposal of restricted securities for the purpose of reinvestment nor does it apply to a private investment fund's investment in restricted securities. This subsection applies to information regarding a direct purchase, holding, or disposal of restricted securities by the Texas growth fund, created under Section 70, Article XVI, Texas Constitution, that is not listed in Section 552.0225(b).

(d)   For the purposes of this chapter:

   (1) "Private investment fund" means an entity, other than a governmental body, that issues restricted securities to a governmental body to evidence the investment of public funds for the purpose of reinvestment.

   (2) "Reinvestment" means investment in a person that makes or will make other investments.

   (3) "Restricted securities" has the meaning assigned by 17 C.F.R. Section 230.144(a)(3).

(e)   Repealed by Acts 2011, 82nd Leg., 1st C.S., ch. 4 (S.B. 1), § 17.05(1)

(f)   This section does not apply to the Texas Mutual Insurance Company or a successor to the company.

There are no cases or formal opinions interpreting this exception. Section 552.0225 makes public certain investment information. The attorney general has determined in an informal letter ruling that section 552.143 is subject to the public disclosure requirements of section 552.0225.[737]

YY. Section 552.144: Working Papers and Electronic Communications of Administrative Law Judges at State Office of Administrative Hearings

Section 552.144 of the Government Code provides as follows:

The following working papers and electronic communications of an administrative law judge at the State Office of Administrative Hearings are excepted from the requirements of Section 552.021:

(1) notes and electronic communications recording the observations, thoughts, questions, deliberations, or impressions of an administrative law judge;

(2) drafts of a proposal for decision;

(3) drafts of orders made in connection with conducting contested case hearings; and

(4) drafts of orders made in connection with conducting alternative dispute resolution procedures.

There are no cases or formal opinions interpreting this exception.

ZZ. Section 552.145: Confidentiality of Texas No-Call List

Section 552.145 of the Government Code provides as follows:

The Texas no-call list created under Subchapter B, Chapter 304, Business & Commerce Code, and any information provided to or received from the administrator of the national do-not-call registry maintained by the United States government, as provided by Sections 304.051 and 304.56, Business & Commerce Code, are excepted from the requirements of Section 552.021.

Section 552.145 applies specifically to the no-call list and information provided to or removed from the administrator of the do-not-call registry.[738]

There are no cases or formal opinions interpreting this exception.

---

[737] Open Records Letter No. 2005-6095 (2005).

[738] *See, e.g.,* Open Records Letter Nos. 2009-10649 (2009), 2009-07316 (2009).

AAA. Section 552.146: Certain Communications with Assistant or Employee of Legislative Budget Board

Section 552.146 of the Government Code provides as follows:

(a) All written or otherwise recorded communications, including conversations, correspondence, and electronic communications, between a member of the legislature or the lieutenant governor and an assistant or employee of the Legislative Budget Board are excepted from the requirements of Section 552.021.

(b) Memoranda of a communication between a member of the legislature or the lieutenant governor and an assistant or employee of the Legislative Budget Board are excepted from the requirements of Section 552.021 without regard to the method used to store or maintain the memoranda.

(c) This section does not except from required disclosure a record or memoranda of a communication that occurs in public during an open meeting or public hearing conducted by the Legislative Budget Board.

There are no cases or formal opinions interpreting this exception.

BBB. Section 552.147: Social Security Numbers

Section 552.147 of the Government Code provides as follows:

(a) Except as provided by Subsection (a-1), the social security number of a living person is excepted from the requirements of Section 552.021, but is not confidential under this section and this section does not make the social security number of a living person confidential under another provision of this chapter or other law.

(a-1) The social security number of an employee of a school district in the custody of the district is confidential.

(b) A governmental body may redact the social security number of a living person from any information the governmental body discloses under Section 552.021 without the necessity of requesting a decision from the attorney general under Subchapter G.

(c) Notwithstanding any other law, a county or district clerk may disclose in the ordinary course of business a social security number that is contained in information held by the clerk's office, and that disclosure is not official misconduct and does not subject the clerk to civil or criminal liability of any kind under the law of this state, including any claim for damages in a lawsuit or the criminal penalty imposed by Section 552.352.

(d) Unless another law requires a social security number to be maintained in a government document, on written request from an individual or the individual's representative the clerk shall redact within a reasonable amount of time all but the last four digits of the individual's social security number from information

maintained in the clerk's official public records, including electronically stored information maintained by or under the control of the clerk. The individual or the individual's representative must identify, using a form provided by the clerk, the specific document or documents from which the partial social security number shall be redacted.

There are no cases or formal opinions interpreting this exception. However, the attorney general has determined in an informal letter ruling that Section 552.147(a-1) makes confidential the social security numbers of both current and former school district employees.[739]

CCC. Section 552.148: Confidentiality of Certain Personal Information Maintained by Municipality Pertaining to a Minor

Section 552.148 of the Government Code provides as follows:

(a) **In this section, "minor" means a person younger than 18 years of age.**

(b) **The following information maintained by a municipality for purposes related to the participation by a minor in a recreational program or activity is excepted from the requirements of Section 552.021:**

  (1) **the name, age, home address, home telephone number, or social security number of the minor;**

  (2) **a photograph of the minor; and**

  (3) **the name of the minor's parent or legal guardian.**

There are no cases or formal opinions interpreting this exception.

DDD. Section 552.149: Confidentiality of Records of Comptroller or Appraisal District Received from Private Entity

Section 552.149 of the Government Code provides as follows:

(a) **Information relating to real property sales prices, descriptions, characteristics, and other related information received from a private entity by the comptroller or the chief appraiser of an appraisal district under Chapter 6, Tax Code, is excepted from the requirements of Section 552.021.**

(b) **Notwithstanding Subsection (a), the property owner or the owner's agent may, on request, obtain from the chief appraiser of the applicable appraisal district a copy of each item of information described by Section 41.461(a)(2), Tax Code, and a copy of each item of information that the chief appraiser took into consideration but does not plan to introduce at the hearing on the protest. In addition, the property owner or**

---

[739] Open Records Letter No. 2013-18655 at 6 (2013).

agent may, on request, obtain from the chief appraiser comparable sales data from a reasonable number of sales that is relevant to any matter to be determined by the appraisal review board at the hearing on the property owner's protest. Information obtained under this subsection:

(1) remains confidential in the possession of the property owner or agent; and

(2) may not be disclosed or used for any purpose except as evidence or argument at the hearing on the protest.

(c) Notwithstanding Subsection (a) or Section 403.304, so as to assist a property owner or an appraisal district in a protest filed under Section 403.303, the property owner, the district, or an agent of the property owner or district may, on request, obtain from the comptroller any information, including confidential information, obtained by the comptroller in connection with the comptroller's finding that is being protested. Confidential information obtained by a property owner, an appraisal district, or an agent of the property owner or district under this subsection:

(1) remains confidential in the possession of the property owner, district, or agent; and

(2) may not be disclosed to a person who is not authorized to receive or inspect the information.

(d) Notwithstanding Subsection (a) or Section 403.304, so as to assist a school district in the preparation of a protest filed or to be filed under Section 403.303, the school district or an agent of the school district may, on request, obtain from the comptroller or the appraisal district any information, including confidential information, obtained by the comptroller or the appraisal district that relates to the appraisal of property involved in the comptroller's finding that is being protested. Confidential information obtained by a school district or an agent of the school district under this subsection:

(1) remains confidential in the possession of the school district or agent; and

(2) may not be disclosed to a person who is not authorized to receive or inspect the information.

(e) This section applies to information described by Subsections (a), (c), and (d) and to an item of information or comparable sales data described by Subsection (b) only if the information, item of information, or comparable sales data relates to real property that is located in a county having a population of more than 50,000.

In *Harris County Appraisal Dist. v. Integrity Title Co., LLC*, the First Court of Appeals addressed, in relevant part, whether otherwise public information provided to a governmental body by a private entity is excepted from disclosure under section 552.149.[740] The Harris County Appraisal District sought to withhold deed document numbers and filing dates received from a private entity under section 552.149; however, the private entity had obtained this information from the Harris County Clerk.[741] The court found section 552.149 protects privately-generated information sold to a governmental body that is not otherwise publicly available and concluded section 552.149 did not except from disclosure the otherwise public information the private entity received from the Harris County Clerk.[742]

EEE. Section 552.150: Confidentiality of Information That Could Compromise Safety of Officer or Employee of Hospital District

Section 552.150 of the Government Code provides as follows:

(a) Information in the custody of a hospital district that relates to an employee or officer of the hospital district is excepted from the requirements of Section 552.021 if:

   (1) it is information that, if disclosed under the specific circumstances pertaining to the individual, could reasonably be expected to compromise the safety of the individual, such as information that describes or depicts the likeness of the individual, information stating the times that the individual arrives at or departs from work, a description of the individual's automobile, or the location where the individual works or parks; and

   (2) the employee or officer applies in writing to the hospital district's officer for public information to have the information withheld from public disclosure under this section and includes in the application:

      (A) a description of the information; and

      (B) the specific circumstances pertaining to the individual that demonstrate why disclosure of the information could reasonably be expected to compromise the safety of the individual.

(b) On receiving a written request for information described in an application submitted under Subsection (a)(2), the officer for public information shall:

   (1) request a decision from the attorney general in accordance with Section 552.301 regarding withholding the information; and

   (2) include a copy of the application submitted under Subsection (a)(2) with the request for the decision.

---

[740] *Harris County Appraisal Dist. v. Integrity Title Co., LLC*, 483 S.W.3d 62, 71 (Tex. App.—Houston [1st Dist.] 2015, pet. denied).

[741] *Harris County Appraisal Dist. v. Integrity Title Co., LLC*, 483 S.W.3d 62, 70 (Tex. App.—Houston [1st Dist.] 2015, pet. denied).

[742] *Harris County Appraisal Dist. v. Integrity Title Co., LLC*, 483 S.W.3d 62, 71 (Tex. App.—Houston [1st Dist.] 2015, pet. denied).

(c) **Repealed by Acts 2011, 82nd Leg., ch. 609 (S.B. 470), § 1.**

There are no cases or formal opinions interpreting this exception. In an informal letter ruling, the attorney general has determined Section 552.150 does not apply to former employees of a hospital district.[743]

FFF. Section 552.151: Confidentiality of Information Regarding Select Agents

Section 552.151 of the Government Code provides as follows:

(a) **The following information that pertains to a biological agent or toxin identified or listed as a select agent under federal law, including under the Public Health Security and Bioterrorism Preparedness and Response Act of 2002 (Pub. L. No. 107-188) and regulations adopted under that Act, is excepted from the requirements of Section 552.021:**

    (1) **the specific location of a select agent within an approved facility;**

    (2) **personal identifying information of an individual whose name appears in documentation relating to the chain of custody of select agents, including a materials transfer agreement; and**

    (3) **the identity of an individual authorized to possess, use, or access a select agent.**

(b) **This section does not except from disclosure the identity of the select agents present at a facility.**

(c) **This section does not except from disclosure the identity of an individual faculty member or employee whose name appears or will appear on published research.**

(d) **This section does not except from disclosure otherwise public information relating to contracts of a governmental body.**

(e) **If a resident of another state is present in Texas and is authorized to possess, use, or access a select agent in conducting research or other work at a Texas facility, information relating to the identity of that individual is subject to disclosure under this chapter only to the extent the information would be subject to disclosure under the laws of the state of which the person is a resident.**

There are no cases or formal opinions interpreting this exception.

---

[743] Open Records Letter No. 2014-15073A at 8 (2014).

GGG. Section 552.152: Confidentiality of Information Concerning Public Employee or Officer Personal Safety

Section 552.152 of the Government Code provides as follows:

Information in the custody of a governmental body that relates to an employee or officer of the governmental body is excepted from the requirements of Section 552.021 if, under the specific circumstances pertaining to the employee or officer, disclosure of the information would subject the employee or officer to a substantial threat of physical harm.

In an informal letter ruling, the attorney general considered a request to the Texas Department of Public Safety for information pertaining to travel expenses incurred by the Governor's security detail.[744] The Texas Department of Public Safety claimed section 552.152 of the Government Code excepted from disclosure travel vouchers and supporting documentation submitted by agents of the Executive Protection Bureau for reimbursement of travel expenses.[745] Relying on representations the Texas Department of Public Safety made about protecting the Governor and his family from physical harm, the attorney general concluded release of the travel vouchers and supporting documentation would subject the Governor and the agents to a substantial threat of physical harm, and therefore, the information must be withheld from disclosure under section 552.152.[746]

HHH. Section 552.153: Proprietary Records and Trade Secrets Involved in Certain Partnerships

Section 552.153 of the Government Code provides as follows:

(a) **In this section, "affected jurisdiction," "comprehensive agreement," "contracting person," "interim agreement," "qualifying project," and "responsible governmental entity" have the meanings assigned those terms by Section 2267.001.**

(b) **Information in the custody of a responsible governmental entity that relates to a proposal for a qualifying project authorized under Chapter 2267 is excepted from the requirements of Section 552.021 if:**

(1) **the information consists of memoranda, staff evaluations, or other records prepared by the responsible governmental entity, its staff, outside advisors, or consultants exclusively for the evaluation and negotiation of proposals filed under Chapter 2267 for which:**

(A) **disclosure to the public before or after the execution of an interim or comprehensive agreement would adversely affect the financial interest or bargaining position of the responsible governmental entity; and**

---

[744] Open Records Letter No. 2014-02048 (2014).

[745] Open Records Letter No. 2014-02048 at 1 (2014).

[746] Open Records Letter No. 2014-02048 at 3-4 (2014).

  (B) the basis for the determination under Paragraph (A) is documented in writing by the responsible governmental entity; or

 (2) the records are provided by a proposer to a responsible governmental entity or affected jurisdiction under Chapter 2267 and contain:

  (A) trade secrets of the proposer;

  (B) financial records of the proposer, including balance sheets and financial statements, that are not generally available to the public through regulatory disclosure or other means; or

  (C) work product related to a competitive bid or proposal submitted by the proposer that, if made public before the execution of an interim or comprehensive agreement, would provide a competing proposer an unjust advantage or adversely affect the financial interest or bargaining position of the responsible governmental entity or the proposer.

(c) Except as specifically provided by Subsection (b), this section does not authorize the withholding of information concerning:

 (1) the terms of any interim or comprehensive agreement, service contract, lease, partnership, or agreement of any kind entered into by the responsible governmental entity and the contracting person or the terms of any financing arrangement that involves the use of any public money; or

 (2) the performance of any person developing or operating a qualifying project under Chapter 2267.

(d) In this section, "proposer" has the meaning assigned by Section 2267.001.

There are no cases or formal opinions interpreting this exception.

III. Section 552.154: Name of Applicant for Executive Director, Chief Investment Officer, or Chief Audit Executive of Teacher Retirement System of Texas

Section 552.154 of the Government Code provides as follows:

> The name of an applicant for the position of executive director, chief investment officer, or chief audit executive of the Teacher Retirement System of Texas is excepted from the requirements of Section 552.021, except that the board of trustees of the Teacher Retirement System of Texas must give public notice of the names of three finalists being considered for one of those positions at least 21 days before the date of the meeting at which the final action or vote is to be taken on choosing a finalist for employment.

There are no cases or formal opinions interpreting this exception.

JJJ. Section 552.155: Confidentiality of Certain Property Tax Appraisal Photographs

Section 552.155 of the Government Code provides as follows:

(a) Except as provided by Subsection (b) or (c), a photograph that is taken by the chief appraiser of an appraisal district or the chief appraiser's authorized representative for property tax appraisal purposes and that shows the interior of an improvement to property is confidential and excepted from the requirements of Section 552.021.

(b) A governmental body shall disclose a photograph described by Subsection (a) to a requestor who had an ownership interest in the improvement to property shown in the photograph on the date the photograph was taken.

(c) A photograph described by Subsection (a) may be used as evidence in and provided to the parties to a protest under Chapter 41, Tax Code, or an appeal of a determination by the appraisal review board under Chapter 42, Tax Code, if it is relevant to the determination of a matter protested or appealed. A photograph that is used as evidence:

  (1) remains confidential in the possession of the person to whom it is disclosed; and

  (2) may not be disclosed or used for any other purpose.

(c-1) Notwithstanding any other law, a photograph described by Subsection (a) may be used to ascertain the location of equipment used to produce or transmit oil and gas for purposes of taxation if that equipment is located on January 1 in the appraisal district that appraises property for the equipment for the preceding 365 consecutive days.

There are no cases or formal opinions interpreting this exception.

KKK. Section 552.156: Confidentiality of Continuity of Operations Plan

Section 552.156 of the Government Code provides as follows:

(a) Except as otherwise provided by this section, the following information is excepted from disclosure under this chapter:

  (1) a continuity of operations plan developed under Section 412.054, Labor Code; and

  (2) all records written, produced, collected, assembled, or maintained as part of the development or review of a continuity of operations plan developed under Section 412.054, Labor Code.

(b) Forms, standards, and other instructional, informational, or planning materials adopted by the office to provide guidance or assistance to a state agency in developing a continuity of operations plan under Section 412.054, Labor Code, are public information subject to disclosure under this chapter.

(c)   A governmental body may disclose or make available information that is confidential under this section to another governmental body or a federal agency.

(d)   Disclosing information to another governmental body or a federal agency under this section does not waive or affect the confidentiality of that information.

There are no cases or formal opinions interpreting this exception.

LLL. Section 552.158: Confidentiality of Personal Information Regarding Applicant for Appointment by Governor

Section 552.158 of the Government Code was added by the 85th Legislature and provides as follows:

The following information obtained by the governor or senate in connection with an applicant for an appointment by the governor is excepted from the requirements of Section 552.021:

(1) the applicant's home address;

(2) the applicant's home telephone number; and

(3) the applicant's social security number.[747]

There are no cases or formal opinions interpreting this exception.

---

[747] Gov't Code § 552.158.

PART THREE: TEXT OF THE TEXAS PUBLIC INFORMATION ACT

GOVERNMENT CODE CHAPTER 552. PUBLIC INFORMATION

SUBCHAPTER A. GENERAL PROVISIONS

§ 552.001.   Policy; Construction

(a) Under the fundamental philosophy of the American constitutional form of representative government that adheres to the principle that government is the servant and not the master of the people, it is the policy of this state that each person is entitled, unless otherwise expressly provided by law, at all times to complete information about the affairs of government and the official acts of public officials and employees. The people, in delegating authority, do not give their public servants the right to decide what is good for the people to know and what is not good for them to know. The people insist on remaining informed so that they may retain control over the instruments they have created. The provisions of this chapter shall be liberally construed to implement this policy.

(b) This chapter shall be liberally construed in favor of granting a request for information.

§ 552.002.   Definition of Public Information; Media Containing Public Information

(a) In this chapter, "public information" means information that is written, produced, collected, assembled, or maintained under a law or ordinance or in connection with the transaction of official business:

   (1)   by a governmental body;

   (2)   for a governmental body and the governmental body:

      (A)   owns the information;

      (B)   has a right of access to the information; or

      (C)   spends or contributes public money for the purpose of writing, producing, collecting, assembling, or maintaining the information; or

   (3)   by an individual officer or employee of a governmental body in the officer's or employee's official capacity and the information pertains to official business of the governmental body.

(a-1) Information is in connection with the transaction of official business if the information is created by, transmitted to, received by, or maintained by an officer or employee of the governmental body in the officer's or employee's official capacity, or a person or entity performing official business or a governmental function on behalf of a governmental body, and pertains to official business of the governmental body.

(a-2) The definition of "public information" provided by Subsection (a) applies to and includes any electronic communication created, transmitted, received, or maintained on any device if the communication is in connection with the transaction of official business.

(b) The media on which public information is recorded include:

   (1)   paper;

   (2)   film;

   (3)   a magnetic, optical, solid state, or other device that can store an electronic signal;

   (4)   tape;

   (5)   Mylar; and

   (6)   any physical material on which information may be recorded, including linen, silk, and vellum.

(c) The general forms in which the media containing public information exist include a book, paper, letter, document, e-mail, Internet posting, text message, instant message, other electronic communication, printout, photograph, film, tape, microfiche, microfilm, photostat, sound recording, map, and drawing and a voice, data, or video representation held in computer memory.

§ 552.003.   Definitions

In this chapter:

(1)   "Governmental body":

   (A)   means:

      (i)   a board, commission, department, committee, institution, agency, or office that is within or is created by the executive or legislative branch of state government and that is directed by one or more elected or appointed members;

      (ii)   a county commissioners court in the state;

      (iii) a municipal governing body in the state;

      (iv)   a deliberative body that has rulemaking or quasi-judicial power and that is classified as a department, agency, or political subdivision of a county or municipality;

      (v)   a school district board of trustees;

      (vi)   a county board of school trustees;

(vii) a county board of education;

(viii) the governing board of a special district;

(ix) the governing body of a nonprofit corporation organized under Chapter 67, Water Code, that provides a water supply or wastewater service, or both, and is exempt from ad valorem taxation under Section 11.30, Tax Code;

(x) a local workforce development board created under Section 2308.253;

(xi) a nonprofit corporation that is eligible to receive funds under the federal community services block grant program and that is authorized by this state to serve a geographic area of the state; and

(xii) the part, section, or portion of an organization, corporation, commission, committee, institution, or agency that spends or that is supported in whole or in part by public funds; and

(B) does not include the judiciary.

(2) "Manipulation" means the process of modifying, reordering, or decoding of information with human intervention.

(2-a) "Official business" means any matter over which a governmental body has any authority, administrative duties, or advisory duties.

(3) "Processing" means the execution of a sequence of coded instructions by a computer producing a result.

(4) "Programming" means the process of producing a sequence of coded instructions that can be executed by a computer.

(5) "Public funds" means funds of the state or of a governmental subdivision of the state.

(6) "Requestor" means a person who submits a request to a governmental body for inspection or copies of public information.

§ 552.0035. Access to Information of Judiciary

(a) Access to information collected, assembled, or maintained by or for the judiciary is governed by rules adopted by the Supreme Court of Texas or by other applicable laws and rules.

(b) This section does not address whether information is considered to be information collected, assembled, or maintained by or for the judiciary.

§ 552.0036. Certain Property Owners' Associations Subject to Law

A property owners' association is subject to this chapter in the same manner as a governmental body:

(1) if:

    (A) membership in the property owners' association is mandatory for owners or for a defined class of owners of private real property in a defined geographic area in a county with a population of 2.8 million or more or in a county adjacent to a county with a population of 2.8 million or more;

    (B) the property owners' association has the power to make mandatory special assessments for capital improvements or mandatory regular assessments; and

    (C) the amount of the mandatory special or regular assessments is or has ever been based in whole or in part on the value at which the state or a local governmental body assesses the property for purposes of ad valorem taxation under Section 20, Article VIII, Texas Constitution; or

(2) if the property owners' association:

    (A) provides maintenance, preservation, and architectural control of residential and commercial property within a defined geographic area in a county with a population of 2.8 million or more or in a county adjacent to a county with a population of 2.8 million or more; and

    (B) is a corporation that:

        (i) is governed by a board of trustees who may employ a general manager to execute the association's bylaws and administer the business of the corporation;

        (ii) does not require membership in the corporation by the owners of the property within the defined area; and

        (iii) was incorporated before January 1, 2006.

§ 552.0038. Public Retirement Systems Subject to Law

(a) In this section, "governing body of a public retirement system" and "public retirement system" have the meanings assigned those terms by Section 802.001.

(b) Except as provided by Subsections (c) through (i), the governing body of a public retirement system is subject to this chapter in the same manner as a governmental body.

(c) Records of individual members, annuitants, retirees, beneficiaries, alternate payees, program participants, or persons eligible for benefits from a retirement system under a retirement plan or program administered by the retirement system that are in the custody of the system or in the custody of an administering firm, a carrier, or another governmental agency, including the comptroller, acting in cooperation with or on behalf of the retirement system are confidential and not subject to public disclosure. The retirement system, administering firm, carrier, or governmental agency is not required to accept or comply with a request for a record or information about a record or to seek an opinion from the attorney general because the records are exempt from the provisions of this chapter, except as otherwise provided by this section.

(d) Records may be released to a member, annuitant, retiree, beneficiary, alternate payee, program participant, or person eligible for benefits from the retirement system or to an authorized attorney, family member, or representative acting on behalf of the member, annuitant, retiree, beneficiary, alternate payee, program participant, or person eligible for benefits. The retirement system may release the records to:

  (1) an administering firm, carrier, or agent or attorney acting on behalf of the retirement system;

  (2) another governmental entity having a legitimate need for the information to perform the purposes of the retirement system; or

  (3) a party in response to a subpoena issued under applicable law.

(e) A record released or received by the retirement system under this section may be transmitted electronically, including through the use of an electronic signature or certification in a form acceptable to the retirement system. An unintentional disclosure to, or unauthorized access by, a third party related to the transmission or receipt of information under this section is not a violation by the retirement system of any law, including a law or rule relating to the protection of confidential information.

(f) The records of an individual member, annuitant, retiree, beneficiary, alternate payee, program participant, or person eligible for benefits from the retirement system remain confidential after release to a person as authorized by this section. The records may become part of the public record of an administrative or judicial proceeding related to a contested case, and the member, annuitant, retiree, beneficiary, alternate payee, program participant, or person eligible for benefits waives the confidentiality of the records, including medical records, unless the records are closed to public access by a protective order issued under applicable law.

(g) The retirement system may require a person to provide the person's social security number as the system considers necessary to ensure the proper administration of all services, benefits, plans, and programs under the retirement system's administration, oversight, or participation or as otherwise required by state or federal law.

(h) The retirement system has sole discretion in determining whether a record is subject to this section. For purposes of this section, a record includes any identifying information about a person, living or deceased, who is or was a member, annuitant, retiree, beneficiary, alternate payee, program participant, or person eligible for benefits from the retirement system under any retirement plan or program administered by the retirement system.

(i) To the extent of a conflict between this section and any other law with respect to the confidential information held by a public retirement system or other entity described by

Subsection (c) concerning an individual member, annuitant, retiree, beneficiary, alternate payee, program participant, or person eligible for benefits from the retirement system, the prevailing provision is the provision that provides the greater substantive and procedural protection for the privacy of information concerning that individual member, annuitant, retiree, beneficiary, alternate payee, program participant, or person eligible for benefits.

§ 552.004. Preservation of Information

A governmental body or, for information of an elective county office, the elected county officer, may determine a time for which information that is not currently in use will be preserved, subject to any applicable rule or law governing the destruction and other disposition of state and local government records or public information.

§ 552.005. Effect of Chapter on Scope of Civil Discovery

(a) This chapter does not affect the scope of civil discovery under the Texas Rules of Civil Procedure.

(b) Exceptions from disclosure under this chapter do not create new privileges from discovery.

§ 552.0055. Subpoena Duces Tecum or Discovery Request

A subpoena duces tecum or a request for discovery that is issued in compliance with a statute or a rule of civil or criminal procedure is not considered to be a request for information under this chapter.

§ 552.006. Effect of Chapter on Withholding Public Information

This chapter does not authorize the withholding of public information or limit the availability of public information to the public, except as expressly provided by this chapter.

§ 552.007. Voluntary Disclosure of Certain Information When Disclosure Not Required

(a) This chapter does not prohibit a governmental body or its officer for public information from voluntarily making part or all of its information available to the public, unless the disclosure is expressly prohibited by law or the information is confidential under law.

(b) Public information made available under Subsection (a) must be made available to any person.

§ 552.008. Information for Legislative Purposes

(a) This chapter does not grant authority to withhold information from individual members, agencies, or committees of the legislature to use for legislative purposes.

(b) A governmental body on request by an individual member, agency, or committee of the legislature shall provide public information, including confidential information, to the requesting member, agency, or committee for inspection or duplication in accordance with this chapter if the requesting member, agency, or committee states that the public information is requested under this chapter for legislative purposes. A governmental body, by providing public information under this section that is confidential or otherwise excepted from required disclosure under law, does not waive or affect the confidentiality of the information for purposes of state or federal law or waive the right to assert exceptions to required disclosure of the information in the future. The governmental body may require the requesting individual member of the legislature, the requesting legislative agency or committee, or the members or employees of the requesting entity who will view or handle information that is received under this section and that is confidential under law to sign a confidentiality agreement that covers the information and requires that:

(1)   the information not be disclosed outside the requesting entity, or within the requesting entity for purposes other than the purpose for which it was received;

(2)   the information be labeled as confidential;

(3)   the information be kept securely; or

(4)   the number of copies made of the information or the notes taken from the information that implicate the confidential nature of the information be controlled, with all copies or notes that are not destroyed or returned to the governmental body remaining confidential and subject to the confidentiality agreement.

(b-1) A member, committee, or agency of the legislature required by a governmental body to sign a confidentiality agreement under Subsection (b) may seek a decision as provided by Subsection (b-2) about whether the information covered by the confidentiality agreement is confidential under law. A confidentiality agreement signed under Subsection (b) is void to the extent that the agreement covers information that is finally determined under Subsection (b-2) to not be confidential under law.

(b-2) The member, committee, or agency of the legislature may seek a decision from the attorney general about the matter. The attorney general by rule shall establish procedures and deadlines for receiving information necessary to decide the matter and briefs from the requestor, the governmental body, and any other interested person. The attorney general shall promptly render a decision requested under this subsection, determining whether the information covered by the confidentiality agreement is confidential under law, not later than the 45th business day after the date the attorney general received the request for a decision under this subsection. The attorney general shall issue a written decision on the matter and provide a copy of the decision to the requestor, the governmental body, and any interested person who submitted necessary information or a brief to the attorney general about the matter. The requestor or the governmental body may appeal a decision of the attorney general under this subsection to a Travis County district court. A person may appeal a decision of the attorney general under this subsection to a Travis County district court if the person claims a proprietary interest in the information affected by the decision or a privacy interest in the information that a confidentiality law or judicial decision is designed to protect.

(c)   This section does not affect:

(1)   the right of an individual member, agency, or committee of the legislature to obtain information from a governmental body under other law, including under the rules of either house of the legislature;

(2)   the procedures under which the information is obtained under other law; or

(3)   the use that may be made of the information obtained under other law.

§ 552.009.   Open Records Steering Committee: Advice to Attorney General; Electronic Availability of Public Information

(a)   The open records steering committee is composed of two representatives of the attorney general's office and:

(1)   a representative of each of the following, appointed by its governing entity:

(A)   the comptroller's office;

(B)   the Department of Public Safety;

(C)   the Department of Information Resources; and

(D)   the Texas State Library and Archives Commission;

(2)   five public members, appointed by the attorney general; and

(3)   a representative of each of the following types of local governments, appointed by the attorney general:

(A)   a municipality;

(B)   a county; and

(C)   a school district.

(b)   The representative of the attorney general designated by the attorney general is the presiding officer of the committee.   The committee shall meet as prescribed by committee procedures or at the call of the presiding officer.

(c)   The committee shall advise the attorney general regarding the office of the attorney general's performance of its duties under Sections 552.010, 552.205, 552.262, 552.269, and 552.274.

(d)   The members of the committee who represent state governmental bodies and the public members of the committee shall periodically study and determine the types of public information for which it would be useful to the public or cost-effective for the government if the type of information were made available by state governmental bodies by means of the

Internet or another electronic format. The committee shall report its findings and recommendations to the governor, the presiding officer of each house of the legislature, and the budget committee and state affairs committee of each house of the legislature.

(e) Chapter 2110 does not apply to the size, composition, or duration of the committee. Chapter 2110 applies to the reimbursement of a public member's expenses related to service on the committee. Any reimbursement of the expenses of a member who represents a state or local governmental body may be paid only from funds available to the state or local governmental body the member represents.

§ 552.010. State Governmental Bodies: Fiscal and Other Information Relating to Making Information Accessible

(a) Each state governmental body shall report to the attorney general the information the attorney general requires regarding:

(1) the number and nature of requests for information the state governmental body processes under this chapter in the period covered by the report; and

(2) the cost to the state governmental body in that period in terms of capital expenditures and personnel time of:

(A) responding to requests for information under this chapter; and

(B) making information available to the public by means of the Internet or another electronic format.

(b) The attorney general shall design and phase in the reporting requirements in a way that:

(1) minimizes the reporting burden on state governmental bodies; and

(2) allows the legislature and state governmental bodies to estimate the extent to which it is cost-effective for state government, and if possible the extent to which it is cost-effective or useful for members of the public, to make information available to the public by means of the Internet or another electronic format as a supplement or alternative to publicizing the information only in other ways or making the information available only in response to requests made under this chapter.

(c) The attorney general shall share the information reported under this section with the open records steering committee.

§ 552.011. Uniformity

The attorney general shall maintain uniformity in the application, operation, and interpretation of this chapter. To perform this duty, the attorney general may prepare, distribute, and publish any materials, including detailed and comprehensive written decisions and opinions, that relate to or are based on this chapter.

§ 552.012. Open Records Training

(a) This section applies to an elected or appointed public official who is:

   (1) a member of a multimember governmental body;

   (2) the governing officer of a governmental body that is headed by a single officer rather than by a multimember governing body; or

   (3) the officer for public information of a governmental body, without regard to whether the officer is elected or appointed to a specific term.

(b) Each public official shall complete a course of training of not less than one and not more than two hours regarding the responsibilities of the governmental body with which the official serves and its officers and employees under this chapter not later than the 90th day after the date the public official:

   (1) takes the oath of office, if the person is required to take an oath of office to assume the person's duties as a public official; or

   (2) otherwise assumes the person's duties as a public official, if the person is not required to take an oath of office to assume the person's duties.

(c) A public official may designate a public information coordinator to satisfy the training requirements of this section for the public official if the public information coordinator is primarily responsible for administering the responsibilities of the public official or governmental body under this chapter. Designation of a public information coordinator under this subsection does not relieve a public official from the duty to comply with any other requirement of this chapter that applies to the public official. The designated public information coordinator shall complete the training course regarding the responsibilities of the governmental body with which the coordinator serves and of its officers and employees under this chapter not later than the 90th day after the date the coordinator assumes the person's duties as coordinator.

(d) The attorney general shall ensure that the training is made available. The office of the attorney general may provide the training and may also approve any acceptable course of training offered by a governmental body or other entity. The attorney general shall ensure that at least one course of training approved or provided by the attorney general is available on videotape or a functionally similar and widely available medium at no cost. The training must include instruction in:

   (1) the general background of the legal requirements for open records and public information;

   (2) the applicability of this chapter to governmental bodies;

   (3) procedures and requirements regarding complying with a request for information under this chapter;

(4)   the role of the attorney general under this chapter; and

(5)   penalties and other consequences for failure to comply with this chapter.

(e)   The office of the attorney general or other entity providing the training shall provide a certificate of course completion to persons who complete the training required by this section. A governmental body shall maintain and make available for public inspection the record of its public officials' or, if applicable, the public information coordinator's completion of the training.

(f)   Completing the required training as a public official of the governmental body satisfies the requirements of this section with regard to the public official's service on a committee or subcommittee of the governmental body and the public official's ex officio service on any other governmental body.

(g)   The training required by this section may be used to satisfy any corresponding training requirements concerning this chapter or open records required by law for a public official or public information coordinator. The attorney general shall attempt to coordinate the training required by this section with training required by other law to the extent practicable.

(h)   A certificate of course completion is admissible as evidence in a criminal prosecution under this chapter. However, evidence that a defendant completed a course of training offered under this section is not prima facie evidence that the defendant knowingly violated this chapter.

SUBCHAPTER B. RIGHT OF ACCESS TO PUBLIC INFORMATION

§ 552.021.   Availability of Public Information

Public information is available to the public at a minimum during the normal business hours of the governmental body.

§ 552.0215.   Right of Access to Certain Information After 75 Years

(a)   Except as provided by Section 552.147, the confidentiality provisions of this chapter, or other law, information that is not confidential but is excepted from required disclosure under Subchapter C is public information and is available to the public on or after the 75th anniversary of the date the information was originally created or received by the governmental body.

(b)   This section does not limit the authority of a governmental body to establish retention periods for records under applicable law.

§ 552.022. Categories of Public Information; Examples

(a) Without limiting the amount or kind of information that is public information under this chapter, the following categories of information are public information and not excepted from required disclosure unless made confidential under this chapter or other law:

   (1) a completed report, audit, evaluation, or investigation made of, for, or by a governmental body, except as provided by Section 552.108;

   (2) the name, sex, ethnicity, salary, title, and dates of employment of each employee and officer of a governmental body;

   (3) information in an account, voucher, or contract relating to the receipt or expenditure of public or other funds by a governmental body;

   (4) the name of each official and the final record of voting on all proceedings in a governmental body;

   (5) all working papers, research material, and information used to estimate the need for or expenditure of public funds or taxes by a governmental body, on completion of the estimate;

   (6) the name, place of business, and the name of the municipality to which local sales and use taxes are credited, if any, for the named person, of a person reporting or paying sales and use taxes under Chapter 151, Tax Code;

   (7) a description of an agency's central and field organizations, including:

      (A) the established places at which the public may obtain information, submit information or requests, or obtain decisions;

      (B) the employees from whom the public may obtain information, submit information or requests, or obtain decisions;

      (C) in the case of a uniformed service, the members from whom the public may obtain information, submit information or requests, or obtain decisions; and

      (D) the methods by which the public may obtain information, submit information or requests, or obtain decisions;

   (8) a statement of the general course and method by which an agency's functions are channeled and determined, including the nature and requirements of all formal and informal policies and procedures;

   (9) a rule of procedure, a description of forms available or the places at which forms may be obtained, and instructions relating to the scope and content of all papers, reports, or examinations;

(10) a substantive rule of general applicability adopted or issued by an agency as authorized by law, and a statement of general policy or interpretation of general applicability formulated and adopted by an agency;

(11) each amendment, revision, or repeal of information described by Subdivisions (7)–(10);

(12) final opinions, including concurring and dissenting opinions, and orders issued in the adjudication of cases;

(13) a policy statement or interpretation that has been adopted or issued by an agency;

(14) administrative staff manuals and instructions to staff that affect a member of the public;

(15) information regarded as open to the public under an agency's policies;

(16) information that is in a bill for attorney's fees and that is not privileged under the attorney-client privilege;

(17) information that is also contained in a public court record; and

(18) a settlement agreement to which a governmental body is a party.

(b) A court in this state may not order a governmental body or an officer for public information to withhold from public inspection any category of public information described by Subsection (a) or to not produce the category of public information for inspection or duplication, unless the category of information is confidential under this chapter or other law.

§ 552.0221. Employee or Trustee of Public Employee Pension System

(a) Information concerning the employment of an employee of a public employee pension system is public information under the terms of this chapter, including information concerning the income, salary, benefits, and bonuses received from the pension system by the employee in the person's capacity as an employee of the system, and is not removed from the application of this chapter, made confidential, or otherwise excepted from the requirements of Section 552.021 by any statute intended to protect the records of persons as members, beneficiaries, or retirees of a public employee pension system in their capacity as such.

(b) Information concerning the service of a trustee of a public employee pension system is public information under the terms of this chapter, including information concerning the income, salary, benefits, and bonuses received from the pension system by the trustee in the person's capacity as a trustee of the system, and is not removed from the application of this chapter, made confidential, or otherwise excepted from the requirements of Section 552.021 by any statute intended to protect the records of persons as members, beneficiaries, or retirees of a public employee pension system in their capacity as such.

(c) Information subject to Subsections (a) and (b) must be released only to the extent the information is not excepted from required disclosure under this subchapter or Subchapter C.

(d)   For purposes of this section, "benefits" does not include pension benefits provided to an individual by a pension system under the statutory plan covering the individual as a member, beneficiary, or retiree of the pension system.

§ 552.0225. Right of Access to Investment Information

(a)   Under the fundamental philosophy of American government described by Section 552.001, it is the policy of this state that investments of government are investments of and for the people and the people are entitled to information regarding those investments. The provisions of this section shall be liberally construed to implement this policy.

(b)   The following categories of information held by a governmental body relating to its investments are public information and not excepted from disclosure under this chapter:

   (1)   the name of any fund or investment entity the governmental body is or has invested in;

   (2)   the date that a fund or investment entity described by Subdivision (1) was established;

   (3)   each date the governmental body invested in a fund or investment entity described by Subdivision (1);

   (4)   the amount of money, expressed in dollars, the governmental body has committed to a fund or investment entity;

   (5)   the amount of money, expressed in dollars, the governmental body is investing or has invested in any fund or investment entity;

   (6)   the total amount of money, expressed in dollars, the governmental body received from any fund or investment entity in connection with an investment;

   (7)   the internal rate of return or other standard used by a governmental body in connection with each fund or investment entity it is or has invested in and the date on which the return or other standard was calculated;

   (8)   the remaining value of any fund or investment entity the governmental body is or has invested in;

   (9)   the total amount of fees, including expenses, charges, and other compensation, assessed against the governmental body by, or paid by the governmental body to, any fund or investment entity or principal of any fund or investment entity in which the governmental body is or has invested;

   (10)   the names of the principals responsible for managing any fund or investment entity in which the governmental body is or has invested;

   (11)   each recusal filed by a member of the governing board in connection with a deliberation or action of the governmental body relating to an investment;

(12) a description of all of the types of businesses a governmental body is or has invested in through a fund or investment entity;

(13) the minutes and audio or video recordings of each open portion of a meeting of the governmental body at which an item described by this subsection was discussed;

(14) the governmental body's percentage ownership interest in a fund or investment entity the governmental body is or has invested in;

(15) any annual ethics disclosure report submitted to the governmental body by a fund or investment entity the governmental body is or has invested in; and

(16) the cash-on-cash return realized by the governmental body for a fund or investment entity the governmental body is or has invested in.

(c) This section does not apply to the Texas Mutual Insurance Company or a successor to the company.

(d) This section does not apply to a private investment fund's investment in restricted securities, as defined in Section 552.143.

§ 552.023. Special Right of Access to Confidential Information

(a) A person or a person's authorized representative has a special right of access, beyond the right of the general public, to information held by a governmental body that relates to the person and that is protected from public disclosure by laws intended to protect that person's privacy interests.

(b) A governmental body may not deny access to information to the person, or the person's representative, to whom the information relates on the grounds that the information is considered confidential by privacy principles under this chapter but may assert as grounds for denial of access other provisions of this chapter or other law that are not intended to protect the person's privacy interests.

(c) A release of information under Subsections (a) and (b) is not an offense under Section 552.352.

(d) A person who receives information under this section may disclose the information to others only to the extent consistent with the authorized purposes for which consent to release the information was obtained.

(e) Access to information under this section shall be provided in the manner prescribed by Sections 552.229 and 552.307.

§ 552.024. Electing to Disclose Address and Telephone Number

(a) Except as provided by Subsection (a-1), each employee or official of a governmental body and each former employee or official of a governmental body shall choose whether to allow public access to the information in the custody of the governmental body that relates to the person's home address, home telephone number, emergency contact information, or social security number, or that reveals whether the person has family members.

(a-1) A school district may not require an employee or former employee of the district to choose whether to allow public access to the employee's or former employee's social security number.

(b)   Each employee and official and each former employee and official shall state that person's choice under Subsection (a) to the main personnel officer of the governmental body in a signed writing not later than the 14th day after the date on which:

(1)   the employee begins employment with the governmental body;

(2)   the official is elected or appointed; or

(3)   the former employee or official ends service with the governmental body.

(c)   If the employee or official or former employee or official chooses not to allow public access to the information:

(1)   the information is protected under Subchapter C; and

(2)   the governmental body may redact the information from any information the governmental body discloses under Section 552.021 without the necessity of requesting a decision from the attorney general under Subchapter G.

(c-1) If, under Subsection (c)(2), a governmental body redacts or withholds information without requesting a decision from the attorney general about whether the information may be redacted or withheld, the requestor is entitled to seek a decision from the attorney general about the matter. The attorney general by rule shall establish procedures and deadlines for receiving information necessary to decide the matter and briefs from the requestor, the governmental body, and any other interested person. The attorney general shall promptly render a decision requested under this subsection, determining whether the redacted or withheld information was excepted from required disclosure to the requestor, not later than the 45th business day after the date the attorney general received the request for a decision under this subsection. The attorney general shall issue a written decision on the matter and provide a copy of the decision to the requestor, the governmental body, and any interested person who submitted necessary information or a brief to the attorney general about the matter. The requestor or the governmental body may appeal a decision of the attorney general under this subsection to a Travis County district court.

(c-2) A governmental body that redacts or withholds information under Subsection (c)(2) shall provide the following information to the requestor on a form prescribed by the attorney general:

(1)   a description of the redacted or withheld information;

(2)   a citation to this section; and

(3) instructions regarding how the requestor may seek a decision from the attorney general regarding whether the redacted or withheld information is excepted from required disclosure.

(d) If an employee or official or a former employee or official fails to state the person's choice within the period established by this section, the information is subject to public access.

(e) An employee or official or former employee or official of a governmental body who wishes to close or open public access to the information may request in writing that the main personnel officer of the governmental body close or open access.

(f) This section does not apply to a person to whom Section 552.1175 applies.

§ 552.025.   Tax Rulings and Opinions

(a) A governmental body with taxing authority that issues a written determination letter, technical advice memorandum, or ruling that concerns a tax matter shall index the letter, memorandum, or ruling by subject matter.

(b) On request, the governmental body shall make the index prepared under Subsection (a) and the document itself available to the public, subject to the provisions of this chapter.

(c) Subchapter C does not authorize withholding from the public or limiting the availability to the public of a written determination letter, technical advice memorandum, or ruling that concerns a tax matter and that is issued by a governmental body with taxing authority.

§ 552.026.   Education Records

This chapter does not require the release of information contained in education records of an educational agency or institution, except in conformity with the Family Educational Rights and Privacy Act of 1974, Sec. 513, Pub. L. No. 93-380, 20 U.S.C. Sec. 1232g.

§ 552.027.   Exception: Information Available Commercially; Resource Material

(a) A governmental body is not required under this chapter to allow the inspection of or to provide a copy of information in a commercial book or publication purchased or acquired by the governmental body for research purposes if the book or publication is commercially available to the public.

(b) Although information in a book or publication may be made available to the public as a resource material, such as a library book, a governmental body is not required to make a copy of the information in response to a request for public information.

(c) A governmental body shall allow the inspection of information in a book or publication that is made part of, incorporated into, or referred to in a rule or policy of a governmental body.

§ 552.028.   Request for Information from Incarcerated Individual

(a)   A governmental body is not required to accept or comply with a request for information from:

   (1)   an individual who is imprisoned or confined in a correctional facility; or

   (2)   an agent of that individual, other than that individual's attorney when the attorney is requesting information that is subject to disclosure under this chapter.

(b)   This section does not prohibit a governmental body from disclosing to an individual described by Subsection (a)(1), or that individual's agent, information held by the governmental body pertaining to that individual.

(c)   In this section, "correctional facility" means:

   (1)   a secure correctional facility, as defined by Section 1.07, Penal Code;

   (2)   a secure correctional facility and a secure detention facility, as defined by Section 51.02, Family Code; and

   (3)   a place designated by the law of this state, another state, or the federal government for the confinement of a person arrested for, charged with, or convicted of a criminal offense.

§ 552.029.   Right of Access to Certain Information Relating to Inmate of Department of Criminal Justice

Notwithstanding Section 508.313 or 552.134, the following information about an inmate who is confined in a facility operated by or under a contract with the Texas Department of Criminal Justice is subject to required disclosure under Section 552.021:

   (1)   the inmate's name, identification number, age, birthplace, department photograph, physical description, or general state of health or the nature of an injury to or critical illness suffered by the inmate;

   (2)   the inmate's assigned unit or the date on which the unit received the inmate, unless disclosure of the information would violate federal law relating to the confidentiality of substance abuse treatment;

   (3)   the offense for which the inmate was convicted or the judgment and sentence for that offense;

   (4)   the county and court in which the inmate was convicted;

   (5)   the inmate's earliest or latest possible release dates;

   (6)   the inmate's parole date or earliest possible parole date;

(7)   any prior confinement of the inmate by the Texas Department of Criminal Justice or its predecessor; or

(8)   basic information regarding the death of an inmate in custody, an incident involving the use of force, or an alleged crime involving the inmate.

SUBCHAPTER C. INFORMATION EXCEPTED FROM REQUIRED DISCLOSURE

§ 552.101.   Exception: Confidential Information

Information is excepted from the requirements of Section 552.021 if it is information considered to be confidential by law, either constitutional, statutory, or by judicial decision.

§ 552.102.   Exception: Confidentiality of Certain Personnel Information

(a)   Information is excepted from the requirements of Section 552.021 if it is information in a personnel file, the disclosure of which would constitute a clearly unwarranted invasion of personal privacy, except that all information in the personnel file of an employee of a governmental body is to be made available to that employee or the employee's designated representative as public information is made available under this chapter. The exception to public disclosure created by this subsection is in addition to any exception created by Section 552.024. Public access to personnel information covered by Section 552.024 is denied to the extent provided by that section.

(b)   Information is excepted from the requirements of Section 552.021 if it is a transcript from an institution of higher education maintained in the personnel file of a professional public school employee, except that this section does not exempt from disclosure the degree obtained or the curriculum on a transcript in the personnel file of the employee.

§ 552.103.   Exception: Litigation or Settlement Negotiations Involving the State or a Political Subdivision

(a)   Information is excepted from the requirements of Section 552.021 if it is information relating to litigation of a civil or criminal nature to which the state or a political subdivision is or may be a party or to which an officer or employee of the state or a political subdivision, as a consequence of the person's office or employment, is or may be a party.

(b)   For purposes of this section, the state or a political subdivision is considered to be a party to litigation of a criminal nature until the applicable statute of limitations has expired or until the defendant has exhausted all appellate and postconviction remedies in state and federal court.

(c)   Information relating to litigation involving a governmental body or an officer or employee of a governmental body is excepted from disclosure under Subsection (a) only if the litigation is pending or reasonably anticipated on the date that the requestor applies to the officer for public information for access to or duplication of the information.

§ 552.104. Exception: Information Related to Competition or Bidding

(a) Information is excepted from the requirements of Section 552.021 if it is information that, if released, would give advantage to a competitor or bidder.

(b) The requirement of Section 552.022 that a category of information listed under Section 552.022(a) is public information and not excepted from required disclosure under this chapter unless expressly confidential under law does not apply to information that is excepted from required disclosure under this section.

§ 552.105. Exception: Information Related to Location or Price of Property

Information is excepted from the requirements of Section 552.021 if it is information relating to:

(1) the location of real or personal property for a public purpose prior to public announcement of the project; or

(2) appraisals or purchase price of real or personal property for a public purpose prior to the formal award of contracts for the property.

§ 552.106. Exception: Certain Legislative Documents

(a) A draft or working paper involved in the preparation of proposed legislation is excepted from the requirements of Section 552.021.

(b) An internal bill analysis or working paper prepared by the governor's office for the purpose of evaluating proposed legislation is excepted from the requirements of Section 552.021.

§ 552.107. Exception: Certain Legal Matters

Information is excepted from the requirements of Section 552.021 if:

(1) it is information that the attorney general or an attorney of a political subdivision is prohibited from disclosing because of a duty to the client under the Texas Rules of Evidence or the Texas Disciplinary Rules of Professional Conduct; or

(2) a court by order has prohibited disclosure of the information.

§ 552.108. Exception: Certain Law Enforcement, Corrections, and Prosecutorial Information

(a) Information held by a law enforcement agency or prosecutor that deals with the detection, investigation, or prosecution of crime is excepted from the requirements of Section 552.021 if:

(1) release of the information would interfere with the detection, investigation, or prosecution of crime;

(2) it is information that deals with the detection, investigation, or prosecution of crime only in relation to an investigation that did not result in conviction or deferred adjudication;

(3) it is information relating to a threat against a peace officer or detention officer collected or disseminated under Section 411.048; or

(4) it is information that:

(A) is prepared by an attorney representing the state in anticipation of or in the course of preparing for criminal litigation; or

(B) reflects the mental impressions or legal reasoning of an attorney representing the state.

(b) An internal record or notation of a law enforcement agency or prosecutor that is maintained for internal use in matters relating to law enforcement or prosecution is excepted from the requirements of Section 552.021 if:

(1) release of the internal record or notation would interfere with law enforcement or prosecution;

(2) the internal record or notation relates to law enforcement only in relation to an investigation that did not result in conviction or deferred adjudication; or

(3) the internal record or notation:

(A) is prepared by an attorney representing the state in anticipation of or in the course of preparing for criminal litigation; or

(B) reflects the mental impressions or legal reasoning of an attorney representing the state.

(c) This section does not except from the requirements of Section 552.021 information that is basic information about an arrested person, an arrest, or a crime.

§ 552.1081. Exception: Confidentiality of Certain Information Regarding Execution of Convict

Information is excepted from the requirements of Section 552.021 if it contains identifying information under Article 43.14, Code of Criminal Procedure, including that of:

(1) any person who participates in an execution procedure, including a person who uses, supplies, or administers a substance during the execution; and

(2) any person or entity that manufactures, transports, tests, procures, compounds, prescribes, dispenses, or provides a substance or supplies used in an execution.

§ 552.1085. Confidentiality of Sensitive Crime Scene Image

(a)   In this section:

    (1)   "Deceased person's next of kin" means:

        (A)   the surviving spouse of the deceased person;

        (B)   if there is no surviving spouse of the deceased, an adult child of the deceased person; or

        (C)   if there is no surviving spouse or adult child of the deceased, a parent of the deceased person.

    (2)   "Defendant" means a person being prosecuted for the death of the deceased person or a person convicted of an offense in relation to that death and appealing that conviction.

    (3)   "Expressive work" means:

        (A)   a fictional or nonfictional entertainment, dramatic, literary, or musical work that is a play, book, article, musical composition, audiovisual work, radio or television program, work of art, or work of political, educational, or newsworthy value;

        (B)   a work the primary function of which is the delivery of news, information, current events, or other matters of public interest or concern; or

        (C)   an advertisement or commercial announcement of a work described by Paragraph (A) or (B).

    (4)   "Local governmental entity" means a county, municipality, school district, charter school, junior college district, or other political subdivision of this state.

    (5)   "Public or private institution of higher education" means:

        (A)   an institution of higher education, as defined by Section 61.003, Education Code; or

        (B)   a private or independent institution of higher education, as defined by Section 61.003, Education Code.

    (6)   "Sensitive crime scene image" means a photograph or video recording taken at a crime scene, contained in or part of a closed criminal case, that depicts a deceased person in a state of dismemberment, decapitation, or similar mutilation or that depicts the deceased person's genitalia.

    (7)   "State agency" means a department, commission, board, office, or other agency that is a part of state government and that is created by the constitution or a statute of this state.

The term includes an institution of higher education as defined by Section 61.003, Education Code.

(b) For purposes of this section, an Internet website, the primary function of which is not the delivery of news, information, current events, or other matters of public interest or concern, is not an expressive work.

(c) A sensitive crime scene image in the custody of a governmental body is confidential and excepted from the requirements of Section 552.021 and a governmental body may not permit a person to view or copy the image except as provided by this section. This section applies to any sensitive crime scene image regardless of the date that the image was taken or recorded.

(d) Notwithstanding Subsection (c) and subject to Subsection (e), the following persons may view or copy information that constitutes a sensitive crime scene image from a governmental body:

   (1) the deceased person's next of kin;

   (2) a person authorized in writing by the deceased person's next of kin;

   (3) a defendant or the defendant's attorney;

   (4) a person who establishes to the governmental body an interest in a sensitive crime scene image that is based on, connected with, or in support of the creation, in any medium, of an expressive work;

   (5) a person performing bona fide research sponsored by a public or private institution of higher education with approval of a supervisor of the research or a supervising faculty member;

   (6) a state agency;

   (7) an agency of the federal government; or

   (8) a local governmental entity.

(e) This section does not prohibit a governmental body from asserting an exception to disclosure of a sensitive crime scene image to a person identified in Subsection (d) on the grounds that the image is excepted from the requirements of Section 552.021 under another provision of this chapter or another law.

(f) Not later than the 10th business day after the date a governmental body receives a request for a sensitive crime scene image from a person described by Subsection (d)(4) or (5), the governmental body shall notify the deceased person's next of kin of the request in writing. The notice must be sent to the next of kin's last known address.

(g) A governmental body that receives a request for information that constitutes a sensitive crime scene image shall allow a person described in Subsection (d) to view or copy the image not later than the 10th business day after the date the governmental body receives the request unless the governmental body files a request for an attorney general decision under Subchapter G regarding whether an exception to public disclosure applies to the information.

§ 552.109. Exception: Confidentiality of Certain Private Communications of an Elected Office Holder

Private correspondence or communications of an elected office holder relating to matters the disclosure of which would constitute an invasion of privacy are excepted from the requirements of Section 552.021.

§ 552.110. Exception: Confidentiality of Trade Secrets; Confidentiality of Certain Commercial or Financial Information

(a) A trade secret obtained from a person and privileged or confidential by statute or judicial decision is excepted from the requirements of Section 552.021.

(b) Commercial or financial information for which it is demonstrated based on specific factual evidence that disclosure would cause substantial competitive harm to the person from whom the information was obtained is excepted from the requirements of Section 552.021.

§ 552.111. Exception: Agency Memoranda

An interagency or intraagency memorandum or letter that would not be available by law to a party in litigation with the agency is excepted from the requirements of Section 552.021.

§ 552.112. Exception: Certain Information Relating to Regulation of Financial Institutions or Securities

(a) Information is excepted from the requirements of Section 552.021 if it is information contained in or relating to examination, operating, or condition reports prepared by or for an agency responsible for the regulation or supervision of financial institutions or securities, or both.

(b) In this section, "securities" has the meaning assigned by The Securities Act (Article 581-1 et seq., Vernon's Texas Civil Statutes).

(c) Information is excepted from the requirements of Section 552.021 if it is information submitted by an individual or other entity to the Texas Legislative Council, or to any state agency or department overseen by the Finance Commission of Texas and the information has been or will be sent to the Texas Legislative Council, for the purpose of performing a statistical or demographic analysis of information subject to Section 323.020. However, this subsection does not except from the requirements of Section 552.021 information that does not identify or tend to identify an individual or other entity and that is subject to required public disclosure under Section 323.020(e).

§ 552.113. Exception: Confidentiality of Geological or Geophysical Information

(a)   Information is excepted from the requirements of Section 552.021 if it is:

    (1)   an electric log confidential under Subchapter M, Chapter 91, Natural Resources Code;

    (2)   geological or geophysical information or data, including maps concerning wells, except information filed in connection with an application or proceeding before an agency; or

    (3)   confidential under Subsections (c) through (f).

(b)   Information that is shown to or examined by an employee of the General Land Office, but not retained in the land office, is not considered to be filed with the land office.

(c)   In this section:

    (1)   "Confidential material" includes all well logs, geological, geophysical, geochemical, and other similar data, including maps and other interpretations of the material filed in the General Land Office:

        (A)   in connection with any administrative application or proceeding before the land commissioner, the school land board, any board for lease, or the commissioner's or board's staff; or

        (B)   in compliance with the requirements of any law, rule, lease, or agreement.

    (2)   "Electric logs" has the same meaning as it has in Chapter 91, Natural Resources Code.

    (3)   "Administrative applications" and "administrative proceedings" include applications for pooling or unitization, review of shut-in royalty payments, review of leases or other agreements to determine their validity, review of any plan of operations, review of the obligation to drill offset wells, or an application to pay compensatory royalty.

(d)   Confidential material, except electric logs, filed in the General Land Office on or after September 1, 1985, is public information and is available to the public under Section 552.021 on and after the later of:

    (1)   five years from the filing date of the confidential material; or

    (2)   one year from the expiration, termination, or forfeiture of the lease in connection with which the confidential material was filed.

(e)   Electric logs filed in the General Land Office on or after September 1, 1985, are either public information or confidential material to the same extent and for the same periods provided for the same logs by Chapter 91, Natural Resources Code. A person may request that an electric log that has been filed in the General Land Office be made confidential by filing with the land office a copy of the written request for confidentiality made to the Railroad Commission of Texas for the same log.

(f)   The following are public information:

(1)   electric logs filed in the General Land Office before September 1, 1985; and

(2)   confidential material, except electric logs, filed in the General Land Office before September 1, 1985, provided, that Subsection (d) governs the disclosure of that confidential material filed in connection with a lease that is a valid and subsisting lease on September 1, 1995.

(g)   Confidential material may be disclosed at any time if the person filing the material, or the person's successor in interest in the lease in connection with which the confidential material was filed, consents in writing to its release. A party consenting to the disclosure of confidential material may restrict the manner of disclosure and the person or persons to whom the disclosure may be made.

(h)   Notwithstanding the confidential nature of the material described in this section, the material may be used by the General Land Office in the enforcement, by administrative proceeding or litigation, of the laws governing the sale and lease of public lands and minerals, the regulations of the land office, the school land board, or of any board for lease, or the terms of any lease, pooling or unitization agreement, or any other agreement or grant.

(i)   An administrative hearings officer may order that confidential material introduced in an administrative proceeding remain confidential until the proceeding is finally concluded, or for the period provided in Subsection (d), whichever is later.

(j)   Confidential material examined by an administrative hearings officer during the course of an administrative proceeding for the purpose of determining its admissibility as evidence shall not be considered to have been filed in the General Land Office to the extent that the confidential material is not introduced into evidence at the proceeding.

(k)   This section does not prevent a person from asserting that any confidential material is exempt from disclosure as a trade secret or commercial information under Section 552.110 or under any other basis permitted by law.

§ 552.114.   Exception: Confidentiality of Student Records

(a)   In this section, "student record" means:

(1)   information that constitutes education records as that term is defined by the Family Educational Rights and Privacy Act of 1974 (20 U.S.C. Section 1232g(a)(4)); or

(2)   information in a record of an applicant for admission to an educational institution, including a transfer applicant.

(b)   Information is confidential and excepted from the requirements of Section 552.021 if it is information in a student record at an educational institution funded wholly or partly by state revenue. This subsection does not prohibit the disclosure or provision of information included in an education record if the disclosure or provision is authorized by 20 U.S.C. Section 1232g or other federal law.

(c)   A record covered by Subsection (b) shall be made available on the request of:

    (1)   educational institution personnel;

    (2)   the student involved or the student's parent, legal guardian, or spouse; or

    (3)   a person conducting a child abuse investigation required by Subchapter D, Chapter 261, Family Code.

(d)   Except as provided by Subsection (e), an educational institution may redact information covered under Subsection (b) from information disclosed under Section 552.021 without requesting a decision from the attorney general.

(e)   If an applicant for admission to an educational institution described by Subsection (b) or a parent or legal guardian of a minor applicant to an educational institution described by Subsection (b) requests information in the record of the applicant, the educational institution shall disclose any information that:

    (1)   is related to the applicant's application for admission; and

    (2)   was provided to the educational institution by the applicant.

§ 552.115.   Exception: Confidentiality of Birth and Death Records

(a)   A birth or death record maintained by the vital statistics unit of the Department of State Health Services or a local registration official is excepted from the requirements of Section 552.021, except that:

    (1)   a birth record is public information and available to the public on and after the 75th anniversary of the date of birth as shown on the record filed with the vital statistics unit or local registration official;

    (2)   a death record is public information and available to the public on and after the 25th anniversary of the date of death as shown on the record filed with the vital statistics unit or local registration official, except that if the decedent is unidentified, the death record is public information and available to the public on and after the first anniversary of the date of death;

    (3)   a general birth index or a general death index established or maintained by the vital statistics unit or a local registration official is public information and available to the public to the extent the index relates to a birth record or death record that is public information and available to the public under Subdivision (1) or (2);

(4)   a summary birth index or a summary death index prepared or maintained by the vital statistics unit or a local registration official is public information and available to the public; and

(5)   a birth or death record is available to the chief executive officer of a home-rule municipality or the officer's designee if:

    (A)   the record is used only to identify a property owner or other person to whom the municipality is required to give notice when enforcing a state statute or an ordinance;

    (B)   the municipality has exercised due diligence in the manner described by Section 54.035(e), Local Government Code, to identify the person; and

    (C)   the officer or designee signs a confidentiality agreement that requires that:

        (i)   the information not be disclosed outside the office of the officer or designee, or within the office for a purpose other than the purpose described by Paragraph (A);

        (ii)   the information be labeled as confidential;

        (iii)   the information be kept securely; and

        (iv)   the number of copies made of the information or the notes taken from the information that implicate the confidential nature of the information be controlled, with all copies or notes that are not destroyed or returned remaining confidential and subject to the confidentiality agreement.

(b)   Notwithstanding Subsection (a), a general birth index or a summary birth index is not public information and is not available to the public if:

(1)   the fact of an adoption or paternity determination can be revealed by the index; or

(2)   the index contains specific identifying information relating to the parents of a child who is the subject of an adoption placement.

(c)   Subsection (a)(1) does not apply to the microfilming agreement entered into by the Genealogical Society of Utah, a nonprofit corporation organized under the laws of the State of Utah, and the Archives and Information Services Division of the Texas State Library and Archives Commission.

(d)   For the purposes of fulfilling the terms of the agreement in Subsection (c), the Genealogical Society of Utah shall have access to birth records on and after the 50th anniversary of the date of birth as shown on the record filed with the bureau of vital statistics or local registration official, but such birth records shall not be made available to the public until the 75th anniversary of the date of birth as shown on the record.

§ 552.116.   Exception: Audit Working Papers

(a) An audit working paper of an audit of the state auditor or the auditor of a state agency, an institution of higher education as defined by Section 61.003, Education Code, a county, a municipality, a school district, a hospital district, or a joint board operating under Section 22.074, Transportation Code, including any audit relating to the criminal history background check of a public school employee, is excepted from the requirements of Section 552.021. If information in an audit working paper is also maintained in another record, that other record is not excepted from the requirements of Section 552.021 by this section.

(b) In this section:

(1)   "Audit" means an audit authorized or required by a statute of this state or the United States, the charter or an ordinance of a municipality, an order of the commissioners court of a county, the bylaws adopted by or other action of the governing board of a hospital district, a resolution or other action of a board of trustees of a school district, including an audit by the district relating to the criminal history background check of a public school employee, or a resolution or other action of a joint board described by Subsection (a) and includes an investigation.

(2)   "Audit working paper" includes all information, documentary or otherwise, prepared or maintained in conducting an audit or preparing an audit report, including:

(A)   intra-agency and interagency communications; and

(B)   drafts of the audit report or portions of those drafts.

§ 552.117.   Exception: Confidentiality of Certain Addresses, Telephone Numbers, Social Security Numbers, and Personal Family Information

(a) Information is excepted from the requirements of Section 552.021 if it is information that relates to the home address, home telephone number, emergency contact information, or social security number of the following person or that reveals whether the person has family members:

(1)   a current or former official or employee of a governmental body, except as otherwise provided by Section 552.024;

(2)   a peace officer as defined by Article 2.12, Code of Criminal Procedure, or a security officer commissioned under Section 51.212, Education Code, regardless of whether the officer complies with Section 552.024 or 552.1175, as applicable;

(3)   a current or former employee of the Texas Department of Criminal Justice or of the predecessor in function of the department or any division of the department, regardless of whether the current or former employee complies with Section 552.1175;

(4)   a peace officer as defined by Article 2.12, Code of Criminal Procedure, or other law, a reserve law enforcement officer, a commissioned deputy game warden, or a corrections

officer in a municipal, county, or state penal institution in this state who was killed in the line of duty, regardless of whether the deceased complied with Section 552.024 or 552.1175;

(5) a commissioned security officer as defined by Section 1702.002, Occupations Code, regardless of whether the officer complies with Section 552.024 or 552.1175, as applicable;

(6) an officer or employee of a community supervision and corrections department established under Chapter 76 who performs a duty described by Section 76.004(b), regardless of whether the officer or employee complies with Section 552.024 or 552.1175;

(7) a current or former employee of the office of the attorney general who is or was assigned to a division of that office the duties of which involve law enforcement, regardless of whether the current or former employee complies with Section 552.024 or 552.1175;

(8) a current or former employee of the Texas Juvenile Justice Department or of the predecessors in function of the department, regardless of whether the current or former employee complies with Section 552.024 or 552.1175;

(9) a current or former juvenile probation or supervision officer certified by the Texas Juvenile Justice Department, or the predecessors in function of the department, under Title 12, Human Resources Code, regardless of whether the current or former officer complies with Section 552.024 or 552.1175;

(10) a current or former employee of a juvenile justice program or facility, as those terms are defined by Section 261.405, Family Code, regardless of whether the current or former employee complies with Section 552.024 or 552.1175;

(11) a current or former member of the Texas military forces, as that term is defined by Section 437.001;

Text of (a)(12), as added by Acts 2017, 85th Leg., ch. 34 (S.B. 1576), § 12

(12) a current or former employee of the Texas Civil Commitment Office or the predecessor in function of the office or a division of the office, regardless of whether the current or former employee complies with Section 552.024 or 552.1175.

Text of (a)(12), as added by Acts 2017, 85th Leg., ch. 190 (S.B. 42), § 17

(12) a current or former federal judge or state judge, as those terms are defined by Section 13.0021(a), Election Code, or a spouse of a current or former federal judge or state judge; or

Text of (a)(12), as added by Acts 2017, 85th Leg., ch. 1006 (H.B. 1278), § 1

(12) a current or former district attorney, criminal district attorney, or county or municipal attorney whose jurisdiction includes any criminal law or child protective services matters,

regardless of whether the current or former attorney complies with Section 552.024 or 552.1175; or

Text of (a)(13), as added by Acts 2017, 85th Leg., ch. 190 (S.B. 42), § 17

(13) a current or former district attorney, criminal district attorney or county attorney whose jurisdiction includes any criminal law or child protective services matter.

Text of (a)(13), as added by Acts 2017, 85th Leg., ch. 1006 (H.B. 1278), § 1

(13) a current or former employee of a district attorney, criminal district attorney, or county or municipal attorney whose jurisdiction includes any criminal law or child protective services matters, regardless of whether the current or former employee complies with Section 552.024 or 552.1175.

(b) All documents filed with a county clerk and all documents filed with a district clerk are exempt from this section.

§ 552.1175. Confidentiality of Certain Personal Information of Peace Officers, County Jailers, Security Officers, Employees of Certain State Agencies or Certain Criminal or Juvenile Justice Agencies or Offices, and Federal and State Judges

(a) This section applies only to:

(1) peace officers as defined by Article 2.12, Code of Criminal Procedure;

(2) county jailers as defined by Section 1701.001, Occupations Code;

(3) current or former employees of the Texas Department of Criminal Justice or of the predecessor in function of the department or any division of the department;

(4) commissioned security officers as defined by Section 1702.002, Occupations Code;

(5) a current or former district attorney, criminal district attorney, or county or municipal attorney whose jurisdiction includes any criminal law or child protective services matters;

(5-a) a current or former employee of a district attorney, criminal district attorney, or county or municipal attorney whose jurisdiction includes any criminal law or child protective services matters;

(6) officers and employees of a community supervision and corrections department established under Chapter 76 who perform a duty described by Section 76.004(b);

(7) criminal investigators of the United States as described by Article 2.122(a), Code of Criminal Procedure;

(8) police officers and inspectors of the United States Federal Protective Service;

(9) current and former employees of the office of the attorney general who are or were assigned to a division of that office the duties of which involve law enforcement;

(10) current or former juvenile probation and detention officers certified by the Texas Juvenile Justice Department, or the predecessors in function of the department, under Title 12, Human Resources Code;

(11) current or former employees of a juvenile justice program or facility, as those terms are defined by Section 261.405, Family Code;

(12) current or former employees of the Texas Juvenile Justice Department or the predecessors in function of the department;

(13) federal judges and state judges as defined by Section 13.0021, Election Code; and

(14) current or former employees of the Texas Civil Commitment Office or of the predecessor in function of the office or a division of the office.

(b) Information that relates to the home address, home telephone number, emergency contact information, date of birth, or social security number of an individual to whom this section applies, or that reveals whether the individual has family members is confidential and may not be disclosed to the public under this chapter if the individual to whom the information relates:

(1) chooses to restrict public access to the information; and

(2) notifies the governmental body of the individual's choice on a form provided by the governmental body, accompanied by evidence of the individual's status.

(c) A choice made under Subsection (b) remains valid until rescinded in writing by the individual.

(d) This section does not apply to information in the tax appraisal records of an appraisal district to which Section 25.025, Tax Code, applies.

(e) All documents filed with a county clerk and all documents filed with a district clerk are exempt from this section.

(f) A governmental body may redact information that must be withheld under Subsection (b) from any information the governmental body discloses under Section 552.021 without the necessity of requesting a decision from the attorney general under Subchapter G.

(g) If, under Subsection (f), a governmental body redacts or withholds information without requesting a decision from the attorney general about whether the information may be redacted or withheld, the requestor is entitled to seek a decision from the attorney general about the matter. The attorney general by rule shall establish procedures and deadlines for receiving information necessary to decide the matter and briefs from the requestor, the governmental body, and any other interested person. The attorney general shall promptly render a decision requested under this subsection, determining whether the redacted or withheld information was excepted from required disclosure to the requestor, not later than the 45th business day after the date the attorney general received the request for a decision under this subsection. The attorney general shall issue a written decision on the matter and provide a copy of the decision to the requestor, the governmental body, and any interested person who submitted necessary information or a brief to the attorney general about the matter. The requestor or the governmental body may appeal a decision of the attorney general under this subsection to a Travis County district court.

(h) A governmental body that redacts or withholds information under Subsection (f) shall provide the following information to the requestor on a form prescribed by the attorney general:

    (1)   a description of the redacted or withheld information;

    (2)   a citation to this section; and

    (3)   instructions regarding how the requestor may seek a decision from the attorney general regarding whether the redacted or withheld information is excepted from required disclosure.

§ 552.1176. Confidentiality of Certain Information Maintained by State Bar

(a) Information that relates to the home address, home telephone number, electronic mail address, social security number, or date of birth of a person licensed to practice law in this state that is maintained under Chapter 81 is confidential and may not be disclosed to the public under this chapter if the person to whom the information relates:

    (1)   chooses to restrict public access to the information; and

    (2)   notifies the State Bar of Texas of the person's choice, in writing or electronically, on a form provided by the state bar.

(b) A choice made under Subsection (a) remains valid until rescinded in writing or electronically by the person.

(c) All documents filed with a county clerk and all documents filed with a district clerk are exempt from this section.

§ 552.118. Exception: Confidentiality of Official Prescription Program Information

Information is excepted from the requirements of Section 552.021 if it is:

    (1)   information on or derived from an official prescription form or electronic prescription record filed with the Texas State Board of Pharmacy under Section 481.075, Health and Safety Code; or

    (2)   other information collected under Section 481.075 of that code.

§ 552.119. Exception: Confidentiality of Certain Photographs of Peace Officers

(a) A photograph that depicts a peace officer as defined by Article 2.12, Code of Criminal Procedure, the release of which would endanger the life or physical safety of the officer, is excepted from the requirements of Section 552.021 unless:

    (1) the officer is under indictment or charged with an offense by information;

    (2) the officer is a party in a civil service hearing or a case in arbitration; or

    (3) the photograph is introduced as evidence in a judicial proceeding.

(b) A photograph excepted from disclosure under Subsection (a) may be made public only if the peace officer gives written consent to the disclosure.

§ 552.120. Exception: Confidentiality of Certain Rare Books and Original Manuscripts

A rare book or original manuscript that was not created or maintained in the conduct of official business of a governmental body and that is held by a private or public archival and manuscript repository for the purpose of historical research is excepted from the requirements of Section 552.021.

§ 552.121. Exception: Confidentiality of Certain Documents Held for Historical Research

An oral history interview, personal paper, unpublished letter, or organizational record of a nongovernmental entity that was not created or maintained in the conduct of official business of a governmental body and that is held by a private or public archival and manuscript repository for the purpose of historical research is excepted from the requirements of Section 552.021 to the extent that the archival and manuscript repository and the donor of the interview, paper, letter, or record agree to limit disclosure of the item.

§ 552.122. Exception: Test Items

(a) A test item developed by an educational institution that is funded wholly or in part by state revenue is excepted from the requirements of Section 552.021.

(b) A test item developed by a licensing agency or governmental body is excepted from the requirements of Section 552.021.

§ 552.123. Exception: Confidentiality of Name of Applicant for Chief Executive Officer of Institution of Higher Education

The name of an applicant for the position of chief executive officer of an institution of higher education, and other information that would tend to identify the applicant, is excepted from the requirements of Section 552.021, except that the governing body of the institution must give public notice of the name or names of the finalists being considered for the position at least 21 days before the date of the meeting at which final action or vote is to be taken on the employment of the person.

§ 552.1235. Exception: Confidentiality of Identity of Private Donor to Institution of Higher Education

(a) The name or other information that would tend to disclose the identity of a person, other than a governmental body, who makes a gift, grant, or donation of money or property to an institution of higher education or to another person with the intent that the money or property be transferred to an institution of higher education is excepted from the requirements of Section 552.021.

(b) Subsection (a) does not except from required disclosure other information relating to gifts, grants, and donations described by Subsection (a), including the amount or value of an individual gift, grant, or donation.

(c) In this section, "institution of higher education" has the meaning assigned by Section 61.003, Education Code.

§ 552.124. Exception: Confidentiality of Records of Library or Library System

(a) A record of a library or library system, supported in whole or in part by public funds, that identifies or serves to identify a person who requested, obtained, or used a library material or service is excepted from the requirements of Section 552.021 unless the record is disclosed:

   (1)   because the library or library system determines that disclosure is reasonably necessary for the operation of the library or library system and the record is not confidential under other state or federal law;

   (2)   under Section 552.023; or

   (3)   to a law enforcement agency or a prosecutor under a court order or subpoena obtained after a showing to a district court that:

      (A) disclosure of the record is necessary to protect the public safety; or

      (B) the record is evidence of an offense or constitutes evidence that a particular person committed an offense.

(b) A record of a library or library system that is excepted from required disclosure under this section is confidential.

§ 552.125. Exception: Certain Audits

Any documents or information privileged under Chapter 1101, Health and Safety Code, are excepted from the requirements of Section 552.021.

§ 552.126. Exception: Confidentiality of Name of Applicant for Superintendent of Public School District

The name of an applicant for the position of superintendent of a public school district is excepted from the requirements of Section 552.021, except that the board of trustees must give public notice of the name or names of the finalists being considered for the position at least 21 days before the date of the meeting at which a final action or vote is to be taken on the employment of the person.

§ 552.127. Exception: Confidentiality of Personal Information Relating to Participants in Neighborhood Crime Watch Organization

(a) Information is excepted from the requirements of Section 552.021 if the information identifies a person as a participant in a neighborhood crime watch organization and relates to the name, home address, business address, home telephone number, or business telephone number of the person.

(b) In this section, "neighborhood crime watch organization" means a group of residents of a neighborhood or part of a neighborhood that is formed in affiliation or association with a law enforcement agency in this state to observe activities within the neighborhood or part of a neighborhood and to take other actions intended to reduce crime in that area.

§ 552.128. Exception: Confidentiality of Certain Information Submitted by Potential Vendor or Contractor

(a) Information submitted by a potential vendor or contractor to a governmental body in connection with an application for certification as a historically underutilized or disadvantaged business under a local, state, or federal certification program is excepted from the requirements of Section 552.021, except as provided by this section.

(b) Notwithstanding Section 552.007 and except as provided by Subsection (c), the information may be disclosed only:

    (1) to a state or local governmental entity in this state, and the state or local governmental entity may use the information only:

        (A) for purposes related to verifying an applicant's status as a historically underutilized or disadvantaged business; or

        (B) for the purpose of conducting a study of a public purchasing program established under state law for historically underutilized or disadvantaged businesses; or

    (2) with the express written permission of the applicant or the applicant's agent.

(c) Information submitted by a vendor or contractor or a potential vendor or contractor to a governmental body in connection with a specific proposed contractual relationship, a specific contract, or an application to be placed on a bidders list, including information that may also have been submitted in connection with an application for certification as a historically underutilized or disadvantaged business, is subject to required disclosure, excepted from required disclosure, or confidential in accordance with other law.

§ 552.129.   Confidentiality of Certain Motor Vehicle Inspection Information

A record created during a motor vehicle emissions inspection under Subchapter F, Chapter 548, Transportation Code, that relates to an individual vehicle or owner of an individual vehicle is excepted from the requirements of Section 552.021.

§ 552.130.   Exception: Confidentiality of Certain Motor Vehicle Records

(a) Information is excepted from the requirements of Section 552.021 if the information relates to:

   (1)   a motor vehicle operator's or driver's license or permit issued by an agency of this state or another state or country;

   (2)   a motor vehicle title or registration issued by an agency of this state or another state or country; or

   (3)   a personal identification document issued by an agency of this state or another state or country or a local agency authorized to issue an identification document.

(b) Information described by Subsection (a) may be released only if, and in the manner, authorized by Chapter 730, Transportation Code.

(c) Subject to Chapter 730, Transportation Code, a governmental body may redact information described by Subsection (a) from any information the governmental body discloses under Section 552.021 without the necessity of requesting a decision from the attorney general under Subchapter G.

(d) If, under Subsection (c), a governmental body redacts or withholds information without requesting a decision from the attorney general about whether the information may be redacted or withheld, the requestor is entitled to seek a decision from the attorney general about the matter. The attorney general by rule shall establish procedures and deadlines for receiving information necessary to decide the matter and briefs from the requestor, the governmental body, and any other interested person. The attorney general shall promptly render a decision requested under this subsection, determining whether the redacted or withheld information was excepted from required disclosure to the requestor, not later than the 45th business day after the date the attorney general received the request for a decision under this subsection. The attorney general shall issue a written decision on the matter and provide a copy of the decision to the requestor, the governmental body, and any interested person who submitted necessary information or a brief to the attorney general about the matter. The requestor or the governmental body may appeal a decision of the attorney general under this subsection to a Travis County district court.

(e) A governmental body that redacts or withholds information under Subsection (c) shall provide the following information to the requestor on a form prescribed by the attorney general:

   (1)   a description of the redacted or withheld information;

   (2)   a citation to this section; and

(3) instructions regarding how the requestor may seek a decision from the attorney general regarding whether the redacted or withheld information is excepted from required disclosure.

§ 552.131.   Exception: Confidentiality of Certain Economic Development Information

(a) Information is excepted from the requirements of Section 552.021 if the information relates to economic development negotiations involving a governmental body and a business prospect that the governmental body seeks to have locate, stay, or expand in or near the territory of the governmental body and the information relates to:

(1) a trade secret of the business prospect; or

(2) commercial or financial information for which it is demonstrated based on specific factual evidence that disclosure would cause substantial competitive harm to the person from whom the information was obtained.

(b) Unless and until an agreement is made with the business prospect, information about a financial or other incentive being offered to the business prospect by the governmental body or by another person is excepted from the requirements of Section 552.021.

(c) After an agreement is made with the business prospect, this section does not except from the requirements of Section 552.021 information about a financial or other incentive being offered to the business prospect:

(1) by the governmental body; or

(2) by another person, if the financial or other incentive may directly or indirectly result in the expenditure of public funds by a governmental body or a reduction in revenue received by a governmental body from any source.

§ 552.132.   Confidentiality of Crime Victim or Claimant Information

(a) Except as provided by Subsection (d), in this section, "crime victim or claimant" means a victim or claimant under Subchapter B, Chapter 56, Code of Criminal Procedure, who has filed an application for compensation under that subchapter.

(b) The following information held by the crime victim's compensation division of the attorney general's office is confidential:

(1) the name, social security number, address, or telephone number of a crime victim or claimant; or

(2) any other information the disclosure of which would identify or tend to identify the crime victim or claimant.

(c) If the crime victim or claimant is awarded compensation under Section 56.34, Code of Criminal Procedure, as of the date of the award of compensation, the name of the crime victim or claimant and the amount of compensation awarded to that crime victim or claimant are public information and are not excepted from the requirements of Section 552.021.

(d) An employee of a governmental body who is also a victim under Subchapter B, Chapter 56, Code of Criminal Procedure, regardless of whether the employee has filed an application for compensation under that subchapter, may elect whether to allow public access to information held by the attorney general's office or other governmental body that would identify or tend to identify the victim, including a photograph or other visual representation of the victim. An election under this subsection must be made in writing on a form developed by the governmental body, be signed by the employee, and be filed with the governmental body before the third anniversary of the latest to occur of one of the following:

    (1)   the date the crime was committed;

    (2)   the date employment begins; or

    (3)   the date the governmental body develops the form and provides it to employees.

(e) If the employee fails to make an election under Subsection (d), the identifying information is excepted from disclosure until the third anniversary of the date the crime was committed. In case of disability, impairment, or other incapacity of the employee, the election may be made by the guardian of the employee or former employee.

§ 552.1325. Crime Victim Impact Statement: Certain Information Confidential

(a) In this section:

    (1)   "Crime victim" means a person who is a victim as defined by Article 56.32, Code of Criminal Procedure.

    (2)   "Victim impact statement" means a victim impact statement under Article 56.03, Code of Criminal Procedure.

(b) The following information that is held by a governmental body or filed with a court and that is contained in a victim impact statement or was submitted for purposes of preparing a victim impact statement is confidential:

    (1)   the name, social security number, address, and telephone number of a crime victim; and

    (2)   any other information the disclosure of which would identify or tend to identify the crime victim.

§ 552.133.   Exception: Confidentiality of Public Power Utility Competitive Matters

(a) In this section, "public power utility" means an entity providing electric or gas utility services that is subject to the provisions of this chapter.

(a-1) For purposes of this section, "competitive matter" means a utility-related matter that is related to the public power utility's competitive activity, including commercial information, and would, if disclosed, give advantage to competitors or prospective competitors. The term:

(1) means a matter that is reasonably related to the following categories of information:

(A) generation unit specific and portfolio fixed and variable costs, including forecasts of those costs, capital improvement plans for generation units, and generation unit operating characteristics and outage scheduling;

(B) bidding and pricing information for purchased power, generation and fuel, and Electric Reliability Council of Texas bids, prices, offers, and related services and strategies;

(C) effective fuel and purchased power agreements and fuel transportation arrangements and contracts;

(D) risk management information, contracts, and strategies, including fuel hedging and storage;

(E) plans, studies, proposals, and analyses for system improvements, additions, or sales, other than transmission and distribution system improvements inside the service area for which the public power utility is the sole certificated retail provider; and

(F) customer billing, contract, and usage information, electric power pricing information, system load characteristics, and electric power marketing analyses and strategies; and

(2) does not include the following categories of information:

(A) information relating to the provision of distribution access service, including the terms and conditions of the service and the rates charged for the service but not including information concerning utility-related services or products that are competitive;

(B) information relating to the provision of transmission service that is required to be filed with the Public Utility Commission of Texas, subject to any confidentiality provided for under the rules of the commission;

(C) information for the distribution system pertaining to reliability and continuity of service, to the extent not security-sensitive, that relates to emergency management, identification of critical loads such as hospitals and police, records of interruption, and distribution feeder standards;

(D) any substantive rule or tariff of general applicability regarding rates, service offerings, service regulation, customer protections, or customer service adopted by the public power utility as authorized by law;

(E)   aggregate information reflecting receipts or expenditures of funds of the public power utility, of the type that would be included in audited financial statements;

(F)   information relating to equal employment opportunities for minority groups, as filed with local, state, or federal agencies;

(G)   information relating to the public power utility's performance in contracting with minority business entities;

(H)   information relating to nuclear decommissioning trust agreements, of the type required to be included in audited financial statements;

(I)   information relating to the amount and timing of any transfer to an owning city's general fund;

(J)   information relating to environmental compliance as required to be filed with any local, state, or national environmental authority, subject to any confidentiality provided under the rules of those authorities;

(K)   names of public officers of the public power utility and the voting records of those officers for all matters other than those within the scope of a competitive resolution provided for by this section;

(L)   a description of the public power utility's central and field organization, including the established places at which the public may obtain information, submit information and requests, or obtain decisions and the identification of employees from whom the public may obtain information, submit information or requests, or obtain decisions;

(M)   information identifying the general course and method by which the public power utility's functions are channeled and determined, including the nature and requirements of all formal and informal policies and procedures;

(N)   salaries and total compensation of all employees of a public power utility; or

(O)   information publicly released by the Electric Reliability Council of Texas in accordance with a law, rule, or protocol generally applicable to similarly situated market participants.

(b) Information or records are excepted from the requirements of Section 552.021 if the information or records are reasonably related to a competitive matter, as defined in this section. Information or records of a municipally owned utility that are reasonably related to a competitive matter are not subject to disclosure under this chapter, whether or not, under the Utilities Code, the municipally owned utility has adopted customer choice or serves in a multiply certificated service area. This section does not limit the right of a public power utility governing body to withhold from disclosure information deemed to be within the scope of any other exception provided for in this chapter, subject to the provisions of this chapter.

(c) The requirement of Section 552.022 that a category of information listed under Section 552.022(a) is public information and not excepted from required disclosure under this chapter unless expressly confidential under law does not apply to information that is excepted from required disclosure under this section.

§ 552.134. Exception: Confidentiality of Certain Information Relating to Inmate of Department of Criminal Justice

(a) Except as provided by Subsection (b) or by Section 552.029, information obtained or maintained by the Texas Department of Criminal Justice is excepted from the requirements of Section 552.021 if it is information about an inmate who is confined in a facility operated by or under a contract with the department.

(b) Subsection (a) does not apply to:

    (1)   statistical or other aggregated information relating to inmates confined in one or more facilities operated by or under a contract with the department; or

    (2)   information about an inmate sentenced to death.

(c) This section does not affect whether information is considered confidential or privileged under Section 508.313.

(d) A release of information described by Subsection (a) to an eligible entity, as defined by Section 508.313(d), for a purpose related to law enforcement, prosecution, corrections, clemency, or treatment is not considered a release of information to the public for purposes of Section 552.007 and does not waive the right to assert in the future that the information is excepted from required disclosure under this section or other law.

§ 552.135. Exception: Confidentiality of Certain Information Held by School District

(a) "Informer" means a student or a former student or an employee or former employee of a school district who has furnished a report of another person's possible violation of criminal, civil, or regulatory law to the school district or the proper regulatory enforcement authority.

(b) An informer's name or information that would substantially reveal the identity of an informer is excepted from the requirements of Section 552.021.

(c) Subsection (b) does not apply:

    (1)   if the informer is a student or former student, and the student or former student, or the legal guardian, or spouse of the student or former student consents to disclosure of the student's or former student's name; or

    (2)   if the informer is an employee or former employee who consents to disclosure of the employee's or former employee's name; or

    (3)   if the informer planned, initiated, or participated in the possible violation.

(d) Information excepted under Subsection (b) may be made available to a law enforcement agency or prosecutor for official purposes of the agency or prosecutor upon proper request made in compliance with applicable law and procedure.

(e) This section does not infringe on or impair the confidentiality of information considered to be confidential by law, whether it be constitutional, statutory, or by judicial decision, including information excepted from the requirements of Section 552.021.

§ 552.136. Confidentiality of Credit Card, Debit Card, Charge Card, and Access Device Numbers

(a) In this section, "access device" means a card, plate, code, account number, personal identification number, electronic serial number, mobile identification number, or other telecommunications service, equipment, or instrument identifier or means of account access that alone or in conjunction with another access device may be used to:

    (1) obtain money, goods, services, or another thing of value; or

    (2) initiate a transfer of funds other than a transfer originated solely by paper instrument.

(b) Notwithstanding any other provision of this chapter, a credit card, debit card, charge card, or access device number that is collected, assembled, or maintained by or for a governmental body is confidential.

(c) A governmental body may redact information that must be withheld under Subsection (b) from any information the governmental body discloses under Section 552.021 without the necessity of requesting a decision from the attorney general under Subchapter G.

(d) If, under Subsection (c), a governmental body redacts or withholds information without requesting a decision from the attorney general about whether the information may be redacted or withheld, the requestor is entitled to seek a decision from the attorney general about the matter. The attorney general by rule shall establish procedures and deadlines for receiving information necessary to decide the matter and briefs from the requestor, the governmental body, and any other interested person. The attorney general shall promptly render a decision requested under this subsection, determining whether the redacted or withheld information was excepted from required disclosure to the requestor, not later than the 45th business day after the date the attorney general received the request for a decision under this subsection. The attorney general shall issue a written decision on the matter and provide a copy of the decision to the requestor, the governmental body, and any interested person who submitted necessary information or a brief to the attorney general about the matter. The requestor or the governmental body may appeal a decision of the attorney general under this subsection to a Travis County district court.

(e) A governmental body that redacts or withholds information under Subsection (c) shall provide the following information to the requestor on a form prescribed by the attorney general:

    (1) a description of the redacted or withheld information;

(2)   a citation to this section; and

(3)   instructions regarding how the requestor may seek a decision from the attorney general regarding whether the redacted or withheld information is excepted from required disclosure.

§ 552.137.   Confidentiality of Certain E-Mail Addresses

(a) Except as otherwise provided by this section, an e-mail address of a member of the public that is provided for the purpose of communicating electronically with a governmental body is confidential and not subject to disclosure under this chapter.

(b) Confidential information described by this section that relates to a member of the public may be disclosed if the member of the public affirmatively consents to its release.

(c) Subsection (a) does not apply to an e-mail address:

(1)   provided to a governmental body by a person who has a contractual relationship with the governmental body or by the contractor's agent;

(2)   provided to a governmental body by a vendor who seeks to contract with the governmental body or by the vendor's agent;

(3)   contained in a response to a request for bids or proposals, contained in a response to similar invitations soliciting offers or information relating to a potential contract, or provided to a governmental body in the course of negotiating the terms of a contract or potential contract;

(4)   provided to a governmental body on a letterhead, coversheet, printed document, or other document made available to the public; or

(5)   provided to a governmental body for the purpose of providing public comment on or receiving notices related to an application for a license as defined by Section 2001.003(2) of this code, or receiving orders or decisions from a governmental body.

(d) Subsection (a) does not prevent a governmental body from disclosing an e-mail address for any reason to another governmental body or to a federal agency.

§ 552.138.   Exception: Confidentiality of Family Violence Shelter Center, Victims of Trafficking Shelter Center, and Sexual Assault Program Information

(a) In this section:

(1)   "Family violence shelter center" has the meaning assigned by Section 51.002, Human Resources Code.

(2)   "Sexual assault program" has the meaning assigned by Section 420.003.

(3)   "Victims of trafficking shelter center" means:

    (A)   a program that:

        (i)   is operated by a public or private nonprofit organization; and

        (ii)   provides comprehensive residential and nonresidential services to persons who are victims of trafficking under Section 20A.02, Penal Code; or

    (B)   a child-placing agency, as defined by Section 42.002, Human Resources Code, that provides services to persons who are victims of trafficking under Section 20A.02, Penal Code.

(b) Information maintained by a family violence shelter center, victims of trafficking shelter center, or sexual assault program is excepted from the requirements of Section 552.021 if it is information that relates to:

    (1)   the home address, home telephone number, or social security number of an employee or a volunteer worker of a family violence shelter center, victims of trafficking shelter center, or sexual assault program, regardless of whether the employee or worker complies with Section 552.024;

    (2)   the location or physical layout of a family violence shelter center or victims of trafficking shelter center;

    (3)   the name, home address, home telephone number, or numeric identifier of a current or former client of a family violence shelter center, victims of trafficking shelter center, or sexual assault program;

    (4)   the provision of services, including counseling and sheltering, to a current or former client of a family violence shelter center, victims of trafficking shelter center, or sexual assault program;

    (5)   the name, home address, or home telephone number of a private donor to a family violence shelter center, victims of trafficking shelter center, or sexual assault program; or

    (6)   the home address or home telephone number of a member of the board of directors or the board of trustees of a family violence shelter center, victims of trafficking shelter center, or sexual assault program, regardless of whether the board member complies with Section 552.024.

(c) A governmental body may redact information maintained by a family violence shelter center, victims of trafficking shelter center, or sexual assault program that may be withheld under Subsection (b)(1) or (6) from any information the governmental body discloses under Section 552.021 without the necessity of requesting a decision from the attorney general under Subchapter G.

(d) If, under Subsection (c), a governmental body redacts or withholds information without requesting a decision from the attorney general about whether the information may be redacted or withheld, the requestor is entitled to seek a decision from the attorney general about the matter. The attorney general by rule shall establish procedures and deadlines for receiving information necessary to decide the matter and briefs from the requestor, the governmental body, and any other interested person. The attorney general shall promptly render a decision requested under this subsection, determining whether the redacted or withheld information was excepted from required disclosure to the requestor, not later than the 45th business day after the date the attorney general received the request for a decision under this subsection. The attorney general shall issue a written decision on the matter and provide a copy of the decision to the requestor, the governmental body, and any interested person who submitted necessary information or a brief to the attorney general about the matter. The requestor or the governmental body may appeal a decision of the attorney general under this subsection to a Travis County district court.

(e) A governmental body that redacts or withholds information under Subsection (c) shall provide the following information to the requestor on a form prescribed by the attorney general:

    (1)   a description of the redacted or withheld information;

    (2)   a citation to this section; and

    (3)   instructions regarding how the requestor may seek a decision from the attorney general regarding whether the redacted or withheld information is excepted from required disclosure.

§ 552.139. Exception: Confidentiality of Government Information Related to Security or Infrastructure Issues for Computers

(a) Information is excepted from the requirements of Section 552.021 if it is information that relates to computer network security, to restricted information under Section 2059.055, or to the design, operation, or defense of a computer network.

(b) The following information is confidential:

    (1)   a computer network vulnerability report;

    (2)   any other assessment of the extent to which data processing operations, a computer, a computer program, network, system, or system interface, or software of a governmental body or of a contractor of a governmental body is vulnerable to unauthorized access or harm, including an assessment of the extent to which the governmental body's or contractor's electronically stored information containing sensitive or critical information is vulnerable to alteration, damage, erasure, or inappropriate use;

    (3)   a photocopy or other copy of an identification badge issued to an official or employee of a governmental body; and

    (4)   information directly arising from a governmental body's routine efforts to prevent, detect, investigate, or mitigate a computer security incident, including information contained in or derived from an information security log.

(b-1) Subsection (b)(4) does not affect the notification requirements related to a breach of system security as defined by Section 521.053, Business & Commerce Code.

(c) Notwithstanding the confidential nature of the information described in this section, the information may be disclosed to a bidder if the governmental body determines that providing the information is necessary for the bidder to provide an accurate bid. A disclosure under this subsection is not a voluntary disclosure for purposes of Section 552.007.

Text of (d), as added by Acts 2017, 85th Leg., ch. 683 (H.B. 8), § 4

(d) When posting a contract on an Internet website as required by Section 2261.253, a state agency shall redact information made confidential by this section or excepted from public disclosure by this section. Redaction under this subsection dos not exempt information from the requirements of Section 552.021.

Text of (d), as added by Acts 2017, 85th Leg., ch. 1042 (H.B. 1861), § 1

(d) A state agency shall redact from a contract posted on the agency's Internet website under Section 2261.253 information that is made confidential by, or excepted from required public disclosure under, this section. The redaction of information under this subsection does not exempt the information from the requirements of Section 552.021 or 552.221.

§ 552.140.   Exception: Confidentiality of Military Discharge Records

(a) This section applies only to a military veteran's Department of Defense Form DD-214 or other military discharge record that is first recorded with or that otherwise first comes into the possession of a governmental body on or after September 1, 2003.

(b) The record is confidential for the 75 years following the date it is recorded with or otherwise first comes into the possession of a governmental body. During that period the governmental body may permit inspection or copying of the record or disclose information contained in the record only in accordance with this section or in accordance with a court order.

(c) On request and the presentation of proper identification, the following persons may inspect the military discharge record or obtain from the governmental body free of charge a copy or certified copy of the record:

(1)   the veteran who is the subject of the record;

(2)   the legal guardian of the veteran;

(3)   the spouse or a child or parent of the veteran or, if there is no living spouse, child, or parent, the nearest living relative of the veteran;

(4)   the personal representative of the estate of the veteran;

(5)   the person named by the veteran, or by a person described by Subdivision (2), (3), or (4), in an appropriate power of attorney executed in accordance with Subchapters A and B, Chapter 752, Estates Code;

(6)   another governmental body; or

(7)   an authorized representative of the funeral home that assists with the burial of the veteran.

(d) A court that orders the release of information under this section shall limit the further disclosure of the information and the purposes for which the information may be used.

(e) A governmental body that obtains information from the record shall limit the governmental body's use and disclosure of the information to the purpose for which the information was obtained.

§ 552.141.   Confidentiality of Information in Application for Marriage License

(a) Information that relates to the social security number of an individual that is maintained by a county clerk and that is on an application for a marriage license, including information in an application on behalf of an absent applicant and the affidavit of an absent applicant, or is on a document submitted with an application for a marriage license is confidential and may not be disclosed by the county clerk to the public under this chapter.

(b) If the county clerk receives a request to make information in a marriage license application available under this chapter, the county clerk shall redact the portion of the application that contains an individual's social security number and release the remainder of the information in the application.

§ 552.142.   Exception: Confidentiality of Records Subject to Order of Nondisclosure

(a) Information is excepted from the requirements of Section 552.021 if an order of nondisclosure of criminal history record information with respect to the information has been issued under Subchapter E-1, Chapter 411.

(b) A person who is the subject of information that is excepted from the requirements of Section 552.021 under this section may deny the occurrence of the criminal proceeding to which the information relates and the exception of the information under this section, unless the information is being used against the person in a subsequent criminal proceeding.

§ 552.1425.   Civil Penalty: Dissemination of Certain Criminal History Information

(a) A private entity that compiles and disseminates for compensation criminal history record information may not compile or disseminate information with respect to which the entity has received notice that:

(1)   an order of expunction has been issued under Article 55.02, Code of Criminal Procedure; or

(2)   an order of nondisclosure of criminal history record information has been issued under Subchapter E-1, Chapter 411.

(b) A district court may issue a warning to a private entity for a first violation of Subsection (a). After receiving a warning for the first violation, the private entity is liable to the state for a civil penalty not to exceed $1,000 for each subsequent violation.

(c) The attorney general or an appropriate prosecuting attorney may sue to collect a civil penalty under this section.

(d) A civil penalty collected under this section shall be deposited in the state treasury to the credit of the general revenue fund.

§ 552.143.   Confidentiality of Certain Investment Information

(a) All information prepared or provided by a private investment fund and held by a governmental body that is not listed in Section 552.0225(b) is confidential and excepted from the requirements of Section 552.021.

(b) Unless the information has been publicly released, pre-investment and post-investment diligence information, including reviews and analyses, prepared or maintained by a governmental body or a private investment fund is confidential and excepted from the requirements of Section 552.021, except to the extent it is subject to disclosure under Subsection (c).

(c) All information regarding a governmental body's direct purchase, holding, or disposal of restricted securities that is not listed in Section 552.0225(b)(2)–(9), (11), or (13)–(16) is confidential and excepted from the requirements of Section 552.021. This subsection does not apply to a governmental body's purchase, holding, or disposal of restricted securities for the purpose of reinvestment nor does it apply to a private investment fund's investment in restricted securities. This subsection applies to information regarding a direct purchase, holding, or disposal of restricted securities by the Texas growth fund, created under Section 70, Article XVI, Texas Constitution, that is not listed in Section 552.0225(b).

(d) For the purposes of this chapter:

(1)   "Private investment fund" means an entity, other than a governmental body, that issues restricted securities to a governmental body to evidence the investment of public funds for the purpose of reinvestment.

(2)   "Reinvestment" means investment in a person that makes or will make other investments.

(3)   "Restricted securities" has the meaning assigned by 17 C.F.R. Section 230.144(a)(3).

(e) Repealed by Acts 2011, 82nd Leg., 1st C.S., ch. 4 (S.B. 1), § 17.05(1).

(f) This section does not apply to the Texas Mutual Insurance Company or a successor to the company.

§ 552.144. Exception: Working Papers and Electronic Communications of Administrative Law Judges at State Office of Administrative Hearings

The following working papers and electronic communications of an administrative law judge at the State Office of Administrative Hearings are excepted from the requirements of Section 552.021:

(1) notes and electronic communications recording the observations, thoughts, questions, deliberations, or impressions of an administrative law judge;

(2) drafts of a proposal for decision;

(3) drafts of orders made in connection with conducting contested case hearings; and

(4) drafts of orders made in connection with conducting alternative dispute resolution procedures.

§ 552.145. Exception: Confidentiality of Texas No-Call List

The Texas no-call list created under Subchapter B, Chapter 304, Business & Commerce Code, and any information provided to or received from the administrator of the national do-not-call registry maintained by the United States government, as provided by Sections 304.051 and 304.56, Business & Commerce Code, are excepted from the requirements of Section 552.021.

§ 552.146. Exception: Certain Communications with Assistant or Employee of Legislative Budget Board

(a) All written or otherwise recorded communications, including conversations, correspondence, and electronic communications, between a member of the legislature or the lieutenant governor and an assistant or employee of the Legislative Budget Board are excepted from the requirements of Section 552.021.

(b) Memoranda of a communication between a member of the legislature or the lieutenant governor and an assistant or employee of the Legislative Budget Board are excepted from the requirements of Section 552.021 without regard to the method used to store or maintain the memoranda.

(c) This section does not except from required disclosure a record or memoranda of a communication that occurs in public during an open meeting or public hearing conducted by the Legislative Budget Board.

§ 552.147. Social Security Numbers

(a) Except as provided by Subsection (a-1), the social security number of a living person is excepted from the requirements of Section 552.021, but is not confidential under this section and this section does not make the social security number of a living person confidential under another provision of this chapter or other law.

(a-1) The social security number of an employee of a school district in the custody of the district is confidential.

(b) A governmental body may redact the social security number of a living person from any information the governmental body discloses under Section 552.021 without the necessity of requesting a decision from the attorney general under Subchapter G.

(c) Notwithstanding any other law, a county or district clerk may disclose in the ordinary course of business a social security number that is contained in information held by the clerk's office, and that disclosure is not official misconduct and does not subject the clerk to civil or criminal liability of any kind under the law of this state, including any claim for damages in a lawsuit or the criminal penalty imposed by Section 552.352.

(d) Unless another law requires a social security number to be maintained in a government document, on written request from an individual or the individual's representative the clerk shall redact within a reasonable amount of time all but the last four digits of the individual's social security number from information maintained in the clerk's official public records, including electronically stored information maintained by or under the control of the clerk. The individual or the individual's representative must identify, using a form provided by the clerk, the specific document or documents from which the partial social security number shall be redacted.

§ 552.148. Exception: Confidentiality of Certain Personal Information Maintained by Municipality Pertaining to a Minor

(a) In this section, "minor" means a person younger than 18 years of age.

(b) The following information maintained by a municipality for purposes related to the participation by a minor in a recreational program or activity is excepted from the requirements of Section 552.021:

    (1) the name, age, home address, home telephone number, or social security number of the minor;

    (2) a photograph of the minor; and

    (3) the name of the minor's parent or legal guardian.

§ 552.149. Exception: Confidentiality of Records of Comptroller or Appraisal District Received from Private Entity

(a) Information relating to real property sales prices, descriptions, characteristics, and other related information received from a private entity by the comptroller or the chief appraiser of an appraisal district under Chapter 6, Tax Code, is excepted from the requirements of Section 552.021.

(b) Notwithstanding Subsection (a), the property owner or the owner's agent may, on request, obtain from the chief appraiser of the applicable appraisal district a copy of each item of information described by Section 41.461(a)(2), Tax Code, and a copy of each item of information that the chief appraiser took into consideration but does not plan to introduce at the hearing on the protest. In addition, the property owner or agent may, on request, obtain from the chief appraiser comparable sales data from a reasonable number of sales that is relevant to any matter to be determined by the appraisal review board at the hearing on the property owner's protest. Information obtained under this subsection:

(1) remains confidential in the possession of the property owner or agent; and

(2) may not be disclosed or used for any purpose except as evidence or argument at the hearing on the protest.

(c) Notwithstanding Subsection (a) or Section 403.304, so as to assist a property owner or an appraisal district in a protest filed under Section 403.303, the property owner, the district, or an agent of the property owner or district may, on request, obtain from the comptroller any information, including confidential information, obtained by the comptroller in connection with the comptroller's finding that is being protested. Confidential information obtained by a property owner, an appraisal district, or an agent of the property owner or district under the subsection:

(1) remains confidential in the possession of the property owner, district, or agent; and

(2) may not be disclosed to a person who is not authorized to receive or inspect the information.

(d) Notwithstanding Subsection (a) or Section 403.304, so as to assist a school district in the preparation of a protest filed or to be filed under Section 403.303, the school district or an agent of the school district may, on request, obtain from the comptroller or the appraisal district any information, including confidential information, obtained by the comptroller or the appraisal district that relates to the appraisal of property involved in the comptroller's finding that is being protested. Confidential information obtained by a school district or an agent of the school district under this subsection:

(1) remains confidential in the possession of the school district or agent; and

(2) may not be disclosed to a person who is not authorized to receive or inspect the information.

(e) This section applies to information described by Subsections (a), (c), and (d) and to an item of information or comparable sales data described by Subsection (b) only if the information, item of information, or comparable sales data relates to real property that is located in a county having a population of more than 50,000.

§ 552.150. Exception: Confidentiality of Information That Could Compromise Safety of Officer or Employee of Hospital District

(a) Information in the custody of a hospital district that relates to an employee or officer of the hospital district is excepted from the requirements of Section 552.021 if:

(1) it is information that, if disclosed under the specific circumstances pertaining to the individual, could reasonably be expected to compromise the safety of the individual, such as information that describes or depicts the likeness of the individual, information stating the times that the individual arrives at or departs from work, a description of the individual's automobile, or the location where the individual works or parks; and

(2) the employee or officer applies in writing to the hospital district's officer for public information to have the information withheld from public disclosure under this section and includes in the application:

  (A) a description of the information; and

  (B) the specific circumstances pertaining to the individual that demonstrate why disclosure of the information could reasonably be expected to compromise the safety of the individual.

(b) On receiving a written request for information described in an application submitted under Subsection (a)(2), the officer for public information shall:

  (1) request a decision from the attorney general in accordance with Section 552.301 regarding withholding the information; and

  (2) include a copy of the application submitted under Subsection (a)(2) with the request for the decision.

(c) Repealed by Acts 2011, 82nd Leg., ch. 609 (S.B. 470), § 1.

§ 552.151. Exception: Confidentiality of Information Concerning Information Regarding Select Agents

(a) The following information that pertains to a biological agent or toxin identified or listed as a select agent under federal law, including under the Public Health Security and Bioterrorism Preparedness and Response Act of 2002 (Pub. L. No. 107-188) and regulations adopted under that Act, is excepted from the requirements of Section 552.021:

  (1) the specific location of a select agent within an approved facility;

  (2) personal identifying information of an individual whose name appears in documentation relating to the chain of custody of select agents, including a materials transfer agreement; and

  (3) the identity of an individual authorized to possess, use, or access a select agent.

(b) This section does not except from disclosure the identity of the select agents present at a facility.

(c) This section does not except from disclosure the identity of an individual faculty member or employee whose name appears or will appear on published research.

(d) This section does not except from disclosure otherwise public information relating to contracts of a governmental body.

(e) If a resident of another state is present in Texas and is authorized to possess, use, or access a select agent in conducting research or other work at a Texas facility, information relating to the identity of that individual is subject to disclosure under this chapter only to the extent the information would be subject to disclosure under the laws of the state of which the person is a resident.

§ 552.152. Exception: Confidentiality of Information Concerning Public Employee or Officer Personal Safety

Information in the custody of a governmental body that relates to an employee or officer of the governmental body is excepted from the requirements of Section 552.021 if, under the specific circumstances pertaining to the employee or officer, disclosure of the information would subject the employee or officer to a substantial threat of physical harm.

§ 552.153. Proprietary Records and Trade Secrets Involved in Certain Partnerships

(a) In this section, "affected jurisdiction," "comprehensive agreement," "contracting person," "interim agreement," "qualifying project," and "responsible governmental entity" have the meanings assigned those terms by Section 2267.001.

(b) Information in the custody of a responsible governmental entity that relates to a proposal for a qualifying project authorized under Chapter 2267 is excepted from the requirements of Section 552.021 if:

(1) the information consists of memoranda, staff evaluations, or other records prepared by the responsible governmental entity, its staff, outside advisors, or consultants exclusively for the evaluation and negotiation of proposals filed under Chapter 2267 for which:

(A) disclosure to the public before or after the execution of an interim or comprehensive agreement would adversely affect the financial interest or bargaining position of the responsible governmental entity; and

(B) the basis for the determination under Paragraph (A) is documented in writing by the responsible governmental entity; or

(2) the records are provided by a proposer to a responsible governmental entity or affected jurisdiction under Chapter 2267 and contain:

(A) trade secrets of the proposer;

(B) financial records of the proposer, including balance sheets and financial statements, that are not generally available to the public through regulatory disclosure or other means; or

(C) work product related to a competitive bid or proposal submitted by the proposer that, if made public before the execution of an interim or comprehensive agreement, would provide a competing proposer an unjust advantage or adversely affect the financial interest or bargaining position of the responsible governmental entity or the proposer.

(c) Except as specifically provided by Subsection (b), this section does not authorize the withholding of information concerning:

  (1) the terms of any interim or comprehensive agreement, service contract, lease, partnership, or agreement of any kind entered into by the responsible governmental entity and the contracting person or the terms of any financing arrangement that involves the use of any public money; or

  (2) the performance of any person developing or operating a qualifying project under Chapter 2267.

(d) In this section, "proposer" has the meaning assigned by Section 2267.001.

§ 552.154. Exception: Name of Applicant for Executive Director, Chief Investment Officer, or Chief Audit Executive of Teacher Retirement System of Texas

The name of an applicant for the position of executive director, chief investment officer, or chief audit executive of the Teacher Retirement System of Texas is excepted from the requirements of Section 552.021, except that the board of trustees of the Teacher Retirement System of Texas must give public notice of the names of three finalists being considered for one of those positions at least 21 days before the date of the meeting at which the final action or vote is to be taken on choosing a finalist for employment.

§ 552.155. Exception: Confidentiality of Certain Property Tax Appraisal Photographs

(a) Except as provided by Subsection (b) or (c), a photograph that is taken by the chief appraiser of an appraisal district or the chief appraiser's authorized representative for property tax appraisal purposes and that shows the interior of an improvement to property is confidential and excepted from the requirements of Section 552.021.

(b) A governmental body shall disclose a photograph described by Subsection (a) to a requestor who had an ownership interest in the improvement to property shown in the photograph on the date the photograph was taken.

(c) A photograph described by Subsection (a) may be used as evidence in and provided to the parties to a protest under Chapter 41, Tax Code, or an appeal of a determination by the appraisal review board under Chapter 42, Tax Code, if it is relevant to the determination of a matter protested or appealed. A photograph that is used as evidence:

  (1) remains confidential in the possession of the person to whom it is disclosed; and

  (2) may not be disclosed or used for any other purpose.

(c-1) Notwithstanding any other law, a photograph described by Subsection (a) may be used to ascertain the location of equipment used to produce or transmit oil and gas for purposes of taxation if that equipment is located on January 1 in the appraisal district that appraises property for the equipment for the preceding 365 consecutive days.

§ 552.156.   Exception: Confidentiality of Continuity of Operations Plan

(a) Except as otherwise provided by this section, the following information is excepted from disclosure under this chapter:

    (1)   a continuity of operations plan developed under Section 412.054, Labor Code; and

    (2)   all records written, produced, collected, assembled, or maintained as part of the development or review of a continuity of operations plan developed under Section 412.054, Labor Code.

(b) Forms, standards, and other instructional, informational, or planning materials adopted by the office to provide guidance or assistance to a state agency in developing a continuity of operations plan under Section 412.054, Labor Code, are public information subject to disclosure under this chapter.

(c) A governmental body may disclose or make available information that is confidential under this section to another governmental body or a federal agency.

(d) Disclosing information to another governmental body or a federal agency under this section does not waive or affect the confidentiality of that information.

§ 552.158.   Exception: Confidentiality of Personal Information Regarding Applicant for Appointment by Governor

The following information obtained by the governor or senate in connection with an applicant for an appointment by the governor is excepted from the requirements of Section 552.021:

    (1) the applicant's home address;

    (2) the applicant's home telephone number; and

    (3) the applicant's social security number.

SUBCHAPTER D. OFFICER FOR PUBLIC INFORMATION

§ 552.201.   Identity of Officer for Public Information

(a) The chief administrative officer of a governmental body is the officer for public information, except as provided by Subsection (b).

(b) Each elected county officer is the officer for public information and the custodian, as defined by Section 201.003, Local Government Code, of the information created or received by that county officer's office.

§ 552.202. Department Heads

Each department head is an agent of the officer for public information for the purposes of complying with this chapter.

§ 552.203. General Duties of Officer for Public Information

Each officer for public information, subject to penalties provided in this chapter, shall:

(1) make public information available for public inspection and copying;

(2) carefully protect public information from deterioration, alteration, mutilation, loss, or unlawful removal; and

(3) repair, renovate, or rebind public information as necessary to maintain it properly.

§ 552.204. Scope of Responsibility of Officer for Public Information

An officer for public information is responsible for the release of public information as required by this chapter. The officer is not responsible for:

(1) the use made of the information by the requestor; or

(2) the release of information after it is removed from a record as a result of an update, a correction, or a change of status of the person to whom the information pertains.

§ 552.205. Informing Public of Basic Rights and Responsibilities Under this Chapter

(a) An officer for public information shall prominently display a sign in the form prescribed by the attorney general that contains basic information about the rights of a requestor, the responsibilities of a governmental body, and the procedures for inspecting or obtaining a copy of public information under this chapter. The officer shall display the sign at one or more places in the administrative offices of the governmental body where it is plainly visible to:

(1) members of the public who request public information in person under this chapter; and

(2) employees of the governmental body whose duties include receiving or responding to requests under this chapter.

(b) The attorney general by rule shall prescribe the content of the sign and the size, shape, and other physical characteristics of the sign. In prescribing the content of the sign, the attorney general shall include plainly written basic information about the rights of a requestor, the responsibilities of a governmental body, and the procedures for inspecting or obtaining a copy of public information under this chapter that, in the opinion of the attorney general, is most useful for requestors to know and for employees of governmental bodies who receive or respond to requests for public information to know.

SUBCHAPTER E. PROCEDURES RELATED TO ACCESS

§ 552.221. Application for Public Information; Production of Public Information

(a) An officer for public information of a governmental body shall promptly produce public information for inspection, duplication, or both on application by any person to the officer. In this subsection, "promptly" means as soon as possible under the circumstances, that is, within a reasonable time, without delay.

(b) An officer for public information complies with Subsection (a) by:

  (1) providing the public information for inspection or duplication in the offices of the governmental body; or

  (2) sending copies of the public information by first class United States mail if the person requesting the information requests that copies be provided and pays the postage and any other applicable charges that the requestor has accrued under Subchapter F.

(b-1) In addition to the methods of production described by Subsection (b), an officer for public information for a governmental body complies with Subsection (a) by referring a requestor to an exact Internet location or uniform resource locator (URL) address on a website maintained by the governmental body and accessible to the public if the requested information is identifiable and readily available on that website. If the person requesting the information prefers a manner other than access through the URL, the governmental body must supply the information in the manner required by Subsection (b).

(b-2) If an officer for public information for a governmental body provides by e-mail an Internet location or uniform resource locator (URL) address as permitted by Subsection (b-1), the e-mail must contain a statement in a conspicuous font clearly indicating that the requestor may nonetheless access the requested information by inspection or duplication or by receipt through United States mail, as provided by Subsection (b).

(c) If the requested information is unavailable at the time of the request to examine because it is in active use or in storage, the officer for public information shall certify this fact in writing to the requestor and set a date and hour within a reasonable time when the information will be available for inspection or duplication.

(d) If an officer for public information cannot produce public information for inspection or duplication within 10 business days after the date the information is requested under Subsection (a), the officer shall certify that fact in writing to the requestor and set a date and hour within a reasonable time when the information will be available for inspection or duplication.

(e) A request is considered to have been withdrawn if the requestor fails to inspect or duplicate the public information in the offices of the governmental body on or before the 60th day after the date the information is made available or fails to pay the postage and any other applicable charges accrued under Subchapter F on or before the 60th day after the date the requestor is informed of the charges.

§ 552.222.   Permissible Inquiry by Governmental Body to Requestor

(a) The officer for public information and the officer's agent may not make an inquiry of a requestor except to establish proper identification or except as provided by Subsection (b), (c), or (c-1).

(b) If what information is requested is unclear to the governmental body, the governmental body may ask the requestor to clarify the request. If a large amount of information has been requested, the governmental body may discuss with the requestor how the scope of a request might be narrowed, but the governmental body may not inquire into the purpose for which information will be used.

(c) If the information requested relates to a motor vehicle record, the officer for public information or the officer's agent may require the requestor to provide additional identifying information sufficient for the officer or the officer's agent to determine whether the requestor is eligible to receive the information under Chapter 730, Transportation Code. In this subsection, "motor vehicle record" has the meaning assigned that term by Section 730.003, Transportation Code.

(c-1) If the information requested includes a photograph described by Section 552.155(a), the officer for public information or the officer's agent may require the requestor to provide additional information sufficient for the officer or the officer's agent to determine whether the requestor is eligible to receive the information under Section 552.155(b).

(d) If by the 61st day after the date a governmental body sends a written request for clarification or discussion under Subsection (b) or an officer for public information or agent sends a written request for additional information under Subsection (c) the governmental body, officer for public information, or agent, as applicable, does not receive a written response from the requestor, the underlying request for public information is considered to have been withdrawn by the requestor.

(e) A written request for clarification or discussion under Subsection (b) or a written request for additional information under Subsection (c) must include a statement as to the consequences of the failure by the requestor to timely respond to the request for clarification, discussion, or additional information.

(f) Except as provided by Subsection (g), if the requestor's request for public information included the requestor's physical or mailing address, the request may not be considered to have been withdrawn under Subsection (d) unless the governmental body, officer for public information, or agent, as applicable, sends the request for clarification or discussion under Subsection (b) or the written request for additional information under Subsection (c) to that address by certified mail.

(g) If the requestor's request for public information was sent by electronic mail, the request may be considered to have been withdrawn under Subsection (d) if:

    (1)   the governmental body, officer for public information, or agent, as applicable, sends the request for clarification or discussion under Subsection (b) or the written request for additional information under Subsection (c) by electronic mail to the same electronic mail address from which the original request was sent or to another electronic mail address provided by the requestor; and

(2)   the governmental body, officer for public information, or agent, as applicable, does not receive from the requestor a written response or response by electronic mail within the period described by Subsection (d).

§ 552.223.   Uniform Treatment of Requests for Information

The officer for public information or the officer's agent shall treat all requests for information uniformly without regard to the position or occupation of the requestor, the person on whose behalf the request is made, or the status of the individual as a member of the media.

§ 552.224.   Comfort and Facility

The officer for public information or the officer's agent shall give to a requestor all reasonable comfort and facility for the full exercise of the right granted by this chapter.

§ 552.225.   Time for Examination

(a)   A requestor must complete the examination of the information not later than the 10th business day after the date the custodian of the information makes it available. If the requestor does not complete the examination of the information within 10 business days after the date the custodian of the information makes the information available and does not file a request for additional time under Subsection (b), the requestor is considered to have withdrawn the request.

(b)   The officer for public information shall extend the initial examination period by an additional 10 business days if, within the initial period, the requestor files with the officer for public information a written request for additional time. The officer for public information shall extend an additional examination period by another 10 business days if, within the additional period, the requestor files with the officer for public information a written request for more additional time.

(c)   The time during which a person may examine information may be interrupted by the officer for public information if the information is needed for use by the governmental body. The period of interruption is not considered to be a part of the time during which the person may examine the information.

§ 552.226.   Removal of Original Record

This chapter does not authorize a requestor to remove an original copy of a public record from the office of a governmental body.

§ 552.227.   Research of State Library Holdings Not Required

An officer for public information or the officer's agent is not required to perform general research within the reference and research archives and holdings of state libraries.

§ 552.228.   Providing Suitable Copy of Public Information Within Reasonable Time

(a) It shall be a policy of a governmental body to provide a suitable copy of public information within a reasonable time after the date on which the copy is requested.

(b) If public information exists in an electronic or magnetic medium, the requestor may request a copy in an electronic medium, such as on diskette or on magnetic tape. A governmental body shall provide a copy in the requested medium if:

   (1)   the governmental body has the technological ability to produce a copy of the requested information in the requested medium;

   (2)   the governmental body is not required to purchase any software or hardware to accommodate the request; and

   (3)   provision of a copy of the information in the requested medium will not violate the terms of any copyright agreement between the governmental body and a third party.

(c) If a governmental body is unable to comply with a request to produce a copy of information in a requested medium for any of the reasons described by this section, the governmental body shall provide a copy in another medium that is acceptable to the requestor. A governmental body is not required to copy information onto a diskette or other material provided by the requestor but may use its own supplies.

§ 552.229.   Consent to Release Information Under Special Right of Access

(a) Consent for the release of information excepted from disclosure to the general public but available to a specific person under Sections 552.023 and 552.307 must be in writing and signed by the specific person or the person's authorized representative.

(b) An individual under 18 years of age may consent to the release of information under this section only with the additional written authorization of the individual's parent or guardian.

(c) An individual who has been adjudicated incompetent to manage the individual's personal affairs or for whom an attorney ad litem has been appointed may consent to the release of information under this section only by the written authorization of the designated legal guardian or attorney ad litem.

§ 552.230.   Rules of Procedure for Inspection and Copying of Public Information

(a) A governmental body may promulgate reasonable rules of procedure under which public information may be inspected and copied efficiently, safely, and without delay.

(b) A rule promulgated under Subsection (a) may not be inconsistent with any provision of this chapter.

§ 552.231. Responding to Requests for Information That Require Programming or Manipulation of Data

(a) A governmental body shall provide to a requestor the written statement described by Subsection (b) if the governmental body determines:

  (1) that responding to a request for public information will require programming or manipulation of data; and

  (2) that:

    (A) compliance with the request is not feasible or will result in substantial interference with its ongoing operations; or

    (B) the information could be made available in the requested form only at a cost that covers the programming and manipulation of data.

(b) The written statement must include:

  (1) a statement that the information is not available in the requested form;

  (2) a description of the form in which the information is available;

  (3) a description of any contract or services that would be required to provide the information in the requested form;

  (4) a statement of the estimated cost of providing the information in the requested form, as determined in accordance with the rules established by the attorney general under Section 552.262; and

  (5) a statement of the anticipated time required to provide the information in the requested form.

(c) The governmental body shall provide the written statement to the requestor within 20 days after the date of the governmental body's receipt of the request. The governmental body has an additional 10 days to provide the statement if the governmental body gives written notice to the requestor, within 20 days after the date of receipt of the request, that the additional time is needed.

(d) On providing the written statement to the requestor as required by this section, the governmental body does not have any further obligation to provide the information in the requested form or in the form in which it is available unless within 30 days the requestor states in writing to the governmental body that the requestor:

  (1) wants the governmental body to provide the information in the requested form according to the cost and time parameters set out in the statement or according to other terms to which the requestor and the governmental body agree; or

  (2) wants the information in the form in which it is available.

(d-1) If a requestor does not make a timely written statement under Subsection (d), the requestor is considered to have withdrawn the request for information.

(e) The officer for public information of a governmental body shall establish policies that assure the expeditious and accurate processing of requests for information that require programming or manipulation of data. A governmental body shall maintain a file containing all written statements issued under this section in a readily accessible location.

§ 552.232.   Responding to Repetitious or Redundant Requests

(a) A governmental body that determines that a requestor has made a request for information for which the governmental body has previously furnished copies to the requestor or made copies available to the requestor on payment of applicable charges under Subchapter F, shall respond to the request, in relation to the information for which copies have been already furnished or made available, in accordance with this section, except that:

   (1)   this section does not prohibit the governmental body from furnishing the information or making the information available to the requestor again in accordance with the request; and

   (2)   the governmental body is not required to comply with this section in relation to information that the governmental body simply furnishes or makes available to the requestor again in accordance with the request.

(b) The governmental body shall certify to the requestor that copies of all or part of the requested information, as applicable, were previously furnished to the requestor or made available to the requestor on payment of applicable charges under Subchapter F. The certification must include:

   (1)   a description of the information for which copies have been previously furnished or made available to the requestor;

   (2)   the date that the governmental body received the requestor's original request for that information;

   (3)   the date that the governmental body previously furnished copies of or made available copies of the information to the requestor;

   (4)   a certification that no subsequent additions, deletions, or corrections have been made to that information; and

   (5)   the name, title, and signature of the officer for public information or the officer's agent making the certification.

(c) A charge may not be imposed for making and furnishing a certification required under Subsection (b).

(d) This section does not apply to information for which the governmental body has not previously furnished copies to the requestor or made copies available to the requestor on payment of applicable charges under Subchapter F. A request by the requestor for information for which copies have not previously been furnished or made available to the requestor, including information for which copies were not furnished or made available because the information was redacted from other information that was furnished or made available or because the information did not yet exist at the time of an earlier request, shall be treated in the same manner as any other request for information under this chapter.

SUBCHAPTER F. CHARGES FOR PROVIDING COPIES OF PUBLIC INFORMATION

§ 552.261. Charge for Providing Copies of Public Information

(a) The charge for providing a copy of public information shall be an amount that reasonably includes all costs related to reproducing the public information, including costs of materials, labor, and overhead. If a request is for 50 or fewer pages of paper records, the charge for providing the copy of the public information may not include costs of materials, labor, or overhead, but shall be limited to the charge for each page of the paper record that is photocopied, unless the pages to be photocopied are located in:

    (1) two or more separate buildings that are not physically connected with each other; or

    (2) a remote storage facility.

(b) If the charge for providing a copy of public information includes costs of labor, the requestor may require the governmental body's officer for public information or the officer's agent to provide the requestor with a written statement as to the amount of time that was required to produce and provide the copy. The statement must be signed by the officer for public information or the officer's agent and the officer's or the agent's name must be typed or legibly printed below the signature. A charge may not be imposed for providing the written statement to the requestor.

(c) For purposes of Subsection (a), a connection of two buildings by a covered or open sidewalk, an elevated or underground passageway, or a similar facility is insufficient to cause the buildings to be considered separate buildings.

(d) Charges for providing a copy of public information are considered to accrue at the time the governmental body advises the requestor that the copy is available on payment of the applicable charges.

(e) Except as otherwise provided by this subsection, all requests received in one calendar day from an individual may be treated as a single request for purposes of calculating costs under this chapter. A governmental body may not combine multiple requests under this subsection from separate individuals who submit requests on behalf of an organization.

§ 552.2615. Required Itemized Estimate of Charges

(a) If a request for a copy of public information will result in the imposition of a charge under this subchapter that exceeds $40, or a request to inspect a paper record will result in the imposition of a charge under Section 552.271 that exceeds $40, the governmental body shall provide the requestor with a written itemized statement that details all estimated charges that will be imposed, including any allowable charges for labor or personnel costs. If an alternative less costly method of viewing the records is available, the statement must include a notice that the requestor may contact the governmental body regarding the alternative method. The governmental body must inform the requestor of the responsibilities imposed on the requestor by this section and of the rights granted by this entire section and give the requestor the information needed to respond, including:

(1)   that the requestor must provide the governmental body with a mailing, facsimile transmission, or electronic mail address to receive the itemized statement and that it is the requestor's choice which type of address to provide;

(2)   that the request is considered automatically withdrawn if the requestor does not respond in writing to the itemized statement and any updated itemized statement in the time and manner required by this section; and

(3)   that the requestor may respond to the statement by delivering the written response to the governmental body by mail, in person, by facsimile transmission if the governmental body is capable of receiving documents transmitted in that manner, or by electronic mail if the governmental body has an electronic mail address.

(b) A request described by Subsection (a) is considered to have been withdrawn by the requestor if the requestor does not respond in writing to the itemized statement by informing the governmental body within 10 business days after the date the statement is sent to the requestor that:

(1)   the requestor will accept the estimated charges;

(2)   the requestor is modifying the request in response to the itemized statement; or

(3)   the requestor has sent to the attorney general a complaint alleging that the requestor has been overcharged for being provided with a copy of the public information.

(c) If the governmental body later determines, but before it makes the copy or the paper record available, that the estimated charges will exceed the charges detailed in the written itemized statement by 20 percent or more, the governmental body shall send to the requestor a written updated itemized statement that details all estimated charges that will be imposed, including any allowable charges for labor or personnel costs. If the requestor does not respond in writing to the updated estimate in the time and manner described by Subsection (b), the request is considered to have been withdrawn by the requestor.

(d) If the actual charges that a governmental body imposes for a copy of public information, or for inspecting a paper record under Section 552.271, exceeds $40, the charges may not exceed:

(1)   the amount estimated in the updated itemized statement; or

(2)   if an updated itemized statement is not sent to the requestor, an amount that exceeds by 20 percent or more the amount estimated in the itemized statement.

(e) An itemized statement or updated itemized statement is considered to have been sent by the governmental body to the requestor on the date that:

(1) the statement is delivered to the requestor in person;

(2) the governmental body deposits the properly addressed statement in the United States mail; or

(3) the governmental body transmits the properly addressed statement by electronic mail or facsimile transmission, if the requestor agrees to receive the statement by electronic mail or facsimile transmission, as applicable.

(f) A requestor is considered to have responded to the itemized statement or the updated itemized statement on the date that:

(1) the response is delivered to the governmental body in person;

(2) the requestor deposits the properly addressed response in the United States mail; or

(3) the requestor transmits the properly addressed response to the governmental body by electronic mail or facsimile transmission.

(g) The time deadlines imposed by this section do not affect the application of a time deadline imposed on a governmental body under Subchapter G.

§ 552.262. Rules of the Attorney General

(a) The attorney general shall adopt rules for use by each governmental body in determining charges for providing copies of public information under this subchapter and in determining the charge, deposit, or bond required for making public information that exists in a paper record available for inspection as authorized by Sections 552.271(c) and (d). The rules adopted by the attorney general shall be used by each governmental body in determining charges for providing copies of public information and in determining the charge, deposit, or bond required for making public information that exists in a paper record available for inspection, except to the extent that other law provides for charges for specific kinds of public information. The charges for providing copies of public information may not be excessive and may not exceed the actual cost of producing the information or for making public information that exists in a paper record available for inspection. A governmental body, other than an agency of state government, may determine its own charges for providing copies of public information and its own charge, deposit, or bond for making public information that exists in a paper record available for inspection but may not charge an amount that is greater than 25 percent more than the amount established by the attorney general unless the governmental body requests an exemption under Subsection (c).

(b) The rules of the attorney general shall prescribe the methods for computing the charges for providing copies of public information in paper, electronic, and other kinds of media and the charge, deposit, or bond required for making public information that exists in a paper record available for inspection. The rules shall establish costs for various components of charges for providing copies of public information that shall be used by each governmental body in providing copies of public information or making public information that exists in a paper record available for inspection.

(c) A governmental body may request that it be exempt from part or all of the rules adopted by the attorney general for determining charges for providing copies of public information or the charge, deposit, or bond required for making public information that exists in a paper record available for inspection. The request must be made in writing to the attorney general and must state the reason for the exemption. If the attorney general determines that good cause exists for exempting a governmental body from a part or all of the rules, the attorney general shall give written notice of the determination to the governmental body within 90 days of the request. On receipt of the determination, the governmental body may amend its charges for providing copies of public information or its charge, deposit, or bond required for making public information that exists in a paper record available for inspection according to the determination of the attorney general.

(d) The attorney general shall publish annually in the Texas Register a list of the governmental bodies that have authorization from the attorney general to adopt any modified rules for determining the cost of providing copies of public information or making public information that exists in a paper record available for inspection.

(e) The rules of the attorney general do not apply to a state governmental body that is not a state agency for purposes of Subtitle D, Title 10.

§ 552.263. Bond for Payment of Costs or Cash Prepayment for Preparation of Copy of Public Information

(a) An officer for public information or the officer's agent may require a deposit or bond for payment of anticipated costs for the preparation of a copy of public information if:

   (1) the officer for public information or the officer's agent has provided the requestor with the written itemized statement required under Section 552.2615 detailing the estimated charge for providing the copy; and

   (2) the charge for providing the copy of the public information specifically requested by the requestor is estimated by the governmental body to exceed:

      (A) $100, if the governmental body has more than 15 full-time employees; or

      (B) $50, if the governmental body has fewer than 16 full-time employees.

(b) The officer for public information or the officer's agent may not require a deposit or bond be paid under Subsection (a) as a down payment for copies of public information that the requestor may request in the future.

(c) An officer for public information or the officer's agent may require a deposit or bond for payment of unpaid amounts owing to the governmental body in relation to previous requests that the requestor has made under this chapter before preparing a copy of public information in response to a new request if those unpaid amounts exceed $100. The officer for public information or the officer's agent may not seek payment of those unpaid amounts through any other means.

(d) The governmental body must fully document the existence and amount of those unpaid amounts or the amount of any anticipated costs, as applicable, before requiring a deposit or bond under this section. The documentation is subject to required public disclosure under this chapter.

(e) For purposes of Subchapters F and G, a request for a copy of public information is considered to have been received by a governmental body on the date the governmental body receives the deposit or bond for payment of anticipated costs or unpaid amounts if the governmental body's officer for public information or the officer's agent requires a deposit or bond in accordance with this section.

(e-1) If a requestor modifies the request in response to the requirement of a deposit or bond authorized by this section, the modified request is considered a separate request for the purposes of this chapter and is considered received on the date the governmental body receives the written modified request.

(f) A requestor who fails to make a deposit or post a bond required under Subsection (a) before the 10th business day after the date the deposit or bond is required is considered to have withdrawn the request for the copy of the public information that precipitated the requirement of the deposit or bond.

§ 552.264.   Copy of Public Information Requested by Member of Legislature

One copy of public information that is requested from a state agency by a member, agency, or committee of the legislature under Section 552.008 shall be provided without charge.

§ 552.265.   Charge For Paper Copy Provided by District or County Clerk

The charge for providing a paper copy made by a district or county clerk's office shall be the charge provided by Chapter 51 of this code, Chapter 118, Local Government Code, or other applicable law.

§ 552.266.   Charge For Copy of Public Information Provided by Municipal Court Clerk

The charge for providing a copy made by a municipal court clerk shall be the charge provided by municipal ordinance.

§ 552.2661.   Charge for Copy of Public Information Provided by School District

A school district that receives a request to produce public information for inspection or publication or to produce copies of public information in response to a requestor who, within the preceding 180 days, has accepted but failed to pay written itemized statements of estimated charges from the district as provided under Section 552.261(b) may require the requestor to pay the estimated charges for the request before the request is fulfilled.

§ 552.267. Waiver or Reduction of Charge for Providing Copy of Public Information

(a) A governmental body shall provide a copy of public information without charge or at a reduced charge if the governmental body determines that waiver or reduction of the charge is in the public interest because providing the copy of the information primarily benefits the general public.

(b) If the cost to a governmental body of processing the collection of a charge for providing a copy of public information will exceed the amount of the charge, the governmental body may waive the charge.

§ 552.268. Efficient Use of Public Resources

A governmental body shall make reasonably efficient use of supplies and other resources to avoid excessive reproduction costs.

§ 552.269. Overcharge or Overpayment for Copy of Public Information

(a) A person who believes the person has been overcharged for being provided with a copy of public information may complain to the attorney general in writing of the alleged overcharge, setting forth the reasons why the person believes the charges are excessive. The attorney general shall review the complaint and make a determination in writing as to the appropriate charge for providing the copy of the requested information. The governmental body shall respond to the attorney general to any written questions asked of the governmental body by the attorney general regarding the charges for providing the copy of the public information. The response must be made to the attorney general within 10 business days after the date the questions are received by the governmental body. If the attorney general determines that a governmental body has overcharged for providing the copy of requested public information, the governmental body shall promptly adjust its charges in accordance with the determination of the attorney general.

(b) A person who overpays for a copy of public information because a governmental body refuses or fails to follow the rules for charges adopted by the attorney general is entitled to recover three times the amount of the overcharge if the governmental body did not act in good faith in computing the costs.

§ 552.270. Charge for Government Publication

(a) This subchapter does not apply to a publication that is compiled and printed by or for a governmental body for public dissemination. If the cost of the publication is not determined by state law, a governmental body may determine the charge for providing the publication.

(b) This section does not prohibit a governmental body from providing a publication free of charge if state law does not require that a certain charge be made.

§ 552.271. Inspection of Public Information in Paper Record if Copy Not Requested

(a) If the requestor does not request a copy of public information, a charge may not be imposed for making available for inspection any public information that exists in a paper record, except as provided by this section.

(b) If a requested page contains confidential information that must be edited from the record before the information can be made available for inspection, the governmental body may charge for the cost of making a photocopy of the page from which confidential information must be edited. No charge other than the cost of the photocopy may be imposed under this subsection.

(c) Except as provided by Subsection (d), an officer for public information or the officer's agent may require a requestor to pay, or to make a deposit or post a bond for the payment of, anticipated personnel costs for making available for inspection public information that exists in paper records only if:

    (1) the public information specifically requested by the requestor:

        (A) is older than five years; or

        (B) completely fills, or when assembled will completely fill, six or more archival boxes; and

    (2) the officer for public information or the officer's agent estimates that more than five hours will be required to make the public information available for inspection.

(d) If the governmental body has fewer than 16 full-time employees, the payment, the deposit, or the bond authorized by Subsection (c) may be required only if:

    (1) the public information specifically requested by the requestor:

        (A) is older than three years; or

        (B) completely fills, or when assembled will completely fill, three or more archival boxes; and

    (2) the officer for public information or the officer's agent estimates that more than two hours will be required to make the public information available for inspection.

§ 552.272. Inspection of Electronic Record if Copy Not Requested

(a) In response to a request to inspect information that exists in an electronic medium and that is not available directly on-line to the requestor, a charge may not be imposed for access to the information, unless complying with the request will require programming or manipulation of data. If programming or manipulation of data is required, the governmental body shall notify the requestor before assembling the information and provide the requestor with an estimate of charges that will be imposed to make the information available. A charge under this section must be assessed in accordance with this subchapter.

(b) If public information exists in an electronic form on a computer owned or leased by a governmental body and if the public has direct access to that computer through a computer network or other means, the electronic form of the information may be electronically copied from that computer without charge if accessing the information does not require processing, programming, or manipulation on the government-owned or government-leased computer before the information is copied.

(c) If public information exists in an electronic form on a computer owned or leased by a governmental body and if the public has direct access to that computer through a computer network or other means and the information requires processing, programming, or manipulation before it can be electronically copied, a governmental body may impose charges in accordance with this subchapter.

(d) If information is created or kept in an electronic form, a governmental body is encouraged to explore options to separate out confidential information and to make public information available to the public through electronic access through a computer network or by other means.

(e) The provisions of this section that prohibit a governmental entity from imposing a charge for access to information that exists in an electronic medium do not apply to the collection of a fee set by the supreme court after consultation with the Judicial Committee on Information Technology as authorized by Section 77.031 for the use of a computerized electronic judicial information system.

§ 552.274. Report by Attorney General on Cost of Copies

(a) The attorney general shall:

   (1)   biennially update a report prepared by the attorney general about the charges made by state agencies for providing copies of public information; and

   (2)   provide a copy of the updated report on the attorney general's open records page on the Internet not later than March 1 of each even-numbered year.

(b) Repealed by Acts 2011, 82nd Leg., ch. 1083 (S.B. 1179), § 25(62).

(c) In this section, "state agency" has the meaning assigned by Sections 2151.002(2)(A) and (C).

§ 552.275. Requests That Require Large Amounts of Employee or Personnel Time

(a) A governmental body may establish reasonable monthly and yearly limits on the amount of time that personnel of the governmental body are required to spend producing public information for inspection or duplication by a requestor, or providing copies of public information to a requestor, without recovering its costs attributable to that personnel time.

(a-1) For the purposes of this section, all county officials who have designated the same officer for public information may calculate the amount of time that personnel are required to spend collectively for purposes of the monthly or yearly limit.

(b) A yearly time limit established under Subsection (a) may not be less than 36 hours for a requestor during the 12-month period that corresponds to the fiscal year of the governmental body. A monthly time limit established under Subsection (a) may not be less than 15 hours for a requestor for a one-month period.

(c) In determining whether a time limit established under Subsection (a) applies, any time spent complying with a request for public information submitted in the name of a minor, as defined by Section 101.003(a), Family Code, is to be included in the calculation of the cumulative amount of time spent complying with a request for public information by a parent, guardian, or other person who has control of the minor under a court order and with whom the minor resides, unless that parent, guardian, or other person establishes that another person submitted that request in the name of the minor.

(d) If a governmental body establishes a time limit under Subsection (a), each time the governmental body complies with a request for public information, the governmental body shall provide the requestor with a written statement of the amount of personnel time spent complying with that request and the cumulative amount of time spent complying with requests for public information from that requestor during the applicable monthly or yearly period. The amount of time spent preparing the written statement may not be included in the amount of time included in the statement provided to the requestor under this subsection.

(e) Subject to Subsection (e-1), if in connection with a request for public information, the cumulative amount of personnel time spent complying with requests for public information from the same requestor equals or exceeds the limit established by the governmental body under Subsection (a), the governmental body shall provide the requestor with a written estimate of the total cost, including materials, personnel time, and overhead expenses, necessary to comply with the request. The written estimate must be provided to the requestor on or before the 10th day after the date on which the public information was requested. The amount of this charge relating to the cost of locating, compiling, and producing the public information shall be established by rules prescribed by the attorney general under Sections 552.262(a) and (b).

(e-1) This subsection applies only to a request made by a requestor who has made a previous request to a governmental body that has not been withdrawn, for which the governmental body has located and compiled documents in response, and for which the governmental body has issued a statement under Subsection (e) that remains unpaid on the date the requestor submits the new request. A governmental body is not required to locate, compile, produce, or provide copies of documents or prepare a statement under Subsection (e) in response to a new request described by this subsection until the date the requestor pays each unpaid statement issued under Subsection (e) in connection with a previous request or withdraws the previous request to which the statement applies.

(f) If the governmental body determines that additional time is required to prepare the written estimate under Subsection (e) and provides the requestor with a written statement of that determination, the governmental body must provide the written statement under that subsection as soon as practicable, but on or before the 10th day after the date the governmental body provided the statement under this subsection.

(g) If a governmental body provides a requestor with the written statement under Subsection (e) and the time limits prescribed by Subsection (a) regarding the requestor have been exceeded, the governmental body is not required to produce public information for inspection or duplication or to provide copies of public information in response to the requestor's request unless on or before the 10th day after the date the governmental body provided the written statement under that subsection, the requestor submits a payment of the amount stated in the written statement provided under Subsection (e).

(h) If the requestor fails or refuses to submit payment under Subsection (g), the requestor is considered to have withdrawn the requestor's pending request for public information.

(i) This section does not prohibit a governmental body from providing a copy of public information without charge or at a reduced rate under Section 552.267 or from waiving a charge for providing a copy of public information under that section.

(j) This section does not apply if the requestor is and individual who, for a substantial portion of the individual's livelihood or for substantial financial gain, gathers, compiles, prepares, collects, photographs, records, writes, edits, reports, investigates, processes, or publishes news or information for and is seeking the information for:

    (1) dissemination by a new medium or communications service provider, including:

        (A) an individual who supervises or assists in gathering, preparing, and disseminating the news or information; or

        (B) an individual who is or was a journalist, scholar, or researcher employed by an institution of higher education at the time the person made the request for information; or

    (2) creation or maintenance of an abstract plant as described by Section 2501.004, Insurance Code.

(k) This section does not apply if the requestor is an elected official of the United States, this state, or a political subdivision of this state.

(l) This section does not apply if the requestor is a representative of a publicly funded legal services organization that is exempt from federal income taxation under Section 501(a), Internal Revenue Code of 1986, as amended, by being listed as an exempt entity under Section 501(c)(3) of that code.

(m) In this section"

    (1) "Communication service provider" has the meaning assigned by Section 22.021, Civil Practice and Remedies Code.

    (2) "News Medium" means a newspaper, magazine or periodical, a book publisher, a news agency, a wire service, an FCC-licensed radio or television station or network of such stations, a cable, satellite, or other transmission system or carrier or channel, or a channel or programming service for a station, network, system, or carrier, or an audio or audiovisual production company or Internet company or provider, or the parent, subsidiary, division, or affiliate of that entity, that disseminates news or information to the public by any means, including:

(A) print;

(B) television;

(C) radio;

(D) photographic;

(E) mechanical;

(F) electronic; and

(G) other means, known or unknown, that are accessible to the public.

SUBCHAPTER G. ATTORNEY GENERAL DECISIONS

§ 552.301. Request for Attorney General Decision

(a) A governmental body that receives a written request for information that it wishes to withhold from public disclosure and that it considers to be within one of the exceptions under Subchapter C must ask for a decision from the attorney general about whether the information is within that exception if there has not been a previous determination about whether the information falls within one of the exceptions.

(a-1) For the purposes of this subchapter, if a governmental body receives a written request by United States mail and cannot adequately establish the actual date on which the governmental body received the request, the written request is considered to have been received by the governmental body on the third business day after the date of the postmark on a properly addressed request.

(b) The governmental body must ask for the attorney general's decision and state the exceptions that apply within a reasonable time but not later than the 10th business day after the date of receiving the written request.

(c) For purposes of this subchapter, a written request includes a request made in writing that is sent to the officer for public information, or the person designated by that officer, by electronic mail or facsimile transmission.

(d) A governmental body that requests an attorney general decision under Subsection (a) must provide to the requestor within a reasonable time but not later than the 10th business day after the date of receiving the requestor's written request:

(1) a written statement that the governmental body wishes to withhold the requested information and has asked for a decision from the attorney general about whether the information is within an exception to public disclosure; and

(2)   a copy of the governmental body's written communication to the attorney general asking for the decision or, if the governmental body's written communication to the attorney general discloses the requested information, a redacted copy of that written communication.

(e) A governmental body that requests an attorney general decision under Subsection (a) must within a reasonable time but not later than the 15th business day after the date of receiving the written request:

(1)   submit to the attorney general:

(A)   written comments stating the reasons why the stated exceptions apply that would allow the information to be withheld;

(B)   a copy of the written request for information;

(C)   a signed statement as to the date on which the written request for information was received by the governmental body or evidence sufficient to establish that date; and

(D)   a copy of the specific information requested, or submit representative samples of the information if a voluminous amount of information was requested; and

(2)   label that copy of the specific information, or of the representative samples, to indicate which exceptions apply to which parts of the copy.

(e-1) A governmental body that submits written comments to the attorney general under Subsection (e)(1)(A) shall send a copy of those comments to the person who requested the information from the governmental body not later than the 15th business day after the date of receiving the written request. If the written comments disclose or contain the substance of the information requested, the copy of the comments provided to the person must be a redacted copy.

(f) A governmental body must release the requested information and is prohibited from asking for a decision from the attorney general about whether information requested under this chapter is within an exception under Subchapter C if:

(1)   the governmental body has previously requested and received a determination from the attorney general concerning the precise information at issue in a pending request; and

(2)   the attorney general or a court determined that the information is public information under this chapter that is not excepted by Subchapter C.

(g) A governmental body may ask for another decision from the attorney general concerning the precise information that was at issue in a prior decision made by the attorney general under this subchapter if:

(1)   a suit challenging the prior decision was timely filed against the attorney general in accordance with this chapter concerning the precise information at issue;

(2)   the attorney general determines that the requestor has voluntarily withdrawn the request for the information in writing or has abandoned the request; and

(3)   the parties agree to dismiss the lawsuit.

§ 552.302.   Failure to Make Timely Request for Attorney General Decision; Presumption that Information Is Public

If a governmental body does not request an attorney general decision as provided by Section 552.301 and provide the requestor with the information required by Sections 552.301(d) and (e-1), the information requested in writing is presumed to be subject to required public disclosure and must be released unless there is a compelling reason to withhold the information.

§ 552.303.   Delivery of Requested Information to Attorney General; Disclosure of Requested Information; Attorney General Request for Submission of Additional Information

(a) A governmental body that requests an attorney general decision under this subchapter shall supply to the attorney general, in accordance with Section 552.301, the specific information requested. Unless the information requested is confidential by law, the governmental body may disclose the requested information to the public or to the requestor before the attorney general makes a final determination that the requested information is public or, if suit is filed under this chapter, before a final determination that the requested information is public has been made by the court with jurisdiction over the suit, except as otherwise provided by Section 552.322.

(b) The attorney general may determine whether a governmental body's submission of information to the attorney general under Section 552.301 is sufficient to render a decision.

(c) If the attorney general determines that information in addition to that required by Section 552.301 is necessary to render a decision, the attorney general shall give written notice of that fact to the governmental body and the requestor.

(d) A governmental body notified under Subsection (c) shall submit the necessary additional information to the attorney general not later than the seventh calendar day after the date the notice is received.

(e) If a governmental body does not comply with Subsection (d), the information that is the subject of a person's request to the governmental body and regarding which the governmental body fails to comply with Subsection (d) is presumed to be subject to required public disclosure and must be released unless there exists a compelling reason to withhold the information.

§ 552.3035. Disclosure of Requested Information by Attorney General

The attorney general may not disclose to the requestor or the public any information submitted to the attorney general under Section 552.301(e)(1)(D).

§ 552.304.   Submission of Public Comments

(a) A person may submit written comments stating reasons why the information at issue in a request for an attorney general decision should or should not be released.

(b) A person who submits written comments to the attorney general under Subsection (a) shall send a copy of those comments to both the person who requested the information from the governmental body and the governmental body. If the written comments submitted to the attorney general disclose or contain the substance of the information requested from the governmental body, the copy of the comments sent to the person who requested the information must be a redacted copy.

(c) In this section, "written comments" includes a letter, a memorandum, or a brief.

§ 552.305.   Information Involving Privacy or Property Interests of Third Party

(a) In a case in which information is requested under this chapter and a person's privacy or property interests may be involved, including a case under Section 552.101, 552.104, 552.110, or 552.114, a governmental body may decline to release the information for the purpose of requesting an attorney general decision.

(b) A person whose interests may be involved under Subsection (a), or any other person, may submit in writing to the attorney general the person's reasons why the information should be withheld or released.

(c) The governmental body may, but is not required to, submit its reasons why the information should be withheld or released.

(d) If release of a person's proprietary information may be subject to exception under Section 552.101, 552.110, 552.113, or 552.131, the governmental body that requests an attorney general decision under Section 552.301 shall make a good faith attempt to notify that person of the request for the attorney general decision. Notice under this subsection must:

   (1)   be in writing and sent within a reasonable time not later than the 10th business day after the date the governmental body receives the request for the information; and

   (2)   include:

      (A)   a copy of the written request for the information, if any, received by the governmental body; and

      (B)   a statement, in the form prescribed by the attorney general, that the person is entitled to submit in writing to the attorney general within a reasonable time not later than the 10th business day after the date the person receives the notice:

         (i)   each reason the person has as to why the information should be withheld; and

         (ii)   a letter, memorandum, or brief in support of that reason.

(e) A person who submits a letter, memorandum, or brief to the attorney general under Subsection (d) shall send a copy of that letter, memorandum, or brief to the person who requested the information from the governmental body. If the letter, memorandum, or brief submitted to the attorney general contains the substance of the information requested, the copy of the letter, memorandum, or brief may be a redacted copy.

§ 552.306. Rendition of Attorney General Decision; Issuance of Written Opinion

(a) Except as provided by Section 552.011, the attorney general shall promptly render a decision requested under this subchapter, consistent with the standards of due process, determining whether the requested information is within one of the exceptions of Subchapter C. The attorney general shall render the decision not later than the 45th business day after the date the attorney general received the request for a decision. If the attorney general is unable to issue the decision within the 45-day period, the attorney general may extend the period for issuing the decision by an additional 10 business days by informing the governmental body and the requestor, during the original 45-day period, of the reason for the delay.

(b) The attorney general shall issue a written opinion of the determination and shall provide a copy of the opinion to the requestor.

§ 552.307. Special Right of Access; Attorney General Decisions

(a) If a governmental body determines that information subject to a special right of access under Section 552.023 is exempt from disclosure under an exception of Subchapter C, other than an exception intended to protect the privacy interest of the requestor or the person whom the requestor is authorized to represent, the governmental body shall, before disclosing the information, submit a written request for a decision to the attorney general under the procedures of this subchapter.

(b) If a decision is not requested under Subsection (a), the governmental body shall release the information to the person with a special right of access under Section 552.023 not later than the 10th business day after the date of receiving the request for information.

§ 552.308. Timeliness of Action by United States Mail, Interagency Mail, or Common Contract Carrier

(a) When this subchapter requires a request, notice, or other document to be submitted or otherwise given to a person within a specified period, the requirement is met in a timely fashion if the document is sent to the person by first class United States mail or common or contract carrier properly addressed with postage or handling charges prepaid and:

(1) it bears a post office cancellation mark or a receipt mark of a common or contract carrier indicating a time within that period; or

(2) the person required to submit or otherwise give the document furnishes satisfactory proof that it was deposited in the mail or with a common or contract carrier within that period.

(b) When this subchapter requires an agency of this state to submit or otherwise give to the attorney general within a specified period a request, notice, or other writing, the requirement is met in a timely fashion if:

 (1) the request, notice, or other writing is sent to the attorney general by interagency mail; and

 (2) the agency provides evidence sufficient to establish that the request, notice, or other writing was deposited in the interagency mail within that period.

§ 552.309. Timeliness of Action by Electronic Submission

(a) When this subchapter requires a request, notice, or other document to be submitted or otherwise given to the attorney general within a specified period, the requirement is met in a timely fashion if the document is submitted to the attorney general through the attorney general's designated electronic filing system within that period.

(b) The attorney general may electronically transmit a notice, decision, or other document. When this subchapter requires the attorney general to deliver a notice, decision, or other document within a specified period, the requirement is met in a timely fashion if the document is electronically transmitted by the attorney general within that period.

(c) This section does not affect the right of a person or governmental body to submit information to the attorney general under Section 552.308.

SUBCHAPTER H. CIVIL ENFORCEMENT

§ 552.321. Suit for Writ of Mandamus

(a) A requestor or the attorney general may file suit for a writ of mandamus compelling a governmental body to make information available for public inspection if the governmental body refuses to request an attorney general's decision as provided by Subchapter G or refuses to supply public information or information that the attorney general has determined is public information that is not excepted from disclosure under Subchapter C.

(b) A suit filed by a requestor under this section must be filed in a district court for the county in which the main offices of the governmental body are located. A suit filed by the attorney general under this section must be filed in a district court of Travis County, except that a suit against a municipality with a population of 100,000 or less must be filed in a district court for the county in which the main offices of the municipality are located.

§ 552.3215. Declaratory Judgment or Injunctive Relief

(a) In this section:

 (1) "Complainant" means a person who claims to be the victim of a violation of this chapter.

(2) "State agency" means a board, commission, department, office, or other agency that:

(A) is in the executive branch of state government;

(B) was created by the constitution or a statute of this state; and

(C) has statewide jurisdiction.

(b) An action for a declaratory judgment or injunctive relief may be brought in accordance with this section against a governmental body that violates this chapter.

(c) The district or county attorney for the county in which a governmental body other than a state agency is located or the attorney general may bring the action in the name of the state only in a district court for that county. If the governmental body extends into more than one county, the action may be brought only in the county in which the administrative offices of the governmental body are located.

(d) If the governmental body is a state agency, the Travis County district attorney or the attorney general may bring the action in the name of the state only in a district court of Travis County.

(e) A complainant may file a complaint alleging a violation of this chapter. The complaint must be filed with the district or county attorney of the county in which the governmental body is located unless the governmental body is the district or county attorney. If the governmental body extends into more than one county, the complaint must be filed with the district or county attorney of the county in which the administrative offices of the governmental body are located. If the governmental body is a state agency, the complaint may be filed with the Travis County district attorney. If the governmental body is the district or county attorney, the complaint must be filed with the attorney general. To be valid, a complaint must:

(1) be in writing and signed by the complainant;

(2) state the name of the governmental body that allegedly committed the violation, as accurately as can be done by the complainant;

(3) state the time and place of the alleged commission of the violation, as definitely as can be done by the complainant; and

(4) in general terms, describe the violation.

(f) A district or county attorney with whom the complaint is filed shall indicate on the face of the written complaint the date the complaint is filed.

(g) Before the 31st day after the date a complaint is filed under Subsection (e), the district or county attorney shall:

(1) determine whether:

(A) the violation alleged in the complaint was committed; and

(B)   an action will be brought against the governmental body under this section; and

(2)   notify the complainant in writing of those determinations.

(h) Notwithstanding Subsection (g)(1), if the district or county attorney believes that that official has a conflict of interest that would preclude that official from bringing an action under this section against the governmental body complained of, before the 31st day after the date the complaint was filed the county or district attorney shall inform the complainant of that official's belief and of the complainant's right to file the complaint with the attorney general. If the district or county attorney determines not to bring an action under this section, the district or county attorney shall:

(1)   include a statement of the basis for that determination; and

(2)   return the complaint to the complainant.

(i)   If the district or county attorney determines not to bring an action under this section, the complainant is entitled to file the complaint with the attorney general before the 31st day after the date the complaint is returned to the complainant. A complainant is entitled to file a complaint with the attorney general on or after the 90th day after the date the complainant files the complaint with the district or county attorney if the district or county attorney has not brought an action under this section. On receipt of the written complaint, the attorney general shall comply with each requirement in Subsections (g) and (h) in the time required by those subsections. If the attorney general decides to bring an action under this section against a governmental body located only in one county in response to the complaint, the attorney general must comply with Subsection (c).

(j)   An action may be brought under this section only if the official proposing to bring the action notifies the governmental body in writing of the official's determination that the alleged violation was committed and the governmental body does not cure the violation before the fourth day after the date the governmental body receives the notice.

(k)   An action authorized by this section is in addition to any other civil, administrative, or criminal action provided by this chapter or another law.

§ 552.322.   Discovery of Information Under Protective Order Pending Final Determination

In a suit filed under this chapter, the court may order that the information at issue may be discovered only under a protective order until a final determination is made.

§ 552.3221.   In Camera Inspection of Information

(a) In any suit filed under this chapter, the information at issue may be filed with the court for in camera inspection as is necessary for the adjudication of the case.

(b) Upon receipt of the information at issue for in camera inspection, the court shall enter an order that prevents release to or access by any person other than the court, a reviewing court of appeals, or parties permitted to inspect the information pursuant to a protective order. The order shall further note the filing date and time.

(c) The information at issue filed with the court for in camera inspection shall be:

(1) appended to the order and transmitted by the court to the clerk for filing as "information at issue";

(2) maintained in a sealed envelope or in a manner that precludes disclosure of the information; and

(3) transmitted by the clerk to any court of appeal as part of the clerk's record.

(d) Information filed with the court under this section does not constitute "court records" within the meaning of Rule 76a, Texas Rules of Civil Procedure, and shall not be made available by the clerk or any custodian of record for public inspection.

(e) For purposes of this section, "information at issue" is defined as information held by a governmental body that forms the basis of a suit under this chapter.

§ 552.323. Assessment of Costs of Litigation and Reasonable Attorney Fees

(a) In an action brought under Section 552.321 or 552.3215, the court shall assess costs of litigation and reasonable attorney fees incurred by a plaintiff who substantially prevails, except that the court may not assess those costs and fees against a governmental body if the court finds that the governmental body acted in reasonable reliance on:

(1) a judgment or an order of a court applicable to the governmental body;

(2) the published opinion of an appellate court; or

(3) a written decision of the attorney general, including a decision issued under Subchapter G or an opinion issued under Section 402.042.

(b) In an action brought under Section 552.324, the court may assess costs of litigation and reasonable attorney's fees incurred by a plaintiff or defendant who substantially prevails. In exercising its discretion under this subsection, the court shall consider whether the conduct of the governmental body had a reasonable basis in law and whether the litigation was brought in good faith.

§ 552.324. Suit by Governmental Body

(a) The only suit a governmental body may file seeking to withhold information from a requestor is a suit that:

(1) is filed in a Travis County district court against the attorney general in accordance with Section 552.325 and

   (2)   seeks declaratory relief from compliance with a decision by the attorney general issued under Subchapter G.

(b) The governmental body must bring the suit not later than the 30th calendar day after the date the governmental body receives the decision of the attorney general determining that the requested information must be disclosed to the requestor. If the governmental body does not bring suit within that period, the governmental body shall comply with the decision of the attorney general. If a governmental body wishes to preserve an affirmative defense for its officer of public information as provided in Section 552.353(b)(3), a suit must be filed within the deadline provided in Section 552.353(b)(3).

§ 552.325.   Parties to Suit Seeking to Withhold Information

(a) A governmental body, officer for public information, or other person or entity that files a suit seeking to withhold information from a requestor may not file suit against the person requesting the information. The requestor is entitled to intervene in the suit.

(b) The governmental body, officer for public information, or other person or entity that files the suit shall demonstrate to the court that the governmental body, officer for public information, or other person or entity made a timely good faith effort to inform the requestor, by certified mail or by another written method of notice that requires the return of a receipt, of:

   (1)   the existence of the suit, including the subject matter and cause number of the suit and the court in which the suit is filed;

   (2)   the requestor's right to intervene in the suit or to choose to not participate in the suit;

   (3)   the fact that the suit is against the attorney general in Travis County district court; and

   (4)   the address and phone number of the office of the attorney general.

(c) If the attorney general enters into a proposed settlement that all or part of the information that is the subject of the suit should be withheld, the attorney general shall notify the requestor of that decision and, if the requestor has not intervened in the suit, of the requestor's right to intervene to contest the withholding. The attorney general shall notify the requestor:

   (1)   in the manner required by the Texas Rules of Civil Procedure, if the requestor has intervened in the suit; or

   (2)   by certified mail or by another written method of notice that requires the return of a receipt, if the requestor has not intervened in the suit.

(d) The court shall allow the requestor a reasonable period to intervene after the attorney general attempts to give notice under Subsection (c)(2).

§ 552.326. Failure to Raise Exceptions Before Attorney General

(a) Except as provided by Subsection (b), the only exceptions to required disclosure within Subchapter C that a governmental body may raise in a suit filed under this chapter are exceptions that the governmental body properly raised before the attorney general in connection with its request for a decision regarding the matter under Subchapter G.

(b) Subsection (a) does not prohibit a governmental body from raising an exception:

    (1)   based on a requirement of federal law; or

    (2)   involving the property or privacy interests of another person.

§ 552.327. Dismissal of Suit Due to Requestor's Withdrawal or Abandonment of Request

A court may dismiss a suit challenging a decision of the attorney general brought in accordance with this chapter if:

    (1)   all parties to the suit agree to the dismissal; and

    (2)   the attorney general determines and represents to the court that the requestor has voluntarily withdrawn the request for information in writing or has abandoned the request.

SUBCHAPTER I. CRIMINAL VIOLATIONS

§ 552.351. Destruction, Removal, or Alteration of Public Information

(a) A person commits an offense if the person willfully destroys, mutilates, removes without permission as provided by this chapter, or alters public information.

(b) An offense under this section is a misdemeanor punishable by:

    (1)   a fine of not less than $25 or more than $4,000;

    (2)   confinement in the county jail for not less than three days or more than three months; or

    (3)   both the fine and confinement.

(c) It is an exception to the application of Subsection (a) that the public information was transferred under Section 441.204.

§ 552.352. Distribution or Misuse of Confidential Information

(a) A person commits an offense if the person distributes information considered confidential under the terms of this chapter.

(a-1) An officer or employee of a governmental body who obtains access to confidential information under Section 552.008 commits an offense if the officer or employee knowingly:

    (1)   uses the confidential information for a purpose other than the purpose for which the information was received or for a purpose unrelated to the law that permitted the officer or employee to obtain access to the information, including solicitation of political contributions or solicitation of clients;

    (2)   permits inspection of the confidential information by a person who is not authorized to inspect the information; or

    (3)   discloses the confidential information to a person who is not authorized to receive the information.

(a-2) For purposes of Subsection (a-1), a member of an advisory committee to a governmental body who obtains access to confidential information in that capacity is considered to be an officer or employee of the governmental body.

(b) An offense under this section is a misdemeanor punishable by:

    (1)   a fine of not more than $1,000;

    (2)   confinement in the county jail for not more than six months; or

    (3)   both the fine and confinement.

(c) A violation under this section constitutes official misconduct.

§ 552.353. Failure or Refusal of Officer for Public Information to Provide Access to or Copying of Public Information

(a) An officer for public information, or the officer's agent, commits an offense if, with criminal negligence, the officer or the officer's agent fails or refuses to give access to, or to permit or provide copying of, public information to a requestor as provided by this chapter.

(b) It is an affirmative defense to prosecution under Subsection (a) that the officer for public information reasonably believed that public access to the requested information was not required and that:

    (1)   the officer acted in reasonable reliance on a court order or a written interpretation of this chapter contained in an opinion of a court of record or of the attorney general issued under Subchapter G;

(2)   the officer requested a decision from the attorney general in accordance with Subchapter G, and the decision is pending; or

(3)   not later than the 10th calendar day after the date of receipt of a decision by the attorney general that the information is public, the officer or the governmental body for whom the defendant is the officer for public information filed a petition for a declaratory judgment against the attorney general in a Travis County district court seeking relief from compliance with the decision of the attorney general, as provided by Section 552.324, and the cause is pending.

(c) It is an affirmative defense to prosecution under Subsection (a) that a person or entity has, not later than the 10th calendar day after the date of receipt by a governmental body of a decision by the attorney general that the information is public, filed a cause of action seeking relief from compliance with the decision of the attorney general, as provided by Section 552.325, and the cause is pending.

(d) It is an affirmative defense to prosecution under Subsection (a) that the defendant is the agent of an officer for public information and that the agent reasonably relied on the written instruction of the officer for public information not to disclose the public information requested.

(e) An offense under this section is a misdemeanor punishable by:

(1)   a fine of not more than $1,000;

(2)   confinement in the county jail for not more than six months; or

(3)   both the fine and confinement.

(f) A violation under this section constitutes official misconduct.

PART FOUR: RULES PROMULGATED BY THE ATTORNEY GENERAL

TEXAS ADMINISTRATIVE CODE, TITLE 1, CHAPTER 63

Subchapter A.   Confidentiality of Information Requested for Legislative Purposes

§ 63.1.   Definition, Purpose, and Application

(a)   In this subchapter, "legislative requestor" means an individual member, agency, or committee of the legislature.

(b)   This subchapter governs the procedures by which the attorney general shall render a decision sought by a legislative requestor under Texas Government Code § 552.008(b-2).

(c)   Texas Government Code § 552.308 applies to all deadlines established in this subchapter.

§ 63.2.   Request for Attorney General Decision Regarding Confidentiality

(a)   If a governmental body that receives a written request for information from a legislative requestor under Texas Government Code § 552.008 determines the requested information is confidential and requires the legislative requestor to sign a confidentiality agreement, the legislative requestor may ask for an attorney general decision about whether the information covered by the confidentiality agreement is confidential under law.

(b)   A request for an attorney general decision must:

(1)   be in writing and signed by the legislative requestor;

(2)   state the name of the governmental body to whom the original request for information was made; and

(3)   state the date the original request was made.

(c)   The legislative requestor must submit a copy of the original request with the request for a decision. If the legislative requestor is unable to do so, the legislative requestor must include a written description of the original request in the request for a decision.

(d)   The legislative requestor may submit written comments to the attorney general stating reasons why the requested information should not be considered confidential by law. The written comments must be labeled to indicate whether any portion of the comments discloses or contains the substance of the specific information deemed confidential by the governmental body. A legislative requestor who submits written comments to the attorney general shall send a copy of those comments to the governmental body.

(e)   The deadlines in § 63.3 and § 63.6 of this subchapter commence on the date on which the attorney general receives from the legislative requestor all of the information required by subsections (b) and (c) of this section.

§ 63.3.   Notice

(a)   The attorney general shall notify the governmental body in writing of a request for a decision and provide the governmental body a copy of the request for a decision within a reasonable time but not later than the 5th business day after the date of receiving the request for a decision.

(b)   The attorney general shall provide the legislative requestor a copy of the written notice to the governmental body, excluding a copy of the request for a decision, within a reasonable time but not later than the 5th business day after the date of receiving the request for a decision.

§ 63.4.   Submission of Documents and Comments

(a)   Within a reasonable time but not later than the 10th business day after the date of receiving the attorney general's written notice of the request for a decision, a governmental body shall:

(1)   submit to the attorney general:

(A)   written comments stating the law that deems the requested information confidential and the reasons why the stated law applies to the information;

(B)   a copy of the written request for information; and

(C)   a copy of the specific information deemed confidential by the governmental body, or representative samples of the information if a voluminous amount of information was requested; and

(2)   label the copy of the specific information, or the representative samples, to indicate which laws apply to which parts of the copy; and

(3)   label the written comments to indicate whether any portion of the comments discloses or contains the substance of the specific information deemed confidential by the governmental body.

(b)   A governmental body that submits written comments to the attorney general shall send a copy of those comments to the legislative requestor within a reasonable time but not later than the 10th business day after the date of receiving the attorney general's written notice of the request for a decision.

(c) If a governmental body determines a person may have a property interest in the requested information, the governmental body shall notify that person in accordance with Texas Government Code § 552.305(d). The governmental body shall notify the affected person not later than the 10th business day after receiving written notice of the request for a decision.

(d) If a person notified in accordance with Texas Government Code § 552.305 decides to submit written comments to the attorney general, the person must do so not later than the 10th business day after receiving the notice. The written comments must be labeled to indicate whether any portion of the comments discloses or contains the substance of the specific information deemed confidential by the governmental body.

(e) Any interested person may submit written comments to the attorney general stating why the requested information is or is not confidential. The written comments must be labeled to indicate whether any portion of the comments discloses or contains the substance of the specific information deemed confidential by the governmental body.

(f) A person who submits written comments under subsection (d) or (e) of this section shall send a copy of those comments to both the legislative requestor and the governmental body.

§ 63.5. Additional Information

(a) The attorney general may determine whether a governmental body's submission of information under § 63.4(a) of this subchapter is sufficient to render a decision.

(b) If the attorney general determines that information in addition to that required by § 63.4(a) of this subchapter is necessary to render a decision, the attorney general shall give written notice of that fact to the governmental body and the legislative requestor.

(c) A governmental body notified under subsection (b) of this section shall submit the necessary additional information to the attorney general not later than the seventh calendar day after the date the notice is received.

§ 63.6. Rendition of Attorney General Decision; Issuance of Written Decision

(a) The attorney general shall promptly render a decision requested under this subchapter, not later than the 45th business day after the date of receiving the request for a decision.

(b) The attorney general shall issue a written decision and shall provide a copy of the decision to the legislative requestor, the governmental body, and any interested person who submitted necessary information or a brief to the attorney general about the matter.

Subchapter B.   Review of Public Information Redactions

§ 63.11. Purpose and Application

(a)   This subchapter governs the procedures by which the attorney general shall render a decision sought by a requestor under Texas Government Code §§ 552.024(c-1), 552.1175(g), 552.130(d), 552.136(d), or 552.138(d).

(b)   Texas Government Code § 552.308 and § 552.309 apply to all deadlines established in this subchapter.

§ 63.12. Request for Review by the Attorney General

(a)   If a governmental body redacts or withholds information under Texas Government Code §§ 552.024(c)(2), 552.1175(f), 552.130(c), 552.136(c), or 552.138(c) without requesting a decision from the attorney general about whether the information may be redacted or withheld, the requestor may ask the attorney general to review the governmental body's determination that the information at issue is excepted from required disclosure.

(b)   A request for review by the attorney general must:

    (1)   be in writing and signed by the requestor;

    (2)   state the name of the governmental body to whom the original request for information was made; and

    (3)   state the date the original request was made.

(c)   The requestor must submit a copy of the original request with the request for review. If the requestor is unable to do so, the requestor must include a written description of the original request in the request for review.

(d)   The requestor may submit written comments to the attorney general stating reasons why the information at issue should be released.

(e)   The deadlines in § 63.13 and § 63.16 of this subchapter commence on the date on which the attorney general receives from the requestor all of the information required by subsections (b) and (c) of this section.

§ 63.13. Notice

(a)   The attorney general shall notify the governmental body in writing of a request for review and provide the governmental body a copy of the request for review not later than the 5th business day after the date of receiving the request for review.

(b)   The attorney general shall provide the requestor a copy of the written notice to the governmental body, excluding a copy of the request for review, not later than the 5th business day after the date of receiving the request for review.

§ 63.14. Submission of Documents and Comments

(a) A governmental body shall provide to the attorney general within a reasonable time but not later than the 10th business day after the date of receiving the attorney general's written notice of the request for review:

    (1) an unredacted copy of the specific information requested, or representative samples of the information if a voluminous amount of information was requested;

    (2) a copy of the specific information requested, or representative samples of the information if a voluminous amount of information was requested, illustrating the information redacted or withheld;

    (3) written comments stating the reasons why the information at issue was redacted or withheld;

    (4) a copy of the written request for information; and

    (5) a copy of the form letter the governmental body provided to the requestor as required by Texas Government Code §§ 552.024(c-2), 552.1175(h), 552.130(e), 552.136(e), and 552.138(e).

(b) A governmental body that submits written comments to the attorney general shall send a copy of those comments to the requestor within a reasonable time but not later than the 10th business day after the date of receiving the attorney general's written notice of the request for review. If the written comments disclose or contain the substance of the information at issue, the copy of the comments provided to the requestor must be a redacted copy.

(c) A person may submit written comments to the attorney general stating why the information at issue in a request for review should or should not be released.

(d) A person who submits written comments under subsection (c) of this section shall send a copy of those comments to both the requestor and the governmental body. If the written comments disclose or contain the substance of the information at issue, the copy of the comments sent to the requestor must be a redacted copy.

§ 63.15. Additional Information

(a) The attorney general may determine whether a governmental body's submission of information under § 63.14(a) of this subchapter is sufficient to render a decision.

(b) If the attorney general determines that information in addition to that required by § 63.14(a) of this subchapter is necessary to render a decision, the attorney general shall give written notice of that fact to the governmental body and the requestor.

(c) A governmental body notified under subsection (b) of this section shall submit the necessary additional information to the attorney general not later than the 7th calendar day after the date the notice is received.

§ 63.16. Rendition of Attorney General Decision; Issuance of Written Decision

(a) The attorney general shall promptly render a decision requested under this subchapter, not later than the 45th business day after the date of receiving the request for review.

(b) The attorney general shall issue a written decision and shall provide a copy of the decision to the requestor, the governmental body, and any interested person who submitted necessary information or a brief to the attorney general about the matter.

Subchapter C. Electronic Submission of Request for Attorney General Open Records Decision

§ 63.21. Definitions

The following words and terms, when used in this subchapter, shall have the following meanings:

(1) "Governmental body" means a governmental body as defined in Texas Government Code § 552.003(1).

(2) "Request for decision" means a request for an attorney general open records decision made by a governmental body pursuant to Texas Government Code § 552.301 and § 552.309.

(3) "Requestor" means a requestor as defined in Texas Government Code § 552.003(6).

(4) "Interested Third Party" means any third party who wishes to submit comments, documents, or other materials for consideration in the attorney general's open records decision process under Texas Government Code § 552.304 or § 552.305.

(5) "Attorney General's Designated Electronic Filing System" means the online, electronic filing system designated by the attorney general as the system for submitting documents and other materials to the attorney general under Texas Government Code § 552.309.

§ 63.22. Electronic Submission of Request for Attorney General Decision

(a) A governmental body that requests a decision from the attorney general under Texas Government Code § 552.301 about whether requested public information is excepted from public disclosure may submit that request for decision to the attorney general through the attorney general's designated electronic filing system.

(b) The governmental body's request for decision must comply with the requirements of Texas Government Code § 552.301.

(c)   The deadlines in Texas Government Code § 552.301 and § 552.303 are met if the governmental body timely submits the required documents and other materials through the attorney general's designated electronic filing system within the time prescribed.

(d)   The governmental body must comply with the requirements of Texas Government Code § 552.301(d) and (e-1), and § 552.305 regardless of whether the request for attorney general decision is submitted electronically or through another permissible method of submission.

(e)   To use the attorney general's designated electronic filing system, the governmental body must agree to and comply with the terms and conditions of use as outlined on the attorney general's designated electronic filing system website.

(f)   The confidentiality of Texas Government Code § 552.3035 applies to information submitted under Texas Government Code § 552.301(e)(1)(D) through the attorney general's designated electronic filing system.

§ 63.23. Electronic Submission of Documents or other Materials by Interested Third Party

(a)   An interested third party may submit, through the attorney general's designated electronic filing system, the reasons why the requested public information should be withheld or released along with any necessary supporting documentation for consideration in the attorney general's open records decision process.

(b)   The deadline in Texas Government Code § 552.305(d)(2)(B) is met if the interested third party timely submits the reasons why the requested public information should be withheld or released along with any necessary supporting documentation through the attorney general's designated electronic filing system within the time prescribed.

(c)   The interested third party must comply with the requirements of Texas Government Code § 552.305(e) regardless of whether the interested third party submits materials electronically or through another permissible method of submission.

(d)   To use the attorney general's designated electronic filing system, the interested third party must agree to and comply with the terms and conditions of use as outlined on the attorney general's designated electronic filing system website.

TEXAS ADMINISTRATIVE CODE, TITLE 1, CHAPTER 70

Chapter 70. Cost of Copies of Public Information

§ 70.1. Purpose

(a) The Office of the Attorney General (the "Attorney General") must:

    (1) Adopt rules for use by each governmental body in determining charges under Texas Government Code, Chapter 552 (Public Information) Subchapter F (Charges for Providing Copies of Public Information);

    (2) Prescribe the methods for computing the charges for copies of public information in paper, electronic, and other kinds of media; and

    (3) Establish costs for various components of charges for public information that shall be used by each governmental body in providing copies of public information.

(b) Governmental bodies must use the charges established by these rules, unless:

    (1) Other law provides for charges for specific kinds of public information;

    (2) They are a governmental body other than a state agency, and their charges are within a 25 percent variance above the charges established by the Attorney General;

    (3) They request and receive an exemption because their actual costs are higher; or

    (4) In accordance with Chapter 552 of the Texas Government Code (also known as the Public Information Act), the governmental body may grant a waiver or reduction for charges for providing copies of public information pursuant to § 552.267 of the Texas Government Code.

        (A) A governmental body shall furnish a copy of public information without charge or at a reduced charge if the governmental body determines that waiver or reduction of the fee is in the public interest because furnishing the information primarily benefits the general public; or

        (B) If the cost to the governmental body of processing the collection of a charge for a copy of public information will exceed the amount of the charge, the governmental body may waive the charge.

§ 70.2. Definitions

The following words and terms, when used in these sections, shall have the following meanings, unless the context clearly indicates otherwise.

(1) Actual cost—The sum of all direct costs plus a proportional share of overhead or indirect costs. Actual cost should be determined in accordance with generally accepted methodologies.

(2) Client/Server System—A combination of two or more computers that serve a particular application through sharing processing, data storage, and end-user interface presentation. PCs located in a LAN environment containing file servers fall into this category as do applications running in an X-window environment where the server is a UNIX based system.

(3) Attorney General—The Office of the Attorney General of Texas.

(4) Governmental Body—An entity as defined by § 552.003 of the Texas Government Code.

(5) Mainframe Computer—A computer located in a controlled environment and serving large applications and/or large numbers of users. These machines usually serve an entire organization or some group of organizations. These machines usually require an operating staff. IBM and UNISYS mainframes, and large Digital VAX 9000 and VAX Clusters fall into this category.

(6) Midsize Computer—A computer smaller than a Mainframe Computer that is not necessarily located in a controlled environment. It usually serves a smaller organization or a sub-unit of an organization. IBM AS/400 and Digital VAX/VMS multi-user single-processor systems fall into this category.

(7) Nonstandard copy—Under § 70.1 through § 70.11 of this title, a copy of public information that is made available to a requestor in any format other than a standard paper copy. Microfiche, microfilm, diskettes, magnetic tapes, CD-ROM are examples of nonstandard copies. Paper copies larger than 8 1/2 by 14 inches (legal size) are also considered nonstandard copies.

(8) PC—An IBM compatible PC, Macintosh or Power PC based computer system operated without a connection to a network.

(9) Standard paper copy—Under § 70.1 through § 70.11 of this title, a copy of public information that is a printed impression on one side of a piece of paper that measures up to 8 1/2 by 14 inches. Each side of a piece of paper on which information is recorded is counted as a single copy. A piece of paper that has information recorded on both sides is counted as two copies.

(10) Archival box—A carton box measuring approximately 12.5" width x 15.5" length x 10" height, or able to contain approximately 1.5 cubic feet in volume.

§ 70.3. Charges for Providing Copies of Public Information

(a)   The charges in this section to recover costs associated with providing copies of public information are based on estimated average costs to governmental bodies across the state. When actual costs are 25% higher than those used in these rules, governmental bodies other than agencies of the state, may request an exemption in accordance with § 70.4 of this title (relating to Requesting an Exemption).

(b)   Copy charge.

   (1)   Standard paper copy. The charge for standard paper copies reproduced by means of an office machine copier or a computer printer is $.10 per page or part of a page. Each side that has recorded information is considered a page.

   (2)   Nonstandard copy. The charges in this subsection are to cover the materials onto which information is copied and do not reflect any additional charges, including labor, that may be associated with a particular request. The charges for nonstandard copies are:

      (A)   Diskette—$1.00;

      (B)   Magnetic tape—actual cost

      (C)   Data cartridge—actual cost;

      (D)   Tape cartridge—actual cost;

      (E)   Rewritable CD (CD-RW)—$1.00;

      (F)   Non-rewritable CD (CD-R)—$1.00;

      (G)   Digital video disc (DVD)—$3.00;

      (H)   JAZ drive—actual cost;

      (I)   Other electronic media—actual cost;

      (J)   VHS video cassette—$2.50;

      (K)   Audio cassette—$1.00;

      (L)   Oversize paper copy (e.g.: 11 inches by 17 inches, greenbar, bluebar, not including maps and photographs using specialty paper—see also § 70.9 of this title)—$.50;

      (M)   Specialty paper (e.g.: Mylar, blueprint, blueline, map, photographic—actual cost).

(c)   Labor charge for programming. If a particular request requires the services of a programmer in order to execute an existing program or to create a new program so that requested information may be accessed and copied, the governmental body may charge for the programmer's time.

    (1)   The hourly charge for a programmer is $28.50 an hour. Only programming services shall be charged at this hourly rate.

    (2)   Governmental bodies that do not have in-house programming capabilities shall comply with requests in accordance with § 552.231 of the Texas Government Code.

    (3)   If the charge for providing a copy of public information includes costs of labor, a governmental body shall comply with the requirements of § 552.261(b) of the Texas Government Code.

(d)   Labor charge for locating, compiling, manipulating data, and reproducing public information.

    (1)   The charge for labor costs incurred in processing a request for public information is $15 an hour. The labor charge includes the actual time to locate, compile, manipulate data, and reproduce the requested information.

    (2)   A labor charge shall not be billed in connection with complying with requests that are for 50 or fewer pages of paper records, unless the documents to be copied are located in:

        (A)   Two or more separate buildings that are not physically connected with each other; or

        (B)   A remote storage facility.

    (3)   A labor charge shall not be recovered for any time spent by an attorney, legal assistant, or any other person who reviews the requested information:

        (A)   To determine whether the governmental body will raise any exceptions to disclosure of the requested information under the Texas Government Code, Subchapter C, Chapter 552; or

        (B)   To research or prepare a request for a ruling by the attorney general's office pursuant to § 552.301 of the Texas Government Code.

    (4)   When confidential information pursuant to a mandatory exception of the Act is mixed with public information in the same page, a labor charge may be recovered for time spent to redact, blackout, or otherwise obscure confidential information in order to release the public information. A labor charge shall not be made for redacting confidential information for requests of 50 or fewer pages, unless the request also qualifies for a labor charge pursuant to Texas Government Code, § 552.261(a)(1) or (2).

(5)   If the charge for providing a copy of public information includes costs of labor, a governmental body shall comply with the requirements of Texas Government Code, Chapter 552, § 552.261(b).

(6)   For purposes of paragraph (2)(A) of this subsection, two buildings connected by a covered or open sidewalk, an elevated or underground passageway, or a similar facility, are not considered to be separate buildings.

(e)   Overhead charge.

(1)   Whenever any labor charge is applicable to a request, a governmental body may include in the charges direct and indirect costs, in addition to the specific labor charge. This overhead charge would cover such costs as depreciation of capital assets, rent, maintenance and repair, utilities, and administrative overhead. If a governmental body chooses to recover such costs, a charge shall be made in accordance with the methodology described in paragraph (3) of this subsection. Although an exact calculation of costs will vary, the use of a standard charge will avoid complication in calculating such costs and will provide uniformity for charges made statewide.

(2)   An overhead charge shall not be made for requests for copies of 50 or fewer pages of standard paper records unless the request also qualifies for a labor charge pursuant to Texas Government Code, § 552.261(a)(1) or (2).

(3)   The overhead charge shall be computed at 20% of the charge made to cover any labor costs associated with a particular request. Example: if one hour of labor is used for a particular request, the formula would be as follows: Labor charge for locating, compiling, and reproducing, $15.00 x .20 = $3.00; or Programming labor charge, $28.50 x .20 = $5.70. If a request requires one hour of labor charge for locating, compiling, and reproducing information ($15.00 per hour); and one hour of programming labor charge ($28.50 per hour), the combined overhead would be: $15.00 + $28.50 = $43.50 x .20 = $8.70.

(f)   Microfiche and microfilm charge.

(1)   If a governmental body already has information that exists on microfiche or microfilm and has copies available for sale or distribution, the charge for a copy must not exceed the cost of its reproduction. If no copies of the requested microfiche or microfilm are available and the information on the microfiche or microfilm can be released in its entirety, the governmental body should make a copy of the microfiche or microfilm. The charge for a copy shall not exceed the cost of its reproduction. The Texas State Library and Archives Commission has the capacity to reproduce microfiche and microfilm for governmental bodies. Governmental bodies that do not have in-house capability to reproduce microfiche or microfilm are encouraged to contact the Texas State Library before having the reproduction made commercially.

(2)   If only a master copy of information in microfilm is maintained, the charge is $.10 per page for standard size paper copies, plus any applicable labor and overhead charge for more than 50 copies.

(g)   Remote document retrieval charge.

    (1)   Due to limited on-site capacity of storage documents, it is frequently necessary to store information that is not in current use in remote storage locations. Every effort should be made by governmental bodies to store current records on-site. State agencies are encouraged to store inactive or non-current records with the Texas State Library and Archives Commission. To the extent that the retrieval of documents results in a charge to comply with a request, it is permissible to recover costs of such services for requests that qualify for labor charges under current law.

    (2)   If a governmental body has a contract with a commercial records storage company, whereby the private company charges a fee to locate, retrieve, deliver, and return to storage the needed record(s), no additional labor charge shall be factored in for time spent locating documents at the storage location by the private company's personnel. If after delivery to the governmental body, the boxes must still be searched for records that are responsive to the request, a labor charge is allowed according to subsection (d)(1) of this section.

(h)   Computer resource charge.

    (1)   The computer resource charge is a utilization charge for computers based on the amortized cost of acquisition, lease, operation, and maintenance of computer resources, which might include, but is not limited to, some or all of the following: central processing units (CPUs), servers, disk drives, local area networks (LANs), printers, tape drives, other peripheral devices, communications devices, software, and system utilities.

    (2)   These computer resource charges are not intended to substitute for cost recovery methodologies or charges made for purposes other than responding to public information requests.

    (3)   The charges in this subsection are averages based on a survey of governmental bodies with a broad range of computer capabilities. Each governmental body using this cost recovery charge shall determine which category(ies) of computer system(s) used to fulfill the public information request most closely fits its existing system(s), and set its charge accordingly. Type of System—Rate: mainframe—$10 per CPU minute; Midsize—$1.50 per CPU minute; Client/Server—$2.20 per clock hour; PC or LAN—$1.00 per clock hour.

    (4)   The charge made to recover the computer utilization cost is the actual time the computer takes to execute a particular program times the applicable rate. The CPU charge is not meant to apply to programming or printing time; rather it is solely to recover costs associated with the actual time required by the computer to execute a program. This time, called CPU time, can be read directly from the CPU clock, and most frequently will be a matter of seconds. If programming is required to comply with a particular request, the appropriate charge that may be recovered for programming time is set forth in subsection (d) of this section. No charge should be

made for computer print-out time. Example: If a mainframe computer is used, and the processing time is 20 seconds, the charges would be as follows: $10 / 3 = $3.33; or $10 / 60 \times 20 = $3.33.

    (5)   A governmental body that does not have in-house computer capabilities shall comply with requests in accordance with the § 552.231 of the Texas Government Code.

(i)   Miscellaneous supplies. The actual cost of miscellaneous supplies, such as labels, boxes, and other supplies used to produce the requested information, may be added to the total charge for public information.

(j)   Postal and shipping charges. Governmental bodies may add any related postal or shipping expenses which are necessary to transmit the reproduced information to the requesting party.

(k)   Sales tax. Pursuant to Office of the Comptroller of Public Accounts' rules sales tax shall not be added on charges for public information (34 TAC, Part 1, Chapter 3, Subchapter O, § 3.341 and § 3.342).

(l)   Miscellaneous charges: A governmental body that accepts payment by credit card for copies of public information and that is charged a "transaction fee" by the credit card company may recover that fee.

(m)   These charges are subject to periodic reevaluation and update.

§ 70.4. Requesting an Exemption

(a)   Pursuant to § 552.262(c) of the Public Information Act, a governmental body may request that it be exempt from part or all of these rules.

(b)   State agencies must request an exemption if their charges to recover costs are higher than those established by these rules.

(c)   Governmental bodies, other than agencies of the state, must request an exemption before seeking to recover costs that are more than 25% higher than the charges established by these rules.

(d)   an exemption request must be made in writing, and must contain the following elements:

    (1)   A statement identifying the subsection(s) of these rules for which an exemption is sought;

    (2)   The reason(s) the exemption is requested;

    (3)   A copy of the proposed charges;

    (4)   The methodology and figures used to calculate/compute the proposed charges;

(5)   Any supporting documentation, such as invoices, contracts, etc.; and

(6)   The name, title, work address, and phone number of a contact person at the governmental body.

(e)   The contact person shall provide sufficient information and answer in writing any questions necessary to process the request for exemption.

(f)   If there is good cause to grant the exemption, because the request is duly documented, reasonable, and in accordance with generally accepted accounting principles, the exemption shall be granted. The name of the governmental body shall be added to a list to be published annually in the *Texas Register.*

(g)   If the request is not duly documented and/or the charges are beyond cost recovery, the request for exemption shall be denied. The letter of denial shall:

(1)   Explain the reason(s) the exemption cannot be granted; and

(2)   Whenever possible, propose alternative charges.

(h)   All determinations to grant or deny a request for exemption shall be completed promptly, but shall not exceed 90 days from receipt of the request by the Attorney General.

§ 70.5.   Access to Information Where Copies Are Not Requested

(a)   Access to information in standard paper form. A governmental body shall not charge for making available for inspection information maintained in standard paper form. Charges are permitted only where the governmental body is asked to provide, for inspection, information that contains mandatory confidential information and public information. When such is the case, the governmental body may charge to make a copy of the page from which information must be edited. No other charges are allowed except as follows:

(1)   The governmental body has 16 or more employees and the information requested takes more than five hours to prepare the public information for inspection; and

(A)   Is older than five years; or

(B)   Completely fills, or when assembled will completely fill, six or more archival boxes.

(2)   The governmental body has 15 or fewer full-time employees and the information requested takes more than two hours to prepare the public information for inspection; and

(A)   Is older than three years; or

(B)   Completely fills, or when assembled will completely fill, three or more archival boxes.

(3)   A governmental body may charge pursuant to paragraphs (1)(A) and (2)(A) of this subsection only for the production of those documents that qualify under those paragraphs.

(b)   Access to information in other than standard form. In response to requests for access, for purposes of inspection only, to information that is maintained in other than standard form, a governmental body may not charge the requesting party the cost of preparing and making available such information, unless complying with the request will require programming or manipulation of data.

§ 70.6.   Format for Copies of Public Information

(a)   If a requesting party asks that information be provided on computer-compatible media of a particular kind, and the requested information is electronically stored and the governmental body has the capability of providing it in that format and it is able to provide it at no greater expense or time, the governmental body shall provide the information in the requested format.

(b)   The extent to which a requestor can be accommodated will depend largely on the technological capability of the governmental body to which the request is made.

(c)   A governmental body is not required to purchase any hardware, software or programming capabilities that it does not already possess to accommodate a particular kind of request.

(d)   Provision of a copy of public information in the requested medium shall not violate the terms of any copyright agreement between the governmental body and a third party.

(e)   if the governmental body does not have the required technological capabilities to comply with the request in the format preferred by the requestor, the governmental body shall proceed in accordance with § 552.228(c) of the Public Information Act.

(f)   If a governmental body receives a request requiring programming or manipulation of data, the governmental body should proceed in accordance with § 552.231 of the Public Information Act. Manipulation of data under § 552.231 applies only to information stored in electronic format.

§ 70.7.   Estimates and Waivers of Public Information Charges

(a)   A governmental body is required to provide a requestor with an itemized statement of estimated charges if charges for copies of public information will exceed $40, or if a charge in accordance with § 70.5 of this title (relating to Access to Information Where Copies Are Not Requested) will exceed $40 for making public information available for inspection. The itemized statement of estimated charges is to be provided before copies are made to enable requestors to make the choices allowed by the Act. A governmental body that fails to provide the required statement may not collect more than $40. The itemized statement must be provided free of charge and shall contain the following information:

(1)   The itemized estimated charges, including any allowable charges for labor, overhead, copies, etc.;

(2)   Whether a less costly or no-cost way of viewing the information is available;

(3)   A statement that the requestor must respond in writing by mail, in person, by facsimile if the governmental body is capable of receiving such transmissions, or by electronic mail, if the governmental body has an electronic mail address;

(4)   A statement that the request will be considered to have been automatically withdrawn by the requestor if a written response from the requestor is not received within ten business days after the date the statement was sent, in which the requestor states that the requestor:

   (A)   Will accept the estimated charges;

   (B)   Is modifying the request in response to the itemized statement; or

   (C)   Has sent to the Attorney General a complaint alleging that the requestor has been overcharged for being provided with a copy of the public information.

(b)   If after starting the work, but before making the copies available, the governmental body determines that the initially accepted estimated statement will be exceeded by 20% or more, an updated statement must be sent. If the requestor does not respond to the updated statement, the request is considered to have been withdrawn by the requestor.

(c)   If the actual charges exceed $40, the charges may not exceed:

   (1)   The amount estimated on the updated statement; or

   (2)   An amount that exceeds by more than 20% the amount in the initial statement, if an updated statement was not sent.

(d)   A governmental body that provides a requestor with the statement mentioned in subsection (a) of this section, may require a deposit or bond as follows:

   (1)   The governmental body has 16 or more full-time employees and the estimated charges are $100 or more; or

   (2)   The governmental body has 15 or fewer full-time employees and the estimated charges are $50 or more.

(e)   If a request for the inspection of paper records will qualify for a deposit or a bond as detailed in subsection (d) of this section, a governmental body may request:

   (1)   A bond for the entire estimated amount; or

   (2)   A deposit not to exceed 50 percent of the entire estimated amount.

(f) A governmental body may require payment of overdue and unpaid balances before preparing a copy in response to a new request if:

   (1) The governmental body provided, and the requestor accepted, the required itemized statements for previous requests that remain unpaid; and

   (2) The aggregated unpaid amount exceeds $100.

(g) A governmental body may not seek payment of said unpaid amounts through any other means.

(h) A governmental body that cannot produce the public information for inspection and/or duplication within 10 business days after the date the written response from the requestor has been received, shall certify to that fact in writing, and set a date and hour within a reasonable time when the information will be available.

§ 70.8. Processing Complaints of Overcharges

(a) Pursuant to § 552.269(a) of the Texas Government Code, requestors who believe they have been overcharged for a copy of public information may complain to the Attorney General.

(b) The complaint must be in writing, and must:

   (1) Set forth the reason(s) the person believes the charges are excessive;

   (2) Provide a copy of the original request and a copy of any correspondence from the governmental body stating the proposed charges; and

   (3) Be received by the Attorney General within 10 business days after the person knows of the occurrence of the alleged overcharge.

   (4) Failure to provide the information listed within the stated timeframe will result in the complaint being dismissed.

(c) The Attorney General shall address written questions to the governmental body, regarding the methodology and figures used in the calculation of the charges which are the subject of the complaint.

(d) The governmental body shall respond in writing to the questions within 10 business days from receipt of the questions.

(e) The Attorney General may use tests, consultations with records managers and technical personnel at the Attorney General and other agencies, and any other reasonable resources to determine appropriate charges.

(f) If the Attorney General determines that the governmental body overcharged for requested public information, the governmental body shall adjust its charges in accordance with the determination, and shall refund the difference between what was charged and what was determined to be appropriate charges.

(g)   The Attorney General shall send a copy of the determination to the complainant and to the governmental body.

(h)   Pursuant to § 552.269(b) of the Texas Government Code, a requestor who overpays because a governmental body refuses or fails to follow the charges established by the Attorney General, is entitled to recover three times the amount of the overcharge if the governmental body did not act in good faith in computing the charges.

§ 70.9.   Examples of Charges for Copies of Public Information

The following tables present a few examples of the calculations of charges for information:

(1)   TABLE 1 (Fewer than 50 pages of paper records): $.10 per copy x number of copies (standard-size paper copies); + Labor charge (if applicable); + Overhead charge (if applicable); + Document retrieval charge (if applicable); + Postage and shipping (if applicable) = $ TOTAL CHARGE.

(2)   TABLE 2 (More than 50 pages of paper records or nonstandard copies): $.10 per copy x number of copies (standard-size paper copies), or cost of nonstandard copy (e.g., diskette, oversized paper, etc.); + Labor charge (if applicable); + Overhead charge (if applicable); + Document retrieval charge (if applicable); + Actual cost of miscellaneous supplies (if applicable); + Postage and shipping (if applicable) = $ TOTAL CHARGE.

(3)   TABLE 3 (Information that Requires Programming or Manipulation of Data): Cost of copy (standard or nonstandard, whichever applies); + Labor charge; + Overhead charge; + Computer resource charge; + Programming time (if applicable); + Document retrieval charge (if applicable); + Actual cost of miscellaneous supplies (if applicable); + Postage and shipping (if applicable) = $ TOTAL CHARGE.

(4)   TABLE 4 (Maps): Cost of paper (Cost of Roll/Avg. # of Maps); + Cost of Toner (Black or Color, # of Maps per Toner Cartridge); + Labor charge (if applicable); + Overhead charge (if applicable) + Plotter/Computer resource Charge; + Actual cost of miscellaneous supplies (if applicable); + Postage and shipping (if applicable) = $ TOTAL CHARGE.

(5)   TABLE 5 (Photographs): Cost of Paper (Cost of Sheet of Photographic Paper/Avg. # of Photographs per Sheet); + Developing/Fixing Chemicals (if applicable); + Labor charge (if applicable); + Overhead charge (if applicable); + Postage and shipping (if applicable) = $ TOTAL CHARGE.

§ 70.10. The Attorney General Charge Schedule

The following is a summary of the charges for copies of public information that have been adopted by the Attorney General.

   (1)   Standard paper copy—$.10 per page.

   (2)   Nonstandard-size copy:

       (A) Diskette: $1.00;

       (B) Magnetic tape: actual cost;

       (C) Data cartridge: actual cost;

       (D) Tape cartridge: actual cost;

       (E) Rewritable CD (CD-RW)—$1.00;

       (F) Non-rewritable CD (CD-R)—$1.00;

       (G) Digital video disc (DVD)—$3.00;

       (H) JAZ drive—actual cost;

       (I) Other electronic media—actual cost;

       (J) VHS video cassette—$2.50;

       (K) Audio cassette—$1.00;

       (L) Oversize paper copy (e.g.: 11 inches by 17 inches, greenbar, bluebar, not including maps and photographs using specialty paper)—$.50;

       (M) Specialty paper (e.g.: Mylar, blueprint, blueline, map, photographic)—actual cost.

   (3)   Labor charge:

       (A) For programming—$28.50 per hour;

       (B) For locating, compiling, and reproducing—$15 per hour.

   (4)   Overhead charge—20% of labor charge.

   (5)   Microfiche or microfilm charge:

       (A) Paper copy—$.10 per page;

    (B)   Fiche or film copy—Actual cost.

(6)   Remote document retrieval charge—Actual cost.

(7)   Computer resource charge:

    (A)   mainframe—$10 per CPU minute;

    (B)   Midsize—$1.50 per CPU minute;

    (C)   Client/Server system—$2.20 per clock hour;

    (D)   PC or LAN—$1.00 per clock hour.

(8)   Miscellaneous supplies—Actual cost.

(9)   Postage and shipping charge—Actual cost.

(10)   Photographs—Actual cost as calculated in accordance with § 70.9(5) of this title.

(11)   Maps—Actual cost as calculated in accordance with § 70.9(4) of this title.

(12)   Other costs—Actual cost.

(13)   Outsourced/Contracted Services—Actual cost for the copy. May not include development costs.

(14)   No Sales Tax—No Sales Tax shall be applied to copies of public information.

§ 70.11. Informing the Public of Basic Rights and Responsibilities Under the Public Information Act

(a)   Pursuant to Texas Government Code, Chapter 552, Subchapter D, § 552.205, an officer for public information shall prominently display a sign in the form prescribed by the Attorney General.

(b)   The sign shall contain basic information about the rights of requestors and responsibilities of governmental bodies that are subject to Chapter 552, as well as the procedures for inspecting or obtaining a copy of public information under said chapter.

(c)   The sign shall have the minimum following characteristics:

    (1)   Be printed on plain paper.

    (2)   Be no less than 8 1/2 inches by 14 inches in total size, exclusive of framing.

    (3)   The sign may be laminated to prevent alterations.

(d)   The sign will contain the following wording:

(1)   The Public Information Act. Texas Government Code, Chapter 552, gives you the right to access government records; and an officer for public information and the officer's agent may not ask why you want them. All government information is presumed to be available to the public. Certain exceptions may apply to the disclosure of the information. Governmental bodies shall promptly release requested information that is not confidential by law, either constitutional, statutory, or by judicial decision, or information for which an exception to disclosure has not been sought.

(2)   Rights of Requestors. You have the right to:

(A)   Prompt access to information that is not confidential or otherwise protected;

(B)   Receive treatment equal to all other requestors, including accommodation in accordance with the Americans with Disabilities Act (ADA) requirements;

(C)   Receive certain kinds of information without exceptions, like the voting record of public officials, and other information;

(D)   Receive a written itemized statement of estimated charges, when charges will exceed $40, in advance of work being started and opportunity to modify the request in response to the itemized statement;

(E)   Choose whether to inspect the requested information (most often at no charge), receive copies of the information, or both;

(F)   A waiver or reduction of charges if the governmental body determines that access to the information primarily benefits the general public;

(G)   Receive a copy of the communication from the governmental body asking the Attorney General for a ruling on whether the information can be withheld under one of the accepted exceptions, or if the communication discloses the requested information, a redacted copy;

(H)   Lodge a written complaint about overcharges for public information with the Attorney General. Complaints of other possible violations may be filed with the county or district attorney of the county where the governmental body, other than a state agency, is located. If the complaint is against the county or district attorney, the complaint must be filed with the Attorney General.

(3)   Responsibilities of Governmental Bodies. All governmental bodies responding to information requests have the responsibility to:

(A)   Establish reasonable procedures for inspecting or copying public information and inform requestors of these procedures;

(B) Treat all requestors uniformly and shall give to the requestor all reasonable comfort and facility, including accommodation in accordance with ADA requirement;

(C) Be informed about open records laws and educate employees on the requirements of those laws;

(D) Inform requestors of the estimated charges greater than $40 and any changes in the estimates above 20 percent of the original estimate, and confirm that the requestor accepts the charges, has amended the request, or has sent a complaint of overcharges to the Attorney General, in writing before finalizing the request;

(E) Inform the requestor if the information cannot be provided promptly and set a date and time to provide it within a reasonable time;

(F) Request a ruling from the Attorney General regarding any information the governmental body wishes to withhold, and send a copy of the request for ruling, or a redacted copy, to the requestor;

(G) Segregate public information from information that may be withheld and provide that public information promptly;

(H) Make a good faith attempt to inform third parties when their proprietary information is being requested from the governmental body;

(I) Respond in writing to all written communications from the Attorney General regarding complaints about the charges for the information and other alleged violations of the Act.

(4) Procedures to Obtain Information

(A) Submit a request by mail, fax, email or in person, according to a governmental body's reasonable procedures.

(B) Include enough description and detail about the information requested to enable the governmental body to accurately identify and locate the information requested.

(C) Cooperate with the governmental body's reasonable efforts to clarify the type or amount of information requested.

(5) Information to be released.

(A) You may review it promptly, and if it cannot be produced within 10 business days the public information officer will notify you in writing of the reasonable date and time when it will be available;

(B)   Keep all appointments to inspect records and to pick up copies. Failure to keep appointments may result in losing the opportunity to inspect the information at the time requested;

(C)   Cost of Records.

(i)   You must respond to any written estimate of charges within 10 business days of the date the governmental body sent it or the request is considered automatically withdrawn;

(ii)   If estimated costs exceed $100.00 (or $50.00 if a governmental body has fewer than 16 full time employees) the governmental body may require a bond, prepayment or deposit;

(iii)   You may ask the governmental body to determine whether providing the information primarily benefits the general public, resulting in a waiver or reduction of charges;

(iv)   Make timely payment for all mutually agreed charges. A governmental body can demand payment of overdue balances exceeding $100.00, or obtain a security deposit, before processing additional requests from you.

(6)   Information that may be withheld due to an exception.

(A)   By the 10th business day after a governmental body receives your written request, a governmental body must:

(i)   Request an Attorney General Opinion and state which exception apply;

(ii)   Notify the requestor of the referral to the Attorney General; and

(iii)   Notify third parties if the request involves their proprietary information;

(B)   Failure to request an Attorney General opinion and to notify the requestor within 10 business days will result in a presumption that the information is open unless there is a compelling reason to withhold it.

(C)   Requestors may send a letter to the Attorney General arguing for release, and may review arguments made by the governmental body. If the arguments disclose the requested information, the requestor may obtain a redacted copy.

(D)   The Attorney General must issue a decision no later than the 45th business day after the Attorney General received the request for a decision. The Attorney General may request an additional 10 business days extension.

(E)   Governmental bodies may not ask the Attorney General to "reconsider" an opinion.

(7)   Additional Information on Sign.

    (A)   The sign must contain information of the governmental body's officer for public information, or the officer's agent, as well as the mailing address, phone and fax numbers, and email address, if any, where requestors may send a request for information to the officer or the officer's agent. The sign must also contain the physical address at which requestors may request information in person.

    (B)   The sign must contain information of the local county attorney or district attorney where requestors may submit a complaint of alleged violations of the Act, as well as the contact information for the Attorney General.

    (C)   The sign must also contain contact information of the person or persons with whom a requestor may make special arrangements for accommodation pursuant to the American with Disabilities Act.

(e)   A governmental body may comply with Texas Government Code, § 552.205 and this rule by posting the sign provided by the Attorney General.

§ 70.12. Allowable Charges Under Section 552.275 of the Texas Government Code

(a)   A governmental body shall utilize the methods established in 1 TAC § 70.3(c) - (e) when calculating allowable charges under Section 552.275 of the Texas Government Code.

(b)   When calculating the amount of time spent complying with an individual's public information request(s) pursuant to Section 552.275 of the Texas Government Code, a governmental body may not include time spent on:

(1)   Determining the meaning and/or scope of the request(s);

(2)   Requesting a clarification from the requestor;

(3)   Comparing records gathered from different sources;

(4)   Determining which exceptions to disclosure under Chapter 552 of the Texas Government Code, if any, may apply to information that is responsive to the request(s);

(5)   Preparing the information and/or correspondence required under Sections 552.301, 552.303, and 552.305 of the Government Code;

(6)   Reordering, reorganizing, or in any other way bringing information into compliance with well established and generally accepted information management practices; or

(7)   Providing instruction to, or learning by, employees or agents of the governmental body of new practices, rules, and/or procedures, including the management of electronic records.

§ 70.13. Fee for Obtaining Copy of Body Worn Camera Recording

    (a)   This section provides the fee for obtaining a copy of body worn camera recording pursuant to § 1701.661 of the Government Code.

        (1)   Section 1701.661 of the Government Code is the sole authority under which a copy of a body worn camera recording may be obtained from a law enforcement agency under the Public Information Act, Chapter 552 of the Government Code, and no fee for obtaining a copy of a body worn camera recording from a law enforcement agency may be charged unless authorized by this section.

        (2)   This section does not apply to a request, or portions of a request, seeking to obtain information other than a copy of a body worn camera recording. Portions of a request seeking information other than a copy of a body worn camera recording are subject to the charges listed in § 70.3 of this chapter.

    (b)   The charge for obtaining a copy of a body worn camera recording shall be:

        (1) $10.00 per recording responsive to the request for information; and

        (2) $1.00 per full minute of body worn camera video or audio footage responsive to the request for information, if identical information has not already been obtained by a member of the public in response to a request for information.

    (c)   A law enforcement agency may provide a copy without charge, or at a reduced charge, if the agency determines waiver or reduction of the charge is in the public interest.

    (d)   If the requestor is not permitted to obtain a copy of a requested body worn camera recording under § 1701.661 of the Government Code or an exception in the Public Information Act, Chapter 552 of the Government Code, the law enforcement agency may not charge the requestor under this section.

PART FIVE: TABLE OF CASES

PART SIX: TABLE OF STATUTES, RULES, REGULATIONS

Texas Health & Safety Code

PART SEVEN: RULES OF JUDICIAL ADMINISTRATION

Rule 12. Public Access to Judicial Records

12.1 Policy. The purpose of this rule is to provide public access to information in the judiciary consistent with the mandates of the Texas Constitution that the public interests are best served by open courts and by an independent judiciary. The rule should be liberally construed to achieve its purpose.

12.2 Definitions. In this rule:

(a) Judge means a regularly appointed or elected judge or justice.

(b) Judicial agency means an office, board, commission, or other similar entity that is in the Judicial Department and that serves an administrative function for a court. A task force or committee created by a court or judge is a "judicial agency".

(c) Judicial officer means a judge, former or retired visiting judge, referee, commissioner, special master, court-appointed arbitrator, or other person exercising adjudicatory powers in the judiciary. A mediator or other provider of non-binding dispute resolution services is not a "judicial officer".

(d) Judicial record means a record made or maintained by or for a court or judicial agency in its regular course of business but not pertaining to its adjudicative function, regardless of whether that function relates to a specific case. A record of any nature created, produced, or filed in connection with any matter that is or has been before a court is not a judicial record. A record is a document, paper, letter, map, book, tape, photograph, film, recording, or other material, regardless of electronic or physical form, characteristics, or means of transmission.

(e) Records custodian means the person with custody of a judicial record determined as follows:

> (1) The judicial records of a court with only one judge, such as any trial court, are in the custody of that judge. Judicial records pertaining to the joint administration of a number of those courts, such as the district courts in a particular county or region, are in the custody of the judge who presides over the joint administration, such as the local or regional administrative judge.

> (2) The judicial records of a court with more than one judge, such as any appellate court, are in the custody of the chief justice or presiding judge, who must act under this rule in accordance with the vote of a majority of the judges of the court. But the judicial records relating specifically to the service of one such judge or that judge's own staff are in the custody of that judge.

> (3) The judicial records of a judicial officer not covered by subparagraphs (1) and (2) are in the custody of that officer.

(4)   The judicial records of a judicial agency are in the custody of its presiding officer, who must act under this rule in accordance with agency policy or the vote of a majority of the members of the agency.

12.3   Applicability. This rule does not apply to:

(a)   records or information to which access is controlled by:

(1)   a state or federal court rule, including:

(A)   a rule of civil or criminal procedure, including Rule 76a, Texas Rules of Civil Procedure;

(B)   a rule of appellate procedure;

(C)   a rule of evidence;

(D)   a rule of administration;

(2)   a state or federal court order not issued merely to thwart the purpose of this rule;

(3)   the Code of Judicial Conduct;

(4)   Chapter 552, Government Code, or another statute or provision of law;

(b)   records or information to which Chapter 552, Government Code, is made inapplicable by statute, rule, or other provision of law, other than Section 552.003(1)(B);

(c)   records or information relating to an arrest or search warrant or a supporting affidavit, access to which is controlled by:

(1)   a state or federal court rule, including a rule of civil or criminal procedure, appellate procedure, or evidence; or

(2)   common law, court order, judicial decision, or another provision of law

(d)   elected officials other than judges.

12.4   Access to Judicial Records.

(a)   *Generally.* Judicial records other than those covered by Rules 12.3 and 12.5 are open to the general public for inspection and copying during regular business hours. But this rule does not require a court, judicial agency, or records custodian to:

> (1)   create a record, other than to print information stored in a computer;

> (2)   retain a judicial record for a specific period of time;

> (3)   allow the inspection of or provide a copy of information in a book or publication commercially available to the public; or

> (4)   respond to or comply with a request for a judicial record from or on behalf of an individual who is imprisoned or confined in a correctional facility as defined in Section 1.07(a), Penal Code, or in any other such facility in any state, federal, or foreign jurisdiction.

(b)   *Voluntary Disclosure.* A records custodian may voluntarily make part or all of the information in a judicial record available to the public, subject to Rules 12.2(e)(2) and 12.2(e)(4), unless the disclosure is expressly prohibited by law or exempt under this rule, or the information is confidential under law. Information voluntarily disclosed must be made available to any person who requests it.

12.5   Exemptions from Disclosure. The following records are exempt from disclosure under this rule:

(a)   *Judicial Work Product and Drafts.* Any record that relates to a judicial officer's adjudicative decision-making process prepared by that judicial officer, by another judicial officer, or by court staff, an intern, or any other person acting on behalf of or at the direction of the judicial officer.

(b)   *Security Plans.* Any record, including a security plan or code, the release of which would jeopardize the security of an individual against physical injury or jeopardize information or property against theft, tampering, improper use, illegal disclosure, trespass, unauthorized access, or physical injury.

(c)   *Personnel Information.* Any personnel record that, if disclosed, would constitute a clearly unwarranted invasion of personal privacy.

(d)   *Home Address and Family Information.* Any record reflecting any person's home address, home or personal telephone number, social security number, or family members.

(e)   *Applicants for Employment or Volunteer Services.* Any records relating to an applicant for employment or volunteer services.

(f)   *Internal Deliberations on Court or Judicial Administration Matters.* Any record relating to internal deliberations of a court or judicial agency, or among judicial officers or members of a judicial agency, on matters of court or judicial administration.

(g)   *Court Law Library Information.* Any record in a law library that links a patron's name with the materials requested or borrowed by that patron.

(h)   *Judicial Calendar Information.*   Any record that reflects a judicial officer's appointments or engagements that are in the future or that constitute an invasion of personal privacy.

(i)   *Information Confidential Under Other Law.* Any record that is confidential or exempt from disclosure under a state or federal constitutional provision, statute or common law, including information that relates to:

   (1)   a complaint alleging misconduct against a judicial officer, if the complaint is exempt from disclosure under Chapter 33, Government Code, or other law;

   (2)   a complaint alleging misconduct against a person who is licensed or regulated by the courts, if the information is confidential under applicable law; or

   (3)   a trade secret or commercial or financial information made privileged or confidential by statute or judicial decision.

(j)   *Litigation or Settlement Negotiations.* Any judicial record relating to civil or criminal litigation or settlement negotiations:

   (1)   in which a court or judicial agency is or may be a party; or

   (2)   in which a judicial officer or member of a judicial agency is or may be a party as a consequence of the person's office or employment.

(k)   *Investigations of Character or Conduct.* Any record relating to an investigation of any person's character or conduct, unless:

   (1)   the record is requested by the person being investigated; and

   (2)   release of the record, in the judgment of the records custodian, would not impair the investigation.

(l)   *Examinations.* Any record relating to an examination administered to any person, unless requested by the person after the examination is concluded.

12.6   Procedures for Obtaining Access to Judicial Records.

(a)   *Request.* A request to inspect or copy a judicial record must be in writing and must include sufficient information to reasonably identify the record requested. The request must be sent to the records custodian and not to a court clerk or other agent for the records custodian. A requestor need not have detailed knowledge of the records custodian's filing system or procedures in order to obtain the information.

(b)   *Time for Inspection and Delivery of Copies.* As soon as practicable—and not more than 14 days—after actual receipt of a request to inspect or copy a judicial record, if the record is available, the records custodian must either:

> (1)   allow the requestor to inspect the record and provide a copy if one is requested; or
>
> (2)   send written notice to the requestor stating that the record cannot within the prescribed period be produced or a copy provided, as applicable, and setting a reasonable date and time when the document will be produced or a copy provided, as applicable.

(c)   *Place for Inspection.* A records custodian must produce a requested judicial record at a convenient, public area.

(d)   *Part of Record Subject to Disclosure.* If part of a requested record is subject to disclosure under this rule and part is not, the records custodian must redact the portion of the record that is not subject to disclosure, permit the remainder of the record to be inspected, and provide a copy if requested.

(e)   *Copying; Mailing.* The records custodian may deliver the record to a court clerk for copying. The records custodian may mail the copy to a requestor who has prepaid the postage.

(f)   *Recipient of Request not Custodian of Record.* A judicial officer or a presiding officer of a judicial agency who receives a request for a judicial record not in his or her custody as defined by this rule must promptly attempt to ascertain who the custodian of the record is. If the recipient of the request can ascertain who the custodian of the requested record is, the recipient must promptly refer the request to that person and notify the requestor in writing of the referral. The time for response prescribed in Rule 12.6(b) does not begin to run until the referral is actually received by the records custodian. If the recipient cannot ascertain who the custodian of the requested record is, the recipient must promptly notify the requestor in writing that the recipient is not the custodian of the record and cannot ascertain who the custodian of the record is.

(g)   *Inquiry to Requestor.* A person requesting a judicial record may not be asked to disclose the purpose of the request as a condition of obtaining the judicial record. But a records custodian may make inquiry to establish the proper identification of the requestor or to clarify the nature or scope of a request.

(h)   *Uniform Treatment of Requests.* A records custodian must treat all requests for information uniformly without regard to the position or occupation of the requestor or the person on whose behalf a request is made, including whether the requestor or such person is a member of the media.

12.7   Costs for Copies of Judicial Records; Appeal of Assessment.

(a)   *Cost.* The cost for a copy of a judicial record is either:

    (1)   the cost prescribed by statute, or

    (2)   if no statute prescribes the cost, the cost the Office of the Attorney General prescribes by rule in the Texas Administrative Code.

(b)   *Waiver or Reduction of Cost Assessment by Records Custodian.* A records custodian may reduce or waive the charge for a copy of a judicial record if:

    (1)   doing so is in the public interest because providing the copy of the record primarily benefits the general public, or

    (2)   the cost of processing collection of a charge will exceed the amount of the charge.

(c)   *Appeal of Cost Assessment.* A person who believes that a charge for a copy of a judicial record is excessive may appeal the overcharge in the manner prescribed by Rule 12.9 for the appeal of the denial of access to a judicial record.

(d)   *Records Custodian Not Personally Responsible for Cost.* A records custodian is not required to incur personal expense in furnishing a copy of a judicial record.

12.8   Denial of Access to a Judicial Record.

(a)   *When Request May be Denied.* A records custodian may deny a request for a judicial record under this rule only if the records custodian:

    (1)   reasonably determines that the requested judicial record is exempt from required disclosure under this rule; or

    (2)   makes specific, non-conclusory findings that compliance with the request would substantially and unreasonably impede the routine operation of the court or judicial agency.

(b)   *Time to Deny.* A records custodian who denies access to a judicial record must notify the person requesting the record of the denial within a reasonable time—not to exceed 14 days—after receipt of the request, or before the deadline for responding to the request extended under Rule 12.6(b)(2).

(c)   *Contents of Notice of Denial.* A notice of denial must be in writing and must:

   (1)   state the reason for the denial;

   (2)   inform the person of the right of appeal provided by Rule 12.9; and

   (3)   include the name and address of the Administrative Director of the Office of Court Administration.

12.9   Relief from Denial of Access to Judicial Records.

(a)   *Appeal.* A person who is denied access to a judicial record may appeal the denial by filing a petition for review with the Administrative Director of the Office of Court Administration.

(b)   *Contents of Petition for Review.* The petition for review:

   (1)   must include a copy of the request to the record custodian and the records custodian's notice of denial;

   (2)   may include any supporting facts, arguments, and authorities that the petitioner believes to be relevant; and

   (3)   may contain a request for expedited review, the grounds for which must be stated.

(c)   *Time for Filing.* The petition must be filed not later than 30 days after the date that the petitioner receives notice of a denial of access to the judicial record.

(d)   *Notification of Records Custodian and Presiding Judges.* Upon receipt of the petition for review, the Administrative Director must promptly notify the records custodian who denied access to the judicial record and the presiding judge of each administrative judicial region of the filing of the petition.

(e)   *Response.* A records custodian who denies access to a judicial record and against whom relief is sought under this section may—within 14 days of receipt of notice from the Administrative Director—submit a written response to the petition for review and include supporting facts and authorities in the response. The records custodian must mail a copy of the response to the petitioner. The records custodian may also submit for in camera inspection any record, or a sample of records, to which access has been denied.

(f)   *Formation of Special Committee.* Upon receiving notice under Rule 12.9(d), the presiding judges must refer the petition to a special committee of not less than five of the presiding judges for review. The presiding judges must notify the Administrative Director, the petitioner, and the records custodian of the names of the judges selected to serve on the committee.

(g)   *Procedure for Review.* The special committee must review the petition and the records custodian's response and determine whether the requested judicial record should be made available under this rule to the petitioner. The special committee may request the records custodian to submit for in camera inspection a record, or a sample of records, to which access has been denied. The records custodian may respond to the request in whole or in part but it not required to do so.

(h)   *Considerations.* When determining whether the requested judicial record should be made available under this rule to petition, the special committee must consider:

(1)   the text and policy of this Rule;

(2)   any supporting and controverting facts, arguments, and authorities in the petition and the response; and

(3)   prior applications of this Rule by other special committees or by courts.

(i)   *Expedited Review.* On request of the petitioner, and for good cause shown, the special committee may schedule an expedited review of the petition.

(j)   *Decision.* The special committee's determination must be supported by a written decision that must:

(1)   issue within 60 days of the date that the Administrative Director received the petition for review;

(2)   either grant the petition in whole or in part or sustain the denial of access to the requested judicial record;

(3)   state the reasons for the decision, including appropriate citations to this rule; and

(4)   identify the record or portions of the record to which access is ordered or denied, but only if the description does not disclose confidential information.

(k)   *Notice of Decision.* The special committee must send the decision to the Administrative Director. On receipt of the decision from the special committee, the Administrative Director must:

(1)   immediately notify the petitioner and the records custodian of the decision and include a copy of the decision with the notice; and

(2)   maintain a copy of the special committee's decision in the Administrative Director's office for public inspection.

(l)   *Publication of Decisions.* The Administrative Director must publish periodically to the judiciary and the general public the special committees' decisions.

(m)   *Final Decision.* A decision of a special committee under this rule is not appealable but is subject to review by mandamus.

(n)   *Appeal to Special Committee Not Exclusive Remedy.* The right of review provided under this subdivision is not exclusive and does not preclude relief by mandamus.

12.10 Sanctions. A records custodian who fails to comply with this rule, knowing that the failure to comply is in violation of the rule, is subject to sanctions under the Code of Judicial Conduct.

Comment to 2008 change:

The Attorney General's rule, adopted in accordance with Section 552.262 of the Government Code, is in Section 70.3 of Title 1 of the Texas Administrative Code.

Comments

1.   Although the definition of "judicial agency" in Rule 12.2(b) is comprehensive, applicability of the rule is restricted by Rule 12.3. The rule does not apply to judicial agencies whose records are expressly made subject to disclosure by statute, rule, or law. An example is the State Bar ("an administrative agency of the judicial department", Tex. Gov't Code § 81.011(a)), which is subject to the Public Information Act. Tex. Gov't Code § 81.033. Thus, no judicial agency must comply with both the Act and this rule; at most one can apply. Nor does the rule apply to judicial agencies expressly excepted from the Act by statute (other than by the general judiciary exception in section 552.003(b) of the Act), rule, or law. Examples are the Board of Legal Specialization, Tex. Gov't Code § 81.033, and the Board of Disciplinary Appeals, Tex. R. Disciplinary App. 7.12. Because these boards are expressly excepted from the Act, their records are not subject to disclosure under this rule, even though no law affirmatively makes their records confidential. The Board of Law Examiners is partly subject to the Act and partly exempt, Tex. Gov't Code § 82.003, and therefore this rule is inapplicable to it. An example of a judicial agency subject to the rule is the Supreme Court Advisory Committee, which is neither subject to nor expressly excepted from the Act, and whose records are not made confidential by any law.

2.   As stated in Rule 12.4, this rule does not require the creation or retention of records, but neither does it permit the destruction of records that are required to be maintained by statute or other law, such as Tex. Gov't Code §§ 441.158-.167, .180-.203; Tex. Local Gov't Code ch. 203; and 13 Tex. Admin. Code § 7.122.

3.   Rule 12.8 allows a records custodian to deny a record request that would substantially and unreasonably impede the routine operation of the court or judicial agency. As an illustration, and not by way of limitation, a request for "all judicial records" that is submitted every day or even every few days by the same person or persons acting in concert could substantially and unreasonably impede the operations of a court or judicial agency that lacked the staff to respond to such repeated requests.

PART EIGHT: PUBLIC INFORMATION ACT DEADLINES FOR GOVERNMENTAL BODIES

Step	Action	Section	Deadline	Due	Done
1	Governmental body must either release requested public information promptly, or if not within ten days of receipt of request, its Public Information Officer ("PIO") must certify fact that governmental body cannot produce the information within ten days and state date and hour within reasonable time when the information will be available.	552.221(a)	Promptly; Within ten business days of receipt of request for information make public information available, **or**		
		552.221(d)	Certify to requestor date and hour when public information will be available.		
2	Governmental body seeking to withhold information based on one or more of the exceptions under Subchapter C must request an attorney general decision stating all exceptions that apply, if there has not been a previous determination.	552.301(b)	Within a reasonable time, but not later than the tenth business day after receipt of the request for information.		
3	Governmental body must provide notice to the requestor of the request for attorney general decision and a copy of the governmental body's request for an attorney general decision.	552.301(d)	Within a reasonable time, but not later than the tenth business day after receipt of the request for information.		
4	Governmental body must submit to the attorney general comments explaining why the exceptions raised in Step 2 apply.	552.301(e)	Within a reasonable time, but not later than the fifteenth business day after receipt of the request for information.		
5	Governmental body must submit to attorney general copy of written request for information.	552.301(e)	Within a reasonable time, but not later than the fifteenth business day after receipt of the request for information.		
6	Governmental body must submit to attorney general signed statement as to date on which written request for information was received.	552.301(e)	Within a reasonable time, but not later than the fifteenth business day after receipt of the request for information.		
7	Governmental body must submit to attorney general copy of information requested or representative sample if voluminous amount of information is requested.	552.301(e)	Within a reasonable time, but not later than the fifteenth business day after receipt of the request for information.		
8	Governmental body must copy the requestor on written comments submitted to the attorney general in Step 4.	552.301 (e-1)	Within a reasonable time, but not later than the fifteenth business day after receipt of the request for information.		
9	a) Governmental body makes a good faith attempt to notify person whose proprietary information may be protected from disclosure under sections 552.101, 552.110, 552.113, or 552.131. Notification includes: 1) copy of written request; 2) letter, in the form prescribed by the attorney general, stating that the third party may submit to the attorney general reasons requested information should be withheld.	552.305(d)	Within a reasonable time, but not later than the tenth business day after date governmental body receives request for information.		
	b) Third party may submit brief to attorney general.	552.305(d)	Within a reasonable time, but not later than the tenth business day of receiving notice from governmental body.		
10	Governmental body must submit to attorney general additional information if requested by attorney general.	552.303(d)	Not later than the seventh calendar day after date governmental body received written notice of attorney general's need for additional information.		

Step	Action	Section	Deadline	Due	Done
11	Governmental body desires attorney general reconsideration of attorney general decision.	552.301(f)	Public Information Act prohibits a governmental body from seeking the attorney general's reconsideration of an open records ruling.		
12	Governmental body files suit challenging the attorney general decision.	552.324	Within thirty calendar days after the date governmental body receives attorney general decision.		
13	Governmental body files suit against the attorney general challenging the attorney general decision to preserve an affirmative defense to prosecution for failing to produce requested information.	552.353(b)	Within ten calendar days after governmental body receives attorney general's decision that information is public.		

PART NINE: NOTICE STATEMENT TO PERSONS WHOSE
               PROPRIETARY INFORMATION IS REQUESTED

(A governmental body must provide this notice to a person whose proprietary interests may be affected by release of information within ten business days after receipt of the written request for information.)

NOTE: This notice is updated periodically. Please check the OAG website http://www.texasattorneygeneral.gov for the latest version.

Date

Third Party Address

Dear M:

We have received a formal request to inspect or copy some of our files. A copy of the request for information is enclosed. The requested files include records we received from you or from your company. The Office of the Attorney General is reviewing this matter, and they will issue a decision on whether Texas law requires us to release your records. Generally, the Public Information Act (the "Act") requires the release of requested information, but there are exceptions. As described below, you have the right to object to the release of your records by submitting written arguments to the attorney general that one or more exceptions apply to your records. You are not required to submit arguments to the attorney general, but if you decide not to submit arguments, the Office of the Attorney General will presume that you have no interest in withholding your records from disclosure. In other words, if you fail to take timely action, the attorney general will more than likely rule that your records must be released to the public. If you decide to submit arguments, **you must do so not later than the tenth business day after the date you receive this notice.**

If you submit arguments to the attorney general, you must:

    a) identify the legal exceptions that apply,

    b) identify the specific parts of each document that are covered by each exception, and

    c) explain why each exception applies.

Gov't Code § 552.305(d). A claim that an exception applies without further explanation will not suffice. Attorney General Opinion H-436 (1974). You may contact this office to review the information at issue in order to make your arguments. We will provide the attorney general with a copy of the request for information and a copy of the requested information, along with other material required by the Act. The attorney general is generally required to issue a decision within 45 business days.

Please send your written comments to the Office of the Attorney General at the following address:

> Office of the Attorney General
> Open Records Division
> P.O. Box 12548
> Austin, Texas 78711-2548

If you wish to submit your written comments electronically, you may only do so via the Office of the Attorney General's eFiling System. An administrative convenience charge will be assessed for use of the eFiling System. No other method of electronic submission is available. Please visit the attorney general's website at http://www.texasattorneygeneral.gov for more information.

In addition, you are required to provide the requestor with a copy of your communication to the Office of the Attorney General. Gov't Code § 552.305(e). You may redact the requestor's copy of your communication to the extent it contains the substance of the requested information. Gov't Code § 552.305(e).

Commonly Raised Exceptions

In order for a governmental body to withhold requested information, specific tests or factors for the applicability of a claimed exception must be met. Failure to meet these tests may result in the release of requested information. We have listed the most commonly claimed exceptions in the Government Code concerning proprietary information and the leading cases or decisions discussing them. This listing is not intended to limit any exceptions or statutes you may raise.

Section 552.101: Information Made Confidential by Law

> Open Records Decision No. 652 (1997).

Section 552.104: Confidentiality of Information Relating to Competition

> *Boeing Co. v. Paxton*, 466 S.W. 3d 831 (Tex. 2015).

Section 552.110: Confidentiality of Trade Secrets and Commercial or Financial Information

Trade Secrets:

> *In re Bass*, 113 S.W.3d 735 (Tex. 2003).
> *Hyde Corp. v. Huffines*, 314 S.W.2d 763, 776 (Tex.), *cert. denied*, 358 U.S. 898 (1958).
> Open Records Decision No. 552 (1990).

Commercial or Financial Information:

> *Birnbaum v. Alliance of Am. Insurers*, 994 S.W.2d 766 (Tex. App.—Austin 1999, pet. filed) (construing previous version of section 552.110), *abrogated by In re Bass*, 113 S.W.3d 735 (Tex. 2003).
> Open Records Decision No. 639 (1996).
> Open Records Decision No. 661 (1999).

Section 552.113: Confidentiality of Geological or Geophysical Information

Open Records Decision No. 627 (1994).

Section 552.131: Confidentiality of Certain Economic Development Negotiation Information

If you have questions about this notice or release of information under the Act, please refer to the *Public Information Act Handbook* published by the Office of the Attorney General, or contact the attorney general's Open Government Hotline at (512) 478-OPEN (6736) or toll-free at (877) 673-6839 (877-OPEN TEX). To access the *Public Information Act Handbook* or Attorney General Opinions, including those listed above, please visit the attorney general's website at http://www.texasattorneygeneral.gov.

Sincerely,

Officer for Public Information or Designee
Name of Governmental Body

Enclosure: Copy of request for information

cc: Requestor
     address
     (w/o enclosures)

     Open Records Division
     Office of the Attorney General
     P.O. Box 12548
     Austin, Texas 78711-2548
     (w/o enclosures)

PART TEN: TEXAS GOVERNMENT CODE SECTION 552.024 PUBLIC ACCESS OPTION FORM

[Note: This form should be completed and signed by the employee no later than the 14th day after the date the employee begins employment, the public official is elected or appointed, or a former employee or official ends employment or service.]

_____
(Name)

The Public Information Act allows employees, public officials and former employees and officials to elect whether to keep certain information about them confidential. Unless you choose to keep it confidential, the following information about you may be subject to public release if requested under the Texas Public Information Act. Therefore, please indicate whether you wish to allow public release of the following information.

	PUBLIC ACCESS?	
	NO	YES
Home Address		
Home Telephone Number		
Social Security Number		
Emergency Contact Information		
Information that reveals whether you have family members		

_____
(Signature)

_____
(Date)

www.ingramcontent.com/pod-product-compliance
Lightning Source LLC
Chambersburg PA
CBHW081412270326

41931CB00015B/3248

* 9 7 8 1 9 5 4 2 8 5 4 9 1 *